DIMENSIONS OF

DETECTIVE FICTION

LARRY N LANDRUM
PAT BROWNE
RAY B. BROWNE

DIMENSIONS OF DETECTIVE FICTION

POPULAR PRESS

Library of Congress Catalog Card Number: 76-14646

ISBN: 0-87972-123-5 CB
0-87972-124-3 PB

TABLE OF CONTENTS

Larry N. Landrum
Pat Browne
Ray B. Browne

INTRODUCTION

The detective story is well over a hundred years old if we date it from Edgar Allan Poe. Though the conventional elements were available as far back as classical times in the form of identifiable motifs, many plots and aspects of characters including the detective, Poe was able to gather these together in a series of stories which gave them a new and larger meaning. The mystery plot in one form or another can be traced back through many literatures and is found in folklore throughout the world. Poe's eccentric M. Dupin has the mannerisms and dapper style of many earlier literary characters extending back into Restoration comedy. Scenes, minor characters, motifs such as intrigue in high places, incompetent law enforcement and the incorporation of current news items and other details had long been available to authors. Poe's contribution, however, was no less than the narrative paradigm for what we now recognize as the detective genre. Though numerous variations have resulted in forms bearing little resemblance to Poe's short stories, the heritage is clear enough. He provided stories which oriented readers to a particular form of tension between the ordinary and the bizarre, between sentiment and reason, and between appearance and reality. From Poe detective fiction emerged as a form which has achieved a complex metaphorical significance which goes far beyond the materials of its conventions. In its many variations it has provided people not only with hours of pleasurable reading, but also with unique ways of understanding the world. In 1922 during the early peak of detective fiction Walter Lippmann wrote in another context about "the world outside and the pictures in our heads." In many ways detective fiction is concerned with precisely this distinction between reality and image. It tends to create situations in which images of reality are in conflict or with that reality dictated by a killer whose particular madness is suddenly thrust upon the world. The resulting story provides a way of knowing or understanding or of achieving retribution.

Historically three established forms lent characteristic structure to the detective story as we know it today. The adventure story evolved in its popular form with the picaresque story, usually an open ended initiation tale emphasizing action and exploration through a boldly drawn central character. Gothic fiction produced images of hazily defined substrata of horror loosely associated with the decline of traditional belief systems, the rise of the individual and the emergence of applied technology which threatened both the former. The third form, domestic fiction, focused on manners and eventually brought into question traditional patriarchal authority in the face of declining family units and the separation of work and home. The infatuation with technology and the growing influence of merchants, manufacturers and technicians helped popularize puzzles and ingenious mechanical devices. Jigsaw puzzles and mechanical toys were among the middle class substitutes for mannerist gardens and illusionist art in the eighteenth century.

In England from the latter eighteenth century and later in the United States, fiction associated with hearth and home grew more adventuresome. Heavily didactic, popular fiction of the time began to follow the interests of the new middle class women. Popular romances, gothics and domestic novels flooded bookstalls in England. The characteristic mystery evolved—a loosely structured vehicle for initiation into the social world and extended sentimental ratiocination. This form was parallel to a growing interest in popular male literature in utopian, travel literature and colonial fiction on the one hand, and lost race and exotic adventure fiction on the other. In a sense these tendencies in England served some of the same purposes as the western in the United States, but with significant differences. In England the colonial novel would turn inward into the psychological symbolism of Joseph Conrad, while the western world focused on the internal cultural problems of an evolving civilization. In both cases, however, the heroes would remain outside what they would see as the general tendencies of their fellow men. In retrospect it appears obvious that Ian Fleming would emerge in England and Mickey Spillane in the United States. But before these somewhat dubious heroes could emerge, they would be preceded by Arthur Conan Doyle and Dashiell Hammett.

Doyle did little to modify the evolved style of popular fiction in England, but like Poe he synthesized a form from a variety of sources, adding his own genius to a multitude of available conventions. Dozens of imitations and further variations followed. By the turn of the century classical detective fiction was firmly established in England and was becoming an integral part of the fiction popular with Americans.

Adventure stories grew with the spread of literacy and popular media in the eighteenth century as visions of an open-ended geography seemed a viable alternative to urban-industrial collectivization. One figure in particular is of interest to us here. The quasi-authentic highwayman in broadsides, chapbooks and newspaper fiction was an enormously popular hero as akin to the Trickster figure in folklore as to his literary cousins in picaresque fiction. In England penny dreadfuls told of the thrilling exploits of such men as Jack Shepherd, Tom King, Dick Turpin, Sixteen String Jack and Paul Clifford. Chapbooks told the story of Turpin's celebrated ride to York jumping all the toll gates along the way, and at least one broadside details with illustration Jack Shepherd's escape from Newgate prison. While the highwayman was far from a detective, he had two qualities which would be important to the detective. He was an outsider, in a sense para-establishment because he was continuing the expression of freedom on the land which was rapidly vanishing in the mid-eighteenth century in the face of closure and urbanization. He was seen as a Robin Hood who in serving his own interests also served those of the masses by providing entertainment and the illusion of generosity. In addition to being an outsider he understood and exploited a variety of skills and social graces, enabling him to move freely through a wide range of society. His was a deadly game with the gallows as the consolation prize, but if he played with bravado he would earn the respect and loyalty of many common people who saw in him their imaginative alter egoes.

In America fiction was still being reprinted in rural newspapers as late as the Second World War. From 1850 newspapers exclusively devoted to fiction were widely circulated in urban areas and dime novels were available through the mail from 1860. By 1870 story papers were running as many as eight concurrent serials. Both of these forms gave way to pulp fiction and comic strips around the turn of the century. Through the gradual process of cumulation and attrition of popular stories, borrowing from successful efforts, the change in the backgrounds of the writers, and more rapid processes of production and circulation which made current interests available to writers, popular fiction gradually evolved into distinct genres. During the period from 1860 to 1898 in the United States the firm of Beadle and Adams published over 3,000 dime novels. These were sold to middle and lower class youth and many adults. Interestingly, only about ten percent deal with detectives and the action for about half of these takes place in the west or southwest, the setting for about half of all dime novel fiction. The five percent which deal with an urban detective treat him primarily as an adventure hero, as in John Russell Coryell's *The Old Detective's Pupil* (1876). By the 1890's he is likely to be a Pinkerton man, foreshadowing Dashiell Hammett's Continental Op, but lacking his complexity.

Dime novels were restricted in complexity by several factors including their heavily juvenile orientation. Most were written by solidly conventional writers, many of whom were school teachers, ministers, magazine editors and others whose imagination was not likely to exceed their moral reach. Although dime novels were full of violence, it was the kind of bloodless allegorical violence which justified the wholesale slaughter of characters designated as evil by definition of stereotype. Pulps, on the other hand, were more often written by men who received much of their education on the streets. Pulp writers included journalists, hack writers who learned their trade by copying earlier pulp work, and professional writers working at finger cramping pace under a variety of pseudonyms. By the turn of the century New York City was teeming with aspiring writers and immigrant youth were learning to read by hiding pulps, story papers and other ephemera between the covers of hardbound books in the warmth of public libraries. *Argosy* magazine, generally regarded as the first pulp magazine, began in 1896 a scant two years before the demise of Beadle and Adams. The pulps were born at the tail of one depression and endured another to be finally worn down by television in the fifties. During their peak in the twenties and thirties when about 400 writers wrote most of the stories for around 200 pulps, formulas were refined, new stereotypes emerged and heroes hardened into competitive professionals like their authors. The heroes were young, opportunistic and hard. Those who did not shape up to this ideal were the straw men the heroes exposed. By the early thirties, detective pulps led all other categories of fiction.

Contemporary fictional detectives are surrogate heroes whose styles relate not only to the conventions of the genre, but perhaps more significantly to representative ways of perceiving reality through the illusions of contrived deceptions. Like the cowboy's before him within the structure of the genre, the fictional detective's motivations, most of his acts and his conscious image of the world exist outside established authority, legal procedure and enforcement. He also lives on the fringes of crime, which area is usually pictured as a somewhat dirty mirror of the moral or legal authority structure or indeed a part of it. As the central dynamic image of the story, the detective understands and often experiences the distribution and ranges of power within both of these systems. As an outsider the detective avoids both assimilation and entrapment by them. When a detective figure is assimilated into the legal system the story is an occupational biography, a courtroom drama or a procedural describing a way of doing rather than knowing. If the detective strays too far afield from the legal/crime structures the story becomes another related type of adventure, such as the spy story.

Though the detective often breaks laws and may kill in his pursuit of the criminal, he exists in that part of the imagination reflecting the real world where personal or interpersonal morality supersedes formal legal procedures. Stories which highlight criminal activity by detective figures are usually "justified" by the terms of the story, as in spy fiction, anti-espionage fiction and the criminal procedural. Each of these forms requires a suspension or displacement of conventional moral judgment. When the detective figure is consciously opposed to these systems or their methods the story is usually a form of thesis fiction, such as the expose or propaganda story. Nothing in the formula really dictates that the detective be legally pure, though the formula demands a moral understanding between author and reader. This understanding is based at least partially on the semi-imaginary nature of the detective's profession. He is shown as neither a "peeper" nor a policeman with a staff and a rationalized set of procedures.

The detective is in some ways vulnerable as an outsider to the system of manners and conventions. Here morality is closely related to matters of taste and judgment, where assimilation and capture are more subtle threats. This is the point Sam Spade was trying to make to Effie Perine about Brigid O'Shaughnessy in *The Maltese Falcon.* Sentimentality leads to illusion because the perspective of the outsider is lost. To retain his independence the detective draws on the skills of the confidence man, priest, inquisitor or fool, using any technique suitable to the situation and his pursuit of knowledge of the crime. His game is pursuit and he must gather information, process it, make decisions and act. In the best detective fiction these things pervade the background creating a web of suspense which heightens the usually episodic action of the story. As a dynamic moral and intellectural (or ideological) force, the detective must be relatively free of distractions and commitments. He necessarily commands a high degree of personal freedom and mobility. He has often become as a result a loner as well as an outsider. But not always. At times he works with a partner in the form of a sidekick or spouse and in a more complex way with his client or contact.

Such conditions of survival and profession, taken out of the story context, may be associated with other adventure heroes such as the spy or western gunfighter as well as the detective. The particular characteristics and orientations of the detective vary widely with cultural distribution, ideological bias and literary taste. While the detective is usually single and free to devote considerable time to his work, he is relatively at ease in a broad range of social situations and his acquaintances often range throughout the social classes. The detective remains on the fringe of this system, substituting the force of his character and the sancitity of his purpose for social amenities and the talismen of status. Then, too, he often uses large measures of bluff, physical force or bravado.

Though some detectives are brought into plots by their own curiosity, most modern detectives are acquainted with the circumstances of the crime by a client or confidant. In a sense this person defines how the reader is to relate to the detective and the ensuing story. The detective's character and actions—especially if he is a series detective—are somewhat predictable to the reader. Clients and their problems are not as familiar and predictable, and these lead the detective and the reader into fresh scenes. This may evolve in the form of a subplot featuring love elements, comedy, sexploitation, initiation or other popular themes. The more literary detective writers tend to use this relationship to explore character or to generalize about human or cultural conditions.

Witnesses are a rich source, not only of information important to plots, but as representative types. We meet workers, servants, professionals, rich and poor, old wealthy and *nouveau riché*. As George Grella observes, the description of manners is one of the most important aspects of the formal detective story, and we find it in a wide range of hard-boiled fiction as well. While some writers barely manage enough information for crude stereotypes, some are able to catch the mannerism or phrase which transforms a type into an individual. In either case witnesses are more than extensions of the landscape. Minor characters in detective stories have to carry the scrutiny of the reader as detective, often a reader who in following the surface game of the story depends upon his own judgments about the honesty, the facts or conjectures witnesses offer and their general reliability. Even in Poe's earliest stories witnesses were used to make the crimes seem unsolvable. Today witnesses are likely to assume a less direct purpose, providing a complex emotional and social as well as factual or intellectual matrix. They sometimes become confessors, unburdening repressed feelings and beliefs onto the detective out of fear or simply because they have needed someone to talk to. Like clients, they are seldom free of feelings of guilt even though they may not be criminals. At the core of the detective is the professional. Whether he has the attributes of the dandy or bumbler or adventurer he embodies the tension between what Jacques Ellul has called "technic," or efficiency, and the associative patterns of exploration. It is a delicate balance. Emphasis on technic favors the procedural, as in Robert Thorpe's *The Detective*, while emphasis on associative exploration favors comic, romantic or ratiocinative development, as in the Shell Scott, the longer Chandler novels and Dorothy Sayers' best known novels.

The future of the detective genre is bound to be filled with modifications—there is too much activity within the field to predict anything else. Exactly where the lines will develop is hard to prophesy. Undoubtedly there will remain much endeavor in conventional types, but there will also be new efforts to widen the scope. Our collection, selected to allow the greatest flexibility possible, accommodates all varieties within the present and the future. Most of the essays in this book are published for the first time. For convenience and through a loose logic we have divided the essays into three categories.

∮ THE GENRE

The essays in this section explore the form, interpretation and characteristics of the genre itself.

Van Meter, in "Sophocles and the Rest of the Boys in the Pulps: Myth and the Detective Novel," realizing that the very basis of detective fiction is myth, argues that the murder mystery contains a "social component" as important as the psychological, and it has always "moved closer to the fringe of the social novel as it simultaneously moves closer to its ritual beginnings."

Elliot L. Gilbert, in "McWatters' Law: The Best Kept Secret of the Secret Service," advances the thesis that the detective in the nineteenth century—as he is today—was an "agent of disorder" rather than of order, that he was, and is, a critic of order rather than a celebrant of it.

In "Murder and Manners: The Formal Detective Novel," George Grella argues that the puzzle theory, though obviously important to detective fiction, does not provide the "chief source of appeal" of the genre. The true power of the formal detective novel, in the twentieth century as it was earlier, lies in its being a "thriller of manners," a comedy of manners.

Geraldine Pederson-Krag, in her "Detective Stories and the Primal Scene," takes a somewhat different approach. In her Freudian interpretation, the detective tale provides us with a reliving of our past. The reader "tries actively to relive and master traumatic infantile experiences he once had to endure passively." Thus the story provides therapy.

In a revealing study, "George Orwell and the Detective Story," Patrick Parrinder discusses Orwell's essay "Grandeur et Decadence du Roman Policier Anglais," published in 1944 when the study of popular literature was held in disrepute. Orwell insisted that the detective thriller had reached its zenith in the 80s and 90s during a "secure and leisured society," which, as Parrinder asserts, really reveals Orwell's political bias and his distrust of the readers of detective fiction.

On a somewhat different tack, William O. Aydelotte in "The Detective Story as a Historical Source," argues that the detective story is obviously unrealistic and its great charm for contemporary readers lies in its use of convention, its repetition of formula. But it is this use of unrealism and formula which makes the genre important to the historian, as indices to the fantasies of society, people's day-dreams, and through them the stories "may reveal political attitudes which shed a flood of light on the motivation behind political, social, and economic history."

Centering on the hard-boiled detective, Edward Margolies in "The American Detective Thriller and the Idea of Society," insists that no matter how overdone he is, the hard-nosed detective recognizes the importance of the individual and society, yet he views himself as "engaged in some kind of moral, if not metaphysical, quest."

∮ ∮ STYLES

The essays in this section deal primarily with individual authors and their accomplishments.

In "Sherlock Holmes and Nero Wolfe: The Role of the 'Great Detective' in Intellectual History," D. F. Rauber studies the so-called "great detective" of the last hundred years and concludes, what might be startling to some readers, that this detective "can be seen as a vulgarization of the scientist, a popular surrogate for the less glamorous figure of the austere investigator of nature" and therefore the detective figure demonstrates how a culture views science. Nero Wolfe reveals our attitude toward physics.

In a needed switch from male to female detective fiction, Nancy Y. Hoffman, in "Mistresses of Malfeasance," ponders the question why women, from Anna Katharine Green to Agatha Christie, have successfully created crime fiction. Surprisingly she feels such fiction has run its course and will be replaced by science fiction.

Ronald J. Ambrosetti, in the first of our studies of individual authors, "The World of Eric Ambler: From Detective to Spy," examines the world of Eric Ambler. Ambler's seeming contribution to literature may be his development of the spy genre, a spin-off development of detective fiction during the Cold War. Ambler's argument, according to Ambrosetti, "resides in the dangerously thin veneer of protection that civilization offers to modern man." But actually Ambler's "contribution specifically lies in his initial linking of the spy genre to the legacy of popular literature —the tale of detection."

In a rare and much-needed study of Race Williams, created by Carroll John Daly for *Black Mask,* Allen B. Crider, in "Race Williams—Private Investigator," demonstrates that this early hard-boiled detective was influential as well as significant in his own right.

In the first of two essays on Mickey Spillane, Kay Weibel, in "Mickey

Spillane as a Fifties Phenomenon," discovers Spillane's novels bedded deep in the society of his time, "at the intersection of sex and motherhood, where sexual adventure meets redeeming social value." As such they "attempt to resolve for men the two-way image of male/female roles provided by the popular media."

On a different tack, R. Jeff Banks, in the second study of the same author, "Spillane's Anti-Establishmentarian Heroes," chronicles Spillane's fights with the Establishment throughout his books and asserts that Spillane's works although considered obvious by many critics really merit further study.

Until recently Black authors were virtually ignored by critics. In an effort to rectify this grievous oversight, Darwin Turner, in "The Rocky Steele Novels of John B. West," fills in our scanty picture of a Black author who instead of creating a Black detective modeled his hero on Spillane's Mike Hammer, muscling him with "the brutality and violence which Anglo-European culture has posited for its most respected heroes."

R. Gordon Kelly, in "The Precarious World of John D. MacDonald," believes that this detective writer works within "certain tenets of late 19th-century naturalism, . . . ideas which have generally been discarded by intellectuals in this century." Like most of us MacDonald is deeply concerned with the questions of society and the individual, as Kelly traces the development in MacDonald's works.

A fascinating and much-needed study of a Black author is Raymond Nelson's "Domestic Harlem: The Detective Fiction of Chester Himes." Nelson demonstrates that anger can beget effective detective fiction, for when he started writing about Harlem detectives Coffin Ed Johnson and Grave Digger Jones, Himes was one of the angriest of the Black writers. The resulting books of "grotesque comedy of violence" and "sparse, descriptive style" resulted in one of the "most compelling images of our time."

Whereas Himes' detective work may have gone unappreciated, from the beginning Ross Macdonald has been driving hard toward respectability. Few writers have earned the respect accorded Macdonald. In the first of two essays on the author, Elmer Pry, in "Lew Archer's 'Moral Landscape'," points out how Macdonald is profoundly affected by and addicted to his landscape, which he sees as the microcosm of America, a world of rogues and fools and saints and lost souls all searching for something.

In the second paper on the same author, Sam Grogg, Jr., lets Macdonald speak for himself in a revealing interview about a probing mind viewing his world and his craft.

∮ ∮ ∮ THE GENRE EXTENDED

For years the "formula" of detective fiction has been undergoing strain as authors tried to broaden and enrich it, some with success, some with noted failure. Precisely where the development will extend is difficult to prophesy. But critics are not reluctant to speculate, as the essays in this third section of the book demonstrate.

In "Strangers Within, Enemies Without: Alienation in Popular Mafia Fiction," Charles R. Carlisle speculates in a broad survey how Mafia fiction fits into the tradition of popular fiction and develops "one of the most salient literary themes of our time: alienation."

In a subject that is getting increasing attention—almost to the point of obsession—these days, Richard Gid Powers, in "J. Edgar Hoover and the Detective Hero," approaches the former head of the FBI as a "phenomenon without parallel in American history." In surveying his career as America's number one crime fighter, Powers wonders if Hoover contributed to the nation's understanding of itself, its problems and its needs" or if he blinded Americans to "vital facts about their society and so helped to create a heritage of unresolved social tensions." These, and other questions, will reverberate throughout this nation for the remainder of this century if not forever.

The switch from Hoover to William Faulkner is without doubt great. Both people played to different constituencies. But Faulkner, a favorite with "elite" critics for years, belongs also in studies of detective fiction, as Mick Gidley in "Elements of the Detective Story in William Faulkner's Fiction," the first of two studies on the same author, demonstrates. Faulkner did not write detective fiction but he used the ingredients of such stories to enrich his fiction in general.

Elaborating somewhat on the same subject, but in an extension that adds much to the subject, Douglas G. Tallack, in "William Faulkner and the Tradition of Tough-Guy Fiction," picks up the tradition of the tough-guy school and demonstrates how Faulkner utilized the techniques to strengthen his own style.

The collection ends with the promise of one of the greater outreaches in detective fiction, that of Ishmael Reed's experimental mystery fiction. Steven R. Carter, in "Ishmael Reed's Neo-Hoodoo Detection," demonstrates that like Faulkner and many other authors, Reed was aiming for something different but hit upon the detective fiction and crime novel form and thus should be considered "one of the foremost practitioners of experimental mystery fiction."

The essays in this book do not cover all writers in the various genres represented here. No single book could do so with any degree of depth. But our coverage and depth reveal how profoundly detective fiction is a part of our lives and what it reveals about us. Therefore, we feel, much of the genre's accomplishment and promise—its future—stands here before the critical eye of concerned students and readers.

THE GENRE

Jan R. Van Meter

SOPHOCLES AND THE REST OF THE BOYS IN THE PULPS: MYTH AND THE DETECTIVE NOVEL

One of the best professors I had in graduate school always began teaching *Oedipus Rex* as a murder mystery. "At its very heart," he always said, "it is the story of the master detective in search of the master criminal." Choubert in Ionesco's *Victims of Duty* says the same thing.

All the plays that have ever been written, from Ancient Greece to the present day, have never really been anything but thrillers. Drama's always been realistic and there's always been a detective about. Every play's an investigation brought to a successful conclusion. There's a riddle, and it's solved in the final scene. Sometimes earlier. You seek, and then you find.[1]

Yet what is strange here is that the critical prejudice against the detective novel is so great that when it is admired or even acclaimed, it ceases to become a detective novel at all in our minds. Borges' story "Death and the Compass," Dostoevski's *Crime and Punishment*, or Dickens' *Bleak House* are, after all, at very base detective novels. The rest, from Dashiell Hammett's *Red Harvest* or Collins' *Woman in White* to Ross Macdonald's *Underground Man* or Maj Sjöwall and Per Wahlöö's *The Laughing Policeman*, if they are ever dealt with at all, are treated as objects of popular culture, a faintly derisive category containing comic books, operettas, and baseball. Yet what we must first recognize is that the detective story is in fact one of the oldest forms of literature—for *Oedipus Rex* is a detective story—and that to understand both its nature and its appeal we must first understand it as a variety of myth which is central to our culture.

In his discussion of the psychology of the audience for art, Kenneth Burke makes an important distinction between the psychology of form and the psychology of information, between, in effect, music and a Merck Manual.

One reason why music can stand repetition so much more sturdily than correspondingly good prose is that music, of all the arts, is by its nature least suited to the psychology of information, and has remained closer to the psychology of form. Here form cannot atrophy. Every dissonant chord cries for its solution, and whether the musician resolves or refuses to resolve this dissonance into the chord which the body cries for, he is dealing in human appetites. Correspondingly good prose, however, more prone to the temptations of pure information, cannot so much bear repetition since the aesthetic value of information is lost once that information is imparted. If one returns to such a work again it is purely because, in the chaos of modern life, he has been able to forget it. With a desire, on the other hand, its recovery is as agreeable as its discovery.[2]

The literature which most appeals to the psychology of information is, as Burke points out, the detective novel. Yet within this most "informative" of literatures, there exists a form which is crucial to its literary enjoyment and a form which is revealed in its connections to myth, both stylistically and psychologically.

Sophocles' play, which is not myth itself but myth dramatized in the most artificial and artistic sense of that word, must be read or viewed at first as a detective story. There Oedipus has become king because he has been able to solve a mystery—the riddle of the Sphinx—and thus lift a curse from the kingdom. Yet his very arrival brings a new curse, and as the responsible authority it is his duty to seek out and bring justice to the former king's murderer. With his country undergoing physical decay which is at the same time a moral decay, Oedipus undertakes his search for the criminal with a ruthless honesty and unrelenting curiosity. Slowly but inexorably, rumors are examined, witnesses questioned, and answers pieced together, until in one crashing climax Oedipus reveals himself as the criminal and exacts punishment.

The obvious objection to such a reading, of course, is that the end of the mystery is known before the play begins. Only the actors in their roles do not know who killed King Laius. Our pleasure, if it can be called that, in rereading the play or the Greek pleasure in reviewing it comes from the terrifying inevitability of the ending and in the psychological tensions which the play invokes in the audience itself. In Burke's terms, when the plot is known, pleasure comes from the form itself, the creation and resolution of dissonances. Yet *Oedipus Rex* remains a murder story whose plot is the myth of the search.

Like the detective novel, myth is at base a "literature" of information, as all plots must be. The first time through any art is a reading or listening or seeing for plot, and the foundation of plot is always "what happened" and "how did it happen." Myth is a plot of "naming," of explanation. It does not necessarily, though it may, reveal the patterns behind the chaos of the world, nor does it necessarily simplify the world. What myth does is to provide us with a comprehension of the "what" and "how" of man and his world. The "why" is to a large extent irrelevant, for to provide a "why" is to give characters a personality. Oedipus, in fact, has no motivation for his actions in Sophocles' play or in the original myths. Oedipus kills his father, marries his mother, fathers his brothers and sisters, and blinds himself for no other reason than his "Oedipus-ness"—it is his Fate and his fate to do so. Acting out of inner and outer necessity, Oedipus has motivation, in our sense of the term, only to the extent that the audience supplies it as a projection of their own motivations. Figures of myth *need* no motives because they *are* motives.

Saying, though, that myth is a literature which relies on the psychology of information, at least at first, does not preclude myth from having form as well. As Philip Slater has shown in his *Glory of Hera*, the Greek myths can be read as variations of the same plot—the family plot of fifth-century Greece with its strong mother-son hostilities.[3] While it is the variation which makes the myths and plays interesting and makes their creations artistic, it is the repetition of "information" which makes them significant as myth, as learning device, as plot.

What we are talking about then is a different kind of psychology of form from Burke, for he is discussing a form which operates within a single work. It is in the idea of repetition over the whole of a genre that a literature of information can take its psychology of form. Consciously or unconsciously we demand of a specific literature a form of plot which varies only in its details, but whose essential movements are both known ahead of time and demanded by its audience.

> The charm of detective stories lies neither in originality nor in artistic merit, though they may possess both these qualities. It consists rather in the repetition of a formula that through trial and error has been found pleasing. We read these books, not to have a new experience, but to repeat in slightly different form an experience we have had already. Thus, for example, the "surprise" ending is not really a surprise. It is the ending we expect and demand, and we would feel outraged if any other kind of ending were offered to us.[4]

Thus the murder mystery has a known and predictable formulation. There is a murder or the suspicion that one may be done. The detective is called in and investigates. During the course of his investigation more murders may be done and lives disrupted, but by the end the murder is solved. The pattern, while not invariable, is almost always followed; only the details and the place are changed to reveal the guilty.

It is, then, the formulaic quality which is necessary for the detective novel and the myth alike, a repetition of form over the whole of the genre. There is also the repetition of form within each novel or mythic representation conditioned by the genre itself. At the center of Greek myth, there is, as Slater shows, the recurrence of intra-sexual, intra-generational struggle: Oedipus against his mother, Jocasta against Laius, a struggle brought to focus by the initial murder. At the center of the detective novel is also the murder, for it is death itself which forms the interest here. As in the Victorian novel from which the murder mystery directly springs and to which it has the strongest ties, the murder mystery affirms the significance of life by affirming the importance of death. Indeed, it is rarely that the victim has any real significance in life—his importance lies in the catalytic value his death gives to events around him, uncovering motives, exposing the past, giving anonymities names.

While we are used to seeing the death of the victim in the detective novel as a chance for the detective, and through him the reader, to reveal as simple the complexities of life and to enable the good to triumph over the evil, the mysteries themselves reveal otherwise. To unravel one set of involved causation and motivation is not, in fact, to reveal the world as a basically simple, understandable place. Indeed, Sherlock Holmes has become a remnant in today's detective novels for increasingly the repetition of the pattern reveals only the innumerable number of patterns to be unravelled and the final realization that motives are never simple or sure. Murder and death, then, become not the agent of social purification, or the catalyst to such purification, but the symptom of the impossibility of such a purification.

Such a pattern of complexity is enforced, or perhaps created, by the atmosphere which is increasingly being generated by the best of the mystery novelists. Originally the detective novel used place only as atmosphere or as information incidental to the actual events of the story. The background of the French Riviera supplied a new area of information for the readers in the same manner that a murder involving rare Chinese vases did. Both provided the author with a chance of displaying his special knowledge and the reader with a chance to become superficially and vicariously versed in the arcana of place or profession. But the actual fact of place—despite the fact that it often provided the twist at the end of the novel—was irrelevant in any real sense.

For three of the best writers currently writing detective novels, however, place is far more than atmosphere and information. In Ross Macdonald's Southern California and in Maj Sjöwall's and Per Wahlöö's Sweden, the environment spawns murder. For these novels society itself provides an impetus for violence in the fragmenting of the social fabric. Macdonald sees this fragmentation as a result of the collapse of the social institutions of the capitalist state; Sjöwall and Wahlöö as the collapse of the social institutions of the socialist state. But most importantly, crime has become not a threat to the state—as it was for example in Mickey Spillane's novels—but an irremediable symptom of a society which has already disintegrated beyond anyone's ability to piece it together.

These attitudes are most clearly in evidence when one compares an early novel of Ross Macdonald's, a novel which is clearly tied to an earlier tradition of American detective novels, *Trouble Follows Me*, with Per Wahlöö's first novel, *The Thirty-First Floor.* In Macdonald's novel

Sam Drake, a naval ensign on leave tracks down a Japanese spy ring responsible for murders in Hawaii, Detroit, on a train in the mid-West, and in Mexico. With the help of an ever-efficient FBI, Drake rids the country of the gang and is ready to return to fight for a united country against its enemies.

In Wahlöö's novel, Chief Inspector Jensen is called in to investigate a bomb threat in the building which houses the nation's publishing combine. Except for Jensen, no one in the novel has a name, and as he probes further and further, surrounded by the ever-increasing suicides and alcoholics, he can find motives but no criminal. At long last he discovers the person who has sent the note because the combine has been responsible for the death of society itself, but there is another note. As the novel closes, Jensen waits for the bomb to explode which has been set by the chiefs of the combine to destroy the last remnants of independence, a group of dissident intellectuals who produce dummy journals on the top floor of the building. The murder has not yet happened; the criminals will never be caught, for the real murder is that of society itself and the victims continue living. The specific crime, like the recurrent suicides and drunkards, has as its real cause society's disintegration in the midst of ever-increasing centralization.

A similar atmosphere is invoked in Macdonald's later novels with the use of symbols like the wandering tribe of surfers in *The Zebra Striped Hearse*, the pestilential oil wells in *The Drowning Pool* or the sirocco-like wind and the forest fire in *The Underground Man.*

> Before we reached Santa Teresa I could see the smoke. Then I could see it dragging like a veil across the face of the mountain behind the city.
>
> Under and through the smoke I caught glimpses of fire like the flashes of heavy guns too far away to be heard. The illusion of war was completed by an old two-engine bomber which flew in low over the mountain's shoulder. The plane was lost in the smoke for a long instant, then climbed out trailing a pastel red cloud of fire retardant.[5]

The atmosphere which Macdonald creates here is more than the miasma of evil which pervades Conan Doyle's *The Hound of the Baskervilles* or the background of tough and ready violence of Hammett's novels. It is instead the essential condition of both the novel and society, for these novels are social novels in which crime and murder are the inevitable products of a disordered society.

It is true that these novels reveal a change in the nature of the detective hero. Earlier versions were generally either amateurs like Holmes or Margery Allingham's Albert Campion or private eyes from Hammett's Continental Op and Raymond Chandler's Philip Marlowe to Spillane's Mike Hammer. The movements in these earlier versions are largely revealing of social preference—the English for amateurs for example—or changing social ideology—the shift to increasing physical and sexual violence in Spillane or in England's Ian Fleming. No matter the change, though, these detectives are all united in their two-dimensionality. Macdonald's Lew Archer and Sjöwall and Wahlöö's Martin Beck are attempts at more developed characters. Parts of their personal lives are revealed as are their emotions and attitudes. Indeed in the nine novels of what is planned to be a ten volume "novel," Beck has grown steadily older, has gotten a divorce from an exasperating wife, has seen some of his friends slowly drop away, and has begun a new personal life.

Even given this important attempt to develop the detective into a person, what remains are undeveloped, two-dimensional figures who are unknowable outside of their function. Significantly it is the rule for the detective to be unmarried, or to assure the audience of their heterosexuality, divorced. Simenon's Inspector Maigret or Hammett's Nick and Nora Charles are exceptions. Such an isolation is crucial to the detective, for as a part of the myth pattern we cannot know them too well. As Raymond Chandler has written in his superb essay, "The Simple Art of Murder":

> He is the hero; he is everything. He must be a complete man and a common man and yet an unusual man. He must be, to use a rather weathered phrase, a man of honor—by instinct, by inevitability, without thought of it, and certainly without saying it. He must be the best man in his world and a good enough man for any world. I do not care much about his private life; he is neither a eunuch nor a satyr; I think he might seduce a duchess and I am quite sure he would not spoil a virgin; if he is a man of honor in one thing, he is that in all things. . . . He is a lonely man and his pride is that you will treat him as a proud man or be very sorry you ever saw him.[6]

Yet while the detective's isolation is necessary for him to be in a position to act as solver and resolver, it is even more critical for as detective he enters into a crucial and unrecognized relationship with the criminal. The detective is created, like the rest of the characters in the detective novel, solely by the criminal.

Just as Oedipus is the only person who can identify King Laius' murderer and the sole person who is pledged to the discovery in order to rid Thebes of the pollution which pervades it, so the detective is uniquely capable for his job. Indeed, "the crime is tailored to fit the detective. It finally proves to be exactly the kind of crime that is best suited to his peculiar and unique talents."[7] The relationship here in *Oedipus Rex* is obvious for Oedipus' existence defines his guilt; the criminal and detective are mutually and spontaneously created. In the detective novel, though, this relationship is diluted in the division of labor.

If we assume for the moment that Chandler is right in asserting that the detective is hero, representative of the social code, of right, we can also assume that the criminal is a symptom of the social malaise and thus a scapegoat for a society which does not recognize its own symptoms as symptoms. The act of murder, crystallizing as it does both the desires of the society as a whole and the desires of the plot itself, acts to socialize the murderer as representative and at the same time to isolate him as an individual. In the anonymous social system which surrounds them, only the criminal and the detective have managed identity, even the identity of mythic figures. So powerful is that act of crime that those whose presence takes them in the paths of these two figures similarly gain an identity, only to lose it in further death or when the murderer is caught and the crime is solved. They have no extra identity, for the detective cannot give it–he remains alone.

Yet murder as an act of individuation is only understood as such by the detective. Not only has he too performed such an isolating act in his choice of profession, but he, like the criminal, is a social scapegoat. Chandler, then, is wrong in his choice of words, or rather we have been wrong in our conception of the position of the detective hero in regards to the society which he is supposed to be motivated to defend. Loaded with the criminal burden of society, isolated and even exiled from the social system by inclination, design, and the curious combination of awe and hatred with which police are always regarded, the detective is both above and outside the law, an individual both despite and because of himself. He has always been seen as the mirror-image of the criminal both by sociologists and the mystery writers, symbolized occasionally by pairings–Batman and the Joker, Sherlock Holmes and Moriarty–and often by the action and description itself. But the link between detective and murderer is more than the murderer as "negative representative" of the detective as Kenneth Burke would have it. Rather the two are the same person whose opposite roles are merely accident, like those children of the slums who become either cops, priests, or gangsters. It is this identity of the seeming opposite which makes the detective uniquely suited to his job.

Even further than this identity of qualities, the detective and the murderer are also related in function–needing each other and at the same time dually needed by society itself. The crime by its existence and by society's response to it reaffirms the existence of the social compact no matter how moribund. The crowd which defines itself in chasing a criminal has no need to distinguish Oliver Twist from Bill Sikes. The outlaw exists to define the mass just as the detective does.

Such a need for definition makes it imperative that we comprehend neither the criminal nor the detective. Indeed, it is not for the reasons of mystery and problem solving that have been the hall-marks of the genre that we are kept in the dark throughout the course of the novel. As many critics have demonstrated, logic is constantly violated in the most "logical" of novels and often only the facade of evidence and solution is maintained. Often we are asked to accept strange and even illogical premises for the solution to work out at all. While the search for the murderer's identity is the pretext for the novel, we are first prevented from knowing the criminal because he has no identity outside of the crime itself—as mythic figure he is crime rather than motivation, Fate rather than fate—and second because with knowledge must come some degree of empathy. Above all it is important that we do not know the murderer, that he as a motivated person remain concealed, because we are dealing here, as in *Oedipus Rex*, with ritual disguised, with a ritual which the repetition of the genre reveals. One cannot empathize with the bull or the meaning of the bullfight is lost.

In two discussions of the psychological significance of the murder mystery, both Geraldine Pederson-Krag and Charles Rycroft base their analyses on the Oedipus myth.[8] For Pederson-Krag, the murder mystery centers on the primal scene where the child witnesses his parents in intercourse. The murder victim then becomes the parent for whom the child has hostility and the detective becomes "personified by the great detective, [who] can look, remember and correlate without fear and without reproach in utter contrast to the ego of the terrified infant witnessing the primal scene."[9] Rycroft essentially agrees with Pederson-Krag's analysis with one exception and one addition. He doubts the necessity of the reader having actually witnessed the primal scene and he stresses the identification by the reader with the detective *and* the criminal. For Rycroft, the reader of the murder mystery "is living a fantasy of being in omnipotent control of the internalized parents."[10] While I do not wish to deny the value of these interpretations, for I think they are correct in their analysis of the underlying psychological significance of the murder mystery, what I do wish to suggest is that the ritual of the murder mystery contains a social component which is as important, if not more so, than the psychological.

As Edmund Leach has shown, ritual contains both a psychological and a social component.[11] The psychological component is that aspect of the ritual which an individual participating responds to. But each individual may respond from different personal causes. The social component is that aspect of the ritual to which the group responds and for which the ritual has been created. Thus, for example, Christian communion may invoke the primal desire to devour and share the power of the father, but it does, on a far simpler level, affirm the community, the solidarity of the group against those who cannot or will not share in the ritual.

The social meaning of the Oedipus myth and the murder mystery thus rests in the identification by the reader with both the detective and the criminal, for as I have discussed, they enable him to define the group of which he is a part and at the same time violate that group by moving outside of it. He can participate in the violation of those standards which are necessary to his existence while remaining safe from the violation. The murder, the most basic of violations of the social code as the act of incest is the most basic of violations of the psychological code, then acts to break and heal the social system simultaneously. Such a social interpretation of the appeal of the ritual of the murder mystery better explains the appeal of the genre for those who are not "addicts."

Increasingly, therefore, the best mysteries concentrate not on who the murderer is, but rather on what brought a specific individual to isolate himself in violence. Simenon's Maigret, Lew Archer, and Martin Beck all seek to understand the criminal act and its roots in the past. The concentration is rarely on alternative suspects, except as a means of complication, but on the one unknown suspect; not on greed or women, but on the ever-deepening layers of the past. Legality in this search may be clear, but morality never is. Indeed, increasingly no moral judgment is made or can be made. As Ross Macdonald has said, "Freud deepened our moral judgment and rendered it forever ambivalent." Such a statement may seem a commonplace, yet in the world of the murder mystery where there has been no distinction made between legality and morality, it is not a commonplace. And such an inability to make moral judgments derives from more than merely the gradual intrusion of psychology on the detective novel, but the very conditions of the crime itself. Since the murder has taken place as a condition of society and since the detective and the criminal share their role against and outside of society, moral judgment is impossible, for any judgment is a judgment of the detective himself and any judgment is also a judgment of the very society which gives the detective his legitimacy. Once the environment becomes the cause, no man's motives are sure and must, in their innermost recesses, remain uncertain. When they do emerge, they can only emerge as insanity and death. And in the end, the detective remains alone, for he has not rescued society or redeemed it, but only staved off its final defeat. And because motive recedes into the mind and the past and remains uncertain, the murderer remains a mythic figure—being motive rather than having one.

In this manner, then, the murder mystery has, with few people being aware of it, moved ever closer to the fringe of the social novel as it simultaneously moves closer to its ritual beginnings. As Macdonald has said, he is seeking a form where "psychic reality blends at the edge of social reality."[13] As pure plot, myth and the murder mystery are rigorously about what they are about. The reading of myth as disguised history or as disguised psychology has meaning only for the scholar. For the believer, the bareness of myth, its "whatness," leaves room for exploring the "why" only as the myth embodies a psychological reality. Yet embodying that reality is not exploring it or explaining it. Everything here in the detective novel is implicit and thus powerful; everything means only by being. Our response to myth and to the detective novel—for how can we explain our constant return to a literary product which is so patently patterned but as a response—does not depend in any sense on our comprehending the levels of psychological apperception, but in our acceptance of its vision. And in *Oedipus Rex* and the murder mystery, the detective searches for the criminal—the self searches for the self on the boundaries of the legitimate—constantly affirming the existence of the boundary while at the same time finding that the solutions never solve the real crime, the boundary itself.

Elliot L. Gilbert

McWATTERS' LAW: THE BEST KEPT SECRET OF THE SECRET SERVICE

"The police are not here to create disorder, they're here to preserve disorder."

–Mayor Richard Daley, Chicago, 1968

Some time ago I published a brief essay in *JPC* called "The Detective as Metaphor in the Nineteenth Century" in which I suggested that the professional detective–who did not make his appearance, either in life or in literature, until the nineteenth century–ought to be considered a representative figure of that age and, by extension, of our own time. I then went on to make the point that the detective, contrary to what would ordinarily be supposed, principally represented for the nineteenth century not so much the age's faith in reason and in man's problem-solving abilities as its growing disillusionment with a rationalistic approach to the mystery of the human condition.

To support my idea that the detective embodied a *criticism* of reason rather than a celebration of it, I dealt with such disparate matters as *Hamlet,* Freud, Conan Doyle, *Oedipus,* Dickens' *Bleak House,* and Poe's "Murders in the Rue Morgue," but it was inevitable that in a paper of less than a dozen pages my remarks would have to be more suggestive than definitive and would have to leave whole areas of the subject unexplored.

Among the matters I was able to mention only in passing, for example, were two which bear most particularly on my thesis and which I would like to consider now. The first has to do with the response of people in the nineteenth century to the real detectives they encountered either in person or through reports in the press. Clearly, if the point is to be made that the detective represents in some crucial way the failure of human reason to achieve order, it should be possible to show that that failure was real as well as metaphoric and was recognized to be so by the detective's contemporaries. There is considerable evidence of this.

The second matter which bears importantly on my thesis has to do with the character of the detective in popular art forms. There is no denying the fact that such popular figures as Sherlock Holmes and Hercule Poirot have helped to create, in countless mystery novels and stories, the familiar image of the detective as a triumphant spokesman for human reason, a ratiocinative genius from whom nothing can be hidden and who always succeeds in restoring order to a murderous world. Such an image cannot, of course, be ignored, but it must be properly understood. In my earlier essay I suggested that the popularity of the traditional detective story derives at least in part from the reader's knowledge—conscious or otherwise—that in the "real" world, order is only rarely achieved; from the fact, in other words, that the successful detective of popular fiction is as much a wish-fulfillment fantasy as he is a portrait from life.

What I had time only to hint at earlier, however, was that in recent years, even in the popular arts, and especially in films, the detective has more or less abandoned the role of super-rationalist and has taken on instead many of the characteristics of real nineteenth-century sleuths. In contemporary films, that is, the detective is frequently seen to be—in Mayor Daley's memorable phrase—as much a preserver of disorder as an enemy of it, and it is one intention of this paper to show how the real-life detective of the nineteenth century and the cinematic detective of our own time are strikingly similar figures who depart dramatically from the stereotype of the popular fictional detective as a master reasoner and promoter of order.

That stereotype would very much have surprised the people who first encountered the detective in the real world of the early nineteenth century. The earliest detectives, brought together in such organizations as London's Bow Street Runners, were recruited from the ranks of "reformed" criminals and to the casual eye of the ordinary turn-of-the-century citizen were hardly distinguishable from the felons they were supposed to pursue. Not for such agents the moral scruples or the intellectual achievements of a Sherlock Holmes or a Hercule Poirot. To the Bow Street Runners, "thief-taking" was merely a business, one in which government bounties usually—though not always—made it more profitable to *catch* a thief than to *be* one. Few of these early detectives, however, were averse to combining the two occupations, and bullying and blackmail, often of the weak and innocent, were among their chief weapons. Moreover, on those occasions when a criminal was able to offer more for his freedom than the state was willing to offer for his capture, early operatives had little or no trouble with their consciences. "As a bankrupt thief turns thief-taker in despair, so an unsuccessful author turns critic," wrote Shelley in his original preface to *Adonais,* clearly suggesting that the general opinion of the early detective force was not a flattering one. The romantic "autobiography" of Vidocq, French thief-turned-thief-taker, vividly recreates the world of the first detectives, with its crude methods and rough justice.

Public disapproval soon helped to drive the Bow Street Runners out of business, their replacements being the better controlled and more respectable Metropolitan Police under the direction of Robert Peel. Peel, rejecting ex-criminals, staffed the new force with former military men and in general attempted to raise the moral tone of the enterprise. In part he succeeded, but the old reputation was hard to live down, and the new organization had its own share of difficulties culminating in the scandal of 1878, which led to the dismissal of two-thirds of the force. In 1887, then, when Sherlock Holmes spoke, in *A Study in Scarlet,* of Scotland Yard operatives Gregson and Lestrade as "the pick of a bad lot," readers of the day would certainly have had every reason to assume that Holmes was making an ethical as well as a professional judgment.

Clearly missing from the unfavorable nineteenth-century picture of the professional police agent is the image of the detective as a masterful reasoner. It is true that being a thief-taker had always required a certain shrewdness and that the profession placed a premium on cleverness. The cleverness that was wanted, however, was more often than not the cleverness of the rogue, of the *Eirōn* of classical Greek literature, of Reynard the Fox—a low cunning very unlike the majestic rationality so highly valued in the great detectives of popular mystery fiction.

It might be wondered, therefore, where the idea of the detective as rationalist and promoter of order came from. To be sure, Dupin, Poe's great creation and the official "first detective" of literature, embodied, right from the start, all the well-known qualities of the fictional sleuth. But while Poe was first in the field, he did not himself create the great vogue of the literary detective. Indeed, interest in the detective as a literary figure developed rather slowly during the next few decades and didn't really flower until the last third of the century.

Ironically, one of the most important contributors to that flowering worked as hard as he did to create an image of the detective as noble and brilliant in order to conceal the darker truth about real detectives for which he himself was largely responsible. During the American Civil War, Allan Pinkerton, proprietor of a pioneering detective agency, was hired to run a secret service and espionage organization for the North, and his great success led him to continue his operations after the surrender of the South, developing his agents into a much-feared private army available to industrialists for strike-breaking and other such duties.

It was largely to counteract the bad publicity resulting from these unpopular activities that Pinkerton inaugurated a series of books about the exploits of his operatives designed to show his people in a favorable light. These books, ostensibly written by Pinkerton himself and bearing such titles as *The Gypsies and Detectives; A Double Life and Detectives; The Railroad Forger and Detectives; Burglars, Fate, and Detectives; The*

Expressman and the Detective; and *Strikers, Communists, Tramps, and Detectives,* were collections of cases showing detectives solving mysteries through the application of reason and always acting in the clear interests of public order.

The Pinkerton books successfully fulfilled their primary function—their propaganda function—substituting in the public's mind the detective for the thief-taker, the rational man of law for the crafty ex-criminal, and helping to create a model for the thousands of fictional detectives, public and private, who have since played such an important role in popular literature. Other publishers soon rushed into print with imitations of the Pinkerton casebooks, attesting to the popularity of the originals, and these books too had the effect of replacing the old, unfavorable image of the detective as "preserver of disorder" with the now familiar figure of the detective as master reasoner and solver of mysteries.

All this time, of course, detectives in real life did not change in any dramatic way. As the Metropolitan Police scandal of 1878 makes clear, and as I suggested in my earlier paper, the real-life detective persisted as a metaphor not for the nineteenth-century's faith in reason but for its growing disillusionment with it. At the same time, the fictional detective, developed as a kind of escape from this reality, as a way of maintaining faith in the efficacy of reason, also persisted. It was an extraordinary situation: two diametrically opposed visions of the world represented by two diametrically opposed views of the same figure.

Nowhere is this confusion more clearly expressed than in a little-known but extremely revealing book published in 1881 under the title *The Detectives of Europe and America: A Revelation of the Secret Service.* The physical characteristics of the book are worth considering for a moment. It's a massive volume—848 pages long—with a cover typical of Victorian book manufacture; not a single square inch left unembellished by text or design. The title makes its way down the embossed cloth in a variety of type sizes and styles, some of the letters appearing on gold bars, others on black scrolls, still others graven on shields. In the spaces and corners not filled with this lettering, there are no fewer than five illustrations, two in black, three in gold. These include a man being robbed by two women; another man, with a dark lantern, entering what looks like a vault door; a mail thief being pursued by a pistol-wielding policeman; an old, bearded man languishing in prison; and in the very middle of the cover, an elaborately engraved human eye in gold, complete with golden eyebrow, beneath which is a scroll with the inscription "Wide Awake." Finally, on the spine of the book there appears, in addition to an abridgement of the title, the words "Celebrated Cases," a figure in gold of Justice, blindfolded, and the motto "Punishing the Guilty Protects the Innocent."

Everything about the appearance of this book, an anthology of some thirty-five true-life detective adventures drawn from police annals all over the world, testifies to its publisher's desire to cash in on the popularity of the Pinkerton series by emphasizing the success and the benignity of the Secret Service. The motto on the spine, for example, is clearly meant to suggest the value to the social order of the whole detective enterprise, the pictures of criminals being caught and punished imply the inevitability of that fate befalling all wrongdoers who come up against the detective force, and the large gold eye, with its motto "Wide Awake," is similar enough to Pinkerton's own famous trademark eye, with its motto "We Never Sleep," to have led careless book buyers to suppose that they were getting one of the authentic Pinkerton volumes. The table of contents continues the theme of the detective as a man of reason serving the best interests of society. From one of the long chapter synopses we learn, for instance, of a

> Drama of the Street Vaurigard, No. 58, in Paris—a saving mother-in-law and an expensive son-in-law—the widow Houet mysteriously disappears—letters received intimating that she has committed suicide—are they forged?—an able detective, M. Chouard, traces the affair during twelve years—Bastien's extortions—Robert, the coward with an unquiet conscience—arrested at last—condemning evidence in the criminal's pocket—who is the murderer?—a skeleton as a witness in the case—startling discoveries of science—phrenology does miracles—murder will out!

All of these elements and many others, including the promise of the title page that the book will offer a "revelation of struggles and triumphs," are clearly intended to present the detective in the most attractive possible light. It is particularly strange, therefore, that in its last chapter *The Detectives of Europe and America* should proceed to undermine its more than eight hundred pages of favorable propaganda with one of the most devastating attacks ever levelled at the professional detective. But this is in fact what the book does, that attack being the work of a man named George S. McWatters, identified on the title page as "late member of the American Secret Service." The title page also describes McWatters as editor of the book, though his name is not to be found anywhere on the outside of the volume. (Even a careless book buyer might have been alerted to the fact that he was not getting a Pinkerton book had some other author's name appeared on the cover.) How much this book was really McWatters' own and how much he might merely have been lending his name to someone else's compilation is not clear. What is clear is that the book's last chapter is an intensely personal statement about the detective profession by someone who was a part of it for many years and who at the end of his career felt compelled to speak a most unexpected truth.

That chapter, entitled "The Detective System," begins unspectacularly enough with Officer McWatters reporting the publisher's request that he prepare an essay on his views of the detective system in general to conclude the volume. We can only wonder what publisher J. B. Burr of Hart-ford may have expected would result from this suggestion. What he got was the following statement:

There are but two great classes in civilization—the oppressed and the oppressors, the trampled upon and the tramplers. To the latter class belongs the detective. He is dishonest, crafty, unscrupulous, when necessary to be so. . . . He is the outgrowth of a diseased and corrupted state of things, and is, consequently, morally diseased himself. He is a miserable snake, not in paradise, but in the social hell. He is a thief and steals into men's confidences to ruin them. He makes friends in order to reap the profits of betraying them.

To account for this remarkable indictment of his profession, McWatters paints an even blacker picture of the society within which the detective must operate. "Everywhere," he says,

I see injustice and wrong triumphing over justice and the right; . . . [The child] is taught that it is no matter how he gets [his] gold, so that he avoids all legal difficulties in the way; and he is further instructed that when he shall have acquired a certain amount of gold he need fear no law, for he can buy juries and judges then, and be "a law unto himself."

In such a world, McWatters continues, the detective cannot be expected to be better than he is. "Whatever is bad in the detective's career," he writes, with an almost Swiftian bitterness,

society has created for him to perform, and compelled him to do it. However unpleasant to himself his business may be, he has the happiness of knowing that in its results it is good—that is, if it be good to preserve the present order of things. For without the detective, the laws, such as they are, could not well be enforced . . . and allowed to pursue their business uninterrupted, the pickpockets, forgers, and bank robbers would soon monopolize the business of the country to the [detriment] of the land speculators, the usurers, the railroad robbers [and] the private bankers, who, with less keen talent than the independent pickpocket proper, are obliged to have laws framed to help them in their iniquity. [Thus is the detective] often degraded to a sort of watchman. . . .

In the light of such a savage judgment as this of his profession, Officer McWatters' valedictory is only what we might expect.

Between the philosophers and the general public I leave the detective system, unwilling to presume to decide for others whether, on the whole, it *fell* from "heaven" or sprang from "hell." But while I would not undertake to determine for others the metaphysical question above raised, I feel it proper to add for myself that though most of my relations with the police during my whole period of office were pleasant enough . . . yet the duties of my position were frequently obnoxious to my taste and—perhaps I will be pardoned for so expressing myself—to my better nature. My adoption of and continuance in the profession were not acts of choice . . . but were rather the results of the "force of circumstances," in conflict with which I was powerless. And I felt relieved of a great burden when fate permitted me at last to forego my honors as a detective.

It is in this remarkable way that the promise of the title page to present us with the "triumphs" of the detective profession is fulfilled.

Statements such as I have quoted from *The Detectives of Europe and America* invite speculation. One thought is that in Officer McWatters we may perhaps have the prototype of a figure familiar today both in detective fiction and detective fact: the embittered policeman, soured by years of association with the worst elements of society, hardened by too much exposure to human misery, disgusted by the discrepancies between pious theories of justice and cynical practice. Interviews with just such police officers as this appear frequently in newspapers and magazines, and the hard-boiled detective has for years been a prominent character in crime and mystery movies and fiction.

There is at least one crucial difference, however, between the vision of the embittered detective we get from McWatters' memoir and the one that emerges from the fiction of, let us say, Dashiell Hammett. Sam Spade is certainly as tough, as cynical, as manipulative, as unsentimental as Officer McWatters reveals himself to be, but on one essential point he differs from the real-life operative. Consider Spade's famous speech to Brigid O'Shaughnessy at the end of *The Maltese Falcon.* Brigid, who murdered Spade's partner Miles Archer, has been counting both on Spade's dislike of Archer and his love for her to save her. But Spade rejects her appeal. "Listen," he says,

> This isn't a damned bit of good. You'll never understand me, but I'll try once more and then we'll give it up. Listen. When a man's partner is killed he's supposed to do something about it. It doesn't make any difference what you thought of him. He was your partner and you're supposed to do something about it. Then it happens we were in the detective business. Well, when one of your organization gets killed it's bad business to let the killer get away with it. It's bad all around—bad for that one organization, bad for every detective everywhere.

The speech goes on, displaying all the cynicism and bitterness we find in McWatters, but displaying also—at least in the passage I quoted—one idea that appears nowhere in McWatters, the idea that through his action and self-sacrifice, Spade is making a definite contribution to the sum total of good, of order in the world. "He was your partner and you're supposed to do something about it" strikes an oddly touching Platonic note in the otherwise tawdry universe of *The Maltese Falcon,* as does Spade's insistence that he has a serious obligation to all detectives everywhere to make their lot better which transcends any merely personal obligation he may have to himself.

It is this notion that the detective's job is to add to the total sum of order in society which is entirely missing from McWatters' last chapter. Indeed, McWatters' point is just the opposite. If, he tells us, the detective succeeds in upholding the law, then he increases the amount of wickedness and disorder in the world, since it is the wicked who "have laws framed to help them in their iniquity." If the detective, through brilliant deductions and hard work, brings small thieves to justice, he in fact increases the amount of injustice in the world, since the people whom he is hired to protect against the small thieves are the big thieves. Necessarily, then—in this view—the detective is an agent of disorder or, as another writer, quoted by McWatters, puts it, a "Purveyor of Hell." Such an unexpectedly bleak vision of the detective business as this surely deserves a name and a proper formulation. I would like to propose both. First, I would like to suggest that we give this concept the name "McWatters' Law," and second, I would like to offer the following statement of that law: "Every effort made by a detective to increase the amount of good and order in any portion of society has the inevitable effect of increasing the amount of evil and disorder in the society as a whole."

Plainly, McWatters' Law has ramifications beyond the comparatively narrow world of the detective. Indeed, the discovery of the universal operation of that law may be said to have been the chief philosophical business of the nineteenth century, of which period the detective, therefore, is a key metaphor. Howard Haycraft, in *Murder for Pleasure,* emphasizes the intimate relationship between the detective and the nineteenth century, writing

> that the first systematic experiments in professional crime detection were naturally made in the largest centers of population, where the need was greatest. And so the early 1800's saw the growth of criminal investigation departments in the police systems of great metropolises such as Paris and London.

Such departments were made necessary by a population growth in the early 1800's very different from the sort of increases which had characterized previous centuries. In earlier years, the increases had been gradual and relatively orderly. By the beginning of the nineteenth century, however, with a mushrooming industrialism demanding large pools of manpower concentrated in a few centers, the population increase became rapid and chaotic. Urban communities could no longer absorb newcomers in an orderly way, anonymous masses of people began to flood the cities, and, cut off from their rural pasts and alienated from their neighbors, people began to find themselves in just that condition of uncertainty, fear, disorganization and mistrust which, in mystery stories, precedes the arrival of the detective.

There is a notable irony here. The industrialism, which led to the social disorientation, which in turn led to the creation of the detective, had originally been intended to *in*crease not *de*crease the order and security of human life. As offspring of the triumphant rationalism of the eighteenth-century, nineteenth-century industrialism had set out to build a new society with improved standards of living for all, only to build great sprawling slums instead. And from these slums there sprang a new kind of crime—impersonal, anonymous—that required for the first time great hordes of impersonal, anonymous policemen for its detection, policemen who, simply by undertaking to solve these crimes and reestablish order, became themselves unwilling dwellers in the disorderly slums that reason had built. A fine instance of McWatters' Law in operation.

In my earlier essay, I discussed the frequency with which the first fictional detectives symbolized the failure rather than the triumph of rationalism. Dickens' Inspector Bucket, for example, brings to mind George McWatters' condemnation of police agents who "steal into men's confidences to ruin them; [who] make friends in order to reap the profits of betraying them"; who, in the name of order, sow disorder. Hugo's Javert is another futile figure, fated, in his pursuit of the sewer-dwellers, to plunge into the sewers himself. And Poe's Dupin, the proud master reasoner, created, according to Joseph Wood Krutch, to keep his author from going mad, fails signally to defeat the ape of insanity prowling the Rue Morgue of the writer's mind.

It might be useful, in this connection, to consider whether there ever really was a possibility of Dupin rescuing Poe from his "madness." Krutch's comment suggests that there was, but his notion is perhaps a little simplistic. It is based on the idea, popularized by commercial mystery fiction, of the detective as a restorer of order and safety, and it therefore sees Poe's detective stories as a potential cure for the disease represented by the author's nightmare tales. But since this cure very obviously did not work, we are perhaps justified in questioning Krutch's analysis of the situation. It is unusual, after all, for a body which has long been producing a substance poisonous to itself to begin suddenly producing the antidote to that poison, and it would therefore be much more reasonable to see the detective story in Poe's work not as part of the author's cure but rather as part of his disease, not as the antidote for the toxin of despair but as itself the poison.

This view is most convincingly expressed by D. H. Lawrence in his famous essay on Poe in *Studies in Classic American Literature.* For Lawrence, the great disease of the nineteenth century in general, and of Poe in particular, was rationalism and especially the analytic process, which is the pride of detective fiction. Poe "never sees anything in terms of life," Lawrence writes,

> [but] always in terms of force, scientific. [With a woman] he wishes to analyze her, till he knows all her component parts, till he has got her all in his consciousness. . . . It is easy to see why each man kills the thing he loves. To *know* a living thing is to kill it. You have to kill a thing in order to know it satisfactorily. . . . Man does so horribly want to master the secret of life and of individuality *with his mind.* It is like the analysis of protoplasm. You can only analyze *dead* protoplasm, and know its constituents. It is a death process. . . . Edgar Allan probed and probed. So often he seemed on the verge. But [his characters] went over the verge of death before he came over the verge of knowledge. And it is always so. . . . Man is always sold in his search for final KNOWLEDGE.

But if this is true, then Poe's detective stories, with their passion for analysis, represent not a healthy alternative to the nightmare tales but a fulfillment of their worst tendencies. For if to analyze is to kill, then there is metaphysically no difference between the detective and the murderer. Both, on the profoundest level, are victims of the analytic impulse, the killer's desire to master and the detective's desire to know being one and the same. No wonder it did no good in the end to send Dupin in pursuit of the ape. Poe was merely sending one murderer after another. The results were inevitable and quite in keeping with McWatters' Law. The more Poe labored to achieve order and safety in the corner of his life devoted to the detective story, the more disorder and danger increased in his life as a whole.

Poe's experience paralleled that of the nineteenth century, which was also preoccupied with the idea of order, with the desire to subdue and control the universe through the application of reason. What the age discovered, however, in its quest for order and control—and what it powerfully symbolized in the detective—was not man's ability to achieve that order but rather his inability to do so. Further, it discovered that nearly every effort, however laudable, to increase the order anywhere in the system inevitably had the effect of increasing the amount of disorder in the system as a whole.

No lesson of the nineteenth century has been taken more to heart by the twentieth than this one. The old faith in technology, with its roots in a more optimistic age, is tarnished in our own time. Scientists, technicians, engineers—all detectives in spirit with their passion for order, their urge to solve mysteries, and their reliance on reason—trouble the ecologists we have all become. We still acknowledge the orderly structures these men can create, but now we are nervous about the price we must pay for them, and we wonder—on occasion, perhaps sentimentally—if we really want order at such a price. More energy seems always to go out than to come in. We consume the resources of ten generations to make one generation comfortable—and are troubled at the bargain. Anxiously, we search for something we can *do,* only to discover that whatever we do seems to make matters worse.

A passage from a recent newspaper story sums up the dilemma. "In the light of the present population problem," reporter Clair Sterling writes,

> we may think it simple common sense to get cracking on planet-wide birth control. Far from helping, though, that could make matters worse. A lower birth-rate would mean more food and capital investment available per person. . . . This could accelerate the pollution crisis and encourage a quick rise in the birth-rate again to take advantage of the extra food.[1]

Here is McWatters' Law with a vengeance, only a McWatters' Law grown far beyond its original limits of application to the detective. Grown so much, in fact, as to begin to merge with another much broader and much more famous law, Newton's Second Law of Thermodynamics, the Law of Entropy, the real spectre which haunted the nineteenth century and which haunts our own century as well; the Law of Entropy which warns that in any system, physical or metaphysical, energy is always lost and disorder always increases.

In the face of such cosmic despair, the continuing popularity of the commercial detective story is very understandable. Just as Pinkerton's true life detective adventures were written to distract people from the author's nefarious professional activities, so the last hundred years of popular mystery fiction, inspired by the Pinkerton books, can be said to have been written in large part to distract readers from the nefarious activities of the universe.

Certainly the world of the commercial detective story differs markedly—and pleasantly—from the real world in which we otherwise live. In most such stories, for example, the detective is depicted as a bringer of order out of chaos. The typical plot begins with that most disorderly of all acts—murder. Disorder soon spreads through the community like an epidemic; people lose their everyday sense of safety, for a killer is abroad and no one knows who he is, why he has struck, or where he might strike next. People also lose their old confidence in one another, for the murderer may be anyone: a friend, a relative, a lover. Into this totally disorganized world steps the detective. With his devotion to analysis and reason, he soon places the facts of the case in their proper relationship to one another, and from this ordering of the facts he goes on to the reordering of society. The murderer is identified and is isolated, uncertainty yields to certainty, safety and trust are restored; for the unsettling puzzle there is substituted the reassuring solution.

The real world clearly doesn't work like this. In the real world, for instance, disorder *in*creases, where in the detective story it *de*creases. In the real world, everything—obeying the Law of Entropy—moves *toward* death, where in the detective story everything moves *away* from death. Death stands at the beginning of the tale, as we've seen, and the author quickly substitutes for the dark mystery of dissolution, the much simpler puzzle of "whodunit." Death is disarmed; for the time that we are reading, we are relieved. "It's a diverting little murder," says the great detective, "but I'm sure that amid the blood we shall find the solution." And we curl up with the book, anticipating a cozy hour, insulated, during the time we are reading, from the real world in which murders are not cozy. For however conscientiously the mystery writer labors to create the illusion of reality, combing police records and medical encyclopedias for precise, even squalid details, the world of the popular mystery story, even the hard-boiled and apparently realistic world of *The Maltese Falcon,* remains hermetically sealed and self-contained, a world in which the tides of the universe are made to flow backwards.

Quite recently, however, a change has begun to occur in the role of the detective in the popular arts. While the market for the traditional detective story continues strong, a very different sort of detective has started to appear in fiction and films. He is not so much a new detective as an old one, a detective of the sort who might have been found on the roster of the Bow Street Runners or who could pass for a near-relative of Dickens' Bucket or Hugo's Javert or even of George S. McWatters. Why such a change is occurring at this moment in time we probably don't have enough perspective to say. Perhaps people have by now lived long enough with McWatters' Law not to require constant protection from it anymore. Whatever the reason, it is clear that in the strange stories of Jorge Luis Borges, in the plays and novels of Ionesco, Duerenmatt, Butor, Robbe-Grillet, and many others, and especially in recent motion pictures, the detective undertakes a different role and the detective story a different function. In these new works, detectives become, very frankly, symbols of man's impotence in the face of the Law of Entropy, and their stories are all illustrations of McWatters' Law—namely, that "every effort made by a detective to increase the amount of order in any portion of society has the inevitable effect of increasing the amount of disorder in the society as a whole."

The direction of movement in these new stories is just the reverse of that in more traditional detective fiction. Instead of beginning with a complex tangle of events and then moving toward a moment of clarity, they begin with something perfectly simple—an easy job, an uncomplicated idea—and then ramify into mysteries so complex that the mind is unable to contemplate them, much less find solutions for them. In Borges' stories, the recurring image is the labyrinth, which the characters enter lightly, not realizing they are lost with the very first step they take. In Duerenmatt's novel *The Pledge,* we meet a detective who has been given a very simple assignment, to wait at a gas station disguised as an attendant until a particular criminal appears, as he is certain to do. Many years later, with the criminal not yet having shown up, the detective still waits, duty having been carried to the point of insanity. But he is not really a detective anymore; no mind can hold its focus for so long under the dissolving influences of life. He has become what at first he only pretended to be, a gas station attendant, living in a hopelessly complex world which has subverted the purity of his original purpose.

Another well-known contemporary novel, Michel Butor's *Degrees;* epitomizes the new role of the detective or the detective-like figure in literature. The central character embarks lightly on what seems to him to be a relatively simple task, the recording of the events which occur in his classroom. It is not long, however, before the teacher-detective discovers that to record everything that goes on in his class means recording thoughts as well as acts, memories of the previous class, for instance, and mental preparations for the next. To find these things out, he begins interviewing the students but soon discovers that these interviews have aroused anxieties among the pupils, their parents, and the school administrators, and it is not long before he is called upon to defend himself against obscure charges of perverse behavior. These are only a few of the deepening complications of *Degrees,* a novel which, though it begins as a simple investigation, quickly evolves into a mystery so dark and convoluted that only the death of the investigator can bring it—however arbitrarily and unsatisfactorily—to an end. In the recent *PMLA* article about *Degrees,* Jennifer R. Walters points out an irony in the book which is a fine example of McWatters' Law. The critic alludes to the self-defeating nature of the protagonist's enterprise, writing that "by means of his book and his teaching Vernier is attempting to progress in a way which greatly resembles all he deplores in history."[2]

Significantly, many of the most admired detective movies of the recent past have presented the detective in this role of defeated investigator. The movie called *Z*, for example, plays on our expectations that the discovery of truth by a detective necessarily leads to justice. Unhappily, the discoveries which the detective in this film makes prove to be, on every level, trivial and impotent. The doctor-specialists, whose brilliant analysis reveals every aspect of the victim's wound, cannot save the victim's life. The formal instruments of justice are corrupt from the first (as in many mystery stories they are at least incompetent), and when the public prosecutor is obliged to take on the role of "private" detective, in order to discover and reveal the truth, he quickly finds that it is the criminals whom he unmasks who have the real power, including the power, in the end, to imprison the detective. One of the most memorable scenes in the film is the last. Set on a hill overlooking the sea on a bright day, it takes full advantage of the pleasant expectations roused by such imagery as well as by our experience with conventional detective stories, which require the restoration of order, to make the announcement of the defeat of justice particularly devastating.

Alfred Hitchcock's celebrated film *Psycho* could hardly make its primary effect at all if it couldn't play itself off against the conventional detective story. Every step of the way, Hitchcock toys with such conventional expectations of ours as that, for example, the heroine will live to see the world restored to order and sanity and that the detective will succeed in exposing and capturing the criminal. But Hitchcock has really taken for his model in this picture not the neat and optimistic world of commercial mystery fiction but the nihilistic world of George McWatters, and so in *Psycho* we find that the heroine dies horribly hardly more than a third of the way through the film, that the detective is murdered by a psychotic whose identity he cannot begin to guess, and that the only survivor among all the major characters is a madman. More recently, *The French Connection* again portrays the detective as an impotent investigator, more destructive in the end than any of the criminals he pursues and fails to capture. Like Oedipus before him, Popeye the detective, with a Javert-like persistence which is his chief virtue, runs down the killer only to find that it is himself.

Finally, there is the impotent detective to end all impotent detectives in Jules Pfeiffer's play and movie, *Little Murders.* Lt. Practice, a parody of the serious criminal investigator, can't be better described than he describes himself in his last speech in the play. The story is set in New York, which has been suffering an unusual number of disasters–illustrating the failure of man the technician–including 345 unsolved murders in the last six months. When Lt. Practice arrives on the scene, he is shaking.

Practice: I wasn't like this when I met you six months ago, was I? Wasn't I a lot more self-confident? Jees, the way I used to enter the scene of a crime! Like I owned the goddam world! There's going to be a shakeup, you know. When there are 345 murders and none of them get solved. Somewhere there's a logical pattern in this whole business. Sooner or later everything falls into place. I believe that. If I didn't believe that I wouldn't want to wake up to see the sun tomorrow morning. Every crime has its own pattern of logic. Everything has an order. If we can't find that order it's not because it doesn't exist, but only because we've incorrectly observed some vital piece of evidence. Let us examine the evidence.

Number one. In the last six months, 345 homicides have been committed in this city. The victims have ranged variously in sex, age, social status and color. Number two. In none of the 345 homicides have we been able to establish motive. Number three. All 345 homicides remain listed on our books as unsolved. So much for the evidence. A subtle pattern begins to emerge. What is this pattern? What is it that each of these 345 homicides have in common? They have in common three things: a) that they have nothing in common; b) that they have no motive; c) that consequently, they remain unsolved. The pattern becomes clearer.

Orthodox police procedure dictates that the basic question you ask in all such investigations is: who has the most to gain? What could possibly be the single unifying motive behind 345 unconnected homicides? When a case does not jell it is often not because we lack the necessary facts, but because we have observed our facts incorrectly. In each of these 345 homicides we observed our facts incorrectly. Following normal routine, we looked for a cause. And we could find no cause. Had we looked for effect, we would have had our answer that much sooner. What is the effect of 345 unsolved homicide cases? The effect is loss of faith in law-enforcement personnel. That is our motive. The pattern is complete. We are involved here in a far-reaching conspiracy to undermine respect for our basic beliefs and our most sacred institutions. Who is behind this conspiracy? Once again, ask the question: who has the most to gain? People in high places. Their names would astound you. People in low places. Concealing their activities beneath a cloak of poverty. People in all walks of life. Left wing and right wing. Black and white. Students and scholars. A conspiracy of such ominous proportions that we may not know the whole truth in our lifetime.

With this speech of Lt. Practice's, we return to the atmosphere of the last chapter of *The Detectives of Europe and America.* Setting aside matters of language and tone, Lt. Practice and George McWatters make exactly the same complaint, that the detective cannot go about his job of increasing the level of order in society because of the formidable and perhaps even conspiratorial forces arrayed against him. "People in high places, people in low places, people in all walks of life," says Practice; "Pickpockets, forgers, land-speculators, userers, private bankers," says McWatters; "Strikers, Communists, Tramps," says Allan Pinkerton; "Hippies, bleeding hearts, liberals, old ladies in tennis shoes," say today's chiefs of police. One might as well add "the planets, the stars, molecules, atoms," for they too are in on the conspiracy. All things conspire against the man who presumes to solve mysteries. That this should be the theme of so many contemporary works about the detective is surely one of the most interesting facts about mystery fiction today. If the detective defined by Sir Arthur Conan Doyle—the detective as success—fulfilled a need for Victorian readers that he continues to fulfill today, the detective defined by McWatters' Law—the detective as failure—touched the nineteenth-century imagination just as profoundly and is now more than ever a central figure in popular art.

George Grella

MURDER AND MANNERS: THE FORMAL DETECTIVE NOVEL

The formal detective novel, the so called "pure puzzle" or "whodunit," is the most firmly established and easily recognized version of the thriller. Sharing sources with the novel proper, boasting a tradition dating from Poe, and listing among its practitioners a number of distinguished men of letters, the detective novel has enjoyed a long, though slightly illicit, relationship with serious literature. As with literary study, historians and bibliographers of the form, discovering incunabula, repudiating apocrypha, and tracing sources and lineage, have published their findings in a multitude of books and essays, in somewhat learned journals and para-scholarly periodicals. And almost since its inception, critics have been denouncing the rise and announcing the demise of the whodunit. But the detective novel has survived the vicissitudes of literary taste and the sometimes suffocating paraphernalia of scholarship; though it attained its greatest heights of production and consumption in the 1920's and 1930's—the so called Golden Age of the detective story—the best examples of the type retain a remarkable longevity. The whodunit, in fact, has become a kind of classic in the field of popular fiction.

One commentator has rather loosely defined the detective story as "a tale in which the primary interest lies in the methodical discovery, by rational means, of the exact circumstances of a mysterious event or series of events,"[1] which could describe a number of literary works, including *Oedipus Rex, Hamlet, Tom Jones,* and *Absalom, Absalom!*. In reality the form, in Raymond Chandler's words, has "learned nothing and forgotten nothing."[2] It subscribes to a rigidly uniform, virtually changeless combination of characters, setting, and events familiar to every reader in the English speaking world. The typical detective story presents a group of people assembled at an isolated place—usually an English country house—who discover that one of their number has been murdered. They summon

Reprinted from NOVEL with the permission of the editor and the author.

the local constabulary, who are completely baffled; they find either no clues or entirely too many, everyone or no one has had the means, motive, and opportunity to commit the crime, and nobody seems to be telling the truth. To the rescue comes an eccentric, intelligent, unofficial investigator who reviews the evidence, questions the suspects, constructs a fabric of proof, and in a dramatic final scene, names the culprit. This sequence describes almost every formal detective novel, the best as well as the worst; whatever the variations, the form remains, as Chandler says,

> . . . Fundamentally . . . the same careful grouping of suspects, the same utterly incomprehensible trick of how somebody stabbed Mrs. Pottington Postlethwaite III with the solid platinum poniard just as she flatted on the top note of the "Bell Song" from *Lakmé* in the presence of fifteen ill-assorted guests; the same ingénue in fur-trimmed pajamas screaming in the night to make the company pop in and out of doors and ball up the timetable; the same moody silence the next day as they sit around sipping Singapore slings and sneering at each other, while the flatfeet crawl to and fro under the Persian rugs, with their derby hats on.[3]

It is one of the curiosities of literature that an endlessly reduplicated form, employing sterile formulas, stock characters, and innumerable clichés of method and construction, should prosper in the two decades between the World Wars and continue to amuse even in the present day. More curious still, this unoriginal and predictable kind of entertainment appealed to a wide and varied audience, attracting not only the usual public for popular fiction but also a number of educated readers; it became known, in Phillip Guedalla's famous phrase, as "the normal recreation of noble minds." This dual appeal raises an obvious question: why should both ordinary and sophisticated readers enjoy a hackneyed and formula-ridden fiction devoid of sensation or titillation, and frequently without significant literary distinction?

Most readers and writers of detective fiction claim that the central puzzle provides the form's chief appeal. Every reasoning man, they say, enjoys matching his intellect against the detective's, and will quite happily suspend his disbelief in order to play the game of wits. Accordingly, detective novelists have drawn up regulations for their craft forbidding unsportsmanlike conduct of any kind; all relevant facts must be revealed to the reader and, though misdirection is allowed, fair play must be observed at all times. Adherents of the puzzle theory assume that the average reader conscientiously catalogues the alibis, checks the timetables, sifts through the clues, and concludes with the detective that only one person could have caught the 4:17 from Stoke Pogis in time to put the cyanide in the crumpets, maladjust the hands of the grandfather clock, incriminate the nice young gentleman who quite innocently left a 12EEE footprint in the rose garden, and arrive home just in time for high tea. That person is the murderer, no matter how guiltless he may have seemed.

In fact, though many readers discover the murderer—usually that old standby, the Least Likely Person—they do so by guesswork or intuition rather than by following the detective's frequently improbable methods. Because the reader seldom possesses the detective's exotic knowledge and superior reason, the important clues often mean little to him. Since he doesn't know the killing distance of a South American blowgun, the rate at which curare is absorbed into the bloodstream, or the effects of an English summer on the process of *rigor mortis,* he cannot duplicate the sleuth's conclusions.

The writers of the Ellery Queen stories (Frederick Dannay and Manfred B. Lee) so firmly accepted the puzzle theory that at one time they inserted near the end of their books a "challenge to the reader," who now possessed all the information necessary to solve the case himself. Since the Queen novels presented some of the most abstruse problems in detective fiction, few readers, if any, rose to the challenge. (The writers have not used the device for more than twenty years.) In *The Chinese Orange Mystery*, for example, one must figure out why a murderer would turn his victim's clothes back-to-front and how a room could be locked from the outside by a complicated arrangement of weights, strings, and thumbtacks. Similarly, few would arrive at Hercule Poirot's dazzling conclusion, in Agatha Christie's *Murder in the Calais Coach,* that since no single person on a train could have committed a murder, all the passengers must have done it together. "Only a halfwit could guess it," commented Raymond Chandler. The fanciful methods and incredible ingenuity of most fictional murderers elude everyone but the detective. Only he is granted the power to arrive at the correct deduction from the most tenuous or ambiguous evidence; thus, the box of spilled pins in John Dickson Carr's *Till Death Do Us Part* immediately suggests to Gideon Fell yet another method of relocking a room, while to the reader it suggests nothing at all extraordinary. Fell solves another difficult case in *Death Turns the Tables* because he happens to know that Canadian taxidermists stuff mooseheads with red sand, a fact unlikely to be known by the reader and equally unlikely to be thought important.

The puzzle theory demands some credence, if only because so many readers and writers espouse it. It seems clear, however, that although the puzzle is central to the detective novel, it does not in fact provide the chief source of appeal; the reader generally cannot solve it by the detective's means, and thus derives his chief pleasure not from duplicating but from observing the mastermind's work. The novels do not so much challenge human ingenuity as display it to its furthest limits. The reader does not share the detective's ability, rather he marvels at it.

Other, more subtle readers of detective fiction reject the puzzle theory for a psychological and literary explanation. Edmund Wilson argues that in the 1920's and 1930's the world was "ridden by an all-pervasive feeling of guilt and by a fear of impending disaster,"[4] which led to the production and enjoyment of detective fiction: everyone sought release from anxiety in the identification of the scapegoat-criminal, who "is not, after all, a person like you and me." W. H. Auden carries Wilson's thesis a step further, suggesting a literary basis for the whodunit's chief appeal. In his penetrating essay, "The Guilty Vicarage," Auden finds a timelessness in the detective story, derived from its resemblance to Greek tragedy. Its interest, he claims, lies "in the dialectic of innocence and guilt." He identifies as "demonic pride" the murderer's belief that his own intelligence will permit him to elude the punishment of a just universe. Since the murderer's action has implicated a whole society, the detective's task is to locate and expel the particular cause of a general guilt. The expulsion has a cathartic effect, liberating the reader's own latent *hubris* and guilty desires. Auden concludes that "the typical reader of detective stories is, like myself, a person who suffers from a sense of sin."

Both critics, though persuasive, fail to account for the peculiar elements of the detective novel. Wilson does not consider the fact that though the whodunits of the Golden Age remain popular, they no longer dominate light fiction, or that very few classic detective novels are currently written. In the present era, haunted by memories of global conflict and menaced by the spectre of nuclear holocaust, man may well labor under the greatest burden of guilt and anxiety since the Fall; logically, the detective novel should now be enjoying unprecedented popularity, but this is not the case. Wilson carelessly identifies the typical villain of the novels as a criminal ("known to the trade as George Gruesome"). Even a casual reader of detective fiction will recognize Wilson's error: the typical villain is not a criminal but an ordinary and superficially acceptable citizen, "a person like you and me," which, in Wilson's terms, would imply condemnation rather than exculpation of the society. Wilson also fails to account for the peculiar nonviolence of the form. It is not, as he implies, a manhunt, but rather an exploration of a posh and stylized milieu; further, the final accusation is less an attempt to fix guilt than a means of expelling a social offender.

Perhaps because he is a confessed "addict" of detective fiction, Auden comes closer to the truth in recognizing the relevance of the novel's society, but errs in identifying its structure and significance as tragic. Since the reader never learns the murderer's identity until he is revealed, and since the criminal's method is described through an intellectual reconstruction, there is no opportunity to identify with him or sympathize with whatever *hubris*, fear, remorse, or guilt he may suffer. Though the detective novel deals in the materials of human disaster, it steadfastly avoids presenting them in emotional terms, and thus prevents the characteristically emotional engagement of tragedy. It presents no violent disruptions of the social fabric, no sense of universal culpability, but rather a calm and virtually unruffled world, where everything turns out, after all, for the best. With the intellectualization of potentially sensational matters, without any direct involvement, knowledge of the murderer's character, or sense of doom, the reader neither experiences complicity nor requires catharsis. A closer examination of the nature of the detective novel reveals something far different from the conclusions of Wilson and Auden.

As Auden implies, the detective novel's true appeal is literary. Neither a picture of actual crime, a pure game of wits, nor a popular but degenerate version of tragedy, it is a comedy. More specifically, it remains one of the last outposts of the comedy of manners in fiction. Once the comic nature of the detective story is revealed, then all of its most important characteristics betray a comic function. The central puzzle provides the usual complication, which the detective hero must remove; and its difficulty insures a typically comic engagement of the intellect. The whodunit's plot, full of deceptions, red herrings, clues real and fabricated, parallels the usually intricate plots of comedy, which often depend upon mistaken motives, confusion, and dissembling; it also supports the familiar romantic subplot. And the upper class setting of the detective story places it even more precisely in the tradition of the comedy of manners. Like the fiction of Jane Austen, George Meredith, and Henry James, the detective novel presents the necessary "stable and numerous society . . . in which the moral code can in some way be externalized in the more or less predictable details of daily life."[5] The *haut monde* of the whodunit provides not only the accepted subject of the comedy of manners, but also furnishes the perfect place for the observable variations of human behavior to be translated into the significant clues of criminal investigation. The detective thriller maintains the necessary equivalence between the social and the moral code: a minute flaw in breeding, taste, or behavior—the wrong tie, the wrong accent, "bad form" of any sort—translates as a violation of an accepted ethical system and provides grounds for expulsion or condemnation. Because of this system the unofficial investigator succeeds where the police fail. They are ordinary, bourgeois citizens who intrude into a closed, aristocratic society; unable to comprehend the complex and delicate social code, they are invariably stymied. The amateur detective, conversely, always is socially acceptable and comprehends the code of the society he investigates—he can question with delicacy, notice "bad form," or understand lying like a gentleman to the police; therefore, he always triumphs over the mundane ways of the official forces of law and order. In fact, although the most frequent types of detective hero derive superficially from the brilliant eccentrics of nineteenth century detective stories, in reality they owe more to the archetypal heroes of comedy. There is more of Shakespeare, Congreve, and Sheridan than Poe, Conan Doyle, and Chesterton in their creation. Even the characters who dwell in the usual settings of detective fiction share close relationships with the humors characters of literary comedy, which may be why they are so often criticized as mere puppets and stereotypes. Finally, in theme, value, and structure, the formal detective novel displays a close alliance with some of the great works of comic literature of the past; both its peculiar, often-criticized nature and its great popularity result from the attributes and attractions of a particular, stylized, and aristocratic type. Consequently, it would be more appropriate to call the detective novel the "thriller of manners."

The most important personage in any comedy, of course, is the hero, who may not necessarily involve himself, except as a problem solver, in the chief romantic plot, but usually deserves credit for clearing up the obstacles to happiness which comedy traditionally presents. Characters like Prospero, Brainworm, and Tony Lumpkin, for example, are the problem-solvers of their plays, but do not share the romantic hero's rewards. The comic hero of the detective story is the sleuth, often distinctive and prepossessing enough to earn the title of Great Detective, who initially develops from the Poe-Conan Doyle tradition, which may at first seem an unlikely beginning for the comedy of manners.

Poe, it is generally agreed, invented the detective story and established its basic conventions—the murky atmosphere, the insoluble problem, the *outré* method, the incredible deductions, the adoring Boswell, and the gifted being who unravels the most difficult crimes.[6] His prototypical detective, C. Auguste Dupin, possesses a dual temperament, "both creative and . . . resolvent," combining the intuition of the poet with the analytical ability of the mathematician; the fusion gives him extraordinary deductive powers, enabling him, for example, to reconstruct his companion's chain of thought from a few penetrating physical observations ("The Murders in the Rue Morgue"). "Enamored of the Night," he shares unusual tastes with his deferential narrator-stooge—they dwell in a "time-eaten and grotesque mansion" which suits "the rather fantastic gloom of [their] common temper." Not at all a comic figure, Dupin exhibits the striking characteristics of intellectual brilliance and personal eccentricity which indelibly mark all later detective heroes.

From Dupin, with some slight influence from Gaboriau and Wilkie Collins,[7] springs Sherlock Holmes, the most important and beloved sleuth in literature, whose creator took the Poe character and formula, condensed the pompous essays on the ratiocinative faculties, added a more concrete sense of life, dispelled the romantic gloom and substituted a lovingly detailed picture of late Victorian England. Like Dupin, Holmes displays extraordinary deductive powers, inferring an entire life history from the most trivial items (a hat in "The Blue Carbuncle," a watch in *The Sign of Four*, a pipe in "The Yellow Face"). Though endowed with the Dupinesque dual temperament—Wilson calls Holmes a "romantic personality possessed by the scientific spirit"—Holmes is considerably less morbid and more endearing than his prototype; his foibles are the understandable eccentricities of a man of genius. He lives in a state of Bohemian disorder, smokes foul tobacco, relieves his chronic melancholia by playing the violin or taking cocaine, and even shoots a patriotic V. R. on his walls with a heavy calibre pistol. Conan Doyle developed Poe's inventions further, giving his detective varied abilities and wide and exotic interests, especially in the sciences of criminology. (Holmes, for example, is the author of a pamphlet on the one hundred and forty varieties of tobacco ash and of a "trifling monograph" analyzing one hundred and sixty separate ciphers.) He established the convention of singular knowledge symbolizing great knowledge: the unusual, with a certain sleight of hand, passed for the universal. Conan Doyle also expressed in conversational, epigrammatic form his detective's peculiar personality and superior intellect: Holmes caps one solution, for example, with "There were twenty-three other deductions which would be of more interest to experts than to you" ("The Reigate Puzzle"). He compresses into one sentence the principle of all fictional detectives: "Eliminate all other factors, and the one which remains must be the truth" (*The Sign of Four*). Holmes also displays a penchant for memorable phrases which influence the speech patterns of later detectives: "The game's afoot," "You know my methods, Watson," "These are deep waters, Watson," or, in reply to an exclamation of wonder, "Elementary, my dear Watson." He is given to pointing out a subtle and apparently irrelevant clue and deducing an unusual conclusion from it, all in a witty form of dialogue known as the "Sherlockism." The most often quoted of these occurs in "The Silver Blaze." Holmes calls a character's attention

> ". . . to the curious incident of the dog in the night-time."
> "The dog did nothing in the night-time," [is the reply].
> "That was the curious incident."

Whatever their individual differences, all other fictional detectives derive from the Dupin-Holmes tradition. Though many later sleuths may seem eminently unSherlockian in appearance, methods, and personality, they all exhibit the primary qualities of the Great Detective. They generally possess a physical appearance as distinctive as Holmes's hawklike profile—they may be either very tall or very short, very fat or very thin, or they may affect unusual attire. They are usually pronounced eccentrics, enjoying odd hobbies, interests, or life styles, and frequently overindulging in what Auden calls the "solitary oral vices" of eating, drinking, smoking, and boasting. Above all, whatever his particular method of detection, the sleuth is blessed with a penetrating observation, highly developed logical powers, wide knowledge, and a brilliantly synthetic imagination: the detective story, unlike most kinds of popular literature, prizes intellectual gifts above all others.

But to change the Great Detective of short fiction to the comic hero of the novel required more than the Dupin-Holmes tradition. The anti-social bachelor with cranky and exotic interests could not adapt well to the large and complex world of the longer form. The detective of the novel demanded a fuller personal background, a greater cast of characters, a more gradual and intricate development of his investigation than the short story provided. The book that effectively transformed the short detective story into the novel of detection is E. C. Bentley's *Trent's Last Case*, published in 1913, while Sherlock Holmes was still practicing at 221B Baker Street. It is probably the most important work of detective fiction since Conan Doyle began writing in 1887, and has been much praised by critics and practitioners as a nearly perfect example of its type. In her historical study, *The Development of the Detective Novel,* A. E. Murch states the usual view of the book:

> *Trent's Last Case*, a novel written at a period when the short detective story was still the most popular form of the genre, brought to fiction of this kind a more spacious atmosphere, time to consider and reconsider the implications of the evidence, and a new literary excellence.

More important, *Trent's Last Case* is the most influential source for the comedy of manners which came to dominate the formal detective novel. It introduced that favorite English detective, the gentleman amateur, in the person of Philip Trent—artist, popular journalist, lover of poetry, and dabbler in crime—the progenitor of all the insouciant dilettantes who breeze gracefully through detective fiction for the next thirty years. Because Trent is an obvious gentleman—immediately apparent by his whimsical speech and shaggy tweeds—he can succeed where the official police cannot: the characters accept him socially, and his accomplishments (an artist's keen eye, well-bred sympathy, the ability to interrogate the French maid in her native tongue) give him greater mobility. Most important, he understands the social code of the world he investigates; in a significant exchange with the secretary of a murdered millionaire, Trent points the direction of later detective fiction:

> "Apropos of nothing in particular . . . were you at Oxford?"
> "Yes," said the young man. "Why do you ask?"
> "I just wondered if I was right in my guess. It's one of the things you can very often tell about a man, isn't it?" (ch. vii)

Trent's sensitivity to those indecipherable things that characterize the Oxford man (by definition a gentleman) emphasizes his own gentlemanly status; moreover, a value system is established—no Oxford man, naturally, could be a murderer. Following Bentley, the detective novel largely abandoned its atmosphere of gloom and menace—a heritage of the Poe influence—and turned to the comic milieu of the traditional English novel. Its favorite detectives, settings, and characters resembled less and less their subliterary models and showed ever closer relationships with the favorite characters and types of traditional comedy. The Great Detective became a comic hero, as well as a transcendent and infallible sleuth; his solution of a difficult problem became the task of releasing a whole world from the bondage of suspicion and distrust. His task allied him with the archetypal problem-solvers of comedy—the tricky slave, the benevolent elf, the Prospero figure.

After *Trent's Last Case* the gentleman amateur dominates the full-length novel of detection. Although this character exhibits the Holmesian conventions of arcane knowledge, personal eccentricity, and idiosyncratic speech, these traits are diluted in the popular conception of the English gentleman. The sardonic savant becomes the witty connoisseur: wide researches are replaced by dilettantism, and the ironic Sherlockian speech is translated into bright and brittle badinage. Some of the best-known examples of this extremely popular detective are H. C. Bailey's Reginald Fortune, A. A. Milne's Antony Gillingham, Phillip MacDonald's Anthony Gethryn, Anthony Berkeley's Roger Sheringham, Margery Allingham's Albert Campion, Nicholas Blake's Nigel Strangeways, and the Oxonian policemen John Appleby and Roderick Alleyn, the creations of Michael Innes and Ngaio Marsh. The only important American versions of the type, which does not travel well, are S. S. Van Dine's Philo Vance and Ellery Queen's Ellery Queen.

The fusion of gentleman and detective reaches its zenith (some think its nadir) in Dorothy L. Sayers' noble sleuth, Lord Peter Wimsey, a full-fledged aristocrat as well as a fop, a bibliophile, and a gourmet.

> He was a respectable scholar in five or six languages, a musician of some skill and more understanding, something of an expert in toxicology, a collector of rare editions, an entertaining man-about-town, and a common sensationalist. (*Clouds of Witness*, ch. iv)

Lord Peter combines the Great Detective with a familiar comic character. His varied abilities, recondite interests, and high intelligence derive of course from the Holmesian genius; but his attire, languid air, and silly-ass speech ally him with the *gracioso* or dandy figure of comedy. Wimsey is partly a version of Jung's archetypal Wonderful Boy (or, as Auden calls him, "the priggish superman"), partly the "tricky slave" of Roman comedy (as Northrop Frye points out), partly the fop of Restoration comedy. As a detective he is, needless to say, a gentleman, a graduate of the proper schools (Eton and Oxford), aware of the subtle code of the thriller of manners. His consistent desire to make things come right—he is always rescuing people from themselves—translates him from the ludicrous dandy figure of satire to the intelligent mechanic of human complications.

Although the gentleman amateur overshadows all other detective heroes, some important sleuths derive from other comic archetypes. Agatha Christie's Hercule Poirot, perhaps the most famous detective since Sherlock Holmes, combines something of the Holmesian tradition with that of the dandy, yet stands apart from both. Lacking the formidable personality of the Sherlockian genius and the airy manner of the *gracioso,* Poirot is an elf.

> Poirot was an extraordinary looking little man. He was hardly more than five feet, four inches, but carried himself with great dignity. His head was exactly the shape of an egg, and he always perched it a little on one side. His moustache was very stiff and military. The neatness of his attire was almost incredible, I believe a speck of dust would have caused him more pain than a bullet wound. (*The Mysterious Affair at Styles,* ch. ii)

In Poirot individuality of utterance becomes a rather tiresome difficulty with English idioms; his major eccentricity is an overweening faith in his "little gray cells." His short stature, pomposity, avuncular goodness, and his foreign, otherworldly air, place him with the kindly elves of the fairytale, as well as with Puck and Ariel. (Miss Christie's elderly spinster detective, Miss Jane Marple, is a kind of universal aunt or fairy godmother, a female Poirot.) Other elf types, of whom Poirot is the major representative, are G. K. Chesterton's Father Brown and Anthony Gilbert's Arthur Crook. Poirot, naturally, always employs his magic for good purposes, insuring that the fabric of society will be repaired after the temporary disruption of murder. It is not surprising that he especially tries to establish or restore conjugal happiness, a symbol of a newly reintegrated society and the traditional goal of all comedy.

Neither a dandy nor an elf, the third major problem-solver is the wizard. The detectives in this category retain the powerful physical presence and the convincing infallibility of the Sherlockian tradition. Rex Stout's curmudgeonly genius, Nero Wolfe, and John Dickson Carr's Sir Henry Merrivale and, above all, Dr. Gideon Fell, are the most successful examples and closest to the Great Detective. A scholar and lexicographer specializing in Satanism and witchcraft, Dr. Fell usually encounters the "impossible" murder, committed in the traditional hermetically sealed room. In addition to his wizardry, he radiates an immense benevolence and a Falstaffian gusto:

> There was the doctor, bigger and stouter than ever. He wheezed. His red face shone, and his small eyes twinkled over eyeglasses on a broad black ribbon. There was a grin under his bandit's moustache, and chuckling upheavals animated his several chins. On his head was the inevitable black shovel-hat; his paunch projected from a voluminous

black cloak. Filling the stairs in grandeur he leaned on an ash cane with one hand and flourished another cane with the other. It was like meeting Father Christmas or Old King Cole. Indeed, Dr. Fell had frequently impersonated Old King Cole at garden pageants, and enjoyed the role immensely. (*The Mad Hatter Mystery,* ch. i)

His love for the ancient British virtues and his enormous capacity for beer combine in his magnum opus, *The Drinking Customs of England from the Earliest Days.* When not outwitting evildoers, Dr. Fell assiduously pursues research for this book through all the novels in which he appears. His joviality, his resemblance to the kindly father figures of legend, and his expertise in the supernatural ally him with an archetypal wizard, Jung's Wise Old Man, the good magician or Prospero figure.

The usual settings of detective fiction serve a comic as well as a functional purpose. The novel invariably presents murder in isolated and luxurious surroundings, combining the necessities of the whodunit with the manners tradition. The setting limits the suspects to a manageable number and establishes an aura of wealth and gentility, the aristocratic atmosphere of high comedy. The ubiquitous English Country house, whose attraction is confirmed by a glance at titles–*The Red House Mystery, Crooked House, Peril at End House, The Mysterious Affair at Styles, Scandal at High Chimneys, The House at Satan's Elbow*–separates a small, homogeneous, elite group from the rest of the world, performing the same function as the *mise en scène* of writers like Goldsmith, Sheridan, Jane Austen, George Meredith, and Henry James. Other settings serve the same purpose; the charity bazaars, men's clubs, card parties, hunting lodges, university common rooms, and snowbound resort hotels of the detective novel withstand the intrusions of the bourgeois policemen and the tramp who is always initially suspect. This posh and pedigreed society, remote from criminal reality, often irritates detective novel readers, but it offers social forms for the novelist of manners and within those forms, the observable clues to human behavior by which the detective hero can identify the culprit.

Though basically homogeneous, this society does contain variety. Its members, though roughly equal in social standing, are not of the same class, family background, or profession. Within a limited range they comprise an English microcosm. There is always at least one representative of the squirearchy, one professional man–commonly a doctor, but sometimes a lawyer, professor, or schoolmaster–a cleancut young sporting type, and a military man (never below the rank of major), usually a veteran of colonial service. An English vicar, often a muscular Christian, frequently hovers about, providing a link with the Established Church. Like the vicar, the other characters serve an emblematic function, the beef-witted squire speaks for the rural aristocratic virtues, "huntin', shootin', and fishin' " the sporting type exemplifies the "Barbarian" graces of good looks, athletic skill, and intellectual deficiency, and the military man stands for the Empire, bluff British honesty, the officer class.

One of the major criticisms of the detective novel is that its characters are merely stereotyped, cardboard constructions, serving the contrivances of a highly artificial method. Though the novelist often creates mere puppets, he errs in good company: his characters generally are modern versions of the humors characters of Roman, Renaissance, and Restoration comedy, people governed by an emblematic function, a single trait, or a necessity of plot. The cast, for example, usually includes a "smashing," decent girl (poor, but of good family) and a spirited young man, to provide the traditional romantic plot. The circumstances of the murder frequently implicate the girl, so the young man covers up for her by destroying or manufacturing evidence, providing false alibis, and generally behaving like a gentleman. The detective sympathizes with such actions and avoids embarrassing the pair. In addition, he clears up the obstacle of criminal suspicion so that they can marry: they furnish the objective means by which the detective can benefit society. They are usually a pallid and uninteresting pair who possess little intrinsic appeal, but exist largely to reflect the powers of the comic hero.

Another favorite stock character is the obsessed philosopher or comic pedant, a man defined wholly in terms of his ruling passion, like "my uncle Toby" or Emma Woodhouse's father. He appears as Pastor Venables in Dorothy L. Sayers' *The Nine Tailors*; perhaps the most extreme example of the type, Venables' ruling passion is campanology. Others include the mechanically minded hobbyists of *The Problem of the Wire Cage* and *The Problem of the Green Capsule* (John Dickson Carr) and the physician of Agatha Christie's *The Murder of Roger Ackroyd.* Often these hobbyists use their unusual knowledge to fashion infernal machines or strange methods of murder, another example of a respectable comic tradition usefully adapted to functional detective purposes.

The military man owes to his comic archetype, the *miles gloriosus* or braggart soldier, a latent ridiculousness: easily recognizable by his phlegmatic temperament, brusque manner, and peculiar habits of speech, he often provides an object of satire. Sometimes he is used solely for humorous effect, as in Major Blunt's embarrassed wooing in *The Murder of Roger Ackroyd.* His stiff upper lip emphasizes his class and his interests, as Colonel Marchbanks demonstrates while regretting the imprisonment on a murder charge of his host, the Duke of Denver, in Dorothy L. Sayers' *Clouds of Witness*: " 'Awfully unpleasant for him, poor chap, and with the birds so good this year' " (ch. ii). Like the obsessed philosopher or the military man, most of the other characters achieve an almost archetypal level themselves, derived both from their frequent appearance in detective stories and their constant use in comedy. Usually they are defined only by their function, e.g., the young man is no more than a suitor or the squire no more than the conventional *senex iratus.* Just as part of the pleasure of comedy results from the author's skilful handling of his stock characters, so too the enjoyment of a mystery comes from the author's tampering with his stereotypes—the reader wonders which of the perennial group will be the murderer this time.

The comedy of manners generally contains an expulsion of the socially undesirable which insures the continued happiness of those remaining. Similarly, the detective novel features two expulsions of "bad" or socially unfit characters: the victim and the murderer. Because only unlikeable characters are made to suffer permanently in comedy, pains are taken to make the victim worthy of his fate: he must be an exceptionally murderable man. This prevents regret and also insures that all characters have sufficient motive. The favorite victim of the mystery is also the favorite unsympathetic character of comedy—the blocking character, who works against such natural and desirable ends as joining the correctly matched young couple. A frequent victim, therefore, is the negative father or mother (a common comic obstacle) who opposes a marriage, makes an unfair will, or refuses to act his or her age, all actions which cause distress to the young. The squire, being elderly, stupid, and irascible, makes an excellent murderee. His fictional archetype is probably Squire Western, who wouldn't have lasted long if *Tom Jones*, a notable comedy of manners, had also been a detective novel. The victim of *The Murder of Roger Ackroyd* is a *senex iratus* who forces an engagement on his stepson, impeding the path of true love and earning his doom. Old General Fentiman is murdered in Miss Sayers' *The Unpleasantness at the Bellona Club* because he has made a bad will. Sigsbee Manderson in *Trent's Last Case* dies because he is much older than his wife, and a brute besides. The negative mothers, like the gross, evil Mrs. Boynton of Agatha Christie's *Appointment With Death*, also make expendable obstacles: Mrs. Boynton prevents her children from marrying, thus causing her death. Similarly, Mrs. Cavendish of Christie's *The Mysterious Affair at Styles* pays dearly for marrying a man much younger than herself and making an unfair will. All of these victims have hindered the natural course of events, chiefly by obstructing the path of true love. Such obstruction in any form of comedy means eventual defeat or exclusion: and in the exacting code of the detective novel, that exclusion means murder.

Another favorite victim is the ineligible mate, whose impending marriage to the decent young girl would interfere with her natural preference for the eligible young man. Since he is young, this victim is burdened with an even more specific sin: under his attractive exterior he conceals the personality of a bounder, a rotter, and a cad. The young victim of Carr's *The Problem of the Wire Cage* reveals his caddishness by taking advantage of a working class girl and cheating at tennis, offenses implicitly equivalent. Philip Boyes of Miss Sayers' *Strong Poison* earns expulsion by espousing free love, writing experimental novels, and making himself "an excescence and a public nuisance," and (kiss of death) in being "a bit of a cad" (ch. iv). In another Sayers novel, *Clouds of Witness,* the dead man seems at first an inappropriate victim—handsome, dashing, an officer with a distinguished war record. But the coroner's inquest establishes his unfitness: he cheated at cards, which "was regarded as far more shameful than such sins as murder and adultery" (ch. i). Another rotter of the worst sort, Paul Alexis in *Have His Carcase,* meets an untimely end because he is a gigolo who preys on lonely, vulnerable women, a professional cad.

Other common fatal flaws, often indirectly related to the social ethic of the comedy of manners, merit violent exclusion. The victim may be guilty of exploiting the ritual of his society, posing as a gentleman, but hiding a dark, unacceptable secret. Mr. Shaitana of Agatha Christie's *Cards on the Table* exudes evil; in her *Murder in the Calais Coach* the victim is an American kidnapper posing as a philanthropist. The victim in Carr's *The Crooked Hinge* is a false claimant to a considerable country estate, neither a gentleman nor a true squire. Because he may have risen from humble beginnings to achieve the doctor's high status, the professional man—generally the only character who actually works for a living—is also a potential victim. On the rare occasions that a young woman is murdered, she is always revealed as a secret sinner under a respectable façade, like the murdered adulteress in Carr's *The Sleeping Sphinx.* (If she is not an adulteress masquerading as a respectable woman, she will then be an actress, never a very desirable occupation for a woman in English literature.) One other damning trait is a fatal un-Englishness. Foreigners lead dangerous lives in detective novels, and men otherwise exemplary die for merely ethnic reasons. The Mediterraneans of the detective novel never seem true gentlemen, perhaps a result of the Italian villainy of Elizabethan revenge tragedies and Gothic fiction. Anthony Morell is condemned on the fourth page of John Dickson Carr's *Death Turns the Tables*, where the reader is told "you would have taken him for an Italian." Since he is indeed an Italian, a businessman, and a symbol of lower class virility, Morell meets his doom three chapters later. The wealthy peer of *Whose Body?* loses his life because he is a Jew; Paul Alexis of *Have His Carcase* compounds his caddishness by being Russian; and in *Clouds of Witness,* Denis Cathcart's French blood explains his inadequacy. (Hercule Poirot is a rare foreigner, tolerated by his society because he is faintly laughable and—like all detectives—represents no sexual threat.)

Virtually all victims, then, suffer their violent explusion because of some breach of the unwritten social or ethical code of the thriller of manners. Even minute infractions, like ungentlemanliness, incur tremendous penalties. Violations of accepted morality, particularly adultery, are capital crimes; both immoral and ungentlemanly (or unladylike), infidelity usually demands the most rigorous penalty that society can apply. The offense of foreign birth or blood seems too trifling to be murdered for, but Englishmen in general distrust the foreigner, and the comedy of manners, which seems the quintessential representation of a ruling class, follows the prejudices of the society it depicts. The dark, handsome, charming man with gleaming white teeth and glossy black hair (all characteristic of the Latin in the whodunit) is generally marked for murder. Since he attempts also to woo the young girl, he serves a blocking function as well. Murder initiates the action of the detective novel, but its real purpose is to indicate the nature of the society in which it occurs, to provide a complication which requires the abilities of a comic hero, and to exclude a social undesirable.

The murderer, though technically a criminal, is more interesting than his victim and consequently occupies an ambivalent position. On the one hand, he has removed an obstacle, destroyed a rotter posing as a gentleman, or expelled a social evil. On the other hand, he has committed the gravest human crime, an offense against both society and God, and has placed the other members of his group under suspicion. In short, he has created a complication which demands his own dismissal. Because he is intelligent enough to commit an ingenious crime and elude detection for most of the novel, he earns a certain admiration. However, since "good" (*i.e.,* socially valuable) people cannot permanently suffer in comedy, the murderer must turn out to be somehow undesirable himself. Usually the culprit is a more acceptable person than his victim, because he comprehends the elaborate social ritual well enough to pose as an innocent. This sustained pretense of innocence culminates, however, in the unveiling of the murderer's true character; the detective exposes him as an imposter, the *alazon,* a familiar comic figure who, Northrop Frye says, "pretends or tries to be something more than he is." His crime is not the true cause of his defeat, only a symptom of it: like his victim, the murderer has guaranteed his doom by committing some earlier comic, social, or ethical mistake. Occasionally, the murderer's motive grows from an earlier crime shared with the victim–blackmail or adultery. More frequently, the murderer may be yet another blocking character. Dr. Nick, the amiable psychiatrist of *The Problem of the Wire Cage,* is a villainous father surrogate who murders his young ward, tries to pin the crime on the eligible bachelor, and seeks to marry the ingénue himself. His crime, of course, violates moral laws, but it is his initial comic sin of multiple blocking that condemns him.

The physician, perhaps as a result of the many famous doctor-murderers (including Crippen), is always suspect in the detective novel. Familiar with many means of killing, especially poisons, and sharing the priest's knowledge of secrets, the doctor occupies a delicate position. Dr. Sheppard, for example, murders Roger Ackroyd to prevent being revealed as a blackmailer; his violation of professional ethics, more than the murder, disrupts his world. Given the orthodox Christian bias of the whodunit, the medical man is often guilty on the additional grounds of favoring science over religion. Dorothy L. Sayers, the most energetic High Church propagandist among detective novelists, condemns two doctor-murderers—Penberthy of *The Unpleasantness at the Bellona Club* and Sir Julian Freke of *Whose Body?*—because both favor an organic interpretation of metaphysics, contending that the soul is merely an outgrowth of inherent glandular and neurological weaknesses.

Another favorite murderer, as well as favorite victim, is the cad who passes himself off as a gentleman. Though the ordinary detective story reader, for example, may have to wait until the end of Dorothy L. Sayers' *Have His Carcase* to discover the criminal, the student of literature recognizes him in Chapter XIII:

> He stood about five foot eleven—a strongly built, heavyish man with a brick-red all-weather face. Evening dress did not suit him . . . one would expect him to look his best in country tweeds and leggings . . . Wimsey, summing him up with the man of the world's experienced eye, placed him at once as a gentleman-farmer, who was not quite a gentleman and not much of a farmer.

Because he looks like a boor, behaves like a bounder, and is a False Squire to boot ("not much of a farmer"), the murderer arouses Lord Peter's, and thereby society's disapproval, which is tantamount to utter condemnation. Although the rest of the novel is devoted to a number of aimless complications, including a wholly non-functional cipher, the mystery ceases to matter once the murderer has been identified by means of the manners tradition. Another imposter, young Ronald Merrick of Carr's *The Sleeping Sphinx,* appears at first an unlikely murderer, since he conforms to the social ethic. After all, how can a cleancut, athletic public school graduate who wears the approved rustic uniform—disreputable tweeds—be guilty of bad form? But Ronald is a rotter, as his artistic talents indicate and his adulterous affair with his victim confirms. Though his crime rids society of one sinner, normality returns only with his own, obviously well-deserved, removal.

The exclusion of the imposter often can be a relatively bloodless affair, provided certain conditions obtain: the rotter who displays some feeling for the code and the really brilliant murderer who has eliminated an obviously evil person, are often permitted to "do the gentlemanly thing" and commit suicide. Lord Peter provides Penberthy this way out in *The Unpleasantness at the Bellona Club.* The gifted Sir Julian Freke of *Whose Body?* and the murderer of Roger Ackroyd poison themselves. And even Ronald Merrick chooses to kill himself rather than endure a public trial—those disreputable tweeds count for something, after all. Other brilliant, somewhat gentlemanly criminals are even occasionally allowed to escape punishment, provided their victims were inordinately evil, and that they never return to their original society again. This exception, however, applies only to those with a modicum of social awareness who have done their society a great service. Such criminals also help the detective by taking the final action out of his hands and sparing him any possible personal remorse. Such a murderer's ultimate action represents a conscious attempt at benevolence and obviously recommends his moral character more highly than his victim's. And since the detective's major concern lies in establishing the general innocence rather than punishing specific guilt, the actual fate of the criminal matters little, so long as he quits his society.

Once the murderer leaves, the world of the novel begins to approach its former peacefulness. The last chapter resembles the final scene of almost every traditional comedy. The successful sleuth presides over a feast of some kind in an appropriately convivial place and explains his reasoning, to the accompaniment of admiring comments from those assembled. The group usually consists of all the major characters in the novel–minus murderer and victim–who represent their society as it should be, cleansed of guilt, free of complication and obstacles, recreated anew from the shambles of a temporary disorder. They gather around a table in the library, at a pub, a dinner party, or even at a wedding: the rightly matched couple have finally married or made plans to marry, their relationship symbolizing the happy and orderly end toward which the detective has been working. Poirot, for example, manages a happy marriage in *The Mysterious Affair at Styles,* causing his Watson, Captain Hastings, to comment, "Who on earth but Poirot would have thought of a trial for murder as a restorer of conjugal happiness" (ch. xiii). At this feast the detective also explains red herrings, forgives those who (through the best of motives) have misled him, and offers advice for the future. The comic hero employs his greatest gifts: he is an engineer of destiny, with the power to recreate a new society from the ruins of the old. Moreover, his acuity and perception, which had enabled him to penetrate both a social code and a complex mystery, now function as abilities even more magical: he presides over a festival of innocence celebrating a return to the usual normative state, and he distributes the miraculous gift of absolution by establishing the essential goodness and worth of the society that survives. As the tricky slave, the benevolent elf, or the Prospero of a particular world, the detective has rearranged human relationships to insure the reintegration and harmony of an entire social order. This conventional ending re-emphasizes the comic structure and function of the formal detective novel.

Often, in fact, the detective novel moves over into purely comic realms. This movement results quite naturally from the whodunit's origins in the manners traditions. In his book on Henry James, *The Expense of Vision,* Laurence Bedwell Holland has remarked of the novel of manners, "That the genre tends toward stylization is suggested by some of the predecessors which on the surface it most resembles: the literature of courtship, Shakespeare's idyllic comedies, Restoration comedy, and the literature of sensibility." As a highly conventionalized version of the thriller and a further stylization of a highly stylized form, the whodunit frequently exhibits a conscious tampering with conventions and becomes sophisticated self-parody. Anthony Berkeley has produced a number of startling variations on the normal whodunit, all of them skilful and individual: in *Trial and Error,* the murderer finds himself forced to prove his own guilt; in *Before the Fact,* the victim helps plan her own demise; in *The Poisoned Chocolates Case,* six different and utterly plausible solutions for one murder are suggested by six different amateur detectives. Agatha Christie has written one book, *Ten Little Indians,* in which all of the characters, including the murderer, are victims. Her best novel, *The Murder of Roger Ackroyd,* serves a number of purposes: it provides the staple attributes of the detective story, satirizes the tiny rural village of King's Abbot, "rich in unmarried ladies and retired military officers . . . whose hobbies and recreations can be summed up in one word, 'gossip' " (ch. ii), and "tricks" the reader by revealing the narrator to be the murderer, a departure from convention that aroused considerable critical controversy.

Dorothy L. Sayers often wholly subordinates her mystery to a purely literary purpose. *The Nine Tailors* is less a detective novel than a nostalgic picture of life in the fen country of East Anglia. In *Gaudy Night,* Lord Peter plays Mirabell to Harriet Vane's Millamant against the Oxford landscape of a "straight" academic comedy devoted to a rather repellent intellectual-feminist thesis. Though her *Clouds of Witness* seems at first a very complicated and satisfying novel of detection, it actually serves to vindicate the aristocratic way of life: Lord Peter defends his brother, the Duke of Denver, before the House of Lords, redeems the honor of his family, and selects the right mate for his flighty sister, who has a penchant for unsuitable men. Along the way he excludes the socially unfit–bohemians, Socialists, "conchies," and cads–while bringing the right people together; the only complete villain in the novel, which has no murderer, is a lout of a farmer who is conveniently run over by a taxicab. Michael Innes also employs the detective story for comic purposes–a satirical look at academic life in *Seven Suspects,* a humorous picture of the art world in *One Man Show,* a sly Jamesian parody in *Comedy of Terrors*; the highly literate Innes manages to satirize his characters, their world, and the mystery itself, all within the normal framework of the whodunit. Most of these works display not only the usual conditioning exerted by the comedy of manners on the whodunit, but also normal comedy of manners masquerading as the detective novel, further demonstrating the reciprocity between the two forms.

Even the detective himself is not immune to the incidental humor of more orthodox comedy. Lord Peter Wimsey, whose earlier novels satirize a wide variety of subjects, begins as a figure of fun before he eventually becomes a priggish superman. An exaggerated aristocrat in everything he does, Wimsey falls into his very best Bertie Wooster Oxonian even when confronting a poisoner:

"I read a book somewhere which said it was all done by leucocytes—those jolly little white corpuscles, don't you know—which sort of got around the stuff and bustled it along so that it couldn't do any harm . . . the point is that if you go on taking arsenic for a good long time . . . you establish a what-not, an immunity, and you can take six or seven grains at a time without so much as a touch of indijaggers" (*Strong Poison*, ch. xv).

Less satirized in his later novels, Wimsey declines in humor as he develops in ability and personality (some attribute this decline to the author's gradually becoming too much enamored of her own creation to hold him up to ridicule). In the later books he displays superhuman versatility in addition to his already impressive skills—he shows himself, among other things, an expert bellringer, champion cricketer, successful international diplomat, and adept advertising copywriter. But his early books demonstrate the humorous potential within the detective hero, a potential that only faintly survives in Hercule Poirot's ludicrous appearance and mannerisms and Gideon Fell's Falstaffian presence. The detective never fully realized his intrinsic capacity for laughter, perhaps because the whodunit failed to enter wholly into the genre that inspired it.

The formal detective novel may succeed best in England because of its dependence on the mainstreams of the national literary heritage. Its use of the heroes, the characters, the archetypes and patterns of fictional comedy of manners for its major sources of theme and meaning is fully appropriate to that heritage. English fiction most often avoids and condemns the extremes of violence, disorder, or anti-social action, favoring instead wholeness, harmony, and social integration, the stable virtues of an essentially benevolent and correct society. Firmly in the mainstream of English literature, the detective novel shares a strong affinity with the "great tradition" identified by F. R. Leavis as central to British fiction. Since it also favors rural settings and rural (though upper-class) people, the formal detective novel shares with the novels of Jane Austen, George Eliot, Anthony Trollope, and George Meredith a tinge of the pastoral. This pastoralism explains in part the whodunit's characteristic distance from ordinary life: like the conventional pastorals of Spenser or Sydney, the detective novel should be judged in terms of its form, rather than in reference to the life that teems outside its quiet, genteel world.

Again like other forms of English fiction, the whodunit assumes a benevolent and knowable universe. In part imitating Conan Doyle's ability to illuminate and transform the ordinary details of life, detective novelists liberally sprinkle charts, diagrams, timetables, maps, plans, and other concrete evidence throughout their books, indicating the English tradition of empirical thought. This penchant for the tangible implies a world that can be interpreted by human reason, embodied in the superior intellect of the detective. His penetration of facts and clues shows his power to apprehend particular reality and attach significance to the trivial residue of any human action. Finding a meaning in the tiniest clue enables the detective to know the truth; thus, his universe seems explainable, the typical cosmos of English fiction, unlike the extravagant and grotesque realities of the American novel. Like the Gothic novel, which treats the seemingly irrational and inexplicable, the detective novel always provides a plausible and rational explanation of even the most perplexing chain of events.

Though the whodunit lacks verisimilitude, it practices the specific literary realism of its major tradition, not so much true to all observable life, as true to its stylized segment of life and its own assumed vision. Having confined his vision to a particular complex of conventions, the detective novelist attempts only to meet the requirements of those conventions, with no reference to the realities of criminal behavior. The highly artificial nature of the form, combined with its pastoral tendencies, isolates it from the facts of life—a detective novel of thirty or forty years ago seems only slightly dated, if at all. The detective novels of the Golden Age never mention the tensions and dangers that threatened the precarious stability of the Twenties and Thirties. They say nothing of the Depression, the social, economic, and political unrest of that time, but choose to remain within the genteel luxury of an aristocratic world, suffering the intrusions of the police and the initially suspected nameless vagabond before the detective hero turns suspicion on society. Except for these brief intrusions, themselves conventional, the great concern of the detective novel is centripetal; it is a formal minuet leading to an inescapable conclusion, as mannered and unreal as the masque, the sonnet, or the drawing room farce.

Aside from its interest as a disappearing vestige of the comedy of manners, perhaps the most important question that remains involves the reasons for the form's flourishing at its particular moment in history. Its profoundly English nature and heritage supply one answer: the detective novel demonstrates perhaps the last identifiable place where traditional, genteel, British fashions, assumptions, and methods triumph in the twentieth century novel. Another answer to the enigma of the detective novel has been advanced by John Paterson, who feels the form answered a profound cultural need in the troubled times of the Golden Age:

> In the age of the Boom, the Great Depression, flappers and gangsterism, and the Fascist Solution, it recalls the sober gentility and crude optimism of an earlier and more complacent generation; it asserts the triumph of a social order and decorum that have all but passed away.[8]

In that sense, perhaps, the detective novel fulfills not only the functions of comedy, but also the purposes of works like the sonnet or the pastoral eclogue, both of which flourished in an age of violence and rapid change. Just as the Elizabethans often found solace in rigidly conventional, peaceful, and essentially unreal literary forms, so too the twentieth century Briton apparently longed for the aristocratic aura, knowable universe, and unerring truth-teller of the detective novel when poverty threatened the established social order, when the cosmos had lost its infinite meaning, and when the Big Lie drowned out all attempts at truth. Dreaming of luxury, longing for stability, desiring the security of formal rigidity, readers of all classes turned toward the detective story, where significant truth lurked behind the arrangement of cigars in an ashtray, where a timeless society re-established its innocence anew, where nubility triumphed over senility, where a wizard disposed of the bad parent, the impostor, the parvenu, the outsider, and bestowed his magical blessings on decent young women and deserving young men. The twentieth century reader, like the Elizabethan, could turn his back on the ugly reality around him and retreat into the stylized world of literary art. The kind of art that most satisfied him and most fully answered the deepest needs of his nation and time was, not surprisingly, comic.

Geraldine Pederson-Krag

DETECTIVE STORIES AND THE PRIMAL SCENE

The popularity of detective stories in the English-speaking countries is a phenomenon psychoanalytically interesting because of its prevalence and because the reading of such fiction so frequently becomes habitual. About one quarter of all fiction published annually in the United States—some three hundred volumes—is of this type.[1] On two of the major radio networks one third to one half of dramatic programs broadcast deal with death and detection, and a large percentage of moving pictures have plots about the detection of crime. There is little novelty in this vicarious pursuit of criminals. Each mystery drama or detective story is less interesting for specific details than because the gratification lies in certain basic elements which are always present.

The first element is some secret wrongdoing between two people, revealed when one of the participants is discovered to have been murdered. The other, the criminal, is kept hidden from the reader among a cast of characters who are respectable members of society. The next element is a detective whose perception is so acute, whose knowledge so unlimited, whose perseverance so undaunted, that he can expose the criminal and reveal the method by which evil was done. Usually there is also introduced a character, typified by Sherlock Holmes' Dr. Watson, a dullard, dazzled by the detective's brilliance, to whom everything is explained as it must be explained to the reader. The third element is a series of observations and occurrences, trivial, commonplace and apparently unconnected. The detective discovers the significance of these and forges them into a chain of clues that leads to the criminal and finally binds him. The discovery of the criminal and his crime is a logical outcome of the combination of these elements, yet on the surface these elements seem to offer nothing which explains the insatiable demand of so many readers for this formula.

Reprinted from THE PSYCHOANALYTIC QUARTERLY, Vol. 18, with the permission of the editor and the author.

Bellak[2] notes that in detective stories anxieties are built up to be released at the height of tension, providing a pleasant experience for the reader. Bergler[3] observes that there is often a sense of uncanniness which recreates the reader's infantile belief in the omnipotence of his thought. Zulliger[4] reports that his pupils worked through the oedipal anxieties aroused in adolescence by reading sensational literature. Bellak demonstrates that the reader indulges his aggressive impulses by identification with the criminal; while in his identification with the detective, he becomes the mighty, blameless superego (confirmed clinically by Buxbaum[5]), and also enjoys the detective's superior intellectual accomplishments without the trouble of acquiring them. Bergler described identification with the victim, by which the reader could indulge his masochism, against which he would otherwise have to defend himself, and have also the rare pleasure of watching his own funeral and of seeing his enemies get their just deserts.

One does not deny the soundness of these observations; but surely they apply to the gratification in reading every kind of fiction in which the reader identifies himself with one or several of the characters to have any interest in the book at all. In fact, the conventions of detective fiction would seem to make it more difficult than otherwise to become identified with any of the characters delineated. Aggression, for example, has its fullest expression in the adventure rather than in the mystery story. In the latter the crime is committed off stage, and the final punishment is implied. Occasionally there may be a little shooting as an occupational hazard for the detective, but usually his work is described as a safe, tedious routine. Though the detective is a genius and a leader of men, he is often portrayed as addicted to morphine or to drink, excessively fat or thin, foppish or pedantic, or a quaint homespun philosopher. Though authors, oddly enough, seem to think these peculiarities are endearing, they should deter the average reader from imagining himself to be such characters. The victim, too, is almost never a sympathetic personality. In life he was cruel, boorish or miserly. He makes a brief, dramatic appearance as a corpse, but he holds the center of the stage all too briefly before he is removed.

Neither the allaying of anxiety nor identifications with various characters takes into account the unique feature of the mystery story: the intense curiosity it arouses. The circumstance in which the human capacity for curiosity reaches its first and most intense expression is the primal scene. Fenichel[6] states: "The observation of sexual scenes between adults creates a high degree of sexual excitement . . . and the impression that sexuality is dangerous. This impression is caused by the fact that the quantity of excitement is beyond the child's capacity to discharge and is therefore experienced as traumatically painful; the child may also sadistically misinterpret what he perceives, or the sight of adult genitals may give rise to castration fear."

Here is the first element of the detective story—the secret crime. Carrying the parallel further, the victim is the parent for whom the reader (the child) had negative oedipal feelings. The clues in the story, disconnected, inexplicable and trifling, represent the child's growing awareness of details it had never understood, such as the family sleeping arrangements, nocturnal sounds, stains, incomprehensible adult jokes and remarks. The criminal of the detective drama appears innocuous until the final page. In real life he was the parent toward whom the child's positive oedipal feelings were directed, the one whom the child wished least of all to imagine participating in a secret crime.

Throughout the centuries there has been a popular demand for a sadistic return to the primal scene. For our largely illiterate forebears of the sixteenth, seventeenth and eighteenth centuries, witch hunting took the place of mystery stories. There was a need to discover witches lurking in everyday surroundings, detected by trifling blemishes on their persons, by the movements of insects, by the behavior of animals, by the acrimony of unfriendly or irresponsible people, or by their own utterances under torture. This resembles the clues of the mystery tale. There were in those days many avowed witches who were psychopaths or devotees of ancient pre-Christian cults; yet, as in the detective story it is the innocent bystander who bears the brand of Cain, so in those days it was often the improbable person whom the witch-finder made his quarry. The witches were hounded to death for the unforgivable sin of fornication with the Devil. Freud[7] has shown that "the Devil is an image of the father and can act as an understudy for him."

Here too was a re-enactment of the primal scene, evidence that there was, and is, a human compulsion to repeat this experience. The primal scene, the dramatic quintessence of all oedipal and castration fears, is a shockingly traumatic event. How traumatic it is depends on the manner in which it is experienced, on the infant's psychic development at the time, and on the relationship of parents to each other and to the infant. It is noteworthy that whatever the child's reaction, it always entails anxiety, a large expenditure of psychic energy, and thrusts the necessity for several choices upon the unready ego.

First the ego must decide the extent to which it will acknowledge the reality of the happening. Some children try to deny their knowledge and consequently have to obliterate much of the outer world as well. One example of this is the hebephrenic patient of Fenichel who "as a child had frequently witnessed primal scenes. He had developed a sadistic conception of the sexual act, an identification with his mother, and a consequent intensive sexual fear. The original reaction to the primal scene—hostility to both parents, especially toward the father—was warded off by means of an increasing indifference toward the world."

A woman patient, until the age of five, showed precocious interest in other people's private lives and mental processes. Then a small boy told her a kindergarten classic about sexual organs and their functioning. This story served to reactivate for her repressed memories of the primal scene, and she became frightened of the curiosity she had previously tolerated well. She shrank from recognizing anything that would suggest that one person differs from another in any way. In analysis she declared ignorance of the terms by which the gender of domestic animals is designated.

Similar to this is Mahler's case of a boy who chronically forgot what he was told.[8] One reason for this was the wish to deny his knowledge of sexual intercourse between his father and a woman not his wife.

The danger of a child's knowing is exemplified by the story of Little Red Ridinghood who made impertinent comments about the size of her grandmother's organs as seen in bed. Judging from the replies, what really interested her were the functions of these parts. This story warns, "Don't be inquisitive or you will learn more than you want to know"; but the alternative, an acceptance of the primal scene, would entail anxiety and aggression. The child would have to look, overhear, correlate, speculate and theorize, all in an atmosphere of danger derived from its own anxiety and the disapproval of adults. Since such discoveries are incompatible with accepted ideas of the parents, they are repressed, although they can occasionally be recovered with little anxiety. In this category is Bonaparte's patient who as early as the fourth week of analysis produced memories of primal scenes referable to the first two years of life.[9]

Having accepted such knowledge, the ego's task of choosing is not yet over. It must now decide whether to accept the reality of the parents' sexual activities from which the child is excluded, or to have the perilous fantasy of taking part in these activities. Little Hans took the latter course.[10] He said, "In the night there was a big giraffe in the room and a crumpled one; and the big one called out because I took the crumpled one away from it. Then it stopped calling out, and then I sat down on top of the crumpled one." This was interpreted as Hans saying to his father, "Call out as much as you like, but Mummy takes me into bed all the same and Mummy belongs to me!"

A man in analysis had the wish to be the love object of a sadistic father. He imitated his mother's mannerisms, was irresponsible, and financially dependent on his father, later on his wife. He appraised all his acquaintances by the extent to which they could serve as substitute fathers. He repeatedly conjured up possibilities of threat and punishment and on these occasions reacted as he had when overhearing a primal scene: he wanted to escape, was unable to do so, and developed tachycardia and dyspnea. During his first nineteen years this patient shared a room with his parents. His symptoms were the result of his unconscious fantasy of replacing the mother in the father's bed. Fears of castration kept him a passive spectator. This recalls the classic dream of the Wolf-man,[11] in which a window opened and the dreamer saw white wolves, immobile, gazing at him from the boughs of a Christmas tree. Freud, describing the fragment of reality at the core of this dream, said, "He [the dreamer] suddenly woke up and saw in front of him a scene of violent movement at which he looked with strained attention."

Whether the reaction to the primal scene has been denial or acceptance, with or without participation, the repressed memory is in every instance charged to some degree with painful affect. The mystery story attempts to present a more satisfying, less painful primal scene from the standpoint of the unconscious. This fictional primal scene satisfies the voyeur who, like the Wolf-man, gazed with strained attention at the scene of parental coitus.

The voyeur is never entirely satisfied with his peeping which he has the compulsion endlessly to repeat like the detective story addict who rereads the same basic mystery tale without tedium. In the gradual revelation of clues that make up the bulk of the narrative, the reader is presented with one significant detail after another, a protracted visual forepleasure. Finally the crime is reconstructed, the mystery solved, that is, the primal scene is exposed. The reader has no need to take part in this by directly identifying with the characters because the gratification is obtained from being a passive onlooker.

Edgar Allan Poe, the progenitor of all modern mystery and detective fiction, with the publication of Tales of Mystery and Imagination in 1841, was the child of actors. Marie Bonaparte's intensive psychological study of Poe and his works traces in the greatest detail the enormous influence of the primal scene in the genesis of his tales.[12] Sir Arthur Conan Doyle, creator of Sherlock Holmes in 1887, who was an ophthalmologist (frustrated by a lack of patients), was directly inspired by Poe.[13]

In participating in the detective-story version of the primal scene, the reader's ego need fear no punishment for libidinal or aggressive urges. In an orgy of investigation, the ego, personified by the great detective, can look, remember and correlate without fear and without reproach in utter contrast to the ego of the terrified infant witnessing the primal scene.

Bergler observed that the sleuth is seldom a member of the official police; rather, he is a gifted amateur, often a dilettante. An inquiring child, free from anxiety, could hardly conduct official investigations. The peculiarities with which many writers endow their detectives allow the reader, who is a little frightened by what he is doing, to say, "This is not I; don't blame me." It is the child in disguise wearing father's cap or mother's coat to surprise and perhaps frighten the adults before its identity is revealed.

Dr. Watson, Sherlock Holmes' plodding companion, is more important than a literary device. He supplies the reader with a safe defense, for should the punishing superego threaten, the reader can point to this character and say, "This is I. I was simply standing by." In the complete knowledge of the crime, achieved by the detective, the ego may participate as either or both parents in the primal scene. Knowledge, as Chadwick has shown, may be the equivalent of male or female sexuality.[14] However, this second-hand sexuality is often insufficient. In many books the detective or one of his surrogates, by a conspicuous display of stupidity, is made the helpless prisoner of the villain. The reader cannot resist entering the parental bed, dangerous though it is. This prisoner, of course, is always rescued unscathed.

In conclusion, the reader addicted to mystery stories tries actively to relive and master traumatic infantile experiences he once had to endure passively. Becoming the detective, he gratifies his infantile curiosity with impunity, redressing completely the helpless inadequacy and anxious guilt unconsciously remembered from childhood.

Patrick Parrinder

GEORGE ORWELL AND THE DETECTIVE STORY

In the nineteen-forties, popular culture was felt to be an unpromising material both for the political commentator and for the literary critic. George Orwell was one of the first to realize that comic papers, seaside postcards and crime thrillers could be seriously analyzed in literary and ideological terms. Orwell's essays such as "Boys' Weeklies," "The Art of Donald McGill," and "Raffles and Miss Blandish" must be among the most widely read discussions of popular culture in existence. With the publication of his *Collected Essays, Journalism and Letters*[1] in 1968, the canon of his work appeared to be complete, but there is at least one notable essay by Orwell on popular fiction which was omitted from the collection and remains virtually unknown. Its subject is the English detective story, and in particular the work of Conan Doyle.

In 1944 the Free French review *Fontaine*, published in Algiers, produced a 450-page special number surveying English literature from 1918 to 1940. *Fontaine* had many contacts in London and virtually every important modern English writer was represented. The special number consisted mainly of translations of previously published works, but George Orwell responded to the editors' invitation with a 2,500 word article for which no English original is known to exist. It was translated by Fernand Auberjonois, one of the magazine's regular contributors, and appeared under the title "Grandeur et Décadence du Roman Policier Anglais." Copies of *Fontaine* are now fairly rare, and there is at present no prospect of an English version of Orwell's essay becoming available.[2]

"Grandeur et Décadence" was written at the same period as "Raffles and Miss Blandish," which first appeared in *Horizon* in October 1944. While "Raffles and Miss Blandish" deals with the crime thriller, "Grandeur et Décadence" is concerned with the detective story, and Orwell, like most critics, regards the two sub-genres as being quite distinct. A certain overlapping occurs when, in the better-known of the two essays, Orwell turns from the thriller to the detective story to support a general argument about fiction and crime. Thus he notes that both the Raffles and the Sherlock Holmes stories often deal with very petty crimes, while modern novels are far more sensational, and, even in the detective story, murder has become obligatory. This change is symptomatic of a general decline in moral standards, further evidence for which is found in the contrast of Sherlock Holmes and the modern detective heroes of Edgar Wallace. Holmes is the intellectual amateur, solving his problems by logical deduction, while Wallace's ideal is the Scotland Yard detective who catches criminals because he belongs to an all-powerful organization. Both of these points are repeated in "Grandeur et Décadence."

Like most of Orwell's writings on popular culture, these two articles are based upon an almost Manichaean contrast of two periods: the late Victorian and Edwardian period, and that of the 1930s and 1940s—the age of Raffles and the age of Miss Blandish. Orwell begins "Grandeur et Décadence" by pointing out that, although the detective story reached its greatest popularity between 1920 and 1940, it was during this time that the genre fell into decay. Detective stories were mass-produced according to an unvarying formula and became "a universal drug of the same order as tea, aspirin, cigarettes and radio."[3] Despite the intellectual standing of some of their authors, most of these books had no literary merit whatever. Yet in the classic period between 1880 and 1920, the detective story was able to achieve both popularity and aesthetic value. Why was this?

Orwell singles out Conan Doyle and two other writers who are now largely forgotten: Ernest Bramah, author of the Max Carrados stories, and R. Austin Freeman, the creator of Dr. Thorndyke.[4] All three writers owed their inspiration to Poe. Significantly, Orwell ascribes the literary value of their stories to their powers of characterization and of creating "atmosphere," and he argues that these qualities are largely achieved through digressions and superfluous detail. Conan Doyle, as much as Dickens, would despise the rigid economy of the modern short story, and the most memorable of the Holmes-Watson dialogues show the master stupefying his companion with displays of reasoning which have nothing whatever to do with the plot. Plot itself, in Orwell's view, requires no more than a crossword-puzzle ingenuity. "Literature" is something which has to be added, and he says that if the classic stories "are works of literature and not mere 'puzzles' it is largely thanks to the digressions that you find there."[5]

Unlike the crime thriller, he argues, the detective story is an intellectual exercise. Conan Doyle, Bramah and Freeman are further distinguished by the fact that they really believed in their detectives, for in Victorian England the amateur investigator could convincingly be represented as an intellectual giant, while his enemy, the arch-criminal such as Moriarty, seemed as terrifying as Hitler. It was quite plausible to show society as a collection of good men whose security was threatened only by the criminal. Orwell suggests that only two modern writers give the impression of believing in their detectives—G. K. Chesterton and Edgar Wallace. But Chesterton's Father Brown is an instrument of religious propaganda, while Wallace is motivated by sadistic power-worship; both, in other words, reflect the age of totalitarian ideologies. Sherlock Holmes, by contrast, is a Victorian scientific rationalist, the type of the free speculative intellect who towers above his fellows. Holmes and Dr. Thorndyke are bachelors practising a monkish celibacy, and Orwell finds in this one more proof of their superiority.

Conan Doyle, Bramah and Freeman wrote what Orwell elsewhere (following Chesterton) called "good bad books."[6] We have seen what Orwell valued in such books--atmosphere, the power of characterization and a certain stylistic grace. He insisted that to capture the popular imagination you have to create memorable characters, so that his reflections on Sherlock Holmes belong together with his studies of other popular heroes such as the Dickens characters, Jeeves, Bertie Wooster, Raffles, and Billy Bunter. He also noted that the late nineteenth and early twentieth centuries were particularly rich in "good bad books."[7] In fact, Orwell's notion of the kind of literary value that can be found in popular fiction is wholly derived from the late Victorian and Edwardian period. The reading he could draw upon was vast and, if one adds his numerous book reviews and his essays on Kipling, Wells, Yeats, Gissing and Jack London, he is revealed as one of the best literary historians of the period, while in "The Art of Donald McGill," "In Defence of P. G. Wodehouse," and "Boys' Weeklies" he analyzed its strange residual imprint on English life.

Orwell deeply disliked the popular culture of his own age, so much so that in *Nineteen Eighty-Four* the BBC, the television set, war films and rationing are all portrayed among the symptoms of totalitarianism. As a socialist he strove hard to clarify what was involved in his preference for the books of his childhood. The ideological tendency of Edwardian culture as he saw it was either openly reactionary (Kipling, Wodehouse, the *Magnet*) or weakly liberal (Wells, Conan Doyle). Yet in all this work he detected standards of decency and rationality which compared favorably with the double-talk and brutality of right and left in his own time. His essays invariably come round to the statement that liberal imperialism is preferable to Fascism. As cultural criticism, however, this is beside the point. *No Orchids for Miss Blandish* may be "pure Fascism" as Orwell says, but Chase's book was not representative of English values in 1940, nor were the ideals of decency and the gentlemanly amateur dead (Orwell apparently failed to predict the apotheosis in popular culture of the Blitz and the Battle of Britain). Nostalgia for the literature of his childhood and gloom about the future distorted and oversimplified his view of the present.

It is not so easy to prove distortion in his picture of the period 1880-1920. This really was the great period of the sub-genres in English fiction, when the coalition of interests that went into the "universal" novels of Dickens and George Eliot broke up, and writers opted for more specialized modes. Orwell discussed the detective story, the comedy and the thriller; he might have added the romance, the mystery tale, science fiction, the adventure story, and the children's classic—all forms which flourished between 1880 and 1920 and which illustrate his axiom that "Light literature is not necessarily bad literature."[7] Arguing that the detective story has fallen into decay, he suggests that the intellectual ideals and the literary expansiveness of Conan Doyle, Bramah and Freeman were only possible in a more secure and leisured society. But the security and leisure belonged exclusively to the middle classes, and this seems to imply that literary value too is a bourgeois luxury. In the "totalitarian" age, he felt, the writer must resign himself to addressing a "highbrow" public or to doping the masses—or, as Orwell did, he must become political. We may conclude from this that Orwell never quite abandoned the late nineteenth-century belief that art is essentially non-utilitarian, something that is superadded to "plot" or "content," however hard he tried. Hence his ambivalence toward the age of Raffles and Sherlock Holmes. "Grandeur et Décadence" ends on a note of wry nostalgia. In the modern world, he writes,

> It is difficult to believe that the game of Cops and Robbers could still inspire a writer of the calibre of Conan Doyle, not to mention Poe. The detective story as we have known it belongs to the nineteenth century, above all to the end of the nineteenth century. It belongs to the London of 1880 and 1890, to that gloomy and mysterious London where top hats shone in the flickering gaslight and the bells of hansom cabs tinkled in the eternal fogs; it belongs to that period in which English public opinion was more deeply stirred by the exploits of Jack the Ripper than by the problems of Irish Home Rule or the Battle of Majuba.[8]

Is this an attack on Victorian complacency, or an expression of admiration for a period which offered a perfect climate for popular literature? No doubt it is both.

William O. Aydelotte

THE DETECTIVE STORY AS A HISTORICAL SOURCE

One would hardly go to the detective story for an accurate picture of modern life. If a historian five hundred years hence were to base a reconstruction of our twentieth-century civilization solely on the evidence contained in detective stories, he might reach strange conclusions. He would probably infer that the most prominent features of our culture were inefficient or corrupt police forces, a multitude of private detectives, sometimes urbane and sometimes hard-boiled, and a constant series of domestic crimes occurring principally in large country houses and committed exclusively by people of the most harmless and respectable outward appearance. What little realism detective stories possess lies on the surface and does not extend to the characters or to the action. The notion that they give a literal representation of modern society may be rejected at the outset. Far from being realistic, they constitute one of the most conventionalized of literary forms, being exceeded in this respect perhaps only by the comic strip.

This does not argue, however, that detective novels are completely dissociated from the age in which they are written. On the contrary, their immense popularity—it is alleged that one out of every four new works of fiction published in the English language belongs to this category—suggests that they are an impressive portent of our culture. Their popularity is not likely to be accidental. If we can ascertain the reason for it, we may be able to grasp the link between detective literature and the society of which it forms a part.

I suggest that the widespread and sustained popularity of detective stories is principally due to the very elements which make them unrealistic, to their conventions. These conventions (which will be analysed at length in the course of this essay) have been fairly constant in the century-long history of the *genre,* amid all the variations of setting and

Reprinted from THE YALE REVIEW, XXXIX with the permission of the editor and the author.

technique. A substantial number of them appear even in the stories of Poe. The long persistence and regular recurrence of these stereotypes afford at least a presumption that they are essential to the detective story's continued vogue. Their role is of course clear. They are wish-fulfilment fantasies designed to produce certain agreeable sensations in the reader, to foist upon him illusions he wants to entertain and which he goes to this literature to find.

The charm of detective stories lies neither in originality nor in artistic merit, though they may possess both these qualities. It consists rather in the repetition of a formula that through trial and error has been found pleasing. We read these books, not to have a new experience, but to repeat in slightly different form an experience we have had already. Thus, for example, the "surprise" ending is not really a surprise. It is the ending we expect and demand, and we would feel outraged if any other kind of ending were offered to us. It is true that many of these works introduce elements of novelty in the background and setting, and that the best of them unquestionably show considerable skill in writing and construction. Such amenities, however, serve not so much to change the formula as to render it more palatable to the highbrow. The educated part of the detective-story audience shows no unwillingness to accept the formula but merely a fastidious distaste for its cruder expressions.

The interest of detective stories to the historian is that they shed light on the people who read them. By studying the fantasies contained in this literature, one may gather a description of its readers, in terms of their unsatisfied motivational drives. Thus these books are the more illuminating the more unrealistic and inaccurate they are. It is precisely by their inaccuracies that they reveal attitudes and emotions of the audience to which they cater. To the historian concerned with popular opinion, this audience is of particular interest for two reasons. In the first place it is large—the detective story is a mass medium—and in the second place it is extremely varied. Detective novels appeal to different types of readers, highbrows as well as lowbrows. They are read with avidity by intellectuals who despise soap operas and are repelled by the success stories in popular magazines. Some critics even assert that they are written primarily for intellectuals, a claim which is of course invalid in view of the breadth and extent of their circulation. The reading of this literature is, rather, a widespread habit to which the educated also adhere.

The extent and variety of the detective-story audience argue a surprising degree of unity in our culture, at least in respect to the demand for the particular fantasies which this literature purveys. Since these books appeal, not only to many people, but to many different kinds of people, they presumably reflect attitudes and needs that are widely distributed. A study of the stereotypes in the detective story may, therefore, reveal to us attitudes and opinions which, if not universal, at least occur in our age with significant frequency.

Primarily, the detective story presents a view of life which is agreeable and reassuring. By ingenious and long-tested devices, it persuades the reader that the world it describes is simple and understandable, that it is meaningful, and that it is secure.

(1) In place of the complex issues of modern existence, people in a detective story have very simple problems. Life goes along well except for the single point that some crime, usually, in modern stories, a murder, has been committed. (There are some exceptions, particularly among the Sherlock Holmes stories, which are not wholly typical of the modern form of the *genre*: many of these contain no murder, and some involve no crime at all, merely a puzzle.) From this act follow most of the troubles which the sympathetic characters must endure: they may, for example, come under temporary suspicion of murder, or they may have a misunderstanding with their loved ones. Troubles are objectively caused by an external circumstance, the murder, which can and will be resolved, whereupon the troubles will disappear. Once the solution has been reached, most of the other difficulties are ended and the characters go away happy, never apparently to be vexed by the minor worries and neuroses of modern man. The mess, confusion, and frustration of life have been reduced to a simple issue between good and evil, virtue and wickedness. And virtue triumphs.

To carry the argument to the next stage, the simplification of the problem is matched by a corresponding simplification of the solution. Here we come to one of the most universal conventions in the *genre*, the essential clue, the unique significant detail that unlocks the mystery. The detective story makes a distinction between essential and non-essential facts. As Sherlock Holmes puts it, "It is of the highest importance in the art of detection to be able to recognize, out of a number of facts, which are incidental and which vital. Otherwise your energy and attention must be dissipated instead of being concentrated." ("The Reigate Puzzle.") In the unreal world of the detective story, we depart from the intricate currents of causation in life as we know it, and find instead that a whole elaborate plot may be unravelled by discovering the one relevant detail. Furthermore, the factual nature of this detail lends an air of concreteness to the solution: we are led to feel it is the only solution, inevitable, unique, completely certain.

(2) By other commonly used devices the detective story makes life more meaningful and endows the events it describes with significance, even with glamor. To say that detective stories provide a thrill which compensates for the dullness of their readers' lives is only the beginning of the story. It is true that they offer the excitement of adventure, and also capitalize on popular indignations or fetishes in the manner of other types of sensation literature. But they do more than this. In many subtle ways

they help their readers to believe in the existence of a richer and fuller world.

Even the sordid surroundings of crime make their contribution to the atmosphere of richness and meaning. As G. K. Chesterton says, this form of literature succeeds often in getting the romance and poetry of the city, and "the investigator crosses London with something of the loneliness and liberty of a prince in a tale of elfland."

Comparable effects are achieved in other ways. Consider, for example, the following quotation, in which Sherlock Holmes is explaining one of his solutions: "I am only, of course, giving you the leading results now of my examination of the paper. There were twenty-three other deductions which would be of more interest to experts than to you." ("The Reigate Puzzle.")

This is one of many passages in which Conan Doyle contrives to suggest there is a great world of intellectual phenomena, beyond the range of the average man, but really existent for all that and within the competence of the superior mind. Thus, for other illustrations, Holmes deduces a whole life-history from the appearance of a hat or a watch. ("The Blue Carbuncle," "The Sign of Four.") The implication is that life is not the simple and drab affair we ordinarily encounter, but something more extensive and more interesting.

To add further to the reader's sense of new frontiers of meaning and significance, the detective story manages in various ways to cast a glamor on its characters and to convey to the reader that these people count, that they matter in the world. Such an illusion is achieved, for example, when the action takes place in the classical setting of the large English country-house with its atmosphere of butlers and scullery maids, lawns and shrubberies, French windows and guest-wings, and large house parties of elegant guests.

(3) Finally, the detective story introduces us to a secure universe. We find here an ordered world obedient to fixed laws. The outcome is certain and the criminal will without fail be beaten by the detective. In this world man has power to control his own affairs and the problems of life can be mastered by human agency.

Even the handling of the theme of death contributes to this feeling of security. One might not at first expect a form of literature which deals with death by violence to have the cheerful and encouraging effect I have attributed to the detective story. Yet murder is an almost universal feature of these books. From the point of view of literary construction, of course, a murder is useful for the plot and provides the suitable starting-point for an investigation. But there is another reason for including it.

This is that the detective story, by its peculiar treatment of death, contrives to minimize the fear of it. Death is always presented in a rather special way. It is something that happens to somebody else, not to anyone we like or identify ourselves with. The victim, though he is ultimately avenged, is not allowed to be a sympathetic character. The reader's emotions must not become engaged on his behalf. At the least the victim is killed off before his personality has been developed far enough for the reader to take an interest in him or to like him. More often the victim is clearly unattractive, a man who has been injuring the lives of a number of the other characters (which also helps the plot by increasing the list of possible suspects), and his death is good riddance. In many cases, the murder turns out to be the best thing that could have happened. After everything has been straightened out, the lovers, if any, are brought together, the detective has had a chance to prove his worth, all the other characters are now freed from the burden of the late victim's persecution of them, and also purged from the guilt of his murder, since this guilt has now been thrown on an acceptable scapegoat, and everyone is set for a cheerful future.

The detective story uses crime not to make life more horrible but to make it more cheerful. The despair and horror it seems to offer the reader are presented in a very manageable form and really subserve, not a pessimistic view of life, but a view that is exactly the opposite. Its concern with crime and the seamy side of life misleads the observer as to its true impact. Its message is essentially agreeable, almost to the point of being saccharine.

The agreeable view of life presented in the detective story is deepened and enlarged by the actions of its two most important characters, the criminal and the detective. Each plays a standardized role that affords a special kind of satisfaction to the reader. We will consider the criminal first.

The criminal is a scapegoat. He is the cause of and can justly be blamed for all the troubles of the detective-story world, the murder and everything that follows from it. The detective story evades the complex issues of life and saves us the effort of analysing the sources of our difficulties and frustrations by presenting every problem as one of personal morality. The criminal therefore must be a single individual, who can eventually be identified. A detective novel where the murder was due to "conditions" of some sort, and where no individual was responsible, would be quite unsatisfactory.

But the criminal is not only a scapegoat, he is also something more deeply gratifying, a scapegoat that can be beaten. His great charm is that he is conquerable and will infallibly be conquered. He appears for most of the story as a colossus, formidable in his cunning and power. But his strength, though great, is futile, only sham strength. His position is actually unreal, for he has no place nor meaning in an ordered world. If you look closely, the criminal is a miserable creature. He can do little ultimately against organized society which is rapidly closing in on him. If we are terrified of him for a while, because of his apparent cunning and dexterity, that simply enhances the relief we feel when he gets beaten, and also the satisfaction we have in knowing all the time, in our inmost hearts, that he is going to be beaten.

Besides this, I believe the criminal also fulfils another and more subtle purpose. He relieves our feelings of aggression, not only by becoming an object of them himself, but also in a second and quite different way, by committing the murder. As I tried to show earlier, it not infrequently happens that the murder is a good thing; the victim is a menace to the sympathetic characters and the murder starts off the train of events that leads finally to the happy ending. In novels where this is the case, the criminal, by killing the victim, performs a service to society, a service we would not wish, however, to have performed by any sympathetic character because of the penalty that must ensue. The criminal, though he is made to act from selfish and unworthy motives and must therefore be punished, still gratifies us by committing the act we are glad to see done. He shares something of the ambiguous character of the scapegoat of mythology who is both a friend and enemy to society, who commits the act of sin or disobedience that helps us all and then removes the taint or penalty attached thereto by himself undergoing the punishment, a punishment that is occasionally even inflicted by the beneficiaries.

Perhaps the most gratifying function of the detective story, and one that is also achieved through the agency of the criminal, is the illusion the reader obtains of being released from guilt and dissociated from the murderer. This illusion is achieved by bringing a number of the most prominent characters, including any with whom the reader might perhaps identify himself, temporarily under suspicion. For this purpose, the criminal must be a member of the closed circle, the small group affected by or concerned with the crime, so that the possibility of an outside murderer will be excluded and any member of this little society may therefore conceivably be guilty. (Here again the Holmes stories constitute a partial exception to the convention that has crystallized in our own day: in very few cases are there several suspects, and in some cases the criminal is an outsider who does not appear till caught.) The criminal must also be the least likely person, revealed only in the surprise ending, so that, since the identity of the murderer is kept a secret until the end, no single character in the closed circle can be assumed to be assuredly free from guilt. By such means the fear of guilt is temporarily intensified and the reader's relief at the identification of the criminal is increased.

Once the criminal is discovered, everyone else is at once freed from the burden of possible guilt. The suspicious actions of the other characters now turn out to have a perfectly innocent explanation. Yet the temporary suspicion directed against them was in a sense justified, for many of them benefited from the crime and would perhaps have liked to commit it if they could have escaped the consequences. For that reason, their relief is the greater. The satisfaction of the "innocent" characters and the reader at being released from guilt is all the more poignant because they do not deserve it; in thought and feeling, if not in action, they are also guilty. Therefore our gratification when the murder is committed does not conflict with our satisfaction at being ultimately freed from guilt, but on the contrary enhances it.

Besides all this, the criminal has one additional function. He contributes to the illusion of the power of the detective. His crime is thought out in great detail, is indeed perfect except for the single flaw discernible only to the detective's penetrating eye. The botched crime of real life is unknown to the detective story. The criminal shows incredible self-possession and address, and conducts himself with such poise and assurance that he is not suspected until the end. In all this he is a worthy antagonist and gives the detective full scope to demonstrate his talents. However, though the crime is so difficult that it can be solved only by the detective, the detective almost invariably does succeed in solving it. He always has the particular bit of esoteric knowledge on the particular type of intuition that turns out to be just what is needed, the one and only thing that will clear up this particular mystery. The point, as we may now perceive, is that the crime is tailored to fit the detective. It finally proves to be exactly the kind of crime that is best suited to his peculiar and unique talents. The criminal actually serves the detective by offering him just the kind of problem that he is best equipped to deal with. Though a skilful writer seeks to maintain the illusion, the crime is really a setup, and the detective solves it because the author has contrived everything to that end.

The detective contributes even more than the criminal to the good view of life set forth in these books. He makes the world simple, comprehensible, and orderly by discovering the essential clue and solving the murder. He understands the meanings and possibilities of life and reveals its vistas to us. He gives us security, certainty and protection. By unearthing the criminal he sets in motion the scapegoat mechanism which shifts the burden of guilt from our shoulders. He can do all these things because he has control over the world we know and the destinies of men in it.

The most prominent feature of the detective is his power and strength. The fact that he is also represented as an intellectual need not lead us astray about this. He is not the feckless intellectual of popular culture, the absent-minded professor, the man who is cloistered, impractical and ineffective. On the contrary, his talents are used for a concrete practical end, the apprehension of the murderer. Intellect is for him simply a path to power, a means of controlling the external world.

Furthermore, his power is not solely intellectual. There is a tradition that he must be physically as well as mentally competent. Detectives in American stories of the hard-boiled school are supposed to be handy with their fists. Sherlock Holmes, though to some extent a recluse and at times a drug-addict, is an expert singlestick player, boxer, and swordsman. Peter Wimsey, no he-man, is still a famous athlete whose proficiency as a cricketer gives away his identity in "Murder Must Advertise." Even the effeminate Poirot shows a courage and alertness in ticklish situations which fit him a little bit into the type of the hero of adventure. Besides this, the detective works not just by intellect and logic but also by intuition. He often senses something wrong in a situation, and this sense prevents him from acting mistakenly or making a fool of himself, even though the whole truth is not yet revealed to his intellect. He plays his hunches, and they are apt to be right.

To make the detective appear a figure of power the police, like the criminal, are drummed into his service. By their very inadequacy or opposition to him they do more to display his qualities than they could by giving him the most efficient co-operation. The convention of the inept police force helps to establish the unique excellence of the detective, his ability to do things nobody else can do. Thus the superiority of the detective to the police has been a common feature of detective literature from Poe's Dupin to Gardner's Perry Mason. It has become especially prominent in recent books, especially American ones such as those of Geoffrey Homes or Dashiell Hammett. Despite some notable exceptions like Inspector Alleyn or Inspector French, there have been relatively few policeman-heroes, and a substantial number of these are police officers only in name who in practice perform something like the role of a private detective. Ellery Queen plays a lone hand and summons in his father's cohorts only for special tasks; the solution is his work and not theirs. Maigret, too, works mostly alone and excites the enmity or disapproval of his colleagues. In one of the latest of the series, he has retired from the *Sûreté*.

Since our present interest in the detective story is its impact on the reader, the important question to ask about the detective is what kind of fantasy he evokes in the reader's mind. At first glance the issue might seem to be whether the reader's relation to the detective is one of identification or dependence. We might attempt, as Louise Bogan suggests would be possible, to divide detective stories into those written for sadists and those written for masochists. Yet this first and most obvious way of putting the question does violence to the complexity of the reader's emotions and reactions, which for any book are likely to be not simple but ambiguous and multiple. As a matter of fact, identification and dependence do not exclude each other; each refers to a different aspect of the reader's reaction, and both are possible at the same time.

I suggest that the reader probably does identify himself with the detective, make the detective an extension of his ego, but only in very general terms. The detective is on our side. His actions are beneficial to us, and we feel ourselves in some degree represented in them. On the other hand, this representation occurs at a distance. The reader may identify himself with the detective to the extent that he gets a vicarious thrill of power when the detective solves the mystery. But I doubt that he identifies himself with the detective to the larger extent of trying to solve the murder himself. The reader is audience. He is like the spectator at a football game, identifying himself with his team, feeling a personal triumph if they win, yet always aware that it is the players and not himself who do the work on which his satisfaction is based. Though the reader both identifies and depends, the emphasis is on the latter, the significant relationship is dependence.

I would argue, to support this, that the reader does not generally compete intellectually with the detective. A detective story is not an invitation to intellectual exercise or exertion, not a puzzle to which the reader must guess the answer. On the contrary, the claim of detective stories to be puzzle literature is in large part a fraud, and the reader, far from attempting to solve the mystery himself, depends on the detective to do it for him.

This is an extremely controversial point. Many detective stories claim to put all the clues in the reader's hands, to show him everything the detective sees, so that the reader has an equal chance to make something out of it. This is the so-called "gentlemen's agreement," the supposedly best modern practice, according to which, says Miss Sayers, readers demand to be put "on an equal footing with the detective himself, as regards all clues and discoveries." Mr. R. Austin Freeman, who also insists that the satisfaction a detective story offers the reader is primarily an intellectual one, argues that the principal connoisseurs of this literature are theologians, scholars and lawyers. To please this audience of subtle and skilled dialecticians, he thinks a good detective story must have above all two things: accuracy as to external facts, and freedom from fallacies of reasoning.

Unfortunately many detective stories, including some of the best-known ones, have neither one nor the other. Critics have amused themselves for some time now by pointing out errors of fact and deduction in the Sherlock Holmes tales. And the same weaknesses can be found in many other works. If we applied to detective stories the critical attention we give to serious literature, we would find a surprising number that simply do not hang together intellectually. This point is the theme of an important article by Raymond Chandler in the December, 1944, issue of the "Atlantic." Mr. Chandler examines a number of the most famous detective novels of all time, "The Red House Mystery," "Trent's Last Case," "Busman's Honeymoon," "Murder in the Calais Coach," and demonstrates conclusively that none of them is free from important fallacies of reasoning, and that they will not stand up for a moment under strict analysis.

The point should not, however, be pushed too far, for there is a certain amount to be said on the other side. It might be argued that the four stories selected by Mr. Chandler for comment are not a fair sample of the best writing in the *genre*. Furthermore, the very fact that the detective story is popularly regarded as puzzle literature has no doubt influenced writers to try to create puzzles that are fair. Some of these books, particularly including Mr. Freeman's, are well written and articulated, and in fact detective literature at its best demands a good deal in the way of strict construction and technical proficiency, and is not easy to write. Also, I have found a number of readers who insist that they read detective stories as puzzles, and are often able to determine the identity of the murderer in the middle of the story by logical deduction from the clues. And yet, without going into the question of the extent to which these readers may be deceiving themselves, I would doubt that the majority of readers discover the murderer by logical processes of thought before the denouement, and I would doubt that this is even possible in a large number, perhaps the majority, of detective stories.

Any writer of detective fiction who tries to adhere to the "gentlemen's agreement" faces the problem well put by Miss Sayers, "How can we at the same time show the reader everything and yet legitimately obfuscate him as to its meaning?" I submit that what this "legitimate obfuscation" often amounts to is that either the clues are *not* all given to the reader, or, if they are, this is not done in a significant way that will enable him to determine their meaning.

The reader, if he guesses correctly at all, does so not by reasoning from the evidence, but rather by selecting the least probable character, the person the evidence does not point to. The reader's solution is a guess and not a deduction. It is on the level of the speculations of the woman in the Thurber story who knew that, whoever might have murdered Duncan, the deed could not possibly have been done by Macbeth because he was too obvious a suspect, a patent red herring.

For a detective story to have a solution that could readily be guessed by the majority of readers would go clean against the whole nature and character of the *genre*. The solution has to come as a surprise. A story has no punch when the reader can guess the murderer before the denouement. Furthermore, the purpose of the detective novel, as we saw from other evidence, is to comfort the reader, create agreeable illusions for him. If these books described themselves primarily as tests of the reader's intelligence, which the reader would flunk if he did not guess the murderer before the end, many readers would scarcely find detective stories comforting. For, if the puzzles are so difficult that they can be worked out by the most intelligent readers only with some effort, they would be far beyond the less intelligent but more numerous remainder of the audience.

Detective stories are not a test of the reader's intelligence but, at the most, a means of creating in the reader a delusion that he is intelligent and that, by following the steps in the analysis, he has somehow displayed intellectual proficiency. All too often, the "gentlemen's agreement" means in practice nothing more than that the *appearance* of fair play is to be maintained. The good writing, if any, helps to create and maintain this illusion.

This effort to maintain the illusion of the reader's intelligence is simply a device to keep decently concealed what I consider to be the basic feature of the detective story, the reader's dependence on the detective. Our attitude toward dependence is apt to be ambivalent: we may need it, and at the same time resent having to confess this need or having it called to our attention. The pretense that the detective story is an intellectual puzzle helps to hide the feeling of dependence which the reader goes to these books to find but which he hates to acknowledge.

In any case, there seems little doubt about the dependence of the reader, as of all the characters in the story, upon the detective-hero. The attraction of this literature is that, though the problem may be beyond the powers of the reader or of any of the characters in the story, we can always depend on the detective to step in and solve it. We get satisfaction from seeing him do this even before we know how he is going to bring it off, for the interest lies not in the steps of the analysis but in the certainty of the solution. Thus the reader may get a little bored in the middle of the book when one theory after another is tried and discarded, but when Dr. Fell says he now pretty well knows who the murderer was, when Poirot says he of course identified the murderer two days ago and is only waiting to settle the details, when Holmes says the crime is simple and obvious and presents no points of difficulty—the reader's interest is quickened by a thrill of excitement.

The characters in the book, like the reader, prove to be passive under the detective's control. By the end they sometimes become his puppets, doing what he planned without knowing he meant them to. In the denouement scene, a character will make an important statement, or act in a particular manner, or even commit suicide, and after it is all over people will realize that the detective planned it just that way. The detective's interference with the lives of the other characters is almost as self-confident and arbitrary as that of a deity, and the reader is supposed to love it.

The passiveness of the reader is underlined by one of the most famous devices of all, the narration of the story by a confidant, a foil to the detective, of which Dr. Watson is the outstanding example. The reader sees the story through the eyes of Watson or Hastings or whoever it may be, and also shares the confidant's sense of security and stability which comes from his dependence on the detective.

The confidant, though he may be of various types, is generally somewhat stupid, inferior to the detective, and the detective pokes fun at his blunders and obtuseness. But the confidant doesn't object to this. Even Dr. Watson, though he does at times rebel against Holmes' superior manner, shows an almost masochistic streak. He doesn't mind being ordered around by Holmes without explanation; in fact, he gets a thrill out of it. He is delighted to be proved wrong and to have his stupidity shown up. For all this enhances his belief in the infallibility of the detective. The detective becomes a kind of father-image to whom the narrator is occasionally opposed but in general submissive. The Watson-Holmes relationship gives an opening for the instincts of hero-worship.

But what is the historical importance of this? How can such a description as I have attempted here of fantasies and the motivations to which they correspond, even if it is made much more accurate and extensive, be translated into terms of society and politics? The answer to this question, suggested at the beginning of this paper, may now be given more fully. The point of all I have been saying is that the detective story is hokum, a means of arousing in the reader a belief in contrary-to-fact conditions, an opiate and a drug, which protects the reader from the facts of life by covering him with veils upon veils of illusions. The historical value of the detective story is that it describes day-dreams, and describes them with a wealth of documentation extending into innumerable volumes. A knowledge of people's daydreams may enable us to progress to an understanding of their desires. In this way, a careful study of literature of this kind may reveal popular attitudes which shed a flood of light on the motivation behind political, social, and economic history.

The method can be illustrated on the basis of the preliminary survey attempted here, and I will now, finally, indicate by a couple of suggestions how it might work. To take a negative point first, even this cursory examination will enable us to dismiss as uncritical and altogether false the thesis, which has been hazarded by not a few writers, that the detective story is in some fashion a flower of democracy and an embodiment of the democratic way of life. The argument used to support this view is that these books have appeared almost exclusively in democratic countries, chiefly England and America, while by contrast the writings of Agatha Christie and Edgar Wallace were banned by Hitler as "decadent." The reason alleged is that this kind of literature can flourish only in a society where there is due process of law, a non-faulty procedure for handling evidence, public sympathy on the side of order, and an effective police dedicated to finding the truth by objective means.

This argument, in the light of what has so far been said, is obviously nonsense. It is not true, incidentally, that detective literature has appeared solely in democratic societies, for Vidocq published his "Memoirs" in the age of Louis Philippe and Gaboriau wrote mostly under the Second Empire. Nor does the development of effective police forces seem relevant, since the fictional detective works separately from or even against the police, who are represented as anything but effective.

Even if we grant, what is for the most part true, that the *genre* has flourished mainly in England and the United States, it does not follow that it is an illustration of democratic sentiment or a symbol of democratic culture. Our analysis of the detective story would lead to a somewhat less reassuring view. The whole tenor of these books appears to be that they show an enormous demand for gratification, on the level of fantasy, of basic drives which apparently cannot be satisfied in our western society on the level of ordinary reality, and which have an application going rather beyond democratic institutions. The resemblance of the fantasies of dependence and aggression in the detective novel to the two principal political figures of totalitarianism, the dictator and the scapegoat, has been pointed out before this.

Though the detective story appears non-political on the surface, the roles of its two protagonists are saturated with political meanings. The criminal, by the very fact that he is the least likely person, justifies the reader's suspicion that all men, including those who appear most innocent, are really his potential enemies. The reader gets a tremendous vicarious satisfaction when the criminal is identified, for this denouement confirms to the reader that he is right to suspect everybody. The criminal is a fantasy developing out of a competitive, uncohesive society. He is a personalization of our grievances, as we like to personalize them in the atmosphere of political or social crisis in real life. We have toward the criminal the same or comparable feelings that we have toward any one of the commonly accepted scapegoats of our day, the Jew, the labor agitator, Wall Street, the "radical," the capitalist, or whatever other image we have formed the habit of using. And we like to attribute to these bogeymen, as we do to the criminal, sham strength instead of real strength, and to think of them as major threats which, however, we will somehow always be able to counter.

The detective, on the other hand, has many characteristics in common with the modern political leader or agitator. He simplifies life, makes sense out of it and gives it meaning. His strength is real, unlike the criminal's pseudo-strength, for it is based not just on externals but on intuition and a sense of community with the right things in the universe. Like the agitator in Professor Lowenthal's article (in "The Public Opinion Quarterly," Fall, 1948), he is conservative and objects not to the system but to certain people, the criminal or criminals, who seem to be endangering it. And yet the detective is not really a part of the established framework of society, for he neither belongs to the police, the official guardians of the law, nor is he a member of the closed circle or group within which the plot develops. Thus, though he moves in an ordered universe, the order is not that of the police or other regular authorities, but an order that is discovered and imposed by him. The detective may have a kind of democratic aura, for he frequently rises from the ranks and is not distinguished by birth, and although he moves unperturbed among the highly placed he is not one of them. Yet he is indispensable, for he alone can solve the riddle. Therefore the authorities (the family or the police) perforce surrender the controls to him, sometimes reluctantly and occasionally with sharp protest. One could argue that all these qualities add up to a dictator, that the detective is the extra-legal superman who is called in to accomplish by extraordinary measures what is impossible within the traditional organization of society.

Thus a case could be made to show that the detective story is no monument to the strength of democracy but rather a symptom revealing its weaknesses, the insupportable burdens it places on the individual. The detective story does not reflect order, but expresses on the fantasy level a yearning for order; it suggests, then, a disordered world, and its roots are to be sought in social disintegration rather than in social cohesion.

All this is not to suggest that the impulses catered to in this literature made their first appearance in history in the nineteenth century, and never existed before. On the contrary, the fantasies of the detective story appear in recognizable form in the popular culture of other ages, in folklore for example, and the drives they reveal are therefore by no means recent in origin but might rather be regarded as traditional elements of the human character as it has developed in our civilization. Nostalgia for the dependent relationships of childhood is hardly a novelty of our own age. The significant thing is rather that so many people of our age, roughly the era of democratic liberalism, have seemingly come to depend on an enormous literature for the development and even the artificial stimulation of these fantasies. This literature offers disturbing evidence of psychological tensions, and of the prevalence in our modern western culture of elements of character-structure which do not provide adequate support for democratic institutions. The hypothesis toward which a study of these books might tend is that the political arrangements in a democracy, in contrast to the political arrangements in more authoritarian types of government, are simply not adequate to take up this strain.

But perhaps we should beware of taking evidence of this sort too tragically, or of deducing from detective stories nothing but a pessimistic moral. The condemnation of detective stories as drugs or cheap escapism may be pedantic. For, if they are a symptom, they can also be a cure. If we credit the Freudian view that socially dangerous impulses can be got rid of by removing them to the level of fantasy, then detective stories could be described as a harmless safety valve, a wholesome therapy serving a desirable social purpose. And yet one may wonder if this commonly accepted view is entirely correct, if fantasy and real life are actually so unrelated. To some extent we may build our real life around our fantasy and, if this is so, sensation literature may not so much rid us of dangerous drives as reinforce and reshape them.

In any case, if detective stories are not so sinister as they at first appear from analysis, neither are they as frivolous as some critics have judged them. The drives they cater to are compelling and basic, and relate ultimately to the struggle for self-preservation. It is the universal nature of their theme which explains the size and variety of their reading audience. The intellectual, who scorns the cheap fantasies of the popular magazines, is not likely to be able to forgo the fantasies which give him hope for his survival in an alien world. Detective stories deal, in their own way and on their own level, with the most essential and urgent problems in the human situation.

Edward Margolies

THE AMERICAN DETECTIVE THRILLER AND THE IDEA OF SOCIETY

In an essay he wrote in 1944 bewailing the degeneration of the English detective novel, George Orwell laid the onus in large part on the influence of the Americans—or more particularly their pulp fiction.[1] What Orwell found especially distressing was the absence or failure of morality on the part of police and detectives in pursuit of their prey. They were frequently as corrupt, ruthless and sadistic as their criminal enemies. Indeed what chiefly distinguished them from their adversaries was that they were simply more powerful. Power had become an end in itself—a theme Orwell would develop to fuller advantage in his post-war novel, *1984*.

Orwell's anxiety was understandable. England had been a nation of venerable social and political institutions whose relatively stable social classes regarded the externals of behavior as expressing the soul, if not the values, of the culture. Any breakdown of the rules, even on the fantasy level of the detective story, was indeed a troublesome portent. But Orwell was mistaken if he saw the American detective thriller as being an altogether amoral phenomenon, although, of course, one must grant that many American authors have shamelessly exploited the sado-masochistic and prurient elements of their readers' psyches. All the same, the literary, historical and psychological genesis of American tough guy fiction was cultivated on a kind of morality peculiar to the American experience. I shall, in the course of this essay, attempt to suggest how this morality developed and what its social implications may involve for the future of the genre.

One may as well begin with Poe since everyone else does and since Poe's detectives are supposed to be the progenitors of all subsequent private eyes, American and European. But only in the faintest way do I regard Poe's Monsieur Dupin as the great-grandfather of Dashiell Hammett's Continental Op, Raymond Chandler's Philip Marlow, Ross Macdonald's Lew Archer, or any of that host of lesser known hardboiled monosyllabic heroes whose presence in our cities has saved us time and again from utter disaster. What Poe's detective does share with all subsequent American private eyes is a kind of contempt for society which, by a tremendous exercise of intellectual will, he transcends, quite as if all legal or social proprieties, even physical milieu did not exist. It is no paradox then that Poe could easily place his detective in Paris, a city Poe had visited only in his imagination. In his mind M. Dupin not only penetrates the minds of persons he has not met, but climbs in and out of windows, over roofs, and in and out of apartments, examining the closest details of furniture—foreshadowing, as it were, hardboiled twentieth century sleuths who would perform these feats physically, overtly. In his indifference to the laws of the land, the rules of civilized behavior, the prerogatives of social class, M. Dupin is spiritually at one with his tough guy successors. But there, I submit, the relationship ends. Dupin's descendants are more properly Sherlock Holmes, Philo Vance, and the fatty, Nero Wolfe, all three of whom prefer to confront crime as an intellectual puzzle and to remove themselves as much as they can physically from the consequences of violence.[2] The hardboiled dicks, on the other hand, however crass, cynical or illiterate they may sound, frequently perceive themselves as engaged in some kind of moral, if not metaphysical, quest. Their clients may be shady or disagreeable, the dicks may find they are not going to be paid, they are often savagely beaten—yet they relentlessly push on. The test of their integrity is that they get to the bottom of things—the Truth. Thus it may be that the ancestors of M. Dupin derive from the rationalists of the Enlightenment while the ancestors of the hardboiled private eyes derive from those legendary medieval knights who most Americans first got to know via the novels of Scott and nineteenth century gothic romances.

I do not mean that all hardboiled dicks *are* knights on white chargers any more than I would want to suggest that all Sherlock Holmes' deductions are logical. Yet the solitary quest for justice, truth, individual integrity are noble activities which emerge time and again as the heroic theme of myth when civilizations begin to disintegrate and the existing social body no longer appears to nourish spiritual needs. In a certain sense America has from the start proved fertile ground for such quests, partially because older European societies nurtured under different conditions have never successfully transplanted themselves. Until recently a relatively rich and underpopulated continent had yet to be conquered—and perhaps Americans were, by their very nature, suspicious of organized society since this is what they had fled in Europe. As countless literary scholars have pointed out, the flight from the corrupt city westward into the forest in the works of Cooper and his successors, the authors of westerns, is the flight from civilized society which, not surprisingly, Huck

Finn among others identifies with repressive American females like his Aunt Sally and the Widow Douglas. Of course the conquest of the continent was made in the name of the civilization (or women) one was attempting to flee, but we need not dwell on that irony at any length other than to note that if indeed American men were conquering the continent in the name of their women, they were not unlike those who swatted away at giants and dragons in the name of the ladies they left behind.

The main point, however, is, given their distrust of organized society and given the absence of social institutions to guide their behavior outside of organized society, the protagonists of American letters, especially Western heroes, have had to create for themselves in little god-like ways their own code of ethics, their own morality. This may in part account for the reasons Western heroes and their successors, the hardboiled dicks (for the hardboiled dicks are, after all, only the Western lone rangers brought back to the city), blithely ignore society's laws about the sanctity of property, due process, assault and battery and other forms of violence. They have their own fish to fry, thank you, and their own individualized morality, based, one supposes, on eternal Christian principles, is far superior to the piddling inhibitions of society that would prevent a man from doing his duty.

How like knights they are—hard, lean, driven, ascetic—as they tread their inexorable ways through the muck of urban wastelands, replete with malaise and unknown dangers—not to mention vile creatures: gangsters, punks, nubile seductresses, politicians, police officials, even churchmen. Presumably because they had once in the dim past been traumatized by violence, pain, betrayal, especially betrayal by women (again those symbols of social sexual control), they have hardened themselves to all but their singleminded purpose. If they are not celibate, sex is for them a mechanical activity they must undergo in the line of duty. "What could I do," asks Dan Parker, Hollywood detective, as he tumbles out of one bed after another along the way to solving a crime, "I'm only human." More often, though, they express outright hostility to women, who if they are not the primary source of evil are obstacles to its eradication. In this regard the knight's chivalry does not extend to the ladies. Sam Spade turns on his loved one when she is revealed as a murderess.[3] Mike Hammer allows his wicked girl friend to strip naked and then shoots her in the navel.[4] Sometimes our dicks prefer simply to beat them up. For example:

> He took one cat-like step toward her. His fist didn't travel more than six inches and it landed with a large smack on the hinge of her jaw just below the ear. Teresa whirled around with a graceful rustle of silk, fell across the divan and rolled off on the floor.
>
> ....
>
> "This isn't going to hurt me worse than it does you," Latin told her conversationally. "In fact I love to bat people around. You tell me where that film is or you're going to be in the market for store teeth."[5]

Or:

I knocked her arm aside and smacked her flush on the jaw. It was even harder than I intended and I felt a little ashamed about it afterward. Somehow you don't like to hit a woman that hard—even a husky capable woman [who lunges at you] with a surgeon's scalpel.[6]

The test, of course, of the superiority of the private eye *vis a vis* society is whether or not he gets his man, which by a peculiar turn of the screw suggests how dependent he is on the society he presumably loathes. For, after all, what can he do with the bad guy after he catches him (unless he kills him himself) other than turn him over to society for appropriate punishment. Hence we see that for all his sense of being above the law and society, the private eye needs law and society, not simply to flaunt, but to give support to his values, substance to his identity. These ambivalencies (or should we say schizophrenia) about sex, morality and society —are they perhaps all one in the eye's mind?—are compounded and brought to a head in the thrillers of Chester Himes. Himes, a black writer who has been living on and off in Paris for the past 25 years, has written several rather lively novels about a couple of hardboiled police detectives who work in Harlem. Although these novels have their own intrinsic literary merits, in the main they pretty much conform to conventions of the hardboiled genre with rather larger than usual infusions of gore and macabre happenings.[7] But for purposes of this paper our interest lies in the divided and selfcontradictory views of the hero cops. On the one hand they often express contempt for the police for whom they work. (Himes obviously could not make them private dicks. Who, after all, could afford, let alone, would employ black private eyes in Harlem?) They see the force as racist, bathed in corruption and frequently used as an instrument to oppress the black community. Yet for all that, they acknowledge that the police are often the only protectors of Harlem. Conversely, they view the exploited black community as itself corrupt and predatory—an intensified microcosm of the dominant white world.

. . . in the murky waters of fetid tenements, a city of black people . . . are convulsed in desperate living, like the voracious churning of millions of hungry cannibal fish. Blind mouths eating their own guts. Stick in a hand and draw back a nub.

That is Harlem.[8]

Interestingly, Coffin Ed Johnson and Grave Digger Jones (note the names) display far more zeal in beating up black people than they do whites. All of which brings us to Himes's last novel, *Blind Man With A Pistol* (1969) wherein the levels of graft, corruption and venality are laid on so thick that our detectives cannot find the killers and the book ends with cops and Negroes shooting at one another without either knowing why. Now who ever heard of a detective novel where the detective cannot find the killer? Does this mean Himes will write no more thrillers? Does it suggest something about the impasse the thriller may some day reach for white writers as well? Does it say something about the state of mind of all of us? Whatever the answers, perhaps it does signal the recognition that the future of the hard-boiled detective story depends on a more coherent urban social order than now exists.

STYLES

D. F. Rauber

SHERLOCK HOLMES AND NERO WOLFE: THE ROLE OF THE "GREAT DETECTIVE" IN INTELLECTUAL HISTORY

It is by now a commonplace in the study of intellectual history that the "world picture" of an age is more profitably investigated in popular literature than in masterpieces. Our interest is in underlying assumptions, unexamined attitudes, what might be called the ground bass against which the individual melodies of a period are played. Such assumptions are present in great works and works which aim at greatness, but they are blurred by the individuality of the conscious artist. But in popular literature—writing turned out quickly, unpretentiously, and primarily for profit—the problems introduced by individuality are greatly reduced. The popular writer—suffering from no delusions of grandeur, pressed for time, and usually working within a formula—has neither the desire nor the opportunity to impose upon his work strongly individualistic elements. The intellectual assumptions in such works are, for the most part, unplanned; they appear naturally as manifestations of the writer's unreflective view of his age. They constitute, therefore, exactly the kind of evidence we want.

More specifically, it would appear that the detective story of the rationalistic or "great detective" variety offers a fertile field for the study of the general way in which a culture views science. These stories are popular in the sense described above, but what gives them their special interest is that the "great detective" can be seen as a vulgarization of the scientist, a popular surrogate for the less glamorous figure of the austere investigator of nature. Like the scientist, the detective collects data, forms hypotheses, checks these by the equivalent of experiment, and reaches conclusions through a combination of observation and logic. Indeed, at bottom the "great detective" is a fantasy figure of the perfectly functioning mind, pure intellect proceeding inexorably onward, indifferent to, or rather oblivious of, emotional considerations. But on a larger cultural scale this is also the ideal of the scientist, partially as viewed by the

Reprinted from the JOURNAL OF POPULAR CULTURE, VI:3.

scientists themselves and partially as the scientist is apprehended by the outside world. This type of fantasy figure does not, I think, appear in literature until after the emergence of modern experimental science; its nearest counterpart in earlier literature being the necromancer or undifferentiated wise man. It is probably not accidental that the hero of deduction is not found before the eighteenth-century or that the "great detective" does not appear until the heyday of scientific success and prestige in the nineteenth-century.[1]

If the detective is a popularized version of the scientist, then detective stories should reflect changing cultural attitudes toward the nature and practice of science. My intent in this paper is to show that this is so. The argument is that Sherlock Holmes reflects, almost as precisely as a mirror, the basic assumptions and tones of classical physics, while Nero Wolfe, his twentieth-century analogue, exhibits marked differences which correspond, again with considerable precision, to the revolutionary changes in physics produced by the emergence of sub-atomic phenomena. My treatment of shifts in physics will, of course, be partial, derivative, and unoriginal. The interest is not in the changes themselves, but rather in the astonishing way in which they are reproduced in the intellectually unpretentious detective story. I know of no more striking example of the way in which very complex ideas have filtered into the general consciousness.

For my purposes Sherlock Holmes and Nero Wolfe are ideal subjects. Not only are they the outstanding examples of the "great detective" for the nineteenth- and twentieth-centuries, respectively, but there is the added advantage that, as Edmund Wilson noticed some years ago, Wolfe is a deliberate imitation of Holmes. Because Rex Stout so completely reproduced the Doyle formulas and characteristics, it is possible to claim, with only slight exaggeration, that Wolfe *is* Holmes in modern dress. The close imitation and host of similarities furnish us with a common background against which differences can easily be located, and in the light of which differences acquire greater significance.[2]

Let us glance first at the similarities, as summarized nicely by Edmund Wilson:

> Here was simply the old Sherlock Holmes formula reproduced. . . . Here was the incomparable private detective, ironic and ceremonious, with a superior mind and eccentric habits, addicted to overeating and orchid-raising, as Holmes had his enervated indulgence in his cocaine and his violin, yet always prepared to revive for prodigies of intellectual alertness; and here were the admiring stooge, adoring and slightly dense, and Inspector Lestrade of Scotland Yard, energetic but entirely at sea, under the new name of Inspector Cramer of Police Headquarters. . . . It was only when I looked up Sherlock Holmes that I realized how much Nero Wolfe was a dim and distant copy of an original.[3]

While some of these equivalences will later be shown to be superficial and misleading, the general argument is sound. Indeed, it appears that Stout, to emphasize rather wittily his debt to Doyle, deliberately reversed the physical characteristics of detective and assistant. Sherlock Holmes was thin, intense, quick, and nervous; while Watson was heavy and slow-moving in mind and body. In Stout's world, it is Wolfe who has these latter characteristics, and it is the assistant, Archie Goodwin, who is similar to Holmes in physical prowess, alertness, and delight in activity.

The similarities go deeper. Stout has taken over from the Doyle stories not only their outward characteristics but also the secret of their enduring popularity. Christopher Morley has observed, and no fan of Holmes would disagree, that "We read the stories again and again; perhaps most of all for the little introductory interiors which give a glimpse of 221B Baker Street. . . . We have a glimpse of the sitting-room, that room we know so well. There are the great volumes of scrapbook records; the bullet marks on the walls; the mysterious 'gasogene'. . . ." (*Preface*, p. viii) But ambiviance is equally important in the Wolfe stories, with "the brownstone of West 35th Street" exerting the same attraction as the famous lodgings of Holmes. Here also it is the accumulation of detail that we relish—the red leather chair in Wolfe's study which is reserved for the client and surrounded by the less prestigious yellow chairs, the daily routine with the orchids (9 to 11 in the morning, 4 to 6 in the afternoon), the unlighted cigar upon which Inspector Cramer grits his teeth, the explosive "Pfui!" of Wolfe, and on and on.

There is, then, no doubt but that Stout has modelled his whole fictional world, in characters, style, and tone, on that of his predecessor Doyle. The interesting fact, though, is that beneath these obvious and surface similarities, the basic assumptions of the two sets of stories are radically different.

Let us first consider Holmes as a representative of the great empirical scientific tradition which acquired its first victories in the seventeenth-century, became stabilized in the eighteenth, and broke out into another series of triumphs in the nineteenth. A convenient summary of the heart of this science, as represented by its greatest glory, physics, is given by the eminent modern physicist-philosopher, Louis de Broglie:

> In classical physics we had postulated the possibility of describing natural phenomena by figures and by motion in the framework of space and time, and this hypothesis had met with an astonishing success; it had seemed capable of allowing, always and everywhere, the establishment of rigid and precise ties of inevitable succession amongst all natural phenomena, and had thus suggested the hypothesis of a universal determinism.[4]

The basis of Holmes' method is exactly trust in the existence of "rigid and precise ties of inevitable succession." A convenient locus is Chapter 2 of *A Study in Scarlet.* Watson, when first he starts rooming with Holmes, comes across a journal article with "the somewhat ambitious title" of "The Book of Life." The article, though Watson does not know it at the time, was written by Holmes and is a condensed and formal laying out of his basic principles:

. . . it attempted to show how much an observant man might learn by an accurate and systematic examination of all that came in his way. . . . The reasoning was close and intense, but the deductions appeared to me far fetched and exaggerated. The writer claimed by a momentary expression, a twitch of a muscle or a glance of an eye, to fathom a man's inmost thoughts. Deceit, according to him, was an impossibility in the case of one trained to observation and analysis. His conclusions were as infallible as so many propositions of Euclid. . . . "From a drop of water," said the writer, "a logician could infer the possibility of an Atlantic or a Niagara without having seen or heard of one or the other. So all life is a great chain, the nature of which is known whenever we are shown a single link of it." (*A Study in Scarlet,* pp. 12-13)

And in practice, as everyone knows, Holmes produces chains, or to use his favorite word *trains,* of infallible reasoning based upon close and detailed observation. One example will more than suffice; here is Holmes explaining how, when first they met, he knew Watson had come from Afghanistan:

Here is a gentleman of a medical type, but with the air of a military man. Clearly an army doctor, then. He has just come from the tropics, for his face is dark, and that is not the natural tint of his skin, for his wrists are fair. He has undergone hardship and sickness, as his haggard face says clearly. His left arm has been injured. He holds it in a stiff and unnatural manner. Where in the tropics could an English army doctor have seen much hardship and got his arm wounded? Clearly in Afghanistan. (*A Study in Scarlet,* p. 14)

In addition to the Euclidian precision of the reasoning, we are struck by the triumphant nature of the repeated *clearly.*

But it is exactly this clearness which has disappeared from modern physics. De Broglie continues the passage previously quoted in this way: "The intervention of the quantum of action no longer allows us to obtain as clear and also as well determined a picture of the evolution of things; it involves a certain weakness which asserts itself in uncertainties. . . ." (p. 110) Later he elaborates this critical theme:

There is here, therefore, a complete reversal of the old perspectives; it is no longer rigorous determinism and the precise laws of mechanics which, applied to the elementary entities, are at the basis of our physical explanations. This basis is now chance, probability, reigning over the kaleidoscopic world of corpuscles and quanta; the laws of mechanics, with their apparent rigour, are nothing more than a macroscopic illusion due to the complexity of the objects on which our direct experiments bear and to the lack of precision of our measurements. (pp. 199-200)

While it is probably possible to find examples of Wolfe of straight-down-the-track logical constructions, they are certainly rare. In *A Right To Die*, for example, Wolfe solves the crime by noticing a curious pattern in the names of several of the people involved in the case, the recurrence of the diphthong *au.* Two of these repetitions are connected with the murderer, one occurring in her real name, the other in her pseudonym. By following up this intuition, Wolfe exposes her true identity. In an extremely revealing passage, Archie muses on the phenomenon:

I certainly need a nap, but there was something on my mind. Not whether it was in the bag, but how we got it. Had it been luck or genius or what? It had been years since I had given up trying to figure how Wolfe's mind worked, but this was special. I hadn't happened to notice that there was an au in four of the names: Paul, Ault, Maud, and Vaughn, but I might have? anybody might. That was nothing special. The point was, if I *had* noticed it, then what? I would have filed it as just coincidence, and probably Wolfe had too. But although filed, that au in four of the names was still somewhere in his mind later, when it got really tough, so in going over and over it, every detail and every factor, that popped up. Okay, but then what? Did he deliberately team them up? . . . Then did he consider each pair and finally decide that the one that might not be just coincidence was Ault and Maud, because if a woman named Ault changed her name she might pick one that had au in it? No. I could have done that myself. I hadn't, but I could. What had happened in his mind was something that had never happened in mine and never would. He had said "tenuous almost to nullity." But there I was . . . and I knew who had killed Susan Brooke. . . . (pp. 168-169)

The Wolfe technique discussed here has, I contend, virtually nothing in common with the deductive reasoning of Holmes. Indeed, the closest approach to such reasoning, a systematic investigation and screening of the *au* permutations is explicitly denied, and the exact nature of the mental processes employed is left unknown and mysterious. But, in broad outline at least, these processes seem remarkably like those of modern theoretical physicists. There is a common reliance, for instance, upon highly abstract formal patterns far removed from common experience and common sense. In physics this emphasis upon rather esoteric mathematical constructions has even led some observers, such as Lord Russell, to grumble about a revival of "the numerical mysticism of the Pythagoreans."[6] Furthermore, both in the kind of data considered and in the mode of dealing with it, the clear sharp edges of classical science and logic have become blurred; Wolfe has abandoned certainty and deals only with the probabilistic. Within this realm he operates by what appear to be intuitive leaps. His own designation of his thought as "tenuous almost to nullity" is quite consonant with de Broglie's sophisticated view of modern physics as an arena in which at best "the scientist succeeds in snatching from the physical world, which he would like to understand, certain information, always partial, which would allow him to make predictions that are incomplete, and in general, only *probable*." (p. 131) The extent of these reservations and qualifications brings to mind David Hilbert's famous witticism that "physics is becoming too difficult for the physicists."[7]

Worthy of special emphasis is the fact that the evidence used by Wolfe above, and this is quite typical, is nonphysical. Holmes, on the other hand, deals almost completely with physical evidence—footprints, cigar ashes, stains, etc.—and furthermore craves immediate contact with the physical world. He is, among other things, almost the apotheosis of the tracker. Here is a representative picture of Holmes in action:

> As he spoke, he whipped a tape measure and a large round magnifying glass from his pocket. With these two implements he trotted noiselessly about the room, sometimes stopping, occasionally kneeling, and once lying flat upon his face. . . . As I watched him I was irresistibly reminded of a pure-blooded, well-trained foxhound . . . For twenty minutes or more he continued his researches, measuring with the most exact care the distance between marks which were entirely invisible to me, and occasionally applying his tape to the walls in an equally incomprehensible manner. In one place he gathered up very carefully a little pile of gray dust from the floor, and packed it away in an envelope. (*A Study in Scarlet,* pp. 22-23)

But what is this except a manifestation of the root assumption of classical physics that individual objects had an indubitable existence and were uniquely located in space and time?

In modern physics this assumption is, according to de Broglie, "Obscured and subject to revision." (p. 11) We are not surprised, therefore, to find that Wolfe has no interest whatever in *things.* He leaves his house only under the greatest provocation and never willingly. He does not visit the scene of a crime, and he never, never whips "a large round magnifying glass from his pocket." In fact, he is almost always separated from the actual data and circumstances of a case by a considerable distance, physical as well as mental, and receives his information through verbal reports from Archie. On the basis of these reports, he makes suggestions and instigates plans of action, which are carried out by his assistants. In times of crisis he goes into a kind of trance:

> Finding that that wasn't getting us anywhere, he leaned back and closed his eyes, and his lips started working. They pushed out, then drew in, and kept at it—out and in, out and in. . . . Man at work, or possibly genius at work. I never interrupt the lip act because I can't; he's not there. It may last anywhere from half a minute to half an hour; I always time it, since there's nothing else to do. (p. 106)

Not only do Wolfe's procedures reflect the changes in physics regarding the status of objects, but they furthermore seem to me in striking correspondence to the marked division in modern science between the laboratory and the study, between the experimentalists and the theoreticians. The fact is that the modern theoretical physicist is as far from the experimental data and brute matter as Wolfe is from his cases. And this is connected with a major difference in the Holmes and the Wolfe stories, the relation between the detective and his assistant. Watson was pure foil, quite properly described by Wilson as "the admiring stooge, adoring and slightly dense." This is not an accurate description of Archie, who is a much more substantial and important figure. Indeed, Wolfe and Archie constitute a partnership, with Wolfe as the senior partner. But Wolfe cannot exist or operate without Archie, while Holmes had no such dependence on Watson. This is not accidental; rather, the relation between Archie and Wolfe is almost exactly like that between the experimentalist, or gatherer of data, and the theoretical physicist. One can even observe in the Wolfe stories—it is present in the preceding quotation—the curiously mixed feelings which the experimentalist has toward the theoretician. Archie obviously admires and needs Wolfe, but at the same time he views him as hopelessly impractical and difficult. The tone of "genius" as he applies it to Wolfe always hovers somewhere between admiration and contempt. This kind of tension exists rather noticeably in physics as well.

But more than this, in the Wolfe stories we find also a re-creation of the organizational structure of modern physics. Holmes, by way of contrast, is the whole show, and it is completely a one-man show. In this he is like the giants of the earlier science. The Wolfe situation is more complex; it is essentially a group effort, with Wolfe at the center and Archie as manager and organizer. In practice, Archie heads a team of detectives, each of whom has his own specialty; Saul Panzer, for example, is the greatest tailer in the world. The group also has its medical consultant, its legal advisor, and its press representative. In other words, it is very much like the modern research team, and like such teams is a response to a much more complex world.

To conclude this study I would like to attempt a deeper penetration by considering the relation of the scientist to his field and to society. For purposes of simplicity I will rather arbitrarily set aside developments in science centering around the Second World War—the great crises produced by the development of the atomic bomb, the massive underwriting of scientific research by governments, and the uncertainties resulting from the experience that technology creates at least as many problems as it solves. These are simply too complex to be entered into here. Furthermore, I am aware that the things discussed in what follow are not limited to science but have obvious social roots as well. Despite these qualifications and misgivings, however, the subject is worth a few tentative observations.

One of the most prominent attributes of nineteenth-century science was its supreme confidence. In Lord Russell's words, "There prevailed at that time a kind of scientific optimism which made men believe that the Kingdom of Heaven was about to break out on earth. The vast strides accomplished by science and technology made it seem not unplausible that the solution of all problems was close at hand." (p. 374) This bubble soon burst, partly because of developments within science, partially by developments in the political realm. New theoretical structures were, of course, created, and they have turned out to be imposing and magnificent. But the old confidence has not been regained. As the quotations from de Broglie show, the new physics is more sophisticated than the old, but it is also more hesitant and problematic. Because of the enormous complexity of his subject and its distance from the assumptions of common sense and common language, because also of the need for ever increased specialization, the modern theoretical physicist has become ever more withdrawn from other scientists and even more distant from the ordinary world.

Here also, though admittedly the analysis is very rude, the detective stories offer parallels. Holmes is an almost perfect example of the supreme, even the hubristic, confidence of the earlier period. He is imbued with the feeling that the straightforward intellect can set things straight, and he delights in applying his powers within a social context. While he is outside the official police structure, he is not outside his society but is an integral working part of it, with no doubts about his place in society or the value of that society.[8] His confidence is based upon intuitive convictions about the stability of the physical, the mental, and–by indirection–the social worlds.

So strong is the impulse in Holmes to operate in the world that in periods of inactivity he must resort to drugs to dull his pain. "My mind . . . . rebels at stagnation. Give me problems, give me work, give me the most abstruse cryptogram, or the most intricate analysis, and I am in my own proper atmosphere." (*The Sign of Four,* p. 92) Holmes' deepest wish is to be active, and active primarily in society, for in actuality he finds the solving of "abstruse cryptograms" not very satisfying.

Wolfe is completely different. He must be prodded by Archie to accept cases; he must be insulted into applying his mind to the outside world. As a matter of fact, Wolfe uses his intellect mainly to construct a refuge for himself. All his efforts are directed ultimately at excluding the outer world.[9] At bottom he represents intellect on the run, with no confidence whatever in the ability of intellect either to comprehend finally or significantly to affect an almost infinitely complex universe. Almost the essence of the position is contained in this exchange between Archie and Wolfe:

> "Very well. You presumed that I am aware of the situation and I said I am. There isn't one single solitary sensible thing that you can do or I can do or Saul and Fred and Orrie can do."
>
> He nodded. "You're right." He switched the reading light on and picked up the book he was just starting. (p. 126)

Obviously this does not represent the only, perhaps not even the predominant, attitude in modern physics, but it is certainly not a insignificant general orientation. Wolfe emerges finally as an excellent example of the basic uncertainties concerning function and role which pervade not only modern science, but the whole modern intellectual world. His "tenuous almost to nullity" might well serve as its motto, or its epitaph.

Nancy Y. Hoffman

MISTRESSES OF MALFEASANCE

The women who have written and published successfully about *crime* contrast sharply with the few women whose non-crime fictions get printed. Why do so many women write in the crime fiction genre? How did they get started? And how do they sell their works in a field apparently so foreign to the feminine image-makers?

An American, Anna Katharine Green (1846-1935), is the godmother of these mistresses of malfeasance. Her *Leavenworth Case* (1878) is a detective story milestone. After Poe fathered the detective story and established its conventions—the impossible deductions made by a superior being, aided by an amanuensis-imperceptive norm-chief cook and bottle washer, amazingly no American followed his lead until the prolific Green created her naturally (!) male police detective, Ebenezer Gryce. Women people every other aspect of Green's fiction, and even function as possible suspects, despite Gryce's protectively faulty logic. Early in *The Leavenworth Case* he concludes that no woman could have committed the murder, because, "Did you ever know a woman who cleaned a pistol, or who knew the object or use of doing so? No. They can fire them and do; but after firing them they do not clean them."

Gryce's assistant is a woman, Amelia Butterworth, much brighter than any helper of Poe's Monsieur Dupin. Green's Amelia Butterworth, Miss Van Arsdale (who narrates *The Woman in the Alcove* (1906), saves and eventually marries a murder suspect), and even the sometimes-sentimental Leavenworth sisters are vibrant women, who salvage and strengthen men. Still a pioneer in crime fiction, in 1915, Green published the stories of Violet Strange, detective. Strange was probably the first woman detective extant, with disturbingly few successors despite the numbers of women detective writers.

Male historians of the detective story, whose criticism is as male-oriented as the literary criticism of less "popular" genres, are fond of indicting Mary Roberts Rinehart (1856-1958) on the charge that her detectives are less important than her female characters. Her single women deviate from the stereotype of most American novels in which the woman over thirty is a crabby, lonely old maid or widow, "more to be pitied than censured"–but never to be emulated. Spunky widows and staunch middle-aged spinsters populate Rinehart's novels. While it takes them longer than it might have taken a professional detective to put two and two together, they eventually identify the equation that solves the mystery–and before the relatively astute male detective comes to his conclusions. Critics carp that chance plays too prominent a part in Rinehart's fictions without admitting that chance is operative everywhere in both life and literature. Further objections focus on her abundance of "domestic detail," as though domesticity should be removed from the murder scene, and on her too-heavy reliance on the least-likely person. Here, critics condemn Rinehart for the excesses of her imitators (Leslie Ford and Mignon Eberhart are the great abusers of the Had I But Known School). This is a little like condemning Hemingway for Mickey Spillane's imitative stylistic abuses. And the best of Rinehart, *The Man in Lower Ten* (1909), *The Circular Staircase* (1908), *The Door* (1930), and the omnibus grouping, *The Frightened Wife and Other Murder Stories* (1951) is still well worth reading.

If Rinehart is different from her predecessor and contemporary, Green, she is just as dissimilar from her other contemporary, Marie Belloc-Lowndes (1868-1947). Sister of Hillaire Belloc and great-great-granddaughter of Joseph Priestly, Belloc-Lowndes employed the hyphenated married name long before people thought of it in our own time. Her fictions are primarily psychological and sociological studies of the murdering mind, often based on real crime, such as her masterly examination of the Jack the Ripper murders in *The Lodger* (1913). Almost thirty years later, she returned to psychological crime with *Lizzie Borden* in 1941. Here, she focuses on woman as criminal rather than woman as object of criminality, and concludes that "passionate love" drove Lizzie Borden to her double murders.

For better or worse, Rinehart's fictions force reader identification with the narrator, and are centered about the life or death conflict between narrator and criminal. Contrastingly Agatha Christie's (1891-1975) and Dorothy Sayers' (1893-1957) intellectualized puzzles, more literary and formalized, owe much to Conan Doyle's and R. Austin Freeman's tales, where the reader does not participate in the detective's skills; he or she feels protected by and marvels at his (almost always "his" despite the many feminine authors) Nietzchean superman abilities. The reader's anxieties are relieved by the identification of the scapegoat villain, or are not emotionally engaged. He or she is confident that any threat to the social structure will be expelled quickly, calmly, and *non-violently,* and the communal order will be restored promptly. The formal detective story is never radical or revolutionary. Its usually male amateur "gentlemen" detectives are aficionados, preferably sexless ("Mr. Queen, will you be good enough to explain your famous character's sex life, if any" questioned Dashiell Hammett when introducing the composite Queen to a lecture audience) and preferably unpaid. For money and women would taint the gentlemen's incorruptibility and destroy their value as society's conservative standard bearers. Money and sex remain the two major motives for murder in fact and fiction of any age.

If there were virtually no women detectives, there were no Jewish, black or working class detectives either. Whatever was, was right. The privatism of the twenties is reflected in its crime stories of the Golden Age. The Depression and rising Facism in the thirties led to a collectivism in its novels, and to a new male-dominated, male-written crime novel where the criminal and the super strongman became the hero (reflective and prophetic of dictatorship's flexing muscles). Yet the formal detective novel continued to be written and read by men and women up to our own time, when it is in danger of being supplanted by science fiction.

Of the two mistresses of the Golden Age, Agatha Christie began writing earlier and was still going strong, with a new Christie appearing annually or semi-annually until her death. Her publishers, Dodd Mead, refused her first book, *The Mysterious Affair at Styles*, in 1920, but published it ten years later. Dodd Mead has made a fortune from Christie with 200 million copies of her novels and short stories in all sizes, shapes, formats and languages. Her most famous, and most controversial novel, *The Murder of Roger Ackroyd,* ends with a twist that left many crime devotees crying foul. At this late date beyond the Golden Era of the mystery story, it is no breach of confidence to reveal that Dr. Sheppard, physician-narrator of the story and apparent confidante to the reader, is Roger Ackroyd's killer. While Edmund Wilson's grumpy downgrading of the detective story per se is entitled, "Who Cares Who Killed Roger Ackroyd?" Dorothy Sayers defends Christie with the injunction, "It is the reader's business to suspect *everyone*." Sayers thus equates the reader's task with that of the detective's. While apparently upholding society's surface, she questions it, Contrary to the tradition of the formal detective novel, the good guys are confused with the bad.

The elf-like Hercule Poirot dominates a majority of Christie's works. In *Pale Horse* (1962) Mrs. Oliver investigates without Poirot, but a sometime scholar, Mark Easterbrook does the real sleuthing. But Christie's Miss Marple, another of the few triumphs over the stereotypical single woman in fiction, has been knitting and probing her way alone through middle and late vintage Christie, working best in *The Body in the Library* (1942) and *What Mrs. McGillicuddy Saw* (1957). Miss Marple is Christie's answer to Sayers' comment in 1929 that "there still is no really brilliant woman detective," although unfortunately, she doesn't have much company. If Miss Marple is not so brilliant as Holmes, she is less a reflection of her feminine creator's anti-feminism than of a tendency in the detective novel to make detectives more fallible. Victims, villains and inquisitors alike are "more like you and me," as Ngaio Marsh and Margery Allingham demonstrate in their literate detective ficciones from the '30's to the '60's.

Sayers is more difficult to evaluate. Male critics are fond of knocking her. Readers, male and female, still read her works, even though she inexplicably stopped writing crime stories in 1937, in favor of Anglican tracts and scholarly essays. Astute crime critic, creator of the Lord Peter Wimsey stories, fascinated by the potential in the union of crime and medical science—the potential for criminality and for analytic deductions in solving crime, Sayers began her career as a detective novelist in 1923 with *Whose Body?* Sayers indicts two physicians as murderers: Dr. Penberthy of *The Unpleasantness at Bellona Club* (1928) and Sir Julian Freke of *Whose Body?* because both doctors assert the ascendance of the body over the spirit. But if the "ladies" can concern themselves with the murdering proclivities of its most respected citizens (a fact which should give the male image-makers pause), the ladies Christie and Sayers apparently consider themselves "ladies" still: they let their doctor-murderers be "gentlemen," or at least be spared the indignities of a murder trial.

Sayers' medical murderers, Dr. Penberthy and Sir Julian, and Christie's Dr. Sheppard commit suicide with the physician's readily-accessible means—poison. Thus, if the sophisticated female crime inditer is more suspicious of the physician—or of any of society's stalwart preservers of life who become destroyers, she is also more protective. Her villains are not subjected to public calumny. For Christie and Sayers write of crime in a way that seems to assert their faith in the social order. If murder shatters the façade of the social structure, the discovery and expulsion of the murderer reasserts the primacy of the communal order . . . which may account for the woman writer's facility in getting her mysteries published.

It is Sayers who introduced what non-medical mystery addicts consider the perfect crime: murder by injection of an air embolus in *Unnatural Death* (1927). And no amount of medical cavilling about the necessary diameter of the syringe capable of performing the crime can lessen the devoteds' belief in its efficacy. The multiple murderess's "revulsion of the flesh," when she is kissed by Wimsey (one of the early detectives to enact the philosophy of anything for a clue), and her implicit lesbianism, contrary to the Golden Age's lexicon of crime without pain or loss, deserve psychological study. For Sayers always implied more than she said and asked questions while seeming to accept.

Jumping over everybody's special favorites, from Josephine Tey and Patricia Highsmith to Margot Bennet's and Emma Lathen's (pseudonym of Mary Latis and Martha Hennisart) knowledgeable Wall Street mysteries, Jean Dodds Freeman's *Diagnosis: Positive* (1971) reveals the changes in subject matter and tone since Sayers and Christie, Green and Belloc-Lowndes. Still using a male sleuth, Freeman's gynecological resident tracks down death-dealing emboli from birth control pills in a wide array of victims, from a prostitute and a physician's wife to the First Lady—of unknown political persuasion. Far removed from the sexless worlds of Holmes and Poirot—and Miss Marple, or the pseudo-sexual world of Lord Peter Wimsey, the young doctor is tempted to desist from his interrogations by such seductions as bribery and even an affair with the drug manufacturer's wife (shades of Ben Jonson's *Volpone!*). Although the physician egotistically congratulates himself for the lives he has saved, he does so at the funeral of one of the victims. And the evil drug manufacturer escapes from Washington on his Onassian yacht. The identification with the victim's suffering and loss, the facing up to death's unalterable finality, and the villain's escape are relatively new phenomena in the crime genre.

The modern mind, male or female, reader or writer, questions the validity of the superior intellect of the Superman detective, Sherlock Holmes, the puckish Hercule Poirot, the placid Miss Marple, the mechanical *gentilesse* of Lord Peter Wimsey. For the superior intellect that enabled the Great Detective to solve a mystery and restore order is the same intellect that can wreak havoc in the wrong person's hands. Doyle's intellectual giant, created at a time of scientific optimism, is strangely dated. As Dorothy Sayers implicitly predicted in her stories, the modern world fears its scientists while it seeks its cure-alls. Science fiction is replacing the detective story. From Mary Shelley's *Frankenstein* of long ago (and her father, William Godwin's *Calab Williams*), the woman writer and the world in which she lives has traversed a full circle to the science fictions of Joanna Russ. Where the woman mystery writer goes from here will depend on where her world goes from here—and that's anybody's guess.

Ronald Ambrosetti

THE WORLD OF ERIC AMBLER: FROM DETECTIVE TO SPY

Eric Ambler's novels began to appear in the late 1930's, representing the transition from the detective tale to the tale of espionage and international intrigue. Ambler's novels may be the *loci classici* of the traits which are considered traditionalist in the spy genre; yet his novels are not spy novels. The chief reasons for this important distinction are that, first of all, Ambler approaches the theme and matter of espionage through the form of the detective novel; and secondly, his formula has undoubtedly influenced the genre for thirty-five years, but the formula had to await the social context of the Cold War before it achieved a widespread acceptance (both in terms of reading audience and socio-economic relevance). Quite simply, the theme of the Cold War was not available to the writer of the thriller in the 1930's, a distinction indirectly admitted by Ambler himself in 1965. Even as recent as the July 10, 1972 issue of *Newsweek,* in "Search for a Summer Thriller," the book review editor differentiated between the "foreign intrigue story" and the "spy story." The former review discussed the most recent publication of Eric Ambler (*The Levanter*), and the latter category specifically stated the Cold War-ingredient as a necessity for the traditional spy story: "Now that we're chums with the Russians and Chinese, the spy story may be in for heavy weather" (p. 91). The rough sailing ahead for the spy novel is not unexpected, but to see that his novels of "foreign intrigue" have still not been wholly accepted within the purview of the literature of espionage must have been a bit disheartening to Mr. Ambler. But it is a matter of form—Ambler's approach is that of the detective/spy—and the *Newsweek* reviewer's "thematic" categorizations are not completely justified. The crucial distinction lies in form, not matter.

Ambler's significant accomplishment in the spy genre revolves about his transitional sub-genre. Ambler's literary predecessors belong more properly to the mode of detective fiction than the burgeoning tales of espionage as prefigured in Buchan and Maugham. To be sure, the exotic geography of Buchan and the variegated characterizations of Maugham are to be found in the early Ambler novels, but Ambler's peculiar type of novel is still a hybrid born of the cross-species blending. Ambler's spy/detective story is actually a permutation of the detective story which happens to have a spy as the central character and/or foreign intelligence agents as the antagonists. The quintessence of the Ambler spy/detective tale is the *ingenu's* inadvertent involvement in a plot of international intrigue, and his subsequent loss of innocence as he seeks the answers to the "accidental" clues provided. The method of detection is logical and deductive; thus Ambler's typical novel bears imprinting of the older tale of ratiocination.

The fact that Ambler's central character is almost always the innocent amateur is his main connection to the detective story and also severs his future connection to the spy story where professional Cold War secret agents must always know what they are doing. In contrast to the latter-day professionals, part of Ambler's formula demands a dilettante who fumbles his way through the novel to an uneasy survival. The Ambler protagonist does not understand what is happening; he cannot go to the police; he probably will not survive the embroilment; and he must comply with the game-plan of the foe. Somehow he survives (usually, by chance) and emerges a chastened but wiser man. Ambler's formula bears a certain resemblance to the undercurrent ethos of Greek tragedy: the gods will not tolerate a man who is too happy or inordinately comfortable in his position in life. Ambler's protagonists are such men, and they are grimly reminded through tragic circumstances that human happiness is too easily subject to chance and fate. In this sense, the Ambler *ingenu* is chastened and recovers from the harrowing experience as a wiser man.

As a device of realism, the amateur as protagonist succeeds for Ambler by reducing all of the *angst* of international intrigue to a very personal level. The reader's distance is maintained when the dangerous situation is ably managed by the ultra-professional James Bond. But Ambler gets the edge on suspense by making his spy/detective an average person—the reader identifies easily. In this sense, the Ambler novel is more of a "thriller" than the later professional-spy novels.

It is quite easy to envision oneself in the predicament of an Ambler thriller. *A Coffin For Dimitrios* (1939) precipitates a powerful crescendo of suspense when Charles Latimer, an English professor of political economy and well-known author of detective stories, becomes engrossed in the search of the true identity of one "Dimitrios." Latimer learns of the existence of Dimitrios by chance. At a party in Istanbul, Latimer is introduced to Colonel Haki. Unbeknownst to Latimer is the fact that Colonel Haki is the chief of Turkish secret police—a soldier of fortune turned intelligence chief. Haki's intentions are benign, for he has admired Latimer's detective stories, and proposes to give gratis a plot for a novel to Latimer.

Colonel Haki indirectly inaugurates Latimer's involved quest when he pauses, and asks: "I wonder if you are interested in *real* murderers, Mr. Latimer."[1] Haki's undisguised sentiment states, in oblique terms, that art is never a substitute for real life encounters with death, espionage, and experience itself. Colonel Haki enjoys his *romans policiers,* but he definitely believes in the bipolar opposites of art and reality.

'I find the murderer in a *roman policier* much more sympathetic than a real murderer. In a *roman policier* there is a corpse, a number of suspects, a detective and a gallows. That is artistic. The real murderer is not artistic. I, who am a sort of policeman, tell you that squarely.' He tapped the folder on his desk. 'Here is a real murderer. We have known of his existence for nearly twenty years. This is his dossier. We know of one murder he may have committed. There are doubtless others of which we, at any rate, know nothing. This man is typical. A dirty type, common, cowardly, scum. Murder, espionage, drugs—that is the history. There were also two affairs of assassination.' (p. 11)

This opposition is sustained throughout the novel, and Latimer's close brush with death is born from his momentary movement from the aseptic and tidy ideology of academic murder in fiction to the unruly, chaotic real world of smokey bistros where actual murder and assassination are plotted. In short, Latimer progresses from observer to participant, and finds that the neat ground rules in the detective's process of deduction are non-existent in the face of brutal reality.

A philosophy of history is always as important in an Ambler novel as the social context in which the novel is written—one complements the other. *A Coffin For Dimitrios* was written in 1939, on the eve of the Second World War. Ambler's particular philosophy of history reflects his reading of Spengler and concurrent opinion that Europe (and Western civilization) had reached a stage of decadence which was bent on self-destruction. One of the minor ironies of the novel consists in the fact that Latimer, aside from writing detective fiction, is a lecturer in political economy in a minor English university; yet when he moves from his secure sphere of observation out to the role of participant in actual melodrama, he learns a lesson in both politics and economics. Or, more precisely, he learns that it is in the realms of politics and economics where Good and Evil really meet:

Dimitrios was not evil. He was logical and consistent; as logical and consistent in the European jungle as the poison gas called Lewisite and the shattered bodies of children killed in the bombardment of an open town. The logic of Michael Angelo's *David,* Beethoven's quartets and Einstein's physics had been replaced by that of the *Stock Exchange Year Book* and Hitler's *Mein Kampf.* (p. 174-175)

Michael Angelo's *David* had encapsulated all the cosmic harmony of the spheres which bespoke a deep faith in Providence. Beethoven's quartets were composed amid the waning of belief in the providential theory of history and at a time when other systematic explanations were already competing for favor. Napoleon could declare by the beginning of the nineteenth-century that fate had been replaced by politics. In the course of the nineteenth-century, new scientific and positivistic systems offered more appealing and more practical explanations for the haphazard facts of the universe. Meanwhile, in popular polemic, theories of evolution and psychotherapy routed the belief that God's intervention and order were the mainsprings of history. In this atmosphere of the belief in the visible and the physical, Einstein formulated a system of "relativity"—the non-immutable. Einstein, in fact, passed beyond the physics of Newton into a realm of meta-physics. The beauty of Einstein's theory was that it retained enough of the old mysticism to still consider the source of a "providence" in history. But, that civilization should reach such final period of corruption and that a man such as Dimitrios should embody the very spirit of the age, is equally as "logical and consistent" in its grotesquery. The Napoleon's, the Hitler's, and the Dimitrios' had won out over the Beethoven's and the Einstein's. Europe was finally to be reduced to its primordial jungle-state by poison gas and bombardment. Ambler's judgment on Europe in 1939 is quite unmistakable. In one other passage does Ambler give strongest enunciation to the tones of the jeremiad:

> In a dying civilisation, political prestige is the reward not of the shrewdest diagnostician but of the man with the best bedside manner. It is the decoration conferred on mediocrity by ignorance. Yet there remains one sort of political prestige that may still be worn with a certain pathetic dignity; it is that given to the liberal-minded leader of a party of conflicting doctrinaire extremists. His dignity is that of all doomed men: for, whether the two extremes proceed to mutual destruction or whether one of them prevails, doomed he is, either to suffer the hatred of the people or to die a martyr. (p. 52)

It comes as no surprise, then, when Latimer returns to the art of detective fiction after his nightmarish venture to the underworld. His quest had begun when he first viewed the corpse of Dimitrios:

> Latimer stared at the corpse. So this was Dimitrios. This was the man who had, perhaps, slit the throat of Sholem, the Jew turned Moslem. This was the man who had connived at assassinations, who had spied for France. This was the man who had trafficked in drugs, who had given a gun to a Croat terrorist and who, in the end, had himself died by violence. This putty-coloured bulk was the end of an Odyssey. Dimitrios had returned at last to the country whence he had set out so many years before. (p. 19)

Just as the Odyssey of Dimitrios comes full circle in its pursuit of violence, Latimer's own quest was to bear a lesson in the philosophy of history with a renewed knowledge of good and evil. And Latimer also returns to his original point of departure: the art of detective fiction. The conclusion of the novel neatly implies that the antinomy between art and reality might never be resolved. In the outside world of experience, Latimer had seen brutality and selfishness produce assassination, poison gas, and bombardment—all done under the sacrosanct aegis of nationalism and patriotism. Politics and economics—the new theologies—reign supreme; and Dimitrios the Greek had in his own logical way been the incarnate paradigm of the age. Latimer therefore returns to the inner world of art—in particular the detective fiction. The detective story is but an extension of Michael Angelo's *David* and Beethoven's quartets—it is the construct emanating from a new harmony of the sphere. It is a world of limited systems, made up of deductively ordered arrays of facts. The novel of detection is an enclosed world which is cogenial to the refugee from the outer environment of armed hostility and imminent cosmic chaos.

Therefore, when Latimer's philosophical friend, Marukakis, writes a letter in an attempt to explain a man like Dimitrios (one wonders if this is Ambler's own thinly disguised voice), Latimer's reaction is justified. The writer's reaction: "Latimer folded the letter and put it in his pocket. A good fellow, Marukakis. He must write to him when he had the time" (p. 214). But, at the moment, Latimer has more important things to think about—he has that novel that must be finished:

> He needed, and badly, a motive, a neat method of committing a murder and an entertaining crew of suspects. Yes, the suspects must certainly be entertaining. His last book had been a trifle heavy. He must inject a little more humour into this one. As for the motive, money was always, of course, the soundest basis. A pity that Wills and life insurance were so outmoded. Supposing a man murdered an old lady so that his wife should have a private income. It might be worth thinking about. The scene? Well, there was always plenty of fun to be got out of an English country village, wasn't there? The time? Summer; with cricket matches on the village green, garden parties at the vicarage, the clink of teacups and the sweet smell of grass on a July evening. That was the sort of thing people liked to hear about. It was the sort of thing that he himself would like to hear about. (p. 214)

Latimer retreats completely to the inner cosmos of order, sweetness, and light. But as he peers from the train window, "The train ran into the tunnel" (p. 214). Ambler's final symbolic stroke relinquishes the writer's retreat as an escape of ambiguous efficacy. Which is the twentieth-century man, the child of history: Dimitrios or Latimer?

If Ambler's solution to the dilemma of whether the man of thought or the man of action shapes the progression of history is too obliquely stated in *A Coffin For Dimitrios,* the next novel, *Journey Into Fear*[2] (1940), makes that answer more explicit.

A *Journey Into Fear* develops when a British ballistics engineer is dispatched to Turkey to provide the technical data to convert the British armaments for Turkish naval vessels. On the night before he is to return to England, a lone gunman attempts to murder him in his Istanbul hotel. It is late 1940, and Allied forces *must* arm the Turkish vessels before the imminent German Spring offensive. Colonel Haki enters the scene, and convinces Mr. Graham, the engineer, that the safest route back to England is an Italian steamer—and not the Orient Express (shades of Graham Greene). What follows is the "journey into fear."

The Italian steamer, *Sestri Levante,* is a "ship of fools" whereby modern man is displayed in the clinical showcase designed by Darwin and Freud. Ambler is extremely effective in bringing the age-old device of the shipboard community of diverse personalities to the espionage genre. Ambler does in fact outmaneuver the "Orient Express" in the element of suspense (and Anthony Burgess uses the ship community in his 1966 *Tremor of Intent*).

The reality of the Darwinian jungle is ubiquitous, just beneath the surface of appearances. The law of the jungle is also just beneath the surface of man's skin. Graham is forced to realize the existence of his own survival instincts when he is pressed to obtain a gun and is willing to kill in self-defense. He is also willing to entertain thought of a *liaison* with a Spanish dancer, and she forces him to recognize his sexual drives. Ambler indirectly resurrects the Maugham's Ashenden formula of sex and violence: these two elements are never far removed from spy genre.

As in the previous Ambler novel, the thematic core of the work resides in the philosophy of history. In *Journey Into Fear,* the philosophy of history is a hybrid form of combined Frazer and Spengler doctrines, ironically expounded by the chief German agent who is disguised as a German archaeologist. Ambler, writing in 1940, seems to indicate that it is the German nation which has learned the principal lesson of history: might makes right. The background for Ambler's novel is a Europe which is headed for self-destruction, and history is the cosmic working out of the death and resurrection ritual. Because of her power and will to exercise that power, Ambler warns, through the pronunciations of the German agent, that Germany may be the new phoenix to rise from the ashes of Europe's destruction. The German "archaeologist" preaches to the Englishman on the subject of historical destiny.

> 'I used to spend hours standing in the shade by the Propylaea looking at it and trying to understand the men who built it. I was young then and did not know how difficult it is for Western man to understand the dream-heavy classical soul. They are so far apart. The god of superlative shape has been replaced by the god of superlative force and between the two conceptions there is all space. The destiny idea symbolised by the Doric collums is incomprehensible to the children of Faust. For us . . .' He broke off. (p. 125)

At this point, the ventriloquism of Ambler breaks through the German agent, and he momentarily loses his nationality. For the children of Faust are toying with the ultimate Damoclean sword which perpetually hangs above civilization itself.

But the arrayed forces of darkness are held back and, temporarily at least, defeated in the novels of Eric Ambler. His fumbling, non-professional "heroes" survive through some chance occurrence or providential event. Latimer lives because of "a criminal's odd taste in interior decoration" (p. 1), and Graham survives because of his final reliance on instinct and violence. The quiet cognitive processes of deduction and reason singularly fail.

All this adds up to the *raison d'etre* of the spy novel—the literature of espionage. The major premise of Ambler's argument resides in the dangerously thin veneer of protection that civilization offers to modern man. The ages of Medieval faith and Renaissance decorum are past: Darwin, Freud, Frazer, and Spengler have triumphed. The world of the detective—the interlocking, visible puzzle pieces of Newton, Dupin, and Holmes—is totally inadequate in the face of technological warfare. The day of the spy had dawned. The detective writer and the ballistics engineer had to doff the velvet of the man, and temporarily assume the characteristics of Dimitrios and Banat in order to survive. There is a little bit of Dimitrios in everyman—every modern man, that is. Violence and betrayal in the global village—this is the legacy of Dimitrios and the beginning for the spy to pick up the pieces of the shattered Victorian closed-world of rationalism.

After the lapse of exactly thirty years, Charles Latimer reappeared in the 1969 publication of *The Intercom Conspiracy.* In Latimer's absence, Ambler had written ten spy novels, the mammoth glacier of the Cold War had frozen solid and then partially thawed, the Vietnam War had been engaged and lost, and America lost a President and Senator named Kennedy with the further assassinations of two charismatic black leaders. In 1969, if ever the time were more ripe for a recrudescent philosophy of historical doom and despair, Eric Ambler seemingly ignored the opportune moment. *The Intercom Conspiracy* attains style of suspense, characterization, and penchant for plot; and even exceeds the former novels in his experimentation with a Conradian point of view. But gone is the undercurrent philosophy of history. In lieu of a search for a logic in history, Ambler renders history at its face value. And history in this case is the Cold War reality of two super-powers who must both seek a *rapprochement* in maintaining a balance of power. *The Intercom Conspiracy* is, however, not straight Cold War plot. The spark of Ambler's old ingenuity becomes evident when Latimer stumbles on the successful extortion of both the United States *and* Russia by a pair of NATO intelligence chiefs. Both super-powers are eager to stop the leakage of information by paying a handsome ransom, and thereby preserve the equilibrium of power and intelligence-access. Ambler's revelation of this plan again comes through the eyes of the innocent victim (not Latimer this time, though) and the whole method of discovery is still presented in terms of deductive detection. The novel is typical Cold War, but Ambler's *sui generis* formula persists along with his basic detective-novel approach.

But *The Intercom Conspiracy* depicts the final, utter failure of the detective hero in the modern era of Cold War espionage. Latimer is no match for the two traitorous NATO confederates; he is liquidated and silenced forever. The modern, corporate "organization" is both hero and villain in the Cold War setting of "bloc" versus "bloc." There is really nothing heroic in Brand's and Jost's plot to blackmail the super-powers, they are merely successful bureaucrats who possess intimate knowledge of the innermost workings of big organizations:

> What impressed them most about these giants, they ultimately decided, was not their strength, still less the loud and threatening noises they made, but their inherent clumsiness.[3]

The bureaucratic spies are successful because of their cognizance of organizational weaknesses. Their guarded daring is always protected by transactions through Swiss banks and telegrams—the personal confrontation of heroic encounter is totally absent.

In final analysis, Eric Ambler seems out of his medium with the Cold War/organization spy novel. Ambler gave more to the genre in his early efforts than what he has extracted in his later work. He apparently picked up some of Ian Fleming's flare for technical accuracy—the result of the genre going to the professional spy; and his Russian "villain" in *The Intercom Conspiracy* bears a Flemingesque touch in his physical grotesquery. But Eric Ambler should be primarily remembered for what he contributed to the literature's overall generic formula. Ambler's contribution specifically lies in his initial linking of the spy genre to the legacy of popular literature—the tale of detection. The precise elements which were carried over to the spy tale from the larger *genus* of popular formulaic fiction include the invocation of salvific violence which preserves the equilibrium of society (and the global village), the extra-legal necessity to enforce that preservation, and finally the ethical dilemma of the observer of history—what option of active participation may be chosen. For Ambler, the choice is quite basic, yet is as old as the Platonic dialogues and as awe-inspiring as Hamlet's soliloquy: is history the product of an ineluctable process of events, or is there a morality of action which demands a participation of the individual in the flux of society? Perhaps the solution lies in the very birth of the spy novel: it shows a complex world where the putative logician can no longer solve the riddle of the Sphinx. But there is the eternal rub—was Oedipus the logical detective or the man of action? Either way, the result was self-destruction. This is the crucial dilemma of Eric Ambler's novels.

Allen B. Crider

RACE WILLIAMS—PRIVATE INVESTIGATOR

In the revival of interest recently in the literature of the private eye, little attention has been paid to Race Williams, the forerunner of both Ross Macdonald's Lew Archer and Raymond Chandler's Marlowe, not to mention the heroes of Dashiell Hammett.

Race Williams was created by Carroll John Daly in the early 1920's for *Black Mask*, the pulp magazine which was later to publish both Hammett and Chandler. Daly wrote in a graceless, even irritating, style; he had little idea about how to create either characters or suspense, and his stories have little or no plot. In spite of these faults, however (or maybe even because of them), Daly was enormously successful. One *Black Mask* editor is reported to have said that putting Race Williams on the cover of the magazine increased sales by fifteen percent.[1] This fact might seem difficult to believe, but at least once in his career Daly managed to write a genuine grade-Z masterpiece, a work which manages to capture the reader's attention in spite of a ridiculous plot, poor writing and inept characterization. Daly's "masterpiece" is *The Snarl of the Beast*, in which the detective myth is reduced to its barest essentials.

To understand Daly's achievement in *The Snarl of the Beast,* we should first examine his faults. Race Williams was in some ways no more than a city version of the cowboy hero of the pulps, with his own version of *High Noon*: "I have brains, I suppose. We all have. But a sharp eye, a quick draw, and a steady trigger finger drove me into the game. . . . I stand on my own two legs and I'll shoot it out with any gun in the city—any time, any place. Thirty-fourth and Broadway, in the five o'clock rush hour, isn't barred, either."[2] As a matter of fact, Williams even carries two guns.

Also, Daly's way with dialogue leaves a great deal to be desired, as the following speech by a captured woman prowler shows:

"Mr. Williams–Race Williams." She was shaking me by the shoulders as she talked, her words coming in quick, spasmodic jerks. "I wasn't always bad. I have been dragged into a terrible net. Won't you believe me–spare me–not lift my mask? I'll never do anything to harm you; perhaps much to help you. You've seen people who wanted to be good, dragged into the bad" (p. 115).

If the above faults are not enough, there remains Daly's style. He is the kind of writer who cannot often *create* excitement; he compensates by attempting to achieve a breathless pace through the use of almost as many dashes as commas, or, even worse, by *telling* the reader that the story is fast-paced and exciting: "Race Williams–Private Investigator–tells the whole story. Right! Let's go" (p. 12). Daly cannot create suspense, either. His idea of suspense is a situation drawn out as long as possible, a device which usually bores the reader rather than creating tension. Daly uses this device time and again, and not just in *The Snarl of the Beast*. In *The Snarl* (p. 53), Race Williams is talking to a client in a gloomy tenement room. The door behind them begins to open slowly (and in this case "slowly" is the operative word). Who is about to enter the room? The client's madman stepfather, the killer who has already attempted Race Williams' life? No, as we finally learn 650 words later–it is only Milly, "a girl of the night." Daly milks the situation for all it is worth, and then some. By the time Milly does get in the room, the reader does not really care.

However, *The Snarl of the Beast* does have its redeeming features. Daly has indeed managed to capture the essence of the detective myth. The supplicant applies to Race Williams for help: " 'I have heard of you. I need you. I can't come to you. My God! Take a chance and come' " (p. 39). The devil from which this man must be saved is unrelievedly evil, more animal than human: " 'A brute–who murders like the fiend he is. The most feared, the cunningest and cruelest creature that stalks the city streets at night. We call him simply, The Beast' " (p. 128). And there is Race Williams himself, the savior: " 'You're playing the game against all the forces of evil–playing it alone' " (p. 215).

Race Williams, like the private detectives who follow him, plays the game not only alone, but by his own rules. He feels that the police are effective in their own fashion, but that they are bound by rules and thus not as likely to serve justice as Williams himself. (In this case, the police have to ask for Williams' help; he gets the reward, and they get the credit.) Being bound by rules, the police are like a great machine, thorough, but incapable of solving the case. The very name of Race Williams' chief contact on the police force, "Coglin," is suggestive; the machine imagery is strengthened by Coglin's reference to "mechanical department routine" (p. 122), and made explicit by William's description of Coglin as "a wheel in a great machine" (pp. 247-248). Race Williams prefers for himself the frontier values of self-reliance, individual responsibility, and competence:

Under the laws I'm labeled on the books and licensed as a private detective. Not that I'm proud of that license but I do need it, and I've had considerable trouble hanging onto it. My position is not exactly a healthy one. The police don't like me. The crooks don't like me. I'm just a halfway house between the law and crime; sort of working both ends against the middle. Right and wrong are not written on the statutes for me, nor do I find my code of morals in the essays of longwinded professors. My ethics are my own. I'm not saying they're good and I'm not admitting they're bad, and what's more, I'm not interested in the opinions of others on that subject. When the time comes for some quick-drawing gunman to jump me over the hurdles I'll ride to the Pearly Gates on my own ticket. It won't be a pass written on the back of another man's thoughts (p. 12).

When Race Williams speaks of his own ethics, he means primarily his ideas about the right of the individual to bring criminals to justice without benefit of a trial, usually by killing them:[3]

He got what was coming to him. If ever a lad needed one good killing, he was the boy. I'm sorry if I appear hard boiled or cold blooded, but I couldn't get a sympathetic kick when that would-be murderer tumbled to the road. I must admit that I'm strong for a little loose shooting against loose thinkers. There may be laws of the state or of the government that aren't so good, but the laws of God and man can't be improved upon. Them that live by the gun should die by the gun, is good sound twentieth century gospel (p. 93).

Williams' justification of his ideas is just as simple as his solution to the crime problem: ". . . it's results that count in life. You can't make ketchup without busting up a few tomatoes" (pp. 96-97).

Race Williams is, as should be evident by now, what is known as a "hard boiled" detective, the first of a long line. In this context, "hard boiled" means a mental toughness developed as a defense against the kind of world in which the detective exists. His toughness alone keeps him from being too deeply affected by what he sees and experiences. As Race Williams puts it, "I'm hard boiled all right—none more so, I guess, and I've seen so much that my heart is petrified to a granitelike hardness" (p. 61). Williams is also hard boiled for his physical defense, as he tells the reader after threatening to shoot the woman prowler if she refuses to obey him:[4] "Did I mean it? Don't make me laugh. A fine story that dame would have to carry to the underworld. Why, every lad who had a girl would send her gunning for me" (p. 107). "Hard boiled" can also mean physical toughness, which Race Williams has in abundance. In one scene near the end of *The Snarl of the Beast,* Williams is clubbed, kicked, spat on, and shot (three times), only to emerge triumphant.

There are also in *The Snarl of the Beast* three more elements which were to be used more subtly and effectively by later writers. The first of these elements is sexual isolation of the detective: "It isn't pleasant to maul a woman. Women mean nothing in my life. Some old mummy has said, 'He travels farthest who travels alone.' That's me. Venus de Milo or Cleopatra herself couldn't switch me from my purpose" (p. 116). The second element is social comment. Although Race Williams talks primarily about himself, he does see fit occasionally to speak of the injustices he sees:

> I stretch out a hand, found the bannister, ran my fingers along through the dust and followed the unseen trail to the head of the stairs. Dimly from below came the dull flickering glare of the single gas jet. The tenement house laws requiring a light on every other floor didn't disturb this landlord. A wealthy, drunken man at his club, perhaps, who couldn't tell offhand the number, or even the street the disreputable building he owned was on. And I didn't blame him over-much. I'd try to forget that dump myself (pp. 63-64).

The third element is a stylistic device principally associated with Raymond Chandler, used for slightly different purposes by Ross Macdonald, and attempted by almost every hard boiled writer who ever practiced: the particularly apt simile, one which is both descriptive and at the same time fitting to the book's tone. For example, Race Williams sees a street "as empty as a congressman's head" (p. 97); the night is "cold enough to freeze the tail off a brass monkey and dark enough for the monkey not to miss it" (p. 98); a dead man is "as cold as an old maid's smile" (p. 305).

In short, all the hard boiled clichés and mannerisms elaborated on by later writers were present in the fiction of Carroll John Daly, most of them in one now almost forgotten novel, *The Snarl of the Beast,* a book which succeeds in spite of its author's faults in capturing the essence of all private detective stories.

Kay Weibel

MICKEY SPILLANE AS A FIFTIES PHENOMENON

Female readers found expression of their mythic dreams in two sentimental novels of the late eighteenth and mid-nineteenth centuries, Susanna Rowson's *Charlotte Temple* (1797–first U. S.) and Susan Warner's *The Wide, Wide World* (1850), books whose overall sales were not topped until the mid-twentieth century.[1] It remained for the novels of Mickey Spillane, however, to similarly strike the heartbeats of the masses of American males. Between 1947 and 1952, Spillane published seven books which have outsold all other mystery and detective fiction in America.[2] (Six of the seven novels were published between the years 1950 and 1952.) In addition, on the overall bestseller list for the years 1895 to 1965, including sales of both hardbound and paperback books, the same seven titles appear among the top thirty bestsellers.[3] No doubt one reason for the popularity of the early Spillane novels lies in their close mirroring of cultural attitudes of the 1950's. Spillane's treatment of women is particularly significant, moreover, since the hard-boiled detective formula, of which Spillane is the master seller, is the first fictional formula for men to focus explicitly on sexual relationships between men and women. In order to understand the importance of Spillane's definition of women, however, it is first necessary to view the novels as reflectors of fifties' attitudes in general.

Six of Spillane's first seven books have as their protagonist Private Eye Mike Hammer. Mike is a war hero who has re-channeled his violent energies into cleaning up criminal activities in New York City. As opposed to other detectives in the hard-boiled tradition, however, including Sam Spade, Philip Marlowe, Lew Archer and most television crime detectives,[4] Mike Hammer does not actually solve his crimes. In fact, Spillane's Hammer novels are not really about crime detection; they are about war. Mike Hammer is a one-man war machine. He has the blind ideological faith in his cause that warring armies have. He is on the side of righteousness, and the city he is attacking, and by inference everyone in it, is evil. The perpetrators of the crime Mike is allegedly solving are always members of a large corrupt group or organization, and Mike merely maims or kills off everybody who is implicated in the group's activities. The last person left standing is presumed most guilty by Mike in the monologue he delivers before the final execution. Significantly, this last person is almost always female.

It is not surprising or unusual that popular fiction written in a post-war decade should be about war. In 1951, the year that three of Spillane's bestsellers appeared, four hardbound novels with wartime settings were also top bestsellers.[5] The Spillane version of war, however, is a highly glamorized one, in which the impossibility of the hero's defeat is always understood. Though the wartime ethic and wartime activities are retained, the wartime setting is altered. Mike Hammer's war is against inner city New York. In *Vengeance Is Mine*, Mike compares New York City crime to jungle warfare and decides to avenge the murder of an old war buddy.

> Yeah, we were buddies. We weren't long, but we were buddies good. If we had both been in the jungle and some slimy Jap had picked him off I would have rammed the butt of a rifle down the brown bastard's throat for it. He would have done the same for me, too. But we weren't in any damn jungle. We were right here in New York City where murder wasn't supposed to happen and did all the time. (pp. 23-24)[6]

In general, the imagery associated with the city is bleak. In *One Lonely Night*, Mike thinks after coming out of a Communist Party meeting, "The street was the same as before, dark, smelly, unaware of the tumor it was breeding in its belly." (p. 76) Furthermore, much of the action in the novels takes place in inclement weather—usually rain or snow. Mike also makes constant reference to the congested crowds in the New York streets and to the constant din of street noises.

In his hatred of the big city, Mike reflects attitudes that cultural indicators show to be common in the 1950's. The fifties witnessed a massive movement out of large cities and into outlying suburban areas. In 1950, cities with 1,000,000 or more inhabitants represented 11.5 percent of the total population of the U. S.; by 1960, the percentage of the total population living in giant cities had reduced to 9.8 percent.[7] In particular, the trend toward the development of suburbs brought the growth of central cities nearly to a standstill between 1950 and 1960.[8] Many people no doubt thought they were leaving the city for good reasons. In 1950, television brought the Kefauver committee's crime investigation hearings into millions of American homes, with the message that crime was taking over America's cities.[9] In 1956, the Federal Bureau of Investigation reported that more major crimes had been committed that year than in any previous year of U. S. history.[10] And in fact, though crime rates in general soared, the urban crime rate nearly doubled between the years of 1937 and 1957.[11]

In Spillane, crime is always linked to another phenomenon of the fifties: fear of the large organization. Publicity of Communist and of Mafia activity stressed the corrupt and near-invulnerable power that a tight organization can wield. Mike, who frequently refers to himself as a one-man gang, fights the giant organization on his own, successfully bringing down major arms of the Communist Party of America (*One Lonely Night*), the Mafia (*Kiss Me, Deadly*), an international terrorist organization (*The Girl Hunters*), and three blackmailing rings (*I, The Jury, The Big Kill,* and *Vengeance Is Mine*). Johnny McBride, hero of *The Long Wait*, overthrows a small town gambling boss, his gang and the banker/embezzler they all take orders from.

Convinced of the evil of his enemies, Mike himself is full of the power of positive thinking. In his self-assurance, Mike reflects the belief of Americans in general in the post-war decade that God and justice were on the American side. The popularity of such advice books as *The Power of Positive Thinking, Life Is Worth Living,* and *How I Raised Myself from Failure to Success in Selling*, are evidence of the emphasis in the fifties on self-confidence as a means of achieving goals.[12] In his righteousness and his sense of superior justice, Mike considers himself above the law. In *I, The Jury*, he proclaims the following to his policeman friend Pat.

> Jack was about the best friend I ever had. We lived together and fought together. And by Christ, I'm not letting the killer go through the tedious process of the law. You know what happens, damn it. They get the best lawyer there is and screw up the whole thing and wind up a hero! . . . A jury is cold and impartial like they're supposed to be, while some snotty lawyer makes them pour tears as he tells how his client was insane at the moment or had to shoot in self-defense. Swell. The law is fine. But this time I'm the law and I'm not going to be cold and impartial. (p. 7)

In each of the novels, Hammer thinks his mission puts him above the law. His justice is the Old Testament logic, "an eye for an eye and a tooth for a tooth," but his manner of proclamation is like an evangelical minister. Just before the final execution in each of the novels, Mike delivers a sermon to the victims in which he outlines their sins. Mike is a minister of damnation only, though, who allows no opportunity for repentance.

As a man self-confidently at war in a just cause, then, Mike Hammer became the ideal role model for men in the 1950's. Here, between the pages of a paperback novel, was war the way it should have been fought—with the righteous army predestined to be victorious. But in addition, through Mike, the ex-GI could relive the wartime social code as well. Mike is a chain smoker who drinks heavily between skirmishes and who has "no strings" access to eager and aggressive women. The reader in the fifties, however, while keeping his bottle and cigarettes, had left his Tiger Lily overseas and had married the girl next door. The wartime social code, then, had to be modified in the novels to accommodate both the wish and the reality. How Spillane accomplished this will be the subject of the final sections of the paper.

In the decade of the 1950's, men and women were receiving conflicting media definitions of their proper roles. Women were defined alternatively as Mother and as sexual toy; men were defined alternatively as stable provider and as Playboy bachelor.

Images aimed specifically at women were vastly more consistent, however. According to economist J. K. Galbraith, the duties of household administrator and purchaser of goods, prime activities of the mid-twentieth-century housewife, became crucial to the functioning of a consumer-based, planning economy.[13] Naive to her function within the economic process, however, and bored with the routine of household chores, the women of the 1950's needed a rationale to remain at home. Accordingly, what looks in retrospect like a nation-wide propaganda campaign was launched by the schools and popular media in order to sell women on the importance of their roles as home-based mothers.[14] "Mother" became the popular heroine of the 1950's—a young, attractive, crisply dressed matron—like Harriet Nelson, Betty White, Donna Reed or any one of the many popular television mothers.[15]

Affirming the dominance of the heroine/mother image, women married at a younger age than ever before in the 1950's. Further, female professionals and advanced degree recipients declined during the decade and women employed on a full-time basis remained at a low one third of the total female working force.[16] Nonetheless, the number of women who worked outside the home continued to rise during the fifties.[17] The jargon of the feminine mystique, however, totally ignored the fact that most of these women who worked did so out of financial necessity, and articles asking the loaded question "Should women with young children work?" were common fare in women's magazines. Psychiatrists and educators (almost always male) invariably concurred that the woman who worked did so at great peril to the emotional stability and future success of her children.[18] That no hard core statistical data backed up these opinions made no difference to experts or to readers.[19]

In 1954, *McCall's* magazine announced its policy of family "Togetherness." Henceforth, said the editors, *McCall's* would not be aimed for women alone but rather for the entire family. The major change, however, consisted in more dramatic and colorful layouts, featuring pictures of men involved in such homelife activities as barbecuing, gardening or putting in a swimming pool. The philosophy was to preach involvement of men in home activities. This formula was so successful that by the end of the decade, *McCall's* had outdistanced long time leader *Ladies Home Journal* in both subscriptions and advertising.[20] Meanwhile, the *Journal*'s closest competitor for many years, *Woman's Home Companion*, tried an issue-oriented format during the 1950's. Despite increases in sales, which indicated that women were responsive to the approach, advertisers would not support alternative images of women, opting instead to back up *McCall's* togetherness scheme.[21]

Also, in popular books aimed for women the image of the young attractive mother was again put forward as the ideal. For the first time during the 1950's, the sales of nonfiction books outdistanced sales of fiction on a title-for-title basis straight down the bestseller list.[22] Tops on the lists of these nonfiction bestsellers were cookbooks, home care books and a large number of books about children and childcare.[23] In addition, another popular genre which had its birth in the 1950's, the woman's gothic mystery romance, features a heroine who proves herself worthy of the hero's love in major part by showing herself able to handle the "difficult child" in the novel. In these novels, this child is hyperactive or mentally disturbed because of his natural mother's neglect or maltreatment.[24]

While both sexes were soaking up the "Make Room for Daddy" image of men and women, another image emerged as well—this one aimed more specifically at men. During the second world war it became both patriotic and profitable for movie companies to launch campaigns making young starlets into armed services pin-up girls. The careers of Rita Hayworth, Jane Russell and Betty Grable were all launched in this manner. These women differed from previous screen goddesses in two respects: they all had large breasts and very little acting ability. Rita, Jane and Betty led a string of big-busted beauties that included Jayne Mansfield, Kim Novak, Lana Turner, Brigitte Bardot and the pin-up girl supreme, Marilyn Monroe. Even though the image these women portrayed was overtly and sumptuously sexual, the films in which they starred depicted females embroiled in the same rat race as the less sexy viewer: chasing down and catching a man.[25] Thus, while not contradicting feminine mystique notions of monogomy and female dependence, these movies carried the message to men that women were desirable as transient sexual adventures.

On nighttime television, the image of men and women in the drama adventure programs differed from the wholesome young parents' image of the family comedies. In the westerns and emerging crime shows, women were episodes in the hero's life only. Sexual adventure, though, was a much more important part of the drama than it is today. It was common for heroes of such shows as "Cheyenne," "Gunsmoke," "Life and Legend of Wyatt Earp," "Palladin," and "San Francisco Beat" to engage in brief affairs which were terminated at the end of each show. Often the woman was regretfully involved in an illicit relationship with the villain at the time the hero appeared on the scene. The price of this illicit sexuality was almost always death at the end of the show. If not death, then the temporary heroine was banished "back East," where no one would be the wiser.

In the religious decade of the 1950's, however, explicit sexual literature was having legal problems, and the Supreme Court acted to set down criteria that would determine the standards of acceptable sexual literature to the present day. In the Roth case, tried by the Supreme Court in 1956, the court held it unlawful to censor any material as long as it contained "any redeeming social importance" by prevailing community standards.[26] Three years before the Roth decision, Hugh Hefner had launched the nation's most successful pornographic magazine to date. Hefner's *Playboy* magazine evolved a money-winning formula by combining photographs of nude women with "redeeming" social commentary on sexual mores, dating procedures and a few controversial political issues. Hefner was so sure of the ultimate success of his venture that he did not solicit advertising at first. In 1956, only three years after the magazine's inception, Hefner was able to demand the type of high quality advertising he considered compatible with *Playboy*'s image of sophistication.[27]

At the intersection of sex and motherhood, where sexual adventure meets redeeming social value, are located the novels of Mickey Spillane. On the one hand, Mike Hammer is a pious believer in the double standard and in the virtue of domesticity. Although the women in the Spillane novels are good looking and sexually aggressive, Mike is frequently most impressed by their alleged domesticity. Evil women even lull him into nonsuspicion by feigning love of children or of cooking. Charlotte Manning, exotic villain of *I, The Jury*, plans a "coincidental" meeting with Mike in Central Park one day where he finds her taking a friend's baby for a stroll. "Juno" Reeves, female impersonator and villain of *Vengeance Is Mine*, treats Mike to a candlelight dinner in her apartment, an affair that postpones his realizations about not only her homosexuality but her villainy as well. Lily Carver, villain of *Kiss Me, Deadly*, also plays the housewife role for Mike by cooking while hiding out from the Mafia in his apartment. The good but foolish women in the novels, who always end up dead or hospitalized by the end of each book, also have their domestic side. Ethel Brighton, communist turned informant in *One Lonely Night*, is last pictured near death in a hospital but reunited with her wealthy father, whose affection she had previously flaunted. Connie Wales, who pays with her life for the help she gives Mike in *Vengeance Is Mine*, is all too eager to cook and keep house for him. "Will I make somebody a good wife?" she asks Mike. "Somebody," Mike replies. (p. 39)

Velda, Mike's girlfriend, secretary and second gun represents the ideal synthesis of mother and sexual toy in the novels. Velda comforts Mike after his close calls, cries whenever his good name or his life are in danger, and she asks no questions about his sexual escapades. Whether at the office or in her apartment, Velda is always an available home base for Mike. In his first novel, *I, The Jury*, Spillane sets the pattern of behavior that Velda will follow in the subsequent novels. Returning to the office after a little "private" investigating with a female murder suspect, Mike stops at the mirrored door to double check for lipstick marks.

> I went in whistling. Velda took one look at me and her mouth tightened up. 'Now what's the matter?' I could see something was wrong.
>
> 'You didn't get it off your ear,' she said.
>
> Uh-oh. This gal could be murder when she wanted to. I didn't bother to say anything more, but walked into my office. Velda had laid out a clean shirt for me, and an unwrinkled tie. Sometimes I thought she was a mind reader. I kept a few things handy for emergencies, and she generally knew when that would be. (p. 50)

Velda is much more than a mother figure for Mike though. She is also a big-busted, long-legged sexual being "with hair like midnight" who provides Mike with continual reaffirmation of his masculinity. Even while laid up on a hospital bed, recovering from multiple bruises, burns and lesions, Mike is irresistible to Velda.

> Her hands were soft on my face and her mouth a hot, hungry thing that tried to drink me down. Even through the covers I could feel the firm pressure of her breasts, live things that caressed me of their own accord. She took her mouth away reluctantly so I could kiss her neck and run my lips across her shoulders. (*Kiss Me, Deadly*, p. 20)

Despite her aggressive sexuality, however, Velda remains virginal throughout the Spillane novels of the 1950's. Since Velda's duties as second gun private eye require her to gain the intimate confidence of the men Mike is investigating, however, her status as a virgin becomes increasingly ambiguous. Nonetheless, Mike is the only man in her life, and as Mike tells her in *One Lonely Night*, " 'I'm just afraid of myself, kid. You and a bedroom could be too much. I'm saving you for something special.' "

The chastity of the heroine is also an issue in bestseller *The Long Wait*, which tells the story of Johnny McBride, a superhero who resembles Mike Hammer in his love for violence and sexy women. McBride has been wrongly accused of bank embezzlement and murder, and six years later he returns to the old home town to clear his name. Complications arise because Johnny lost his memory while he was in hiding and, to make a long and hardly credible story short, one of the more important things he has forgotten is his marriage to the novel's heroine, Vera West. At the end of the novel, when Johnny discovers Vera's true identity (she's been going under an alias), she asks him, "Did you ever wonder why I let you make love to me?" It's then she pulls out the marriage license. Unbelievably, Johnny's thrilled.

Though Johnny McBride manages to avoid involvement with the other sexy women in *The Long Wait* (after all, he's a married man, whether he knows it or not), Mike Hammer feels perfectly free to engage in sexual relationships with all the women who make themselves available to him. Spillane hereby clearly endorses the double standard of sexual conduct. The implication is, moreover, that men should choose their sexual conquests from among the "lower classes" of women, since the women Mike has affairs with always have questionable pasts and frequently are suspects in the crime he is investigating. These women have something else in common. They exude sexuality—of the Marilyn Monroe, Jane Russell, Brigitte Bardot variety. Mike repeatedly avows his scorn for skinny women—the type that model clothes. He goes for the movie types, though naturally he doesn't put it that way. Despite their experience, furthermore, all of these women are sexually starved. They throw themselves at Mike not because of his good looks (he is careful to let it be known that he is *not* good looking) or because he has a strong line or a way with women; they throw themselves at him because he is violent. All these women know that Mike is a confessed killer, and it is this knowledge that kindles the fires of passion. The message is that the only way to satisfy a truly sexy woman is with violence.

The following episode, from *Vengeance Is Mine*, takes place between Mike and a sexy young woman who models underwear. Mike has grown suspicious about her overzealous desire to help him solve his murder case. When he confronts her, she hits him violently in the face and then confesses her true interest.

> 'I have five brothers,' she said. Her voice had a snarl in it. 'They're big and nasty but they're all men. I have ten other guys who wouldn't make one man put together. Then you come along. I'd like to beat your stupid head off. You have eyes and you can't see. All right, Mike, I'll give you something to look at, and you'll know why all the concern.'
>
> Her hand grabbed her blouse at the neckline and ripped it down. Buttons rolled away at my feet. The other thing she wore pulled apart with a harsh tearing sound and she stood there proudly, her hands on her hips, flaunting her breasts in my face. A tremour of excitement made the muscles under the taught flesh of her stomach undulate, and she let me look at her like that as long as it pleased me.
>
> I had to put my hands down and squeeze the arms of the chair. My collar was too tight all of a sudden, and something was crawling up my spine.
>
> Her teeth were clamped together. Her eyes were vicious.
>
> 'Make me,' she said.
>
> Another trickle of blood ran down my chin, reminding me of what had happened. I reached up and smacked her across the mouth as hard as I could. Her head rocked, but she still stood there, and now her eyes were more vicious than ever. 'Still want me to make you?'
>
> 'Make me,' she said. (pp. 40-41)

The scene related above is not typical of Mike's sexual encounters, however, since the clear implication is that this one ends in brutal but mutually satisfying sexual intercourse. In the scene in the novel which follows the one above, Mike and the woman are pictured having a leisurely meal in a restaurant, clearly recuperating.

In general, however, Mike's sexual episodes are immediately followed by an act of violent assault, usually murder. In addition, these episodes take place in dark, out-of-the-way places: stereotyped settings for rape. Either that or a woman alone in an apartment invites Mike in without knowing for certain who he is. In *I, The Jury*, murder suspect Mary Bellemy lets Mike into her apartment and procedes to make a sexual advance upon him. Later in the novel, she lures him into the woods, takes off all her clothes and seduces him. Mike returns to the tennis match they had left just in time to discover a fresh murder victim—female, of course. In *Kiss Me, Deadly*, Mike picks up a hitchhiker who almost immediately makes a pass at him. Mike resists and soon after his car is run off the road by a car filled with Mafia agents who strip and torture the hitchhiker and then kill her. In *One Lonely Night*, Mike meets a frightened woman being chased down a deserted bridge at night. He kills her pursuer and turns his attention to the woman, with his gun still in his hand. She takes one look at the "kill lust" in Mike's face and jumps over the bridge to her death.

It is no coincidence that the villains of Spillane's novels almost inevitably prove to be women. In his article "The Spillane Phenomenon," John Cawelti talks about the rhythm in Spillane's novels, stating that it reaches its final climax in "violence as orgasm."[28] Since Mike is at war in the novels, a torturous rape would provide the natural climax. In that manner the sexual and violent tensions created by the action in the novels would be resolved simultaneously. Mike Hammer is not allowed this indulgence, however, since he is a believer in female purity and a righteous avenger serving the cause of justice, and atrocities, even in war, are always committed only by the enemy. Denied rape, Mike takes the next best alternative—pumping bullets from the gun that symbolizes his masculinity into the nude body of the villain.

The Spillane novels, then, attempt to resolve for men the two-way image of male/female roles provided by the popular media. On the one hand, men were being told to settle down and be the stable provider for the decade's heroine, Mother. The success of the supersex movie queens and of *Playboy* and its imitators, however, indicated that men had another and contradictory image of themselves as adventure-seeking bachelors. Mike Hammer's solution was simple: take the best of both worlds. Have handy an attractive mother/wife for emergencies and general support, but pursue the adventurous life, including violence and loose women, as well. The unworkability of this formula is revealed metaphorically, however, in the violent death of all the promiscuous women in the novels. Since the real wife/mother would not allow the intrusion of violence and other women in the life of her stable provider, the enjoyment of these adventures must be limited—to the span of time it takes to read a Mickey Spillane novel.

Chronology of Spillane Bestsellers

		copies sold to 1965
1947	I, The Jury*	5,390,105
1950	My Gun Is Quick	4,916,074
	Vengeance Is Mine	4,637,734
1951	The Big Kill	5,098,472
	One Lonely Night	4,873,563
	The Long Wait	4,835,966
1952	Kiss Me, Deadly	4,828,044
1961	The Deep	1,928,513
1962	The Girl Hunters	1,863,260
1964	Day of Guns	1,265,336
	The Snake	1,220,875
1965	Bloody Sunrise	1,290,291

*All books were printed as Signet paperbacks.

R. Jeff Banks

SPILLANE'S ANTI-ESTABLISHMENTARIAN HEROES

"Up the Rebels" is a slogan which may or may not have been tattoed in an interesting location on one of several short lived characters in a recent Pete McGrath mystery.[1] The attitude thus implied toward politico-socio-economic authority, "the Establishment" as it is currently labelled, has pervaded much of literature—both popular and literary—since the time of Aristophanes. It accounts at least in part for the taste which has made some Restoration Drama popular long past the time in which it was written and played, it is the attitude motivating much of the satire of any age, and it provides an important element today in both the most serious and the most amusing espionage novels.[2] Certainly it is one of the key forces controlling the detectives and authors of both the Hard-boiled and Sex and Sadism schools of the detective story.

It would be difficult to imagine a Dashiell Hammett hero who was completely at peace with the *status quo,* and the author's own vigorous struggles against it are so well known as to need neither comment nor documentation. Raymond Chandler's Marlowe may not be an overt rebel against society, but he is certainly dissatisfied with the way it works in relation to him. Travis McGee, the most recent major series character in the field, issues frequent jeremiads against credit cards, which he long refused to own or use. This list could be extended indefinitely.

One only need remember that rebellion is not the exclusive property of the Left in this or any other country to feel no surprise that it is a strong feature of the works of the most popular fiction writer on the Right. Practically all of Mickey Spillane's heroes are anti-Establishment in sentiment, often outspoken in their views, and sometimes activist. The actions taken range from such petty harassment of a police officer as smashing his cigars by a carefully planned accident,[3] through threatening bodily harm to a whole station house full of policemen, some of whom have been attempting to prove to the hero just how "tough" they are,[4] to the actual killing of policemen in three of the stories. The latter will be discussed more fully later.

Any consideration of the Spillane hero must begin with Mike Hammer, but it ends there only for those who are unaware that more than two thirds of the author's books were written after 1960 and that the later books boast quite healthy sales records. Furthermore, any study of Mike Hammer that ends with the Korean War period verges on the same sort of incompleteness that would mark a character study of Perry Mason that considered only *The Case of the Velvet Claws.*

Through all the Hammer books there are bad relations between the hero and successive District Attorneys, but generally the detective is on good terms with the New York City Police Department, especially as it is represented by his oldest and best friend Capt. Pat Chambers. His relations with these two elements of the "Law and Order Establishment" are analogous to the relations of Mike Shayne to the Miami Beach and Miami Police Departments, respectively. Someday someone should do a study comparing technique and mutual influences of the Shayne and Hammer series. Certainly the casual dismissal of Shayne's creator "Brett Helliday [sic]" as a mere prolific hack "who more or less imitate[s] the Spillane recipe without adding much in the way of literary interest"[5] is a too facile approach. However, exploration of Spillane's relationships with Halliday, Philip Atlee (James Atlee Phillips) and several other writers is far beyond the scope of this paper.

We may begin by assuming that the conflicts between Hammer and any District Attorney are little more than an observation by Spillane of one of the familiar conventions of the Hard-boiled detective story. Petty harassments on both sides and shouted exchanges of insults are entertaining to Spillane's millions of readers, but with rare exceptions they are "gut issues" for neither Hammer nor Spillane.[6]

When Pat Chambers has Hammer followed, as he does in *I, the Jury,* the detective makes a little game of making the police look ridiculous. In Chapter 3, for instance, he waits, while Chambers wakes "the tail" from a complacent nap, to tell the man how he recognized him; shortly thereafter he gives the policeman a ride in his own car only to leave him helplessly wedged inside a revolving door.[7] Whenever his activities bring him into contact with police who are merely doing their job and not infringing upon his rights, he performs as a docile good citizen. Obvious examples are the on-the-spot investigations of the hit-and-run murder to which he was an eye witness at the beginning of *The Big Kill* and of the attempt to kill him on the street in Chapter 5 of *One Lonely Night.*

Relations with federal officers are less easygoing. This is due in large part to the wholehearted acceptance by both Spillane and Hammer, along with Chambers and most of Hammer's other friends, of McCarthyism as a political philosophy. This is most apparent among the early works in *One Lonely Night.* However, McCarthyism permeates almost every novel and shorter story Spillane has published. Documentation and comment upon his politics would require booklength treatment, and the political views are so obvious that no attempt at enumeration will be made here.

Hammer's first description of the federal agents prominent in *Kiss Me, Deadly* shows respect for their organization and its reputation. Almost immediately, however, his attitude changes to jealous guardianship of his own rights, including the all-important one of revenge. He stops just short of threatening the F.B.I. men, but otherwise the exchange is not unlike those already mentioned with various District Attorneys. Still in the same chapter, Capt. Chambers bases an appeal for co-operation upon patriotism, to which Hammer responds:

> Patriotism, my back. I don't give a damn if Congress, the President and the Supreme Court told me to lay off [the Mafia]. They're only men and they didn't get sapped and dumped over a cliff. You don't play with guys who pull that kind of stuff. The feds can be as cagey as they like, but when they wrap the bunch up what happens? So they testify. Great. Costello testified and I can show you where he committed perjury in the minutes of the hearing. What happened? Yeah . . . you know what happened as well as I do. They're too big to do anything with. They got too much dough and too much power and if they talk too many people are going to go under. Well, the hell with 'em. . . . If the feds beat me to 'em it's okay by me, but I'll wait, pal. If I don't reach them first I'll wait until they get through testifying or serving that short sentence those babies seem to draw and when I do you won't be having much trouble from them again ever.

Concluding this heated exchange, Chambers contends, "Those government boys are shrewd apples," then he brings out the standard threat to "lift" Hammer's license, even to jail him.[8] A few pages later, Hammer offers a counter-threat:

> "Tomorrow you can remind 'em I'm an incorporated business, a taxpayer and a boy with connections. My lawyer has a judge probably getting up a show cause right now and until they settle the case in court they aren't pulling any bill-of-attainder stuff on me."
>
> "You got a mouthful of words on that one, Mike."
>
> "Uh-huh. And you know what I'm talking about. Nobody, not even a Federal agency is going to pull my tail and not get chewed a little bit. . . . They haven't got one guy in Washington that's smarter than I am . . . not one guy. If they had they'd be making more money than I am and don't fool yourself thinking they're in there for love of the job. It's about the limit they can do."[9]

In Chapter 9, Hammer overcomes two separate pairs of Mafia killers even though he remains disarmed by F.B.I. order. Chambers conveys the official reaction to one of the incidents to him:

> "The feds are pretty sore about it."
>
> "You know what to tell them," I said.
>
> "I did. They don't want to waste time pulling you out of jams."
>
> "Why those apple heads! Who are they supposed to be kidding? They must

have had a tail on me all night to run me down in that joint and they sure waited until it was finished before they came in to get their suits dirty."[10]

However, the attitude of his final comment on federal agents is more respectful. "They'd know. They were the lads you never noticed in a crowd, but they were all eyes and ears and brains. They worked quietly and you never read about them in the papers, but they got things done and they'd know. Maybe they knew a lot more than I thought they'd know."[11] This is the last impression regarding the F.B.I. that Spillane, through Hammer, left with his five million readers.

In destroying one very serious Communist menace with both foreign and domestic agents ranged against him in *One Lonely Night,* Hammer uses characteristic violence. There is characteristic audacity too in his brief, spur-of-the-moment masquerade as an F.B.I. man in Chapter 10. A Spillanean kind of poetic justice appears in Hammer's mass execution of Reds with an F.B.I. tommygun. He even comments on the "cover-up" that this will eventually make necessary.[12]

Survival Zero reworks some of the plot material from *One Lonely Night* and even more from the Tiger Mann series (see below). Hammer is regarded by federal authorities, who are charged with foiling a germ warfare espionage attack, and even temporarily by his friend Capt. Chambers, as an unwanted intruder. He treats the federal men precisely as Tiger Mann has been doing since his first recorded adventure. In Chapter 4, he slyly lets Chambers know that he has long been aware of the supposedly secret location of a suite of government offices, strikes a match to light his cigarette on the face of a federal "No Smoking" sign, deliberately does not use an ashtray in the meeting room, and says defiantly to a convened group of federal men who are supposedly putting him "on the spot," "I don't dig you goons. You're all bureaucratic nonsense, tax happy, self-centered socialistic slobs who think the public's a game you can run for your own benefit. One day you'll realize that its the individual who pulls the strings." The rest of this exchange and a later one involve a familiar Hammer threat to District Attorneys, and one that Tiger Mann has used often against I.A.T.S.: the use of publicity, plus diminution through laughter, of the pompous bureaucrats.[13]

In Chapter 6, Hammer's self-identification as someone the people "living on the perimeter of normalcy" (These are specifically enumerated as including prostitutes, the indigent aged and denizens of a Lower-Lower class bar, but presumably include all the picturesque types that writers of this genre have used to enliven their works since at least the early work of Hammett.) would be willing to talk to in preference to the police, because "I was one of them," opens a possible further insight to the relationship of Spillane's heroes to the Establishment.[14]

Nor is this something new for Hammer. The soliloquy beginning *One Lonely Night* includes these telling bits of introspection: ". . . I was a licensed investigator who knocked off somebody who needed knocking off bad and. . . . So I was a murderer by definition and all the law could do was shake its finger at definitions . . . a big guy with an ugly reputation." Later in the same book he treats Capt. Chambers to a lengthy harrangue against letting duly constituted agencies handle the menace of domestic Communism, putting himself above the law on grounds that he is ruthless enough to deal with the Reds in their own way. "I'm messing with people and letting them see that I'm nobody to mess with," he says in part.[15] A similar reason for taking direct personal action against the Mafia is certainly strongly implied in what has been quoted from *Kiss Me, Deadly,* above. In fact this personal creed of being worse than the worst at their own game is present to some degree in most of the Hammer stories, indeed in most of Spillane, and along with actions designed to prove it, it provides a major objection on the part of the literati to Spillane's works.[16]

Hammer's relationships with "squealers," vital to the investigative technique of most of the Hard-boiled detectives, seem to bear out the claim of a special pipeline of confidences.[17]

Turning to Spillane's other heroes we should first deal with Johnny McBride of *The Long Wait.* This novel completes the original canon of works which seem to be the only sources yet drawn upon by scholarly critics. The hero's goal is to destroy a town in order to avenge a friend. Specifically he strikes out against political and social leaders and the corrupt police force which serves them, what he refers to in the aggregate as "a whole crooked setup in a whole crooked town." The reader not already prejudiced against Spillane would agree with goal and motivation, though he might cavil at some elements of the *modus operandi.*

In the first chapter, the hero and the first policeman he meets, a sadist named Tucker, exchange threats. In the next, the hero and Tucker and Capt. Lindsey, a monomaniac whose purpose in life is to convict the hero of the five-year-old murder of a friend of his, exchange blows; leaving all three requiring hospital treatment. He eludes his police "tail" as easily as Mike Hammer ever did in Chapters 3 and 4. In Chapter 5, he is shot at by the town's leading banker (although he does not learn who did the shooting until near the end of the book), and he exchanges more harsh words with Lindsey. In Chapter 6, he is "taken for a ride" by agents of the Lyncastle Business Group, the corrupters who control the town, and kills two of them in self-defense. By the time the novel ends, he has discredited the city government and police force and either killed or been instrumental in the deaths of the leading banker, the leaders of the Lyncastle Business Group, and others.

The new and larger group of Spillane thrillers began in 1961 with one of his most peculiar books and (up to that time) heroes.

The title character of *The Deep* is a grown-up juvenile delinquent returning to his old territory after 25 years to claim control of the area segment of the underworld following the murder of a boyhood chum who had been the local crime czar. A ward-heeling "Councilman Hugh Peddle" is the slum's political link with the downtown Establishment. In Chapter 6, Deep turns down Peddle's large cash offer to leave quietly and blunts the politician's first threat of violence. He goes further, threatening to use whatever hold his dead friend Bennet had over Peddle to destroy him in Chapter 9. In Chapter 11, he learns that Peddle has imported a pair of "contract killers" to kill him and takes immediate action to find and kill the politician, although others beat him to it.

Motivated by knowledge of Deep's past and what he seems to be at present, ultra-tough police sergeant Hurd gives him the beginnings of a stereotyped "third degree" in Chapter 8, complete with a quick beating. However, the hero does well in the physical exchange, and in the surprise ending it is Hurd who first officially recognizes Deep as a superior in the New York City Police Department. Surely here we have the very type of Norman Mailer's hoodlum-policeman, who is just as surely represented by Hammer in the private detective role. Mailer hinted at the concept as early as Part II of *The Naked and the Dead,* in his characterization of Gallagher, but it was not until one of his recent journalistic writings that he offered the idea fully fleshed:

> Studies based on the usual psychological tests fail to detect a significant difference [between police and criminals]. . . . The criminal attempts to reduce the tension within himself by expressing in the direct language of action whatever is most violent and outraged in his depths. . . . The cop tries to solve his violence by blanketing it with a uniform. That is virtually a commonplace, but it explains why cops will put up with poor salary, public dislike, uncomfortable working conditions and a general sense of bad conscience. They know they are lucky; they know they are getting away with a successful solution to the criminality they can taste in their blood. This taste is practically in the forefront of a cop's brain; he is in a stink of perspiration whenever he goes into action; he can tolerate little in the way of insult [The Spillane hero, of course, can and does tolerate no insult.], and virtually no contradiction; he lies with a simplicity and quick confidence which will stifle the breath of any upright citizen who encounters it innocently for the first time.[18]

Mailer's description fits Hammer, and as shall be demonstrated it fits the rest of Spillane's heroes as well. After all, they are all just the essential Hammer over again, with different names and somewhat different backgrounds.

Shortly after the "rebrith" of Mike Hammer in *The Girl Hunters* in 1962, Spillane introduced a new series hero, Tiger Mann. He was intended to occupy the equivalent position in spy (actually counterspy) fiction to that of Hammer in detective fiction. As preparation for writing counterspy novels, Spillane had already done *One Lonely Night* and *The Girl Hunters* in the Hammer series. He has since had Hammer operating more-

or-less as a counterspy in *The Body Lovers* and *Survival Zero.* Hammer is a private detective; Mann is a private counterspy (surely a unique figure in the crowded spy/counterspy field) on the payroll of oil super-billionaire Martin Grady, a somewhat less obviously insane version of the villain in Len Deighton's *Billion Dollar Brain.* Hammer competes with official law enforcement agencies (especially the New York City District Attorney's office); Mann competes primarily with federal counter-espionage agencies (especially the esoteric I.A.T.S.), although frequent mention is made of his part in Grady's overseas operations around the world. Hammer is the frequent target of gangland killers; Mann is near the top of the highest priority list of people to be assassinated by Communist agents. Over the years Hammer's tendency to kill the villains in his books has been one of the main things that most of his critics and competitors have objected to. Necessity has forced him to always make it possible to claim self-defense; Mann, benefitting from the years of conditioning reading audiences to James Bond's double-zero rating with its built-in "license to kill," kills more casually. Yet in the very nature of things, the reader finds him most frequently killing those who are out to kill him. Pat Chambers is Hammer's source of knowledge, protection and occasional special privilege in the official police camp; Col. (actually Gen., but Mann continues to call him "Colonel," out of World War II nostalgia) Charlie Corbinet, Mann's former commanding officer in the O.S.S., provides the same services for Mann from his high position in I.A.T.S. The list of parallels could be extended for several pages, but this is hardly necessary as any reader at all knowledgeable about Hammer will be able to pick them out easily for himself in the first Tiger Mann book, *The Day of the Guns.*

The very nature of Mann's work and his employer make clear the distrust of the Establishment—especially in the area of defense against Communism—which is the hallmark of this series. His first fictional encounter with I.A.T.S. is described succinctly. "They took turns interrogating me. For two hours I let them waste their time and told them nothing." Then when he was ready to terminate the interview, he showed knowledge of their supposedly secret telephone numbers and code words, plus a considerable degree of immunity from their interference.[19] All this is obviously calculated by hero and author to show disrespect.

In this same first book the Grady organization is shown to be acting in the best interests of the country, despite governmental interference in Chapters 8, 10, and 13 specifically, although that is an attitudinal theme which permeates the entire book and series. In Chapter 2 of *The Death Dealers,* Mann is warned off a domestic operation of C.I.A. and I.A.T.S., but with predictable stubborness declares that he will carry on despite them. In the next chapter, he loses a federal "tail" as easily as Hammer would a city "flatfoot," dismissing the incident with only two sentences before going on to describe the more important steps he took. His easy penetration of an elaborate net of federal security around a foreign potentate in Chapter 4 is symptomatic of the same kind of disrespect shown in his casual display of knowledge of "secret" things mentioned above in the first book. In Chapter 10 of *The Day of the Guns,* he forces the I.A.T.S. to trail a suspect for him; in Chapter 4 of *The Death Dealers,* he forces the agency to put him on the federal payroll, allowing him to provide the protection that the government seems unable to for the visiting oil king. A parallel situation occurs in the next book, *Bloody Sunrise,* when he twice penetrates security provided for a key Russian defector and finds the girl for whom the Russian defected before the federal agencies can. This time he uses these successes and other pressures to have his girlfriend released from federal custody and to give himself "running room" to escape from a New York City Police dragnet.

In the thus far final Tiger Mann adventure, *The By-Pass Control,* he accuses federal foreign policy makers of stupidity in Chapter 1, and persuades the I.A.T.S. to temporarily merge forces with the Martin Grady group in Chapter 2. One of the strangest couplings of unlikely bedfellows in thriller history, the effect of this is to have the government agency providing manpower and resources for the private group's operation. To salvage a fragment of control the federals insist upon reactiviting Mann as their agent. Twice threatened with a court-martial if he makes a mistake, Mann boasts that he hasn't in twenty years, a rather direct dare to the federal men to catch him in the wrong.

The fourth chapter opens with a comment on I.A.T.S. that might well be Hammer's comment on the police. "They were far from inefficient. Hamstrung by directives and stymied by bureaucratic precedents perhaps, but not inefficient."[20] Hardly a page later he threatens a bureau chief of the agency with unwanted publicity, just as Hammer has threatened many a district attorney. Mann made the threat before in *The Day of the Guns,* Chapters 3 and 13; in *The Death Dealers,* Chapter 8; and in *Bloody Sunrise,* Chapter 4.

When Mann's activities are not illegal they are at least extra-legal, thus he is frequently brought into contact with local police forces—of New York City in the first three books and of a small town in Florida in *The By-Pass Control*—and expresses feelings regarding them. The attitude of his statement at the beginning of Chapter 5 in *The Death Dealers,* is more extravangantly worded than is usual, but the sentiments are typical:

> You take all your Federal agencies, your highly trained but obscure intelligence units, your college degrees and your high IQ, hand-selected personnel working under bureau orders sure, you take them. When you want a job done, give me New York's finest in or out of uniform. Give me the beat cop, the plainclothesmen, the dedicated people so imbued with the city and its environs that they can do a character study of anybody in a half second.
>
> They came out of the womb of the city and although they're tied to her apron

> strings by a paycheck, they're the big independents who love her enough to keep her clean. They sweat in the sun at street crossings, they prowl the festered parts of her body because she nursed them in the beginning, they take the abuse of the other sons and never quit. Even when you find a bad one or one on the take, he's still a guy ready to lay his life on the line if he has to, and will go in [sic] a dark alley after a killer with no concern about his own safety. But most are the best. They have to be or they wouldn't be there.
>
> These are the ones who can analyze the population at a glance. They can spot a stranger, single out the wrong character, sense the mood of the city and prepare in advance for what will happen. These are the crime surgeons, the crime deterrents, the ones who answer when you yell for a cop.[21]

Throughout this book he co-operates with the New York City Police in establishing a dragnet for a little known Communist assassin, only to have to kill the fugitive himself in a final shoot-out.

In Chapter 7 of *The By-Pass Control*, he co-operates docilely with a Florida town's police in an investigation of two attempts on his life, although in Chapter 1, he has used connections and federal pressure to literally get away with murder. In Chapters 10 and 11, he uses the same sort of influence to operate more freely in the Florida town and to leave several dead men without explanation when he flies north for the final confrontation. In *Bloody Sunrise*, Chapter 10, he casually eludes a squad of police who are trying to arrest him for murder in an office building.

It should probably also be pointed out that Spillane's praise of the police came shortly after the Radical Left began attacking them. The Leftist attacks probably grew out of some of the excessive behavior of (generally Southern and largely rural) "peace officers" just at the beginning of the Kennedy years. It was heightened, of course, by the assassination of President Kennedy, followed almost immediately by the assassination of the supposed presidential assassin *while under heavy police guard.* It became general and applied to most policemen in most cities during the period between the events in Dallas and the appearance of the first Tiger Mann book. By the time of the 1964 election, the Radical Right had begun a propaganda counter-offensive intended to do more than exonerate the police. Spillane's extravagant praise is in obvious sympathy with the attempt to glorify the police.[22]

Then there are what might be termed the miscellaneous works. Ryan, the hero of "Me, Hood!" and "Return of the Hood" is a criminal by choice. We might take him as yet another fictional elaboration of Mailer's hoodlum policeman idea. He joyfully thumbs his nose at the police until forced to work with them and with federal agents in those two stories. At the end of "Return of the Hood," he realizes that he is a marked man, unable to return to his underworld friends and way of life. He accepts the new role of law abiding citizen with grace, if not with relish.

His earlier disrespect and dislike for the law so permeates both stories as to make attempts to document it practically unnecessary. In the first meeting with the federal agents who want his help, he announces full awareness that they have had him "tailed" for ten days, with none of the agents assigned to follow him aware of his awareness; he boasts that he could have eluded the followers with ease at any time. Ready to end the meeting, he throws down a gauntlet:

"You listen, you stinking, miserable little slob . . . don't tell me to watch my mouth. Don't tell me one lousy little thing to do at all or I'll tell you where to shove it. Don't try to peg me because I have a record. . . ."

In back of me the tall boy stopped smiling and hissed, "Let him say it out."

"Damn right, let me say it out. You got no choice. You're not fooling with a parolee or a hooker who's scared stiff or cops in general and right now you slobs in particular. This little shake has all the earmarks of a frame and brother, you're in over your head if you try it."[23]

A few words later, he adds the now very familiar Spillane hero threat of unfavorable publicity unless he is allowed to leave peaceably and left unmolested. In the final scene of this story, after having accomplished all that he had reluctantly agreed to do, despite some official interference, he tells a recently acquired girlfriend:

. . . Nothing in this whole lousy world is going to shake me up. I like being a hood. To me it's the only way I can tell off this stupid race of slobs. I can keep out of their damned organizations and petty grievances and keep them away from me. I can drink my own kind of poison and be dirty mean when they want me to drink theirs.[24]

At the beginning of the sequel, Ryan takes advantage of an at least partly coincidental disturbance in the street to slip away from a pair of officers who have come to arrest him for a murder. In the second chapter, he calls a policeman who was associated with him in "Me, Hood!" to protest his innocence and to hint at some extenuating circumstances for his failure to surrender to the police. The call is repeated, catching the policeman at home to allow a fuller conversation without the possibility of its being traced, in Chapter 4. In the next chapter, Ryan arranges a meeting with a federal officer from "Me, Hood!" whose help is needed if he is to deliver secret information needed by the government, save the life of the kidnapped agent who passed it to him, and prove his innocence of the murder charge. What he is doing in all these instances, of course, is just what Hammer, Mann, and all the other Spillane heroes do frequently—putting himself above the law. This is a characteristic of his heroes that Spillane fans delight in and that his many outspoken critics deplore.

Resenting an attempt to dismiss him as just "a hood," he characterizes himself. "So I like it this way. I can chisel the chiselers and don't have to pay any respect to the phony politicos who run us into the ground for their own egotistical satisfaction. I don't have to go along with the sheep who cry and bleat about the way things are and can do something about it in my own way. If this was 1776, I'd be a revolutionary and tax collectors would be fair game. I could drop the enemies trying to destroy us and be a wheel . . . I'm not going to be a sheep."[25]

The title characters of *The Deep* and of "The Bastard Bannerman" (*The Tough Guys,* NAL, 1969; second story in *Return of the Hood,* Corgi, 1964, in its original British publication) are, or seem to be, full-fledged gangster types. However, surprise endings in both stories have them turn out to be policemen. The Deep One is a New York City policeman detailed undercover to his old neighborhood to rid it of a long established criminal stranglehold. Bannerman is a West Coast policeman revisiting his Florida hometown to clean up a murder and a Mafia attempt to take over the town during a stopover while en route to pick up a prisoner being held by the New York Police.

Spillane skillfully builds in the reader an impression of disrespect for law and order in the part of the Deep One, but a careful reading shows that all the symptoms belong to his remembered juvenile delinquent days. He is very sentimental about "the old cop on the beat" whom he remembers fondly from his childhood. The one rebellious action that he does engage in is fisticuffs with a vicious policeman bent on giving him an old style "third degree." That device was originated by Mike Hammer in *Vengeance Is Mine* and repeated by George Weston-Johnny McBride in *The Long Wait.* Almost as much a Spillane trademark as the hero's being "taken for a ride" and managing to kill his captors (used more than a half-dozen times in the book length stories), it occurs again in two of the recent Hammer books, *The Girl Hunters* and *The Twisted Thing.* In every case the policeman is clearly in the wrong, and the hero's action is clearly justified as self defense. Following this incident in *The Deep*, the hero further puts the erring policeman in his place by informing him of his "downtown" connections and permission to operate freely in the precinct.[26]

"Killer Mine," title story of Spillane books which also include "Man Alone" in both England (1965) and the United States (1968) repeats a part of the situation in *The Deep*, viewing the plot materials from a different perspective, and providing a radically different surprise ending. The hero, a police lieutenant (the rank held secretly by the Deep One) who returns to his old slum neighborhood to investigate a series of murders, is known to the other characters as a policeman from the beginning. The cover story for his mission is that he is courting a neighborhood girl (his childhood sweetheart) who is secretly a policewoman. The surprise ending is provided by his discovery that the murderer is his long lost (presumed dead) identical twin brother. Protected only by his personal toughness, good reputation on the force and willingness (however reluctantly) to accept the undercover assignment, Lt. Joe Scanlon "tells off" the Police Commissioner by telephone in Chapter 1, adding the stock threat of unpleasant publicity if he is not allowed a free hand.[27] This threat carries reasonable conviction when it is the apolitical (at least in the local sense) Mike Hammer threatening a very political district attorney, even if it is only because it is one of the conventions of the form. (We are used to it and expect it; the competitive tension which brings it about is almost as much a part of such fiction as the murder itself.) It is less convincing in the Tiger Mann series, but if one can suspend his disbelief sufficiently to accept the basic premises of the series, the old familiar threat may be assimilated with the rest easily enough. Finally, it is completely lacking in conviction in "Killer Mine." With this kind of attitude and sufficient honesty and disregard to speak it so freely Scanlon would never have risen from the level of beat-pounder. Assuming that this was his first such outburst, he would soon be pounding a beat again, if indeed he managed to remain on the force, and the story would either have to end there or switch to another hero to solve the killings.

In the second chapter a local political leader (Spillane actually uses the term "ward heeler.") is slapped around and threatened by Scanlon who taunts him, "I come from this place. I know the rules. When I don't like 'em I make up new ones."[28] Surely this is an obviously anti-Establishment position on the neighborhood level, neatly paralleling relations between the Deep One and Councilman Hugh Peddle.

The only other story in this book is "Man Alone." In it the hero is another policeman named Regan. He has been suspended from the force and almost successfully framed for the murder of an important gang lord. Even though the story begins immediately after his winning acquittal in the murder trial, he is clearly convicted in the public mind. In order to win eventual reinstatement as a policeman he must solve the killing operating as a private citizen. One of his first steps is to lay claim to the money which was supposedly a bribe paid to him by the murder victim. Ostensibly his attitude here is that if one is punished for stealing a sheep (his dismissal from the force for taking a bribe) he might as well eat the mutton, but the reader is hastily informed that Regan will use the money to finance his investigation of the killing—using evil against itself in one of the Spillanean varieties of poetic justice.[29]

In Chapter 4, Regan strikes a policeman who insults him in the police station. This bit of anti-Establishment action is seen to be excusable in Chapter 6, first when the policeman is shown to be taking money from prostitutes and then identified as a kidnapper. In the last chapter he is unmasked as a sadist, a killer, and the man who framed Regan to begin with, so that when Regan kills him (in self defense) the reader must feel the act is well justified.[30]

In "Kick It or Kill!" (second of three stories in *Me, Hood!* in the British edition, first of three in *The Tough Guys* in its U. S. publication) the hero is another policeman who is thought by most of the other characters to be a criminal. On leave to remote lake country while recovering from a gunshot wound, he is even thought to be an addict. In the first pages he twice exchanges unfriendly words with a local police captain, ending by threatening both violence and to have the officer arrested. Later he exposes the captain's connections with a criminal element that has taken over the tiny resort town and is using it as a safe location for sexual and sadistic entertainment for its own members and corrupted politicians.[31] The situation parallels that involving the United Nations which was exposed by Mike Hammer in *The Body Lovers,* and it ends in a not dissimilar *gotterdammerung* when hero Kelly Smith destroys all the evildoers with fire.

"The Seven Year Kill" (second story in *The Flier* in England in 1964, and in *The Tough Guys* in the U. S.) has a disgraced newspaper reporter, Phil Rocca, as its hero. Seven years before he wrote an expose that his editor and publisher were afraid to print. Because he knew too much he had been framed (more successfully than Regan in "Man Alone") and when he came out of prison he accepted what had been done to him, becoming a derelict. When coincidence provides him with a hope of exoneration seven years later, he asks politely for, and gets, the cooperation of the District Attorney who as an Assistant District Attorney had prosecuted him. Near Pheonix, Arizona, a local police force is equally co-operative. The story is atypical of Spillane in the hero's friendly relations with the law enforcement arm of the Establishment. It is included here only for the sake of completeness.

Perhaps the best known and most popular of the latter day Spillane works is *The Delta Factor,* also the most recent of his books to be filmed. This is the story of Morgan the Raider, a modernday pirate who is pressed into government service. Spillane himself offers the analogy of the privateers from the age of the real pirates. However, the modern popular culture consumer will see more obvious connections with the recruiting of reluctant federal agents who have highly specialized talents and socially undesirable backgrounds in such TV series as "It Takes a Thief" and "Garrison's Gorillas," such satiric novel series as Ted Mark's "Man from O.R.G.Y." and Troy Conway's "Coxeman." Such a formerly unfriendly critic as Anthony Boucher has praised this as Spillane's best book.

Certainly the hero's hostility towards authority pervades the entire story. Before it begins he has supposedly stolen $40 million, and at the end of it he escapes the spymasters who have used him to try to recover the loot. In the book he has ample opportunity to tell many authority figures what he thinks of them. His appreciation of the meeting at which he is recruited reveals much of his own attitude as he articulates how he thinks "they" feel towards him: "I kept getting those surreptitious glances of distaste from the time they outfitted me in new clothes until they sat me at a corner of the table in the dust-filled room, enough out of line with the others so that I would know that I wasn't one of them, but something dirty yet necessary, like a squeamish woman putting a slimy worm on a hook just to catch a nice clean fish."[32]

Still in the first chapter, like Hammer, Mann and others, Morgan brings up the threat of unfavorable publicity; he repeats it in Chapter 3. In the second chapter, he diverts himself by making faces at his captors in a two-way mirror, and by plotting and executing an elaborate escape just to show them that he can do it no matter what extremes they go to in guarding him. This latter is motivated, he says, by resentment at having a two-way mirror in his bathroom. Leaving the wooden pistol, that made it possible, where it will be found and then brazenly surrendering himself again to their custody are added ways of thumbing his nose at the authority that they represent.

He exchanges gun threats with the regular United States agent who is assigned to him as combination guard and helper in Chapters 4, 5, 6, and 8. He threatens to rape this same agent, a girl who has married him as a part of their cover, in Chapters 3, 7, and 8. That he has a strong personal liking for the girl is apparent in the more sincere development of their relationship by the end of the book. However, that is not allowed to stand in the way of his dislike for her as a representative of the authority of the Establishment which he scorns.

As the final two-thirds (8 chapters) of the book are spent carrying out the assignment, breaking a vital scientist out of an "escape proof" prison and returning him to United States territory and control, that section occurs almost totally abroad. The setting is a Caribbean country much like Cuba just before the Castro revolution. Certainly, there is much in the Establishment there that bears criticism, and Spillane's hero is irrespressively verbal and activist. His activism includes killing a baker's dozen prison guards, a squad of soldiers, the head of the national police force, and the Communist-leaning power-behind-the-government political boss; plus solving and avenging the murder of a girl revolutionary, and helping her cohorts move a much needed short-wave radio station to prevent its discovery by government agents. However, these accomplishments, which are off-hand, secondary activities, and his entirely predictable comments about the governmental and social order of the country, are beyond the scope of the anti-Establishmentarianism typical of a Spillane hero.

At the end of the book, in a final flaunting of our government's authority, he escapes three armed United States agents by parachuting from the airplane which is bringing him back to this country. That his escape is over the open sea and that he expects to be rescued by criminal associates in a motorboat adds the Spillane touch of flamboyance to the ending.[33]

Finally, there are the two Spillane stories published in England, but not yet, as this is written, in the United States. One of them, "The Affair with the Dragon Lady," is far different from anything else he has published. Largely because of that, it will probably never appear in this country. It is like a great deal of what used to appear in the slick magazines of the 1940's, and their cliché "heart warming" fits it exactly. About the only anti-Establishment sentiment in it is expressed by Vern Tice when he refers to marriage (one of the strongest holds of the Establishment upon the individual) as a trap. His change of mind is a major ingredient in the happy ending.

The other is "The Flier," title story of the British book which included "The Seven Year Kill." This is more nearly typical. Like *The Delta Factor* and some of the Tiger Mann series, it makes use of Spillane's Army Air Corps background, doing so more extensively than any of his other works except "The Affair with the Dragon Lady." Cat Fallon, hero-narrator and title character, begins by defying a Florida city police lieutenant and a detective from the State's Attorney's office. He demands that they "quit playing kid games," state their business "or take a walk," and punctuates their conversation with a declaration that the man who appointed the detective had to be "pretty damn dumb."[34]

In Chapter 3, the hero describes a personal reverie. "I laughed a little thinking of Del Reed [the man from the State's Attorney] and the big cop, Lieutenant Trusky. If they wanted a shady past to look into they should try mine. Hell, I'd make old Tuck [a deceased friend who willed Fallon his small airport] look like a Boy Scout. At least Tuck had principles. I never was burdened with any."[35] The unprincipled loner has to be anti-Establishment, as the principles of the average citizen are the foundation stones of the Establishment.

Lest the foregoing self-analysis put the reader off, Fallon puts himself firmly in the militant anti-Communist camp with declarations to Trusky and Reed (page 34) and to a pair of federal agents who question his loyalty (page 66). The latter statement of his principles is the more outspoken, but the former one is sufficient to remove any doubts from the reader's mind. After one of the federal men is killed, the survivor gives Fallon his blessings for an officially unauthorized bombing strike against a Cuban ship which is "secretly" en route to blow up the Panama Canal. This approval of filibustering piracy occurs at the end of Chapter 7.

No attempt is made in this paper to deal with Spillane's magazine fiction. Much of that, after the overwhelming success of the Hammer series, was ghostwritten. The earlier pulp work is inaccessible for serious study, with the current incompleteness of even the best and biggest university library holdings of pulp magazines.

In so far as there are patterns in Spillane's anti-Establishment writings, they may be summarized as follows:

(1) There is the natural tension always present between private and official workers on the side of right. This shows most obviously in the Hammer series in the hero's anti-District Attorney and occasional anti-police actions and statements. However this is such a stock part of the genre of these works that it may be largely discounted. In the Mann series the same tensions exist, but raised to a higher power—international politics. Here they begin to shade over into something else. (See No. 3, below.)

(2) "Good policemen" are to be co-operated with so long as their dedication to routine does not jeopardize success. At that point they should be circumvented, an activity that Hammer, Mann and the various "undercover policemen" heroes have raised to an art. "Bad policemen," on the other hand, should be destroyed. Hammer does just that in *The Twisted Thing,* McBride does it in *The Long Wait,* Regan does it in "Man Alone," and Kelly Smith in "Kick It or Kill" settles for destroying the corrupt police captain's career and forcing him to help bring those who have corrupted him to justice.

(3) In the Mann series generally, in *One Lonely Night* (Hammer), and to a lesser extent in "The Flier," the heroes act to save the country in spite of what militant rightists often refer to a "softness on Communism" which leads official agencies to operate indifferently to (if not actually against the interests of) our national good. Such action, indeed such situations, are a natural corollary to Spillane's often outspokenly stated rightist politics.

(4) Finally, there are the rogues like Ryan (the Hood), and Morgan (the Raider) who somewhat unwillingly operate to support the Establishment. In their cases the anti-Establishmentarian views usually result more from opposition to short-sightedness and inefficiency than from any fundamental desire to upset the *status quo.* Their personal political creeds are always on the side of right (which to Spillane and his heroes means the far right).

Certainly the patterns described here leave some of the specific anti-Establishment views and actions described in this paper unaccounted for. Furthermore, no attempt is made to trace Spillane's influence upon his imitators and other later writers of Hard-boiled detective fiction in the expansion of anti-Establishment expression. That expansion is an obvious fact, opening the way for a fascinating exploration by scholars who may be interested in the works of prominent or obscure writers in this field.

Darwin T. Turner

THE ROCKY STEELE NOVELS OF JOHN B. WEST

Today, black detective heroes are in vogue. As Stokely Carmichael has commented, it might seem that wherever one looks in the world of fantasy, he sees a dark-skinned supercop. On television, Bill Cosby, a CIA superspy, was followed by Barney, the electronics expert on *Mission Impossible.* At least one black face regularly appears in almost any scene of police officers, from Cade's County to Manhattan precincts. An Afro-tressed black youth helps the Mod Squad solve problems for the police, and Ironside and Mannix have black assistants who occasionally assume major roles in investigations. Lieutenant Tibbs and Shaft, created first in novels by white authors–John Ball and Ernest Tidyman–have established the popularity potential of black plainclothesmen and black private investigators in films. In books of fiction, John Brunner, an Englishman, George Baxl, and Ed Lacy are recent creators of black detectives. Truly, a visitor from another planet who explored the films and fiction of the past five years might presume this to be the era of the black supercop–unless he chanced to read one of the infrequent newspaper features pointing to the insignificant percentages of blacks on the police forces of America.

In this paper, however, I wish to lead you to a not-long-ago period, before black detectives or even black writers became fashionable. The years 1956-1959. Recall them. Convinced of its status as leader of the free world, America basked in the watchful serenity of peace. The most recent war–the Korean–had ended, and the world once again was safe from non-democratic, un-American forces as long as America kept a watchful eye and several nuclear bombs focused on the Russian Communists. The Supreme Court had reassured the dubious that all American children would be amalgamated into a unified society which did not concern itself with such trivia as skin color. "Black Power" was merely the title of a

Reprinted from THE ARMCHAIR DETECTIVE, Aug. 1973, with permission of the editor.

Richard Wright book which no one read, and "Negro Literature" and "Negro History" were being voted out of the curricula of Southern Negro colleges, which did not want to be accused of maintaining barriers against the integration of the Negro into American society.

James Baldwin was known only to a few readers of "little" magazines, and *Invisible Man* had not been discovered to be *the* American novel of the generation. John Killens, Paule Marshall, and Julian Mayfield wrote novels, quietly published and quietly received by individuals who saw scant value in identifying the authors as black. Frank Yerby, the most popular Negro novelist of the decade, was rarely revealed to readers except as a slightly blurred, dust-jacket photo of an individual who could claim citizenship in any European nation.

In such a time, it is not surprising that black detectives in fiction were even rarer than in actuality. (In fact, I know none except the detective whom Harry Faggett, a black college teacher, glamorized in the *Baltimore Afro-American* newspaper but could not sell to a major publisher and the Coffin Ed-Gravedigger Jones team with whom Chester Himes excited French readers.) Thus it is not surprising that a Negro who wanted to publish detective fiction in America should have ignored the possibility of a black detective and should have modeled a white detective after the most popular American private eye of the decade, Mickey Spillane's violent, patriotic stud, Mike Hammer. This, I believe, is the perspective from which one must view the six novels in which John B. West detailed the lurid adventures of Rocky Steele.

Unfortunately, biographical information about West is scant. He has been identified as a Negro American. In a preface to his second novel, he identified himself as a physician living in Monrovia, Liberia, and hoping to complete a novel to recoup his gambling losses at Las Vegas. He wrote six novels: *An Eye for an Eye, Cobra Venom, A Taste for Blood, Bullets Are My Business, Death on the Rocks,* and *Never Kill a Cop,* published only in paper by Signet Books. Internal evidence dates the action of the six in a three-year period from 1957 to 1959. The first was published in 1959, the last in 1961. The last three, published from October 1960 to April 1961, appeared after West's death. The probability is that at least five of the six were written between February 1959 and April 1960. All this suggests rather frantic, possibly careless creativity, and the works verify the impression. In characterization, plot, and thought, they follow formulas well known to detective-story enthusiasts. In style they are undistinguished, even when compared only with pulp detective stories of the time.

Such caustic criticism should not suggest that they are worse than the efforts of better known diarists of the escapades of private detectives. To the contrary, they compare favorably with the works of M. E. Chambers, Brett Halliday, or Mickey Spillane. But, with one exception, they demonstrate no individuality to persuade one that he must read about

Rocky Steele rather than about Mike Shayne or Mike Hammer. That one exception–West's final book–is one that I shall consider briefly at the end of this paper. Located in Africa, and the only one which has a black investigator, it is unique among his works.

What can be said about big, brutal Rocky Steele and his adventures? As I stated earlier, Steele is modeled after Spillane's Mike Hammer, who appeared in *I the Jury* twelve years before Rocky Steele first glared from the pages of Signet Books. Named Aloysius Algernon by a father never discussed except as the originator of the hated moniker, Rocky Steele is a 6 ft. 3 in., 190-198 lb. former Commando and former prize fighter, who chain smokes Lucky Strikes, worships a Cadillac given by an unnamed client, and tries vainly to protect his beautiful and expensive new rug from the hoodlums who thoughtlessly drip blood on it. Distinguished from other fictional detectives primarily by his unique ability to define the physical appearances of anyone whose voice he has heard, Rocky harbors talents and skills never mentioned until they become significant to a plot. In *Cobra Venom,* he must disguise from Chinese Communists the fact that he can speak Chinese and is conversant with Chinese culture. *In Bullets Are My Business,* Rocky reveals a diamond dealer's expert knowledge of diamonds and the market. In the same novel, he reveals himself to be an expert pilot just in time to crashland a sabotaged plane. Steele specializes in violence: he may persuade a hoodlum to talk by smashing a heavy book against his face until teeth burst through the upper lip; he bends back the hand of a knife-wielder until the blades cut off the attacker's fingers; he shoots men in the gut with Betsy, his .45; he knees a hoodlum's face into a pulp; he tortures criminals until they scream "like a raped woman who didn't want it." (*An Eye for an Eye*, p. 31) Rocky is even a violent, though satisfying, brute when he is merely engaging in intercourse with several 5 ft. 3 in., 120 lb. blondes who beg him to hurt them. I leave to the imaginative any speculation about whether Rocky's sadism reflects John West's vicarious avenging of the abuse of blacks by America. Such a thesis seems to be refuted by the super-patriot sentiments of Rocky in *Cobra Venom.*

Like Mike Hammer, like the mythical lawmen of the West, Steele is a one-man avenging mob, but he vacillates between anticipated/realized pleasure derived from sadistic methods of eliciting information and perplexed speculation about the reason that so many corpses seem to litter his path. In *I the Jury*, Hammer concludes his oath of vengeance against the murderer of a friend:

> Some day, before long, I'm going to have my rod in my mitt and the killer in front of me. I'm going to watch the killer's face. I'm going to plunk one right in his gut, and when he's dying on the floor I may kick his teeth out. (p. 8)

Less imaginatively but with equal conviction, Steele swears in *An Eye for an Eye*:

> Rough Voice was the one I wanted, and I knew that when I caught up with him, I was gonna kill him, and I was gonna let him have it slow. I wanted to watch his life drain out of him inch by inch while he begged for mercy. Mercy! That rat didn't know what the word meant, and I wasn't gonna teach him. (p. 24)

Nevertheless, in the tradition of the good-guy hired gunman, Rocky is capable of sentiment and admiration. He admires, or at least respects, those killers who can accept his closed-book beatings without whimpering. Sentimentally, he mourns through six, woman-adorned adventures, the death of Norma Cartaret, a wealthy, beautiful aristocrat, whom he failed to protect. Disdaining her fears because she lived in a seemingly unassailable apartment, he left after spending their meeting night in her bed. He returned just in time to hear her killer leave. Sentimentally also, he befriended Tai May Sen, a beautiful fifteen-year-old Chinese fugitive from a whorehouse for Japanese soldiers. With the curious admixture of lust and Puritan morality characteristic of many fictional American detectives, Rocky beds (or tries to bed) every attractive woman he meets except his eager-eyed, tempting, voluptuous, and willing secretary, whose virginity he preserves as zealously as a Victorian father. She is better off because he does avoid her. Although he insists that he must protect their employer-employee relationship, it is demonstrated that, once a woman has intercourse with Rocky, she either tries to kill him or is killed. One might lose too many secretaries that way.

When considering Rocky's fascination with expensive luxuries despite his disdain for wealthy men, one wishes it were possible to infer such a significant conclusion as that John West was reflecting a poor man's fascination with wealth. Unfortunately, here too West is probably merely reflecting that long tradition in which a detective is individualized or glamorized or humanized by his capability as a connoisseur or a collector.

In each novel, Rocky Steele is surrounded by a cast of stereotypes from detective fiction—Vicky Boston, a beautiful secretary, expert in judo and karate, who frequently but unsuccessfully, "with devils dancing in her eyes," implores Rocky, "I wanna get weighed"; Captain Richards, a friendly detective who beseeches Rocky to stop killing people—at least not so many; Inspector Morris, a hostile detective who hopes to be able to put Rocky behind bars but who occasionally saves his life; Jimmy "the Count" Lutz, a gentleman safe-cracker and knife-thrower; and, of course, one beautiful victim or villain whose bared or negligee-shadowed "peaches" engross Rocky and male readers through more than one interesting interlude. Less typical, but certainly not unique in his role is Benny the Dip, a Jewish homosexual clubowner, who supplies Rocky with information from the underworld grapevine.

This cast is repeatedly tossed into corpse-cluttered, predictable plots in which the arch criminal is supposedly the least suspected person. In *An Eye for an Eye,* Rocky is deceived by Boss Charis, only because Charis's voice seems different from that of the mastermind behind the crimes. Steele finally learns that Charis, once a professional impersonator, can disguise his voice. In *Cobra Venom,* the villain is Stephen Greene, a CIA agent who has enlisted Rocky to solve the murder of another agent. In *A Taste of Blood,* the mastermind in a blackmail plot is Hastings, an assistant district attorney who harassed the DA to act against the forces which Hastings controls. In *Never Kill a Cop,* the chief villain is Dancer, a gangster who apparently cannot have killed his boss because he was in jail when the boss supposedly was murdered. West does not slight female murderers. In *Bullets Are My Business,* the mastermind is Penny Carew, who is preparing to enter Rocky's bed shortly before he learns of the murder for which she is responsible. In *Death on the Rocks,* the mastermind behind a plot to secure diamonds is Barbara Stack, who has begged Rocky to protect her from Karl von Stroheim, who is actually Barbara's father and partner in crime.

The plots are further complicated by the fact that, wanting more corpses than Rocky and the major villain can possibly account for, West always adds an obvious suspect, who is the accomplice of the unsuspected villain. The two alibi each other, as the unsuspected villain kills those whom the obvious villain would have reason to murder and vice versa.

The plots are melodramatic, too frequently to the point of absurdity. For the sake of West's reputation, one wishes it were possible to read a spoofing intention into some of the incidents. For instance, a classic scene of recent detective fiction is the conclusion of *I the Jury.* Mike Hammer shoots a gorgeous murderer in the stomach after she has completed a sensuous strip tease designed to lull him into complacency which will permit her to kill him. Twice West extends this semi-absurdity into the ludicrous. In *An Eye for an Eye,* Steele, to avenge Norma Cartaret's death, shoots Boss Charis in the stomach to prolong the agony of Charis's death. Because he has been badly wounded by Charis, however, Rocky faints. While he is unconscious, the mortally wounded but conscious Charis reaches a loaded gun. Rocky is saved only by the fortuitous intervention of Inspector Morris, who hates Rocky. In *Bullets Are My Business,* Penny Carew returns to Rocky's apartment, supposedly to complete their interrupted night of romance but actually to kill him. While Rocky prepares drinks, negligee-clad Penny teases him sexually, then pulls a gun. To entertain herself, she plans to kill him slowly. First she shoots him in the right leg, then the left, then the left shoulder. Before she can fire the last bullet into his forehead, however, she succumbs to the Mickey Finn of sodium pentathol which Rocky mixed into her drink.

Because butlers have been the villains in many mysteries, a butler is the least suspected character in most contemporary mysteries. In *Bullets Are My Business,* however, the obvious suspect is the butler, believed to be Michael Holliday, who has sworn vengeance against the family of Milton Honeywell because Honeywell attempted to kill him, stole his gold mine, and married his wife. Actually, however, the butler is a victim, hired for the part by Honeywell, who actually did kill his partner and who now plans to murder his wife so that he can marry Penny Carew.

Truly, after reading such a story, one wishes to think of John West as a physician who entertained himself by heightening to absurdity the traditional plots of mysteries. Unfortunately, no elements of the novels reveal West to be an author who consciously parodies others rather than one who unconsciously parodies himself.

One cannot say that a study of the thought of John West illuminates the dim corners of the mind. He offers none of the semi-philosophical essays about human personality and human relationships that one reads in John D. MacDonald's work. Unlike Chester Himes, he is not a critic of social relationships, certainly not black-white relationships. He does not even create an avenger who weeps his woes to the world in the manner of post-1960 Mike Hammer. In short, Rocky Steele is not a role for a Humphrey Bogart; Steele is instead a role for a horseless John Wayne, who thinks little beyond his admiration for the wealthy and his hatred of Japanese, Communists, and others who might threaten the "American" way of life.

It may be adjudged unfair to expect significant perception in detective stories. Aside from an occasional justification of speeding or of running through a stop sign, the level of perceptive comment in the Perry Mason stories rarely rises above Paul Drake's diatribes against soggy hamburgers. But John West entices a reader to expect more because of the introductory paragraph to *An Eye for an Eye*:

> Tonight I got to thinking about people—the people who hire me and my gun and my ways, the people I'm hired to find or trap, or beat up, or even kill—and the people who live in safe, comfortable seclusion, never knowing how the other half dies. Maybe, I thought, all these people should get together, and me—I'm just the guy to introduce them to each other because I work with all three types every day. So it occurred to me to try to let the secluded half know what makes the other half tick—and stop ticking. (p. 5)

Unfortunately, West never again concerns himself deeply with the psychological motivation of criminals. His murderers have such simplistic motives that the proverbial little old lady in Pasadena would have no difficulty drawing up such a list of motives before reading any of the novels—a financially troubled gangster wants to save himself $100,000; a double agent protects his secret; an assistant district attorney wants to preserve his blackmail racket; a hustling singer persuades her wealthy lover to murder his wife; two gang lieutenants kill to take over the respective mobs; diamond dealers desire a diamond worth a million dollars. These motives and characters would not surprise "the secluded half."

Stylistically, West vacillates between striving for a lush literary quality and striving for the hardbitten tone of the pulps. In either, he seems incapable of avoiding amusing bathos:

A damp wind blew in through the open window, caught up a lock of her golden hair, and blew it across my face. It was fresh, new cornsilk—so soft and smooth and clinging. And there was a fragrance about it that made my head spin even faster than it was already spinning. I cupped my lower lip and blew hard, blowing that angel hair away from my face, and then I looked at her. She was beautifully undressed in a transparent blue thing she called a negligee, and brother, was it negligent when it came to hiding what she had! From the top of her spun-gold head to the tips of her ruby-red toenails, she was pure gold—twenty-four carat gold. I knew she could be a twenty-four-carat bitch, too, when she wanted to be, and so did everybody else that knew her, but right then, I loved every one of her carats, gold or bitch. (*Bullets Are My Business,* p. 5)

He circled warily around me, and I was laughing in his face all the time. I gave him what looked like a sweet opening, and he made his play. I side-stepped, catching his knife hand in my big paw, and wrapping my fingers around the back of the blade. I squeezed slow, still laughing. When he felt the blade biting into the backs of his fingers, he screamed like a raped virgin who didn't want it, and I kept squeezing slow, laughing all the time. Maybe I was kill-crazy right then. I don't know. All I could think of was cutting the bastard into thin ribbons and broiling 'em over a slow fire. I kept the squeeze on, and then Spike went lax, and slid to the floor, unconscious. But three of his fingers hit the floor before he did, and they weren't tied to his hand any more.

I grabbed a piece of string out of the table drawer and tied it tight around the stumps to keep 'em from bleeding all over my nice new rug, and then I dug out a fag with the hand that wasn't covered with blood, and lit up, shaking some now that it was all over. Then I went in the john and washed up. (*A Taste for Blood,* p. 27)

Eliko stood there just inside the door, holding it ajar, and she was clad only in a gossamer thing as light and airy as moonbeams, her platinum hair falling in shining cascades around her rose-pink shoulders and sparkling through the moonbeams where a woman's hair should sparkle. She was all platinum, from stem to stern. Those two peaches thrust out from her chest like they were trying to push their way through the moonbeams, and I gave 'em some help.

I crushed her soft body against the rock-hard muscles of my chest until it hurt, but she only moaned softly in ecstasy, trying to come closer. Again her tongue was like a fiery serpent, darting in and out against mine. In a moment I pushed her away and started climbing out of the rest of my clothes, thrilling as I watched her hands fumble with the buttons, her body so rigid that it trembled now and then. In a few moments, I stood there beside her with nothing separating us but that moonbeam gown. Then I swept her up in my arms and walked quickly to the big silk-sheeted bed and laid her on it.

"Oh, my darling," she whispered. "Oh, my darling. If I could only tell you what you do to me." "You're telling me without trying, sweetheart," I told her. "Like I hope I'm telling you. Words can't do it." "No, Rocky. They can't. Let me breathe a moment, my darling. Only a moment, then take me close to you again." (*Cobra Venom,* pp. 72-73)

I walked slowly over to stand between them where neither of them could reach me with his feet, swung my right fist suddenly into Two-Ton's belly with all I could put into it, and watched him double up like a jackknife. He didn't make a sound except for the air that made a quick, high whistle as it left his lungs in a rush.

"I got lots more," I told him. "You feel like talking yet?" The sonofabitch spit in my face, and then I really let him have one—right in the same place. No sense in breaking my hands on his head when his belly was so much softer. This time he got a little green around the gills.

"Make it good, Mac," he gasped. "My day will come, and I'm gonna make you remember this." I let him have another one in the same place and watched him puke over my nice, clean rug. It was Prettyboy that winced. He was gonna be the one that would soften up easy, but I'd get around to him later. I picked up a heavy book off the table and slapped Two-Ton across the face with it half a dozen times, rocking his head with each blow, and watching the corners of his mouth split and spurt blood as the edge of the cover caught him in the teeth. He didn't make a sound except for the puking.

"You lousy, dirty bastard," I spat at him, "I'm gonna make you talk or kill you trying." I let him have another brace across the teeth and watched his lips turn into strawberry jam that ran down his chin onto his nice new shirt and suit. It was a real heavy book, and a couple of his teeth were loose. He rolled them around in their sockets with his tongue, glaring at me with more hate than I'd ever seen, and then he got two more in the kisser. The loose teeth weren't loose any more—they were looking up at him from the floor, but he still didn't say a word and he hadn't made a sound. He must have been made of iron all over. (*An Eye for an Eye,* pp. 29-30)

Despite a conventional plot, *Death on the Rocks* is the most individualized of all West's novels. On the way to the ship which will carry him to Africa for a vacation, Rocky Steele, helpless to prevent the killing of a diamond salesman, shoots holes in the tires of the assailants and watches them burn to death. Aboard the ship, Rocky meets Barbara Stack, a platinum blonde en route to Liberia to purchase a 1,012 carat, 4 point, perfect, blue-white diamond for ten million dollars. After refusing her request for assistance, Steele changes his mind when he discovers that "Bobby" Stack is being pursued by a deadly South American syndicate, headed by Karl von Stroheim, a former Nazi. So ends Chapter One. After mutually satisfying sexual intercourse with Bobby, Steele agrees to defend her against von Stroheim, who has boarded the ship. When a Spanish woman is killed in the cabin previously occupied by Bobby Stack, Steele vows to discover and kill the person behind the plot. In Liberia, they are joined by Captain Deegbeh of the Homicide Division of the Liberian National Police, who informs them that the two dealers scheduled to meet Bobby Stack have been killed by a foreigner trying to cast suspicion on the inactive Leopard Society. After escaping from attempted sabotage of the plane which Deegbeh has secured, Steele, convinced that von Stroheim is the murderer, flies to Spain in pursuit. By smashing the face of von Stroheim's man with a copy of *Don Quixote* (appropriate for Spain!), Rocky persuades the employee to lead him to von Stroheim's island stronghold, where he kills von Stroheim after learning that von

Stroheim's daughter is the chief architect of the plot and the murders. In the final chapter Bobby Stack is revealed as von Stroheim's daughter. After Bobby shoots Rocky, he kills her and accidentally finds the $10 million diamond.

Two elements of the book distinguish it from his others. Familiar with Liberia, West not only describes the physical attractions of Monrovia but also sketches customs, secret societies, dances and living habits unique to West Africa. In doing so he infuses the story with a local color far richer and more vivid than that of earlier novels located in Manhattan.

More important is his creation of a black policeman. Just as West was not the first black writer to scribble mysteries about white protagonists, so he was not the first to create a black detective. Nevertheless, a black official of the law was a rarity in American literature of the 1950's. In fact, any respected black character was rare in the mysteries of Erle Stanley Gardner, Ellery Queen, Brett Halliday and other well-known writers who restricted their infrequent portraits to black servants or comic foils who speak a dialect conspicuously different from the standard English of the white characters.

Captain Deegbeh, however, is drawn with a dignity and a respect which West does not seem to extend to non-professional Liberian natives. Educated in America, "a smart cookie" who speaks English better than Rocky Steele does, Deegbeh is an African counterpart of Captain Richards. Identifiably African only in skin color and occasional use of Liberian proverbs, he is a good cop. Except for *Death on the Rocks,* however, the novels of West were imitative; and imitations rarely equal the originals.

The Steele saga ended in 1961. Several years would pass before America would take interest in the fictional black police of Chester Himes and would be willing to accept a scarfaced black Coffin Ed in the one-man role of captor, judge, jury, and executioner. By that time, John West was dead. And few would remember or mourn the passing of a black writer who dared entry into pulp fiction by capsulizing in a pale Mike Hammer the brutality and violence which Anglo-European culture has posited for its most respected heroes.

R. Gordon Kelly

THE PRECARIOUS WORLD OF JOHN D. MacDONALD

Literature—narrative fiction in particular—often seems a tantalizing but illusive kind of source to the historian. Popular narrative formulas such as the detective story or the Western seem especially attractive sources with which to investigate, indirectly, widely shared images of society for which there is little if any systematically generated record. The relative popularity of these formulas at a given time, the sustained popularity of some formulas (such as the detective story), and the decline or occasional disappearance of once-popular formulas (the sentimental novel of seduction, for example) all suggest that such formula narratives serve important social functions beyond those merely of entertainment, diversion, or escape. Conceptions of these functions vary, but historians have often assumed—and rightly so—that popular literature embodies values, attitudes, beliefs, expectations, and implicit psychologies, which are characteristic of large numbers of people, if not of whole societies. Historians have not always been very explicit about how values, for example, are embodied in narratives, and they have generally remained silent about the assumptions governing the process by which values abstracted from popular fiction are imputed to the society in and for which the fiction was produced. Although this essay is intended to outline an explanation for the popularity of a prolific contemporary practitioner in the mystery-suspense field, John D. MacDonald, I hope to suggest as well some conceptual bases for limiting the kinds of generalizations about society often made from analyses of popular materials.

A central element in MacDonald's fiction is a vivid sense of the precariousness and vulnerability underlying life in American society. To illuminate this quality, it is useful to examine a brief passage, the Flitcraft episode, in Dashiell Hammett's *The Maltese Falcon* (1930).[1]

Early in that hard-boiled detective novel, Sam Spade recounts (to

Brigid O'Shaughnessy) the story of Flitcraft, a Tacoma, Washington, real estate man who one day vanished without explanation. Several years afterward, Spade had managed to locate Flitcraft in Spokane, living under the assumed name of Charles Pierce, and there learned from Flitcraft/Pierce, the occasion for his disappearance. Succinctly, and with little interpretive comment, Spade retells Flitcraft's story.

While walking to lunch one day, Flitcraft had nearly been killed by a beam falling from a building under construction. Unhurt but deeply shocked by the experience, Flitcraft suddenly knew, with the force of revelation, that the assumptions and the logic of his conventional life bore little resemblance to the realities of a world in which men "lived only while blind chance spared them." Resolving on the spot to live by his new perception, Flitcraft took to changing his life at random. His new name testifies to his altered perception—his conversion experience. For the next several years Flitcraft/Pierce drifted, but as no more beams fell in his life, he slipped gradually and insensibly into that pattern of customary behavior which had defined his life before the beam had fallen. "He adjusted himself to beams falling, and then no more of them fell, and he adjusted himself to them not falling," Spade concludes.[2]

We need argue no necessary influence in observing that one of the major preoccupations threading the novels of John D. MacDonald is precisely that compelling sense of randomness and unpredictability which Flitcraft experienced most vividly in the moment of his danger and escape, and which necessitated his moving outside of his taken-for-granted world in order to discover an explanation of the event—and to discover principles on which to establish a life consistent with the real world as he had been compelled to perceive it.

Although MacDonald is one of the more prolific popular writers of the post World War II period, *The Executioners* (1957) embodies a vision of the precariousness of life as directly and economically as any of MacDonald's more than fifty novels, and I have chosen in this essay to concentrate on it.[3] The world limned in *The Executioners* is similar to, but more dangerous than, Flitcraft's, for MacDonald has added to a world pervaded by chance the element of malicious intent embodied in the strikingly vicious character of the sadistic villain, Max Cady.

The Executioners begins—and ends—in a setting long since familiar in its outlines to students of American culture—a serene "Middle Landscape" associated with feelings of independence, security, and well-being. In *The Executioners*, the pastoral retreat is a small island in a lake to which Sam Bowden and his family have come for the first picnic of the summer and to which they will return at the end of a summer of terror climaxed by a dark night of violence.

Bowden, married and with three children, practices law in fictional New Essex, a city of about 130,000, but he lives in a remodeled farm house on the edge of a small town a dozen miles from New Essex. A decent, thoughtful man with a touch of saving irony, Bowden is devoted to his family and to the practice of the law, to which he brings a combination of intelligence, idealism, and good sense—qualities which reappear in the portraits of other professional men scattered through MacDonald's works.

The initial mood of pastoral idyll is evoked, however, only to be destroyed. As an Army lieutenant, Bowden had served in the Judge Advocate General's Department during the war. One night, on leave in Melbourne, he had chanced to come on an American soldier raping a young Australian girl in an alley. Bowden knocked the man out with a lucky punch, and subsequently testified at the court-martial proceedings which ended in a life sentence at hard labor for the soldier. When he is paroled after serving thirteen years, Max Cady comes looking for the lieutenant whose sucker punch had put him to hard labor. During his imprisonment, Cady's wife had remarried and his son had been killed in an accident. Blaming Bowden for these losses as well as his years in prison, Cady seeks an appropriate revenge.

Bowden is justifiably alarmed by Cady, whose squat, muscular appearance and savage but controlled malice ally him with a number of psychopathic characters in other MacDonald novels, but Bowden is convinced that there is a relatively simple answer to what at first seems like just another problem to be handled with intelligence and logic. It ought to be possible, he thinks, to let the police and the courts take care of Cady. He quickly discovers, however, that he cannot persuade the police to harass Cady out of the city; and a private detective whom Bowden contacts reports that Cady is too shrewd and wary to be easily trapped into an overt threatening act. Surveillance, he is told, would entail a difficult, prohibitively expensive, and probably futile effort to discover and anticipate Cady's intentions. When the family dog is poisoned with strychnine and dies in agony in front of the three children, Bowden and his wife are convinced that Cady is responsible and that the man is insane. There is no legal way, however, that they can act on that supposition and have Cady examined or committed; his murderous intent, while clear to the Bowdens, effectively lies beyond the purview of the law.

Following the death of the dog, Cady subtly but unmistakably threatens Bowden's oldest child, his fourteen year old daughter—again in a manner that conveys his intention but gives no basis for invoking the law. Shortly after this, Bowden decides to act on the hint of the private detective and have Cady professionally beaten by hired thugs. The man proves too tough even for such desperate tactics as these, but he is sentenced to a month in jail for resisting arrest when police are called to the scene of the melee. The possibility of a second attack on Cady vanishes when the private detective is transferred to another city and the small-time hoodlum whom Bowden was to have contacted to set up the attack suffers a fatal heart attack. At this point MacDonald has effectively closed to his hero the legal and extra-legal institutions which Bowden had taken for granted as sufficient protection for himself and his family. During the respite provided by Cady's month in jail, Bowden applies for and receives a permit to carry a revolver and begins practicing with it. His two oldest children are sent off to camp, while his wife and the youngest child seclude themselves at a summer hotel some distance from their home.

Cady's release renews the family's terror, but a week goes by before anything happens: Bowden's older son is wounded while at camp, saved, it appears, only when the bullet is slightly deflected by a stray gust of wind. On the trip back from the hospital with the boy, the family's station wagon loses a wheel—the lug nuts had been murderously loosened—and turns over. No one is hurt, but Bowden realizes they cannot expect to be so fortunate again, and he begins to think about personally taking the initiative against Cady. For a time, he imagines ways to lure Cady to a spot where he can be killed and the body quietly disposed of, but Bowden sensibly discards the plan as too dangerous, given Cady's evident skills, and as too destructive potentially of the quiet world he and his wife have built.

As a last resort, they make a second appeal to the New Essex police, this time with some success. With the children safely away from the house, Bowden and a young policeman with infantry experience set a trap for Cady, who Bowden is convinced is watching the house. In the explosive conclusion, Cady very nearly succeeds in raping Bowden's wife, but he does mortally wound the policeman and then is wounded in turn by Bowden, snap shooting in the dark, and bleeds to death in the trees behind the house. In the concluding scene, the Bowdens return to their island sanctuary, and the novel ends on the same note of pastoral lyricism with which it began—but cleansed now of the undercurrent of terror. It is not really the same world to which they return, however, for Bowden and his wife now recognize, and explicitly testify to, the contingent and precarious nature of their lives. They are not so much sobered by their new knowledge as filled with a heightened, exhilerated sense of reality: "It's like recovering from a serious illness," Bowden tells his wife. "All the world looks fresh and new. Everything looks special. I feel enormously alive."[4]

It is not simply the pattern of events in *The Executioners* that are worth remarking. What is of interest to the cultural historian are the terms in and through which MacDonald presents the series of events that culminate both in Cady's death and in a reordering, not of Bowden's life (as Flitcraft decisively and immediately reorders his) but of Bowden's perception. Narrative is, if nothing else, a process of selection and ordering, and the manner in which a given writer categorizes—especially—motivation, social institutions, and the chronically vulnerable and often problematic relationship between appearance and reality is of crucial importance to descriptions of cognitive orientations. The fragile, often tenuous, links that are posited between mental activity and overt behavior, constitute one of the most revealing characteristics of a particular culture.

In *The Executioners* these links may be best observed in the portrait of Maxwell Cady. Cady, like Junior Allen in MacDonald's *The Deep Blue Good-bye*, is a distinctive combination of mental qualities matched with physical characteristics that are presumably the appropriate, widely recognized and accepted complements and manifestations of personalities such as his. Without conscience or compassion, these recurrent individuals in MacDonald's fiction are savage, quick, and merciless. Like Cady, they have an instinct for their victim's weak spot and have no scruples about exploiting it. They are sadists, and their assaults are typically sexual. Physically, Cady is stocky, big-boned, and heavily muscled but nevertheless exceptionally fast and agile. MacDonald's initial description of him clearly hints at the link between his physical appearance and his personality and suggests as well an explanation that is reaffirmed throughout the book: "Dark hair grew low on his forehead. Heavy mouth and jaw. Small brown eyes set in deep and simian sockets."[5] From the outset, Cady is presented as congenitally vicious. He comes from "old stock"—southern mountain hill people, specifically—but he is also a reversion to a more primitive stage of human evolution. His "simian" appearance (a term that reverberates throughout MacDonald's books) suggests his cunning, his merciless cruelty, his formidable combination of agility and strength. A "rogue beast,"—MacDonald's term—he exists beyond the law, beyond the terms of civilized persuasion—an outlaw and an outsider in a literal, profound, and ineluctable way.. His death is styled an "execution" at the novel's conclusion, and in our last glimpse of him, Cady is seen to be an "elemental and merciless force" that has been rendered inert. The reader is not encouraged to question Cady's end; his death presumably has been imposed by a more inclusive, if less understood, imperative than statute law. In death, as in life, he lacks humanity.

To this conception of Cady as a "rogue beast," a destructive genetic aberration, MacDonald adds at one point an explanation for the man's violence which is environmental and psychological. In a conversation with his daughter, Bowden explains that Cady had gone from a prolonged period of island fighting, combat of the most intense and savage kind, to a life sentence at hard labor because of his chance encounter with Bowden. Under these circumstances, the man broke, blamed Bowden for his conviction, and irrationally sought revenge when he was paroled. Unlike the "reversion" explanation, however, this implicitly sympathetic account of Cady's malice is not functional in the narrative outside of the conversation in which it occurs and in which it helps to establish Bowden's relationship with his daughter and to reveal his recognition of Cady's suffering.[6] For a moment, Cady is the product of the madness of total war—but the man was violent before he went to war. Temperament, ultimately biological in origin, is the real basis for aggression and violence. The environmental explanation, which carries with it typically the implication of widely diffused responsibility and the possibility of amelioration via environmental manipulation, is never again invoked in *The Executioners.* Cady remains the personification of all the inexplicable "black things" let loose in the world. If he is not precisely evil, he is, by nature and by experience, without conscience or even the possibility of conscience; and references throughout *The Executioners* to Cady's animality, as well as to his probable insanity, remind us that his eventual death is warranted and just.[7]

To the extent that he offers a genetic and evolutionary explanation of Cady's behavior, MacDonald differs significantly from such highly regarded mystery writers as Raymond Chandler or, more recently, Ross Macdonald. These writers accord much more readily with the environmentalism which is at the heart of the liberal reform tradition that has dominated social thought in this century. Nevertheless, the nature/nurture controversy is not dead, as the controversial work of Robin Fox and Lionel Tiger—and especially the recent work of Jensen on intelligence—attests. The bio-psychological element in behavior is conceptually and methodologically difficult to examine, but the issue also raises, and has raised, idiological problems of the most profound kind. The evolution of the neo-cortex, despite its centrality in hominid evolution, is something about which we actually know very little.

MacDonald, to be sure, is not working within the complex framework of neurophysiology. Instead, the terms used to characterize Cady suggest the persistence of certain tenets of late 19th century naturalism, modified in ways that are not completely clear—ideas which have generally been discarded by intellectuals in this century.

MacDonald's work suggests that these ideas function to support an individualistic ethic which is seen to be threatened by centralized, specialized, and highly rationalized organizations. Such organizations appear to rob individuals of functions which, for many people, are linked to deeply-rooted feelings about identity. The references to Cady in *The Executioners* also suggest a sensitivity—born of experiences about which I can only speculate—to the explanatory limits of the environmentalism that characterizes our recent intellectual history. Cady cannot be explained simply or satisfactorily as the product of a particular environment or series of environments. His conscienceless sadism can only be understood, MacDonald suggests, as "natural," and the most readily available category of explanation is some notion of reversion—a genetic accident producing an organism which embodies a more primitive stage of social evolution and which, by definition, is poorly adapted to civilization. In these terms, Cady takes his place alongside characters drawn by Norris and London, earlier literary naturalists obsessed on occasion with the possibility of just such reversions to more primitive modes of behavior. As civilization evolves, however, tending toward complexity and interdependence, its members become increasingly vulnerable to such reversions as Cady whose personality and physique are particularly fitted to the individual struggle for survival characteristic of more primitive social organization. Finally, MacDonald's theme suggests the degree to which violence and aggression, historically of great concern to the middle class, continue to demand explanation, even as they defy it.

The nature of the threat posed by Cady is perhaps best explored in the sequence of events which, as we have seen, isolated the Bowden family from the social institutions charged with their protection, particularly legal institutions, and which reveal and define, in the process, three things: the limits of those agencies; the actual situation of men in the world; and the course of action most appropriate for Bowden to follow, given that situation.

Although MacDonald does not make overt the identification between law and civilization, it seems clear that the law, despite its acknowledged inequities, appropriately symbolizes the cultural distance men have traveled from savagery to civilization. Thus Cady's actions reveal not simply the limits of the law but the limits of civilization as well. By trusting institutions to protect him completely, Bowden has, in fact, gotten out of step—as Flitcraft had—with the principles which really order human experience. At one point Bowden suggests that it would have been easier to handle Cady in a more primitive period of history when institutions, less developed themselves and closer to instinctual processes, were better adapted to the savage challenge embodied by Cady.[8] Moreover, civilization, defined late in the novel specifically in terms of Christian moralism, respect for life, and concern for human dignity, is presented as having interferred in recent history (World War II and Korea) with the ability of significant numbers of Americans to contribute to the defense of their society. The capacity to kill, if one is directly attacked, must be maintained, MacDonald implies.

Despite its acknowledged blessings, civilization tends to soften the very instincts which may be needed to defend it. Individuals continue to be responsible, ultimately, for their own safety and survival and for the security of their families. Manhood is defined in the course of the novel not as professional success—Bowden finds no comfort or safety in his successful legal practice—but as the capacity to defend one's "brood" from the Cadys of the world. Civilization, with its substitution of logic for instinct and dependence for self-reliance, does not define the limits of the real world. A charmed circle of order, civilization is at best a fragile, isolated structure contrived in a universe of chance.

The violent conclusion to *The Executioners* validates the shift in perception that Bowden experiences and legitimizes the measures he has adopted for his self-defense. He has armed himself and become skilled with his weapon. When Cady does finally strike, Bowden goes to confront him but is spared an unequal hand-to-hand struggle. In the darkness, a chance bullet ends what a chance meeting began. Bowden feels no guilt or shame for killing Cady, although he expects to—and perhaps the reader does too. Instead he discovers "only a sense of savage satisfaction, a feeling of strong and primitive fulfillment. All the neat and careful layers of civilized instincts and behavior were peeled back to reveal an intense exultation over the death of an enemy."[9] This appropriate emotional response—appropriate, that is, in the context carefully established for it throughout the novel—is reinforced by the closing chapter.

With order restored in their lives, the Bowden family returns to their island sanctuary for the last picnic of the summer. In a reflective, self-conscious conversation, Bowden and his wife define for each other what they have learned: that the world is not framed for them (or anyone) to be happy in, although that is the universal human delusion. On the contrary, everything is balanced on "a delicate web of incidence and coincidence," and the law, in which Bowden placed too much of his trust, is seen to be merely a tool—limited and specialized, both in its application to and its explanation of human problems.[10]

For the black things loose in the world, we are capable of partial, unsatisfactory explanations only, MacDonald suggests, and a life of conventional morality and success is no buffer against sudden intrusions that threaten the very basis of life.[11] Some of these intrusions, like Cady, can be fought (indeed, they must be fought); others, like the cancers that recur in MacDonald's recent Travis McGee series, for example, can only be endured. Their incidence appears completely, bafflingly incommensurate with the value of the stricken individual, and no subtle casuistry can make clear finally why the attack occurs. Although MacDonald occasionally scouts the idea of design in the universe (see note 3), it is a design which is inapplicable to the fate of individuals. This concept of design fails to answer the anguished *Why*? that is so prominent in MacDonald's work. It is more a hope than a conviction directing the logic of his narratives. In short, it fails to function as explanation—as meaning for the violence and aggression that repeatedly erupt in MacDonald's work.

Although the late nineteenth century locus of scientific naturalism is well established, relatively little is known about the form of, and the extent to which, aspects of naturalistic thought have persisted in the twentieth century, given the tendency of intellectual historians to engage idea systems in their most complete, complex, and subtle forms. Indeed, it is not clear whether John D. MacDonald's ideas represent a migration of concepts from one social group to another or a resurrection of certain concepts or a persistence over two generations within the same strata of American society.[12]

In *The Executioners* the principle naturalistic element is the concept of cultural evolution, as already noted. It functions as a theory of history and of institutional development, provides an explanation of personality, and justifies the moral stance appropriate to the natural laws it identifies and summarizes. This concept does not exist, it should be said, in any systematic fashion in the narrative; rather it is a convenient covering term which best explains a pattern of reference, in the form typically invoked throughout the novel in contexts that relate appearance and reality or ends and means. References to increasing social complexity, the concomitant replacement of instinct by reason as the basis for behavior, the substitution of dependence for independence in social relations, and the recapitulation in children of phylogenic development thus define the matrix in which the events of the story find their principal meanings.[13] (At the same time, in a complex dialectic, the events of *The Executioners* may be said to qualify and particularize the rather conventional naturalistic ideas that may be abstracted from the narrative.) Although not as harshly as some earlier naturalistic thinkers, MacDonald dwarfs his characters against an immense sweep of time and space and shows them subject to forces over which they have no control. But there is none of the buoyant faith in reason and intelligence that characterized some earlier naturalistic thinkers.

Ironically, the notion of reversion to a more primitive stage of cultural development derives from theories originally intended to explain and to rationalize the dynamics of evolution, but in MacDonald's hands reversion defines a nightmare of genetic transmission and is presented as constituting, as we have seen, a very real threat to civilized society in which the maintenance of order, and specifically the protection of life and property, is no longer the responsibility of the individual but the function of specialized, highly rationalized bureaucracies. Given the possibility of cultural reversion, posed in an extreme form by Cady, the individual's salvation lies in facing squarely the fact of randomness and in accepting the continued utility of primitive instincts, especially those implicated in maintaining the security of the nuclear family and the inviolability of one's home place. Civilization notwithstanding, the residual instinct to protect the family must be conserved; it is an imperative that cannot be denied. Obeying it leads neither to shame nor to guilt but to a quick, savage elation which is wholly legitimate and healthy. Had Bowden not accepted the primacy of the protective instincts, however, he would have been unmanned–presumably, even if he had somehow survived Cady's murderous assault.

The limits of reason, the limits of institutionally guaranteed security, then, are clear, and rights are not given in nature and protected by law but are rooted finally in a core of instincts. These have remained stable despite the comparatively recent efflorescence of civilization and define man's inescapable animal heritage. Rights are constituted in what the individual can maintain in the face of chance and desperate malice. Existence, even in civilized society, does not confer automatically the right to happiness or security, however exemplary one's commitment to the normative standards of his society. Instead, MacDonald suggests, we have, at best, a fighting chance in a precarious world. Understanding this, facing it with courage and a wry awareness of his capacity for self-deception, Bowden strikes the appropriate stance in a world not well adapted to sustain individual life, let alone liberty or the pursuit of happiness.

Up to this point, I have suggested that *The Executioners* reveals the persistence of ideas not generally regarded as most characteristic of the dominant intellectual traditions of the twentieth century. There is a more contemporary context, however, which is useful in interpreting the novel. In both the Flitcraft episode and *The Executioners*, an event occurs which appears so radically disparate as to call into question an individual's taken-for-granted assumptions about his world. Underlying Flitcraft's initial world is the assumption that one's experiences are somehow commensurate with the moral, or at least the conventional, definitions of conduct provided by the norms of society. Success is the tribute accorded uprightness. The falling beam brings this assumption to consciousness—and at the same time reveals its absurdity. A new world, ordered on radically different principles, lies suddenly and fully revealed to Flitcraft, and he quickly and consciously accommodates himself to the new and compelling realities.

The Bowdens too are confronted with an anomalous experience, Cady's attack, which reveals a world substantially different in its ordering from their normal one, but a reality which is presented to them with an authority which compels acknowledgment. Their taken-for-granted world—a seemingly predictable, stable, and inclusive world—is shown to be radically precarious and partial. Their experience, moreover, reveals the principles of a yet more inclusive reality which contains the original world *and* the anomalous event and which, by providing the means to relate it to the previously taken-for-granted reality, serves to explain what has happened and to integrate events in a new and more realistic view (of the world.)

In *The Maltese Falcon*, the Flitcraft episode does little more than to suggest an essential quality of the hard-boiled detective hero. Unlike Flitcraft, Sam Spade continues to expect the unexpected. In contrast to Hammett and others who have written in the hard-boiled vein, MacDonald is preoccupied, as we have seen, with the precariousness of social order and individual security. More consistently—perhaps more effectively than other recent popular authors in the mystery-suspense field—MacDonald's explorations of the theme of social precariousness exemplify the process of response in the face of "marginal situations" that Peter Berger and Thomas Luckmann describe in *The Social Construction of Reality*, a recent essay in the sociology of knowledge.[14] Briefly, Berger and Luckmann define marginal situations as those experiences which call into doubt the reality of everyday life. Although their favorite examples are dreams and the death of a "significant other," it is clear that any experience in which an individual's routine cognitive orientation is massively, if temporarily, disrupted may be construed as a marginal situation. Marginality in this sense, it should be noted, does not refer to social status but to an experience, however brief in duration, of anomie, that is, the experience of a profound sense of meaninglessness, isolation, and terror. Moreover, since marginal situations cannot be avoided, they must be integrated conceptually within the structure of everyday reality. Every culture, Berger and Luckmann argue, has its symbolic universe (or universes in complex literate societies) which provides a basis for this essential integration, and which may be invoked to protect the individual from the paralyzing anomic experience triggered by marginal situations. Given the inevitability of marginal experiences and their threat to social continuity, it is clear that the procedures evolved by a group are crucial to an understanding of that group.

Basic to Berger's and Luckmann's essay is a deeply rooted sense of the precariousness of social organization, and more particularly of social meanings. Given man's virtually nonexistent instinctual basis for social behavior, it is necessary, they maintain, to transmit to successive generations every aspect of social life, but most especially the shared meanings, specific to a particular group, which hold social life together. Cultural transmission is at once absolutely essential for social continuity and peculiarly vulnerable, for there is no guarantee that the young can be persuaded that the accepted ways are warranted. For Berger and Luckmann, culture is a precarious enterprise because man is continually making and remaking, justifying and legitimating, the meanings in and through which he must live. Their subtle and elaborate argument, to which no short summary can do justice, analyzes on a high level of generality the processes of reality maintenance that transcend specific cultures; they note, without ascribing ontological reality to, a number of specific integrative schemes that have provided meaning for various groups at various times, and their own work may be viewed as attempting the same integrative function but from a relativistic position that takes the process of legitimation as subject for analysis rather than the content of a particular group's symbolic universe.

The knowledge that Bowden and his wife articulate at the conclusion of *The Executioners* may be understood then as an invocation of specific principles of order which give meaning to the terror and isolation they have experienced and which locate both Cady and themselves in a single symbolic universe—a universe, as we have seen, characterized by the extremely precarious situation of individuals. This is the way things really are, the Bowdens learn, and the wise accept the certainty of uncertainty with courage, if not with evangelical fervor.

Two points remain to be made. First, Bowden's new perception of things-as-they-are represents one of several alternative modes, available in contemporary American culture, for understanding the phenomena described, even if we accept the proposition that many Americans perceive society, even intermittently, as a fragile, precarious system of meanings and relationships. Many assuredly do not (quite the opposite, in fact); and for such persons neither Berger's and Luckmann's analysis nor *The Executioners* may make very much sense.

A second point concerns the extent to which this sense of precariousness is widely felt in American society—and this is the difficult, tantalizing, and generally overlooked problem of audience. To how many persons in American society and distinguished by what characteristics can we impute the meanings abstracted from MacDonald's novel? The answer is by no means clear. Although it appears impossible to specify with any degree of confidence the characteristics of the audience for *The Executioners* merely from the novel's content, several observations do seem worth making. First, MacDonald's popularity over a twenty-five year period suggests a measure of response enjoyed by relatively few authors. The existence of a fanzine devoted exclusively to his work further suggests that he has attracted the sustained loyalty of a few readers to a degree matched by only a handful of popular writers in this century. To the extent that MacDonald's work reveals a preoccupation with the meaning of violence, (and embodies explanations of the sort analyzed above) we may suppose a similar concern in his audience and even an acceptance of the terms in and through which violence is presented and resolved.

It is tempting to argue that MacDonald's evident and sustained popularity tells us something about contemporary American culture, but recent work in cognitive anthropology and the sociology of knowledge, including the essay by Berger and Luckmann, have made the assumption of a unitary American culture dubious at best. MacDonald's work may tell us something about perceptions shared by members of an ill-defined group in American society but nothing, it would seem, about the state of the culture generally. Knowledge, including variations in everyday knowledge, is socially distributed—but in ways that we have hardly begun to analyze systematically. Although the pattern of threat and resolution in *The Executioners* is pervasive in MacDonald's work, and indeed in a great deal of popular fiction, the terms which invoke order in the novel are highly individualized; and it is these terms, functioning as ultimate explanatory constructs, that may well constitute an important part of MacDonald's appeal. On the other hand, to borrow a religious metaphor in keeping with the function attributed to these terms, it is notoriously difficult to read the tracts of a sect different from one's own; and this difficulty, I take it, explains in some measure the academic resistance to the work of a popular writer like Spillane—and may indicate, moreover, a possible reason for MacDonald's failure to attract much academic attention, even from students of popular culture.

If nothing else is clear about MacDonald's audience, assuming the appeal of the resolution of *The Executioners*, it is a well-developed skepticism concerning environmental determinism. This skepticism may be allied to a brand of political conservatism, but it is certainly linked to a nightmare vision born of a vestigial but apparently still powerful evolutionary naturalism.[15] Undoubtedly, to many people, such seemingly outmoded notions are deplorable as examples of the popular misuse of science; but to the extent that they are believed, they constitute a basis for action and hence are very real indeed. Bowden is lucky, we must admit—but he is also successful in defending his family. For many Americans, that alone is enough to make him right—in short to validate the ideas which led logically to the final scene in *The Executioners.*

Raymond Nelson

DOMESTIC HARLEM: THE DETECTIVE FICTION OF CHESTER HIMES

In 1957, four years after he had left the United States to settle in France, Chester Himes began writing a remarkable series of novels about the adventures of Coffin Ed Johnson and Grave Digger Jones, a pair of tough Harlem police detectives. With characteristic irony Himes called this loosely sequential string of bloody narratives his "Harlem Domestic" series. Himes's interest in crime and violence was not new when these detective stories were first brought out for French audiences; he had long been regarded as one of the angriest black writers of the "school" of Richard Wright, and he had behind him several excellent naturalistic novels which must be counted among the most ragingly violent American fictions of our century.

What was new about the Harlem Domestic series was its variety of character-types, its grotesque comedy of violence, and its sparse, descriptive style. Because of these characteristics, and because of Himes's unabashed use of popular-crime formulae, his detective novels were indiscriminately labeled "potboilers," and in an amusingly unconscious confession of their own provincialism several American reviewers speculated that Himes was pandering to some depraved French taste for violence and flocculent sex in a sublimative Afro-America. I hope these lively tales did set Himes's pot to boiling—it was certainly time he made money—but his stories of criminal Harlem are more than commercial ventures. In them Himes moves beyond his earlier naturalism and embraces the rich folk-traditions of Black American culture. Judging from the responses of younger black writers, this shift of emphasis makes the Harlem Domestic series a seminal contribution to contemporary literature.

In an interview conducted by John A. Williams for *Amistad* magazine, Himes cryptically associates the beginning of the detective series with a "change from pessimism to optimism." We will probably have to wait for his autobiography to have that remark explained, but some of the dynam-

Reprinted from the VIRGINIA QUARTERLY REVIEW, 48:2, with the permission of the editor and the author.

ics of their origin can certainly be seen in the detective fictions themselves. Like his friend Richard Wright, Himes had been strongly influenced by the naturalism of the 1930's and 1940's. His earlier work was concerned largely with analyzing social and natural forces which his characters could neither understand fully nor control, but which imprisoned them in their own poverty, futility, and smoldering rage. Himes, however, is just old enough to remember also the 1920's and to have shared in the twilight days of that reinterpretation of Black culture and flowering of Black art known as the Harlem (or Negro) Renaissance. In the *Amistad* interview Himes discusses his experience in that exciting, exuberantly self-conscious Harlem—as much a "place" of the mind as a geographical entity. He knew, then or later, such fine writers of the period as Langston Hughes and Wallace Thurman; he was photographed and catalogued by the ubiquitous Carl Van Vechten. Harlem Renaissance artists refused to be embarrassed by the "Negro characteristics" at which white Americans laughed; they discovered the sources of cultural pride in the folklore and the unique mores of the traditional black community. It would be surprising if a sensitive young writer had not been deeply impressed by their delighted urbanization of Black folk-culture, their hedonistic celebrations of Negro life in the streets and cafés, their loving attention to the intimate details of day-to-day life among black people.

There was more to the Harlem Renaissance, of course, than its superficial primitivism, far more to it than the popular image of happy Negroes who endlessly drank, fought, and danced, but even its most talented apologists soon discovered a frivolity about the period that Himes must have sensed also. When the deadly serious Great Depression ushered in a new literary era, Himes (perhaps regretfully) left Renaissance themes unexplored and turned instead to the literature of protest. In the Harlem Domestic series, however, he recaptures the spirit (without succumbing to the naïveté) of the Harlem Renaissance, and manages to mold the substance of two literary eras into a single balanced response to experience. Without sacrificing his bitter moral outrage, without taking his eyes from the ugly wound at which he has relentlessly pointed for some thirty-five years, he brightens his sordid criminal Harlem with the wild comedy, eccentricity of character, and exotic low-life that he inherited from the celebratory black writers of the twenties. The characters who crowd the pages of the detective stories are shockingly appropriate composites of Bigger Thomas and the lovable picaroons who wander in and out of Langston Hughes's tales of Jesse B. Semple. They are at once depraved and funny, grotesque and amiable, absurd and pragmatic, agonized and witty.

The Harlem Domestic novels (with the exception of the last) were first published in French translation in Gallimard's "Série Noire." The first, "For Love of Imabelle," appeared in 1958 and was followed (in order of composition) by "The Real Cool Killers," "The Crazy Kill," "The Big Gold Dream," "All Shot Up," "The Heat's On," "Cotton Comes to Harlem," and "Blind Man with a Pistol" (1969). Read as a chronologically ordered unit, the series offers a brief, imaginative history of the changing social and psychological orientation of black Americans during two explosive decades. It also shows how Himes has developed, both as an artist and as a man. Such simple inconsistencies as those in the characters of Coffin Ed and Grave Digger, who in the first book "took their tribute, like all real cops, from the established underworld catering to the essential needs of the people," but in the last "hadn't taken a dime in bribes," point to the values by which Himes refocused his vision as his stories grew.

While the first of the Harlem Domestic novels does roar with the frighteningly comic violence, grotesque characterization, and breathtaking "chase" sequences that inform the others, it is a detective story not yet fully realized. Himes's imagination is clearly engaged by the brutal action on which the later tales will depend, but "For Love of Imabelle" still draws its authority primarily from a naturalistic analysis of the invisible pressures that drive and control innocent black lives. He permits himself such images as that which describes Harlem's "Valley":

> . . . waves of gray rooftops distort the perspective like the surface of a sea. Below the surface, in the murky waters of fetid tenements, a city of black people who are convulsed in desperate living, like the voracious churning of millions of hungry cannibal fish. Blind mouths eating their own guts. Stick in a hand and draw back a nub.

The aggressive naturalism of the image, the association of social conditions with malevolent natural forces, would be digressive in the subsequent tales, which can spare no time for analysis.

But essentially "For Love of Imabelle" is not a true detective story because it does not center upon the detectives. Coffin Ed and Grave Digger are important, but tangential characters—decent cops who are forced to be supremely tough by the unspeakable social context in which they work. Rather than the heroic figures they will become, they are themselves victims of an oppressive environment, cynical men seeking a basis for logical action in a brutally irrational world. Their extreme limitations are illustrated by the important waterfront scene in which a combination of accidents, mistaken identities, explosive human emotions, and simple darkness permits a cheap hoodlum the opportunity to throw acid into Coffin Ed's eyes. Blinded, thrashing about in agony, Coffin Ed knocks Grave Digger out with his pistol, and their prisoners escape. "For Love of Imabelle" has its own power and excellence, but it is, finally, less a detective story than a naturalistic novel about criminal sporting-life in Harlem.

In the five succeeding novels, however, Himes develops fully the embryonic form that we recognize in "For Love of Imabelle." He tells *Amistad*'s John A. Williams that these stories grow naturally out of the experience of being black in America, and he argues that the detective novel is a native American genre which, for black people, isolates the most pertinent depravity of American life. Claiming only to have borrowed an ultimately appropriate mode already defined by its culture, Himes says this about his detective fiction:

It's a form, you know, and it's a particularly American form. My French editor says, the Americans have a style of writing detective stories that no one has been able to imitate. . . . There's no reason why the black American, who is also an American, like all other Americans, and brought up in this sphere of violence which is the main sphere of American detective stories, there's no reason why he shouldn't write them. It's just plain and simple violence in narrative form. . . .

. . . no one understands violence or experiences violence like the American civilians do. The only other people in the white community who are violent enough for it are the armed forces . . . But of course they don't write about it. . . .

American violence is public life, it's a public way of life, it became a form, a detective story form. . . . The detective story originally in the plain narrative form—straightforward violence—is an American product. So I haven't created anything whatsoever; I just made the faces black, that's all.

We may be politely skeptical about Himes's disclaimer of originality and still recognize in his statement a confirmation of Edward Margolies' shrewd observation "that the kind of detective fiction he chose to write—implying, as it does, the comic, the violent, and above all the absurd—exactly suited his vision. In a peculiar fashion, for Himes the genre *is* the message."

What we have, then, is a literature of violence, growing naturally out of a particular place and time, and formed, not by self-conscious artistry, but by a more organic esthetic that permits the laws of a specific way of life to find their own expression. The value of this literature is not in the form itself, but in the unique experience that produced it, and it is important to insist upon the specificity of Himes's method. Under his hand, "it could only happen in America" (in this case, only in Harlem) becomes more than a truism. It is a structural principle as well. Only LeRoi Jones, that I know of, has taken the detective fiction seriously enough to recognize the significance of Himes's peculiar brand of regionalism. In his contribution to Herbert Hill's "Anger and Beyond," Jones writes:

It's all there, even to the Raymond Chandler-Dashiell Hammett genre of the detective novel, in Chester Himes' *All Shot Up* or *The Crazy Kill* or *The Real Cool Killers*, which are much more interesting, not only in regard to plot but also in terms of "place," a place wherein such a plot can find a natural existence. So that the Negro writer finally doesn't have to think about his "roots" even literarily, as being subject to some kind of derogatory statement—one has only to read the literature.

Whatever we are to say, however, about their origins or the responsibility of their creator for their form, the five novels Himes wrote between

1958 and 1961 are classic detective stories. Each poses a problem, or a series of problems, usually expressed in hideous physical violence, which extends its corruption into personal and communal life, and threatens the always precarious balance by which individuals survive in Harlem. Each network of dangerous mysteries is explained by a single discovery of guilt, which restores that balance and redefines the worth of those characters with whom we sympathize. The discovery, of course, is made by Grave Digger and Coffin Ed, the heroic figures who embody all the attributes of the traditional literary detective. Opposed by violence and unreason, they struggle courageously to uncover truth; trapped in a hopelessly venal institution, they remain incorruptibly honest; burdened with a body of law ludicrously inappropriate to the conditions of Harlem life, they are lonely dispensers of justice. They implement most of their solutions outside the law; many of their methods defy it. The responsibilities and dangers involved in the search for decency rest upon them personally rather than upon the institutional apparatus which supposedly protects them.

But Grave Digger and Coffin Ed are more than familiar literary heroes; their cultural antecedents ultimately give them the moral authority they exercise. Simply enough, they are the "bad niggers" of Black folklore. They are Nat Turners or Stackalees brought up to date and moved to the city, contemporary avatars of one of the stubbornly pervasive motifs in Black American culture. Like their less sophisticated ancestors, they are aggressively courageous and utterly indifferent to physical danger, willing to submit without complaint to the risk of the same ruthless violence by which they express their own naked force of will. The raw personal power with which the "bad nigger" defies his world has traditionally been celebrated in hyperbole, and there is a (never completely formalized) refrain running through the Harlem Domestic series that rings with unmistakable cultural reference:

> Coffin Ed had killed a man for breaking wind. Grave Digger had shot both eyes out of a man who was holding a loaded automatic. The story was in Harlem that these two black detectives would kill a dead man in his coffin if he so much as moved.

These awesome detectives do not always limit their violence to the guilty—they are, in fact, distressingly quick to beat on almost any black head they encounter—and like all "bad niggers" they may seem at first glance improbable (or undesirable) models for humanity. But the "bad nigger" is an emotionally projected rather than a socially functional figure; he is valuable as a symbol of defiance, strength, and masculinity to a community that has been forced to learn, or at least to sham, weakness and compliance. As "bad niggers" Coffin Ed and Grave Digger are part of the continuing evolution of a black hero, and are thus studies in cultural lore rather than examples of individual character. In the Harlem series they lay all of their traditional qualifications on the line in a desperate fight against the crimes that endanger the integrity, even the collective sanity, of the black community.

And, for all the socially dubious behavior the detectives find necessary, the sense of community is strong in these novels. Himes remembers that he began them in a state of "pure homesickness" as expressions of an exiled memory of America, and he has made them alive with warm evocations of life lived in what is a surprisingly *domestic* Harlem after all. Each story, for example, examines one or more of the peculiar "institutions" through which the criminal activity of Harlem is carried on. At times these oblique social commentaries are morbidly bitter; more often they are softened by at least a hint of fondness. In "The Real Cool Killers" the "institution" is the street gang; in "The Crazy Kill" it is professional gambling. "The Big Gold Dream" looks at both evangelistic Christianity (which, for Himes, is always a racket) and the numbers. "All Shot Up" moves back and forth between politics and Harlem's homosexual subculture, and "The Heat's On," by far the harshest and most grotesque of the series, deals with the heroin trade. None of these "institutions" are used simply as background; they are explained in minute detail, often through portraits of the individual personalities they have helped to shape, and information about them is often offered as much for its own sake as to meet exigencies of plot.

Himes does not depict only the criminal life in his cumulative panorama of Harlem, however; he also presents the less sensational aspects of the place, details of its special patterns of day-to-day life, with an intimacy that can make them either attractive or disgusting. He never tires of elaborate topographical descriptions of particular Harlem streets, the contents of store windows, the larger geography of the area. Famous Harlem landmarks—the Apollo Theater, Small's Paradise, the National Memorial African Book Store—are repeatedly described, both as geographical references and as settings for the action. The graffiti and stenches of slum tenements, the sounds of bars and jazz joints, the oppressive atmosphere of the pool-room and the prison: all add texture and density to the massive violence that moves this extra-legal (or sub-legal) Harlem. Himes's creative memory seems especially excited by the tastes he has left behind in America; the soul-food restaurant and the rich peculiarities of Afro-American cooking recur in sensual images of excess. And finally, of course, there are the street-scenes, the unending parades of Harlem life:

> It was eleven o'clock Sunday morning, and the good colored people of Harlem were on their way to church.
>
> It was a gloomy, overcast day, miserable enough to make the most hardened sinner think twice about the hot, sunshiny streets of heaven before turning over and going back to sleep.
>
> Grave Digger and Coffin Ed looked them over indifferently as they drove toward Harlem hospital. A typical Sunday morning sight, come sun or come rain.
>
> Old white-haired sisters bundled up like bales of cotton against the bitter cold;

their equally white-haired men, stumbling along in oversize galoshes like the last herd of Uncle Toms, toddling the last mile toward salvation on half-frozen feet.

Middle-aged couples and their broods, products of the postwar generation, the prosperous generation, looking sanctimonious in their good warm clothes, going to praise the Lord for the white folks' blessings.

Young men who hadn't yet made it, dressed in light-weight suits and topcoats sold by color instead of quality or weight in the credit stores, with enough brown wrapping paper underneath their pastel shirts to keep them warm, laughing at the strange words of God and making like Solomon at the pretty brownskin girls.

Young women who were sure as hell going to make it or drop dead in the attempt, ashy with cold, clad in the unbelievable colors of cheap American dyes, some at that very moment catching the pneumonia which would take them before that God they were on their way to worship.

Despite its irony and sadness, this processional image is offered with the almost tender affection characteristic of much of Himes's evocation of Harlem culture, and it points to one of the subordinate purposes of his series: to envision a particular place at a particular moment of history—its customs, speech, topography, occupations, even its food—and record it for posterity.

Himes never becomes sentimental about Harlem; he permits himself no unrelieved nostalgia. The most prominent characteristics of the community that he chronicles are fear and brutality. His Harlem is an isolated world motivated and ordered by violence. The novels themselves are in a sense his violent assaults upon his reader. Himes is a fighter, a sort of literary Muhammad Ali (or, perhaps more accurately, Jack Johnson), and he writes with the same intense ferocity with which he might knock a man down. As he told John A. Williams—and the remark can be applied to the method as well as the theme of his series—"After all, Americans live by violence, and violence achieves—regardless of what anyone says, regardless of the distaste of the white community—its own ends." This emphasis on violence as a means—a revolutionary tactic, a method of survival, a mode of communication—helps to explain the troubling brutality with which the profoundly decent Coffin Ed and Grave Digger conduct their investigations. It is the only means at their disposal. They work within a system as closed as those electrical circuits that operate from a power-source since removed from the circuit itself—the works are set going but the first mover is withdrawn. Each problem the detectives face has its origin in the forbidden white city that surrounds Harlem. When Coffin Ed and Grave Digger confront criminal disorder they are thus limited to symptoms; the actual malfunction is inaccessible. Harlem problems are violent; they can be fought locally, and the delicate balance of community life sustained, only by an even more uninhibited violence. It is one of the brilliant ironies of the Harlem Domestic stories that the detective-heroes can express their genuine love for their people, their altruistic hopes for communal peace and decency, only through the crude brutality that has become their bitter way of life.

Himes's descriptions of physical violence itself are exquisitely detailed and deliberately repulsive. He wants to shove his reader's nose into them, and he has something more than mere education or social protest in mind. The violent scenes in the detective novels develop their own systems of imagery and their own concrete "meaning." Ultimately, they are the experiential base on which the fiction rests. Neither Himes nor his characters interpret the action they create—the violence is itself the message—but it is unlikely that recurring similarities of literary terrorism, such as those that define two typically grim scenes from "All Shot Up," are entirely coincidental.

The first of these exemplary scenes describes the death of a tire thief whom Grave Digger and Coffin Ed are pursuing because he has witnessed a murder that is the key to a complicated network of criminal activity. Ignorant of their intentions, however, the thief clings desperately to his instinctive habit of avoiding the police at all costs. He is riding a motorcycle, and as he leads the detectives through the crowded Harlem streets, he plans to squeeze through a narrow break in the traffic with his smaller vehicle, and leave his pursuers behind a truck. But the delicate timing of his maneuver is upset when Coffin Ed shoots out one of the truck's tires:

> He [the tire thief] was pulling up fast behind the car carrying sheet metal when the tire burst and the driver tamped his brakes. He wheeled sharply to the left, but not quickly enough.
>
> The three thin sheets of stainless steel, six feet in width, with red flags flying from both corners, formed a blade less than a quarter of an inch thick. This blade caught the rider above his woolen-lined jacket, on the exposed part of his neck, which was stretched and taut from his physical exertion, as the motorcycle went underneath. He was hitting more than fifty-five miles an hour, and the blade severed his head from his body as though he had been guillotined.
>
> His head rolled halfway up the sheets of metal while his body kept astride the seat and his hands gripped the handlebars. A stream of blood spurted from his severed jugular, but his body completed the maneuver which his head had ordered and went past the truck as planned.
>
> The truck driver glanced from his window to watch the passing truck as he kept braking to a stop. But instead he saw a man without a head passing on a motorcycle with a sidecar and a stream of steaming blood flowing back in the wind.

Himes continues to describe the progress of his grotesque apparition along the streets and on the sidewalks until the corpse finally goes limp, and the motorcycle comes to rest against the grating of a credit jewelry store.

A similarly macabre sequence occurs later in "All Shot Up" when Big Six and George Drake, two sympathetic racketeers, are assigned to protect Casper Holmes as he leaves Harlem Hospital. Holmes is a familiar type: a crooked, a homosexually inclined, but a powerful Harlem politician, who because of the intricate system of checks and balances that keeps Harlem from exploding altogether, is arrogantly beyond the law. After arranging to have his campaign funds stolen and double-crossing his fellow thieves, he is attempting to escape into a private stronghold. As part of his erstwhile accomplices' plan to kidnap Holmes and recover the money, Big Six is lured from his car by an apparently drunken white man who urinates on a fender and spits out a racial insult:

> . . . Big Six reached out a hand to clutch the drunk by the shoulder.
>
> The drunk swung a long arc with his right hand, which he had held out of sight, and plunged the blade of a hunting knife through Big Six's head. It went in above the left temple, and two inches of the point came out on a direct line above the right temple. Big Six went deaf, dumb, and blind, but not unconscious. He teetered slightly and groped about aimlessly like an old blind man.

The narrative turns for a moment to the murder of George Drake, then returns to Big Six as he stumbles through the streets:

> Big Six kept on slowly, lost to the world. "George!" he was calling silently in the rational part of his mind. "George. The mother-raper stuck me."
>
> He started across Seventh Avenue. Snow was banked against the curb, and his foot plowed into the snow bank. He slipped but somehow managed not to fall. He got into the traffic lane. He stepped in front of a fast-moving car. Brakes shrieked.
>
> "Drunken idiot!" the driver cried. Then he saw the knife sticking from Big Six's head.
>
> He jumped from his car, ran forward and took Big Six gently by the arm.
>
> "My God in heaven," he said.
>
> He was a young colored doctor doing his internship in Brooklyn Hospital. They had had a case similar to that a year ago; the other victim had been a colored man, also. The only way to save him was to leave the knife in the wound.

Both of these episodes, however sensationalistic they may be, achieve their horrible intensity by concentrating on the continued function of bodies that have lost their essential consciousness, their essential humanity. They are grim parodies of the "mindless" life. The metaphorical quality of violence, the statement about a generalized cultural lobotomy, that such a paraphrase suggests, however, is only implicit; Himes never offers it as an intellectualized "meaning." We can push Himes's suggestion further by noticing similar patterns in the knifings of Big Six and of Leila, Holmes's wife, who later in "All Shot Up" is stabbed by the same white thug. Coffin Ed and Grave Digger discover her moaning softly, clutching the handle of the knife that has been plunged into her stomach, and "Grave Digger knelt down, pulled her hands away gently and handcuffed them behind her back. 'You can't pull it out,' he said. 'That would only kill you.' " It is as if Himes were saying that his characters, that black Americans in general, are forced to live with knives thrust into the sensitive areas of their bodies: if the blade is left in, it means blindness, impotence, helplessness, and above all pain; if the blade is removed, it is death. But Himes does not say this—at least not explicitly. Neither are these episodes expressions of a consistent thematic development that can be abstracted and analyzed. Rather, they are in effect visual analogues—small, carefully framed pictures which "mean" in and for themselves, but which also represent the "meaning" of "All Shot Up" as a whole.

Perhaps Himes's iconographic method can be seen more clearly in one of the spectacular scenes near the end of "Cotton Comes to Harlem." Grave Digger and Coffin Ed have unearthed two vicious mobsters hiding in a church, and engage them in a gun duel. Because they anticipated fighting in darkness, the detectives had loaded their pistols with tracer bullets, and everything they hit bursts into flame. Himes takes full advantage of his juxtaposition between the sacred objects in the church and the burning criminals, and the passage ends thus:

> Upstairs in the church, light from the burning gunman on the floor lit up the figure of the gunman with his head on fire crouched behind the end of a bench ahead.
>
> On the other side of the church Coffin Ed was standing with his pistol leveled, shouting, "Come out, mother-raper, and die like a man."
>
> Grave Digger took careful aim between the legs of the benches at the only part of the gunman that was visible and shot him through the stomach. The gunman emitted an eerie howl of pain, like a mortally wounded beast, and stood up with his .45 spewing slugs in a blind stream. The screaming had risen to an unearthly pitch, filling the mouths of the detectives with the taste of bile. Coffin Ed shot him in the vicinity of the heart and his clothes caught fire. The screaming ceased abruptly as the gunman slumped across the bench in a kneeling posture, as though praying in fire.

The scene offers an excellent capsulization of Himes's technique. Out of clichéd man's-magazine material, without diluting the fast narrative violence that is his "form," Himes has created a picture that Bosch might have painted of a ragingly moral world.

Despite such compressed flashes of imagistic brilliance, however, "Cotton Comes to Harlem" does not employ the techniques I have been describing with the consistency of the earlier stories. It and "Blind Man with a Pistol," the most recent Harlem Domestic novels, seem to be experiments, and may indicate that Himes is growing restless under the strict limitations of the detective format. In any case, he apparently is attempting to adapt his narratives to an increasingly ambitious symbolic and analytic purpose. His success is at best relative. As Himes himself has said, violence *is* its own form, and the detective story is formulaic and fixed; it brooks no tampering. Once the crisp, efficient rationale, the uninterrupted attention to plot demanded by a search for a single truth is violated, the form collapses into its component clichés and the unity of the work is lost. The "larger" concerns of "Cotton Comes to Harlem" and "Blind Man with a Pistol" (which, significantly, extend criminal investigation into the amorphous gray area beyond Harlem) are admirable in themselves, but they simply blunt the sharp edge of Himes's technique and adulterate the "message" of his genre.

"Cotton Comes to Harlem" parallels the story of the chase after Deke O'Malley, the crooked organizer of a "Back-to-Africa" movement, with a symbolic confrontation of black (the Harlem community in general) and white (an Alabama Colonel with an ideological mission to return the "Nigra" to the cotton-fields). The symbolic apparatus is broadly comic and refreshingly unpretentious, but it defies the fragile system of probabilities on which "belief" in the detective story is based. There is too much explicit racial commentary, too much protest, too much satire to be absorbed by what is fundamentally an anti-intellectual genre. The narrative of Colonel Calhoun and his Back-to-the-Southland movement would itself be irrevocably damaging to the integrity of a detective novel. Not only is the Colonel a preposterously "literary" anachronism in modern Harlem, he is also the victim of implausible plot devices. In one of the primary "mysteries" of the narrative, he brings a symbolic bale of cotton to New York in order to hide in it the money he steals from the Back-to-Africa organization. Himes's attempts to weld together two unlike materials are sometimes hilariously successful, but the seams show, and, finally, the fusion does not hold.

"Blind Man with a Pistol," in some ways the most ambitious novel in the Harlem Domestic series, displays a further disintegration of the detective form. In fact, parts of it read like self-parody. The deterioration of narrative logic is deliberate in this impressively experimental novel; here, the *failure* of the genre is the message. There are several "plots" in "Blind Man with a Pistol"–two dealing with wildly grotesque murder, one with an apparently coincidental series of riots–and they are confusingly juxtaposed, perhaps in order to disturb our complacent sense of chronology. None of the plots go anywhere. Because of institutional pressures the murders are left unsolved; Coffin Ed and Grave Digger are forbidden to follow a path of investigation which would inevitably lead to powerful whites. As the narratives of detective action run down unresolved, the frustrations of the novel explode in a frantically culminative riot, symbolizing the inflammatory emotion the two detectives had once been able to suppress, but which, now released, threatens to destroy forever the delicate balance of life they had painfully sustained. The novel ends with the parable of the blind man with a pistol who, firing aimlessly at a fancied racial slur, touches off what is probably the same climactic riot, seen in another context. Certainly the statement that emerges from this maniacal collision of themes and movements is legitimate, and certainly it demands expression. But, again, it contradicts the faith in the ability of men to discover truth that is a basic precondition of the detective genre. The wide range of reference, the tortuous complexity of motivation inherent in Himes's attempt to bring racist white society explicitly into his novel simply cannot be contained within the limitations of his form.

So the Harlem Domestic series as it now exists ends on a note of decay and frustration. "Blind Man with a Pistol" might almost be considered a literary ruin. But the artist who broke his own detective form is still writing, and we may happily anticipate that he will turn his hand to some new form that will express his genius even more appropriately. One almost wishes that Himes would go backward–repeat himself, and turn out more of these profoundly exciting tales of crime and violence. Whether he does or not, we may be grateful for the substantial achievement he has already wrung from an improbable genre, and salute both the integrity and the force of the imagination that conceived it. If the vehicle itself is small, Himes's accomplishments within it are not, and the residual portrait left by these books—of Coffin Ed and Grave Digger outlined against the dull, lurid light of a criminal city—is one of the compelling images of our time.

Elmer Pry

LEW ARCHER'S "MORAL LANDSCAPE"

"Who is ever quite without his landscape?" asks W. H. Auden in his 1937 poem, "Detective Story," and Auden's readers understand that the "landscape" metaphor throughout his poetry has a fixed meaning. The title of his earlier poem, "*Paysage Moralisé*" (1936), particularizes his meaning of the term: Auden's reference *is* to the "moral landscape," to the painting of an individual life which points out the shadowed patches wherein hidden sins reside. And while poet Auden examines the appeal of the detective tale as it works upon the reader's own dark sense of guilt, the novelist Ross Macdonald conjures up fictions in which the hero himself is a moral agent observing, reporting, and explaining the nexus between the evil and its society in his California moral landscape.

The novelist himself is fully aware of his panorama as "moral landscape." Detective hero Lew Archer makes it perfectly clear in a descriptive summary report in *The Wycherly Woman* (1961):

> A million people live between the Bay and the ridge, in grubby tracts built on fills, in junior-executive ranchhouse developments, in senior-executive mansions, in Hillsborough palaces. I'd had some cases on the Peninsula: violence and passional crime are as much a part of the *moral landscape* [my emphasis] as P.T.A. and Young Republican meetings and traffic accidents. (p49)

Archer is both observer/narrator and a representative citizen of his California milieu. He is middle-aged, divorced, usually companionless, of moderate income and average physical attractiveness; in short, he is all that we have come not to expect of our detective heroes. There are neither Dr. Watsons nor Archie Goodwins, few stereotyped damsels in distress, generally no wrongly-accused innocents. Archer's saving grace, then, as a detective hero, is his strength as a moral agent. Not only, as he reminds us in *The Way Some People Die* (1951), does he regularly transfer his gun from shoulder to holster to pocket in order to lean his "moral

Reprinted from THE ARMCHAIR DETECTIVE, 8:2, with the permission of the editor.

weight on it" (p208), but also, even more importantly, his vision is clear, his judgment sagacious, his awareness of himself and his society incessant and substantive. And his ultimate assessment of the moral landscape seems to be that California had the promise of Eden; that a perversion of values, especially religious values, has precluded the possibility of Paradise; and that the culprit temptation is neither serpent nor Satan, but a complex convergence of Hollywood posturing, of a confusion between love and sex, and of twentieth-century technology.

The potential Paradise is sometimes implicit, more often implied in Archer's narrations. Note the idyllic picture drawn in the opening paragraph of *The Wycherly Woman*:

> Coming over the pass you can see the whole valley spread out below. On a clear morning, when it lies broad and colored under a white sky, with the mountains standing far back on either side, you can imagine it's the promised land. (p1)

Or in the opening lines of *The Instant Enemy* (1968):

> There was a light early morning traffic on Sepulveda. As I drove over the low pass, the sun came up glaring behind the blue crags on the far side of the valley. For a minute or two, before regular day set in, everything looked fresh and new and awesome as creation (p3).

So often, however, it is not direct statement, but the implication of art which draws attention to the lost paradise. Archer's narrative consistently and insistently patterns images of war, of death, and of decay, juxtaposing them with the physical California and its people. Beauty which might be cause for celebration becomes a surrealistic nightmare. For example, in *The Underground Man* (1971), one of Macdonald's finest novels, there are avocado trees in an orchard which might be the subject of a pastoral, but Archer notes that the "fruit hung down from their branches like green hand grenades" (p31); an athletic field near a school—not commonly an ominous threat—here resembles "a staging area just back of the lines in a major battle" (p128); and the handwriting in an old family manuscript "straggles across the lined yellow page like a defeated army" (p147). Thus the most significant Edenic qualities—innocence, beauty in nature, play and leisure, style—are all perverted in the California gardens.

Well, what exactly has happened? Why is Lew Archer's world not a paradise? What are the causes for the violence, for the absence of love and sentiment, for the disturbing sense of futility and danger? In *The Far Side of the Dollar* (1965), Archer suggests diagnosing the illness by examining a prominent symptom: "Somebody with an eye for detail should make a study of automobile graveyards . . . the way they study the ruins and potsherds of vanished civilizations. It could provide a clue as to why our civilization is vanishing" (p43). And perhaps some student of American culture may want to do that sort of research, but for the student of literature, a return to the texts themselves must provide the answers. Fortunately, Ross Macdonald does give us some alternatives to open air analysis of Hudson hubcaps and Bugatti bumpers.

We might, for example, listen to Joseph Tobias, the black student and lifeguard in *The Barbarous Coast*, a 1956 novel. Tobias blames the "big corporations" and Eisenhower's "businessmen's administration," arguing that "Mass production and mass marketing do make for some social benefits, but sheer size tends to militate against the human element. We've reached the point where we should count the human cost" (p470). Archer himself regularly criticizes that idea of progress, of big money, big houses, industrial activity, and swiftly-paced living. In *The Doomsters* (1958), fast living damages the body of society, as "highway traffic thrummed invisibly like a damaged artery" (p23), and later, Archer philosophizes that money may indeed be the root of all evil, for "a house could make people hate each other. A house, or the money it stood for, or the cannibalistic family hungers it symbolized" (p45). And in *Sleeping Beauty* (1973), industry, specifically the oil industry, is condemned by particularizing, when Archer cannot immediately recognize the western grebe carried from the water because it is "so fouled with oil" (p4), and then more broadly attacked through metaphor:

> It lay on the blue water off Pacific Point in a free-form slick that seemed miles wide and many miles long. An offshore oil pattern stood up out of its windward end like the metal handle of a dagger that had stabbed the world and made it spill black blood (p3).

The mentally disturbed Isobel Graff of *The Barbarous Coast* perhaps summarizes most effectively Macdonald's condemnation of the modern pace: "Miracles of modern science. From a greasy spoon in Newark to wealth and decadence in one easy generation. It's the new accelerated pace, with automation" (p456).

Other folk Archer encounters are less inclined to blame an anonymous Big Brother or industrial complex, and more willing to assume personal responsibility for their own mistakes. Carl Trevor, for example, is the admitted murderer in *The Wycherly Woman*, but he also has enough insight to recognize and analyze his motivations: "It grew on me like a disease–the realization that I'd had the one thing worth having. A little warmth and companionship in the void. I'd had it and given it up, in favor of security, I suppose you'd call it. Security. The great American substitute for love" (p275). Valuing security before love is common to the wealthy citizens who populate Archer's landscape, but few are able to recognize their own faults. More are akin to the self-deluded Mrs. Snow, the ironically-named murderess in *The Underground Man*; her moral villainy has its allegorical physical analogues, especially when she stares in "blank apprehension like a blind woman" (p59), since physical blindness is archetypally a sign of moral blindness.

But Archer is quick to indicate that neither greed nor self-delusion can bear the whole blame for society's ills. In *The Moving Target* (1949), he says, "You can't blame money for what it does to people. The evil is in the people, and money is the peg they hang it on. They go wild for money when they've lost their other values" (p182). And if Archer is not himself self-deluded about his own moral biases, he is at least aware that neither has he satisfactorily resolved his own Trevor-like problems: "The problem was to love people, try to serve them, without wanting anything from them. I was a long way from solving that one" (p434, *The Barbarous Coast*). So Lew Archer, more moral agent than secret agent or private eye, makes his ultimate diagnosis of the germ which enters the body of society and produces such chaotic and violent symptoms: a perverse religiosity is the culprit. I do not mean to imply that Lew Archer is himself religious, for he is not; nor does he argue that either his characters or his readers ought to become more religious and church-going. Rather he argues, often metaphorically, that the moral landscape has been overrun by religious rituals and icons and shamans in inappropriate contexts.

Who are the deities in Archer's world? Most often, they are the moneyed classes, the leaders of industry. Observe one of the followers, Clarence Bassett, manager of the exclusive Channel Club at Malibu Beach; Archer reports: "His voice took on a religious coloring whenever he mentioned the members. They might have belonged to a higher race, supermen or avenging angels" (p357). And well he might tremble in awe, for characters like Simon Graff carry themselves as gods, condemning those who disobey the financial lord's commandments to the satanic employees, Leroy Frost and Theodore Marfeld. Virtually every Lew Archer tale has its wealthy god-figure: the head-of-family in *The Underground Man* is long since deceased; but like Colonel Sartoris in Faulkner's novel or Pyncheon in Hawthorne's *House of the Seven Gables*, Robert Driscoll Falconer continues to be the center of the family's attention. After all, as Elizabeth Falconer Broadhurst's manuscript of the family history tells us, the founder of the family fortune had been "a god come down to earth in human guise" (p147).

There are other human beings playing unnatural religious roles: Jerry Kilpatrick, one of the many lost youth rambling across Ross Macdonald's pages, has an enormous head, "like a papier-mache saint's head on a stick" (p76); and his father, Brian, is "a spoiled priest in hiding" (p89). Complementing the human spiritual perversions are the products of modern technology: the "familiar spirit" (p83) for the age is the portable radio, spreading its gospel with the news of violent deaths, poisonous oil spills, and rampaging fires; the mornings begin not with traditional masses, but with services offered by delivery men. Archer reports, "It was nearly eight by my watch, and delivery trucks were honking their matins" (*Way Some People Die*, p216). Telephones, televisons–so many miracles of modern science and technology come under attack as they incorporate religion into their services. Even the contemporary circular king-size bed, with its nine foot diameter, is, to Archer's sensitive probing, a "hopeful altar(s) to old gods" (p557, *Black Money*).

The icons of the twentieth-century Californian's renegade religion are legion in Lew Archer's reports; we shall make it sufficient here to examine but two further examples, in somewhat greater detail. In *The Underground Man*, Mrs. Snow has *apparently* been shielding a guilty man, her imbecilic son, Fritz. After shattering a teacup, she gathers the pieces as if the cup had been "a religious object," perhaps some relic of her life with Fritz, and she is, at the same time, "a faded vestal virgin guarding a shrine" (p63). Well, what sort of a shrine is she guarding? She has been protecting her son, Fritz; Fritz is a nickname for Frederick, and the name Frederick itself means "Abounding in Peace," evidently suggesting Christ. And the irony in Archer's "shrine" becomes clear: modern religiosity's Christ is imbecilic because his worshippers–people like Clarence Bassett, others like Mrs. Snow–make perverse, confused adorations; if we deify Simon Graff (or should that be read as Simony Graft?) or Fritz Snow, then we are not only murderers or fictional characters in detective novels–we are also slayers of morality, maniacal beasts ravaging the moral landscape.

In an earlier novel, *Black Money* (1966), Lew Archer's job involves finding a girl named Kitty; to that end, he interviews the girl's mother, Mrs. Sekjar, at her home. When he arrives, the television set is alive with an afternoon soap-opera.

> Mrs. Sekjar switched it off. On top of the television set were a large Bible and one of those glass balls that you shake to make a snowstorm. The pictures on the walls were all religious, and there were so many of them that they suggested a line of defense against the world (p569).

The juxtaposition of the television, the Bible, and the innocuous snowstorm seems innocent enough, and the religious barrier on the walls properly characterizes the house's only resident. But there are deeper implications here; the presentation is too directly suggestive to allow us to ignore them. The television set, like the radio, is one of those "familiar spirits" already considered; the unopened Bible is also appropriate to Archer's Southern California–better to read an old family manuscript, as the Broadhurst clan does, to discover the truths about the old family gods; the third member of the new Holy Trinity, however, requires some further explanation. The glass ball is a cultural artifact, one of those toys of modern industry, and as such, its presence is contextually appropriate in the novel. But if its presence is natural in that sense, it is unnatural in another, and there is surely a relationship between the naming of Mrs. Snow in *The Underground Man* and the bauble on Mrs. Sekjar's television set here. Our physical landscape, remember, is Southern California, not a setting hospitable to snow. Mrs. Snow was, of course, both unnatural and immoral, and the fantasy snowstorm in this triumvirate, an artificial work of nature, a product of modern technology, is just as unnatural; it is unable to play any role assigned to it as part of the Trinity. And the typical Lew Archer war image extends the irony: the pictures are indeed a "line of defense" for Mrs. Sekjar, protecting her abherrant adoration within from a moral landscape without which is, ironically, just as aberrant.

Thus Lew Archer's world, for all its paradisiacal potential, is clearly not an Eden populated by Adams and Eves; it is occasionally, indeed, a purgatory or hell instead. In *The Way Some People Die*, Archer drives with a sickly villain named Mosquito from San Francisco to Half Moon Bay in search of another from California's low-life, a man known as "Speed."

> We crept on under the smothering gray sky, through the gray cloud-drowned hills. The sun and the other stars had burned out long ago, and Mosquito and I were journeying for our sins through a purgatory of gray space (p301).

Or, if Archer's world is not the garden, it is sometimes the desert. At the Scorpion Club, the boss, Mr. Davis, "moved warily . . . as if his desert-colored office was actual desert, with rattlesnakes under the rug" (*Black Money*, p576). There are not, however, many serpents slithering through Archer's landscapes; there are not even many satan figures. Where, then, is the temptress? How are villains enticed to sin, and the common folk led unto an industrial-technological religion?

The answer is multifarious. Archer clearly implies that Hollywood's influence is one source; perhaps no image so persistently pervades the Archer novels as that of the theatrical mask. In *The Underground Man*, for example, we learn that the rigidly-programmed Kilpatrick family "had been a lonely trio, living like actors on a Hollywood set" (p107); that Martha Crandall is "an actress forbidden to step out through the proscenium into the welter of reality" (p221); that the murdered Al Sweetner, caught in the violent charades of his time and place, grins up in death "like a magician who had pulled off the ultimate trick" (p94); and that Jean Broadhurst, whose son has been kidnapped and husband murdered, has "a harlequin aspect, like a sad clown caught on a poor street under a smoky sky" (p61), and that she is "a lost and widowed Columbine" (p136), a tragicomic figure in a commedia dell'arte. One may choose, of course, to explain the theatre metaphor by reference to Ross Macdonald's statement in his "Foreword" to the *Archer at Large* omnibus; there he argues that the "lords of the military-industrial-academic complex may be as subject to tragic flaws as Shakespeare's kings." He may, therefore, be using the drama images to underscore the sense of tragic drama in his fictions. But the theatre and its favorite son, the television set, which so encourage posturing and artificiality, may well also be the serpent, the embodied Satan creating the hell which is Lew Archer's California landscape.

A second significant force in Archer's world is the blurred union of love and sex. So often an illicit sexual relationship or love in the past becomes the reason for murder in the present: in *The Wycherly Woman*, Carl Trevor's long love affair with Catherine Wycherly, and the twenty-one year old daughter, Phoebe, who thinks Trevor is her uncle, result in Trevor's murder of Catherine; the motive for murder, as it so often is in Ross Macdonald's novels, is love–Trevor loves his daughter, and doesn't want Catherine to tell her that she is illegitimate. In *Sleeping Beauty*, Marian Lennox killed a woman because her seagoing husband spent his last night ashore with the mistress rather than the wife. And, to cite but one more of the many available examples, Mrs. Snow in *The Underground Man*, murdered Leo Broadhurst two decades earlier because, in her words, "he deserved to die. He was a wicked man, a cheat and a fornicator. He got Marty Nickerson pregnant and let my boy take the blame" (p272). Her love for her son and an unsanctioned sexual relationship conjoin to drive her to murder. Perhaps these two deterministic forces, the theatre and sex, are most distinctly propounded by an unnamed visitor at Simon Graff's huge party, who parodies Marx by arguing that "Sex and television are the opium of the people" (p450).

Of course, not all of the characters peopling Archer's moral landscape are either villainous or amoral and insensitive. Archer himself, learning much perhaps because he sees that love itself is so often a motive for murder, may not be didactic persona, but he certainly admits regularly to his own moral idealism. In *The Goodbye Look* (1969), his "passion for justice" is suggested by another character:

> You have a secret passion for justice. Why don't you admit it?
> I have a secret passion for mercy [he responds]. . . . But justice is what keeps happening to people.

And people like Joseph Tobias (in *The Way Some People Die*) and Laurel Russo (in *Sleeping Beauty*) also live by rules which include integrity and honesty as chief commandments. Indeed, one character, Carl Hallman of *The Doomsters*, is a "positive saint," one who wanted to blend religion and modern science in a positive way by becoming what he called a "medical missionary" (p9).

But the "saints" are few, and in the end, when the curtain is drawn on Ross Macdonald's tragicomic scenes, the moral landscape is properly marked off and divided. The villains destroy themselves or are taken away, often like Mrs. Marburg of *The Instant Enemy*, facing a particular sort of hell. As Archer describes her, she "sat looking down . . . in the way I imagine the damned look down, with pity and terror only for themselves" (p239). The innocents, on the other hand, come to recognize the landscape, often trying to escape it. Mrs. Marjorie Fellows, the heavy-set and likeable woman who left her husband George in Toledo, very much regrets her second marriage: "I want to go back to Toledo, where people are nice. I always wanted to live in California but now that I've seen it, it's a hellish place. I've fallen among thieves, that's what I've done. Thieves and murderers and confidence men" (p292). And Archer alone is left as the moral agent observing, evaluating, and reporting on the landscape, as he concludes *The Instant Enemy*:

> I had a second slug to fortify my nerves. Then I got Mrs. Marburg's check out of the safe. I tore it into small pieces and tossed the yellow confetti out the window. It drifted down on the short hairs and the long hairs, the potheads and the acid heads, draft dodgers and dollar chasers, swingers and walking wounded, idiot saints, hard cases, foolish virgins.

All quotations are from Knopf editions of the novels or from Knopf omnibuses of Archer stories, and are cited in the paper by page number only.

Sam L. Grogg, Jr.

INTERVIEW WITH ROSS MACDONALD

G: What do you think of the critical attention which has been recently given to your work? Do you think you deserve it?

M: Yes. Although, I'm surprised by it. You don't always get what you deserve. A writer gets use to not having attention, to inattention. I did.

G: What's most important to you: critical attention or the fact that millions of people read your novels?

M: The second. But I like both. I'll tell you the truth, though, it's good for a writer to spend the greater part of his working life without getting too much attention. I think it's somewhat distracting. It's better just to do your work than be a writer with a capital "W." And I'm still trying to do that. I haven't let this new attention change my way of life at all. I'm living exactly the way I did twenty years ago. Except that I have more money.

G: Can you ever see yourself writing for the critics first and those millions second?

M: I wouldn't know how to write for the critics. All I really know is how to tell my own kind of story. I really wouldn't know how to do anything different.

G: Have you ever had any criticism that has really affected you adversely?

M: Well, my books were frequently dismissed by reviewers.

G: Do you think that was because they were "detective" novels rather than "novel" novels?

M: Partly that and partly the fact that they're in the "hard-boiled" vein.

Reprinted from the JOURNAL OF POPULAR CULTURE, VII:2.

That was regarded as in for a dig for a long time. Below the level of adult attention by some critics. And this was true, unfortunately, of some of the most powerful critics. By critics, I really mean "reviewers." The "critics" really have no part in this at all. And I was hurt by Raymond Chandler's dismissal of my work. But that's understandable, too. We're really quite different.

G: You mentioned the "hard-boiled" tradition. How has that tradition influenced you, and how have you tried to influence it?

M: Well, I think all writers who have any serious interest in writing start out with something that's been done before, a tradition if that's what you want to call it, and gradually make an attempt to infuse that tradition with their own ideas and attitudes. That's what I've been doing. In other words, I've been trying to mold the tradition my own way.

G: George Grella has pointed out that the "hard-boiled" detective novel is appropriate for reflecting American attitudes and values. Do you agree with this idea of appropriateness?

M: Yes. I think the American "hard-boiled" detective novel was invented to reflect American society, which is essentially an equalitarian society. Everything is in the process of change. Whereas, although it's true that things are changing in England and Europe, they are changing very slowly and, so to speak, against the grain. And that grain is represented by the English detective story which is highly formalistic and socially stratified.

G: But your novels, which deal with this "nouveau-riche" society of southern California, seem almost to represent a bridge between the "hard-boiled" and the "formal" detective novel traditions.

M: It's sort of inevitable that that should happen because I was brought up in Canada which is kind of a cultural bridge between England and the United States. I was raised not only on the American "hard-boiled" tradition, but also on the English tradition. There is, I think, in my work a melding of the two, to some extent. With emphasis on the American, though. Incidentally, in a new society where people are rich, they're inevitably "nouveau-riche" and to have a family that goes back three generations of known people or successful people constitutes almost being an aristocrat.

I have certain advantages from having been brought up in two cultures, Canadian and American. They're closely related but, nevertheless, they're different enough so it's like looking through binoculars as compared with looking through a telescope. Having not only studied literature and history, but taught them in Canada before I became an American writer, I can see American life in relation to another culture which I know equally well. I really know the anglo-Canadian culture more deeply and thoroughly than I do the American culture. The things you know best are what you learn between the ages of five and twenty-five. Of course, we write out of our experience. So, I think I can refer to myself as a North American novelist, although nearly all the action of my books takes place in the United States. There's an advantage in being different. You know that Canadian background is really an essential differentia of my books. It would be hard to point out how. For me to point it out. But I know that's the difference.

You can't understand one culture without having known another. This is true of all science and of all knowledge. There has to be a comparison possible. If you just know one culture, there's nothing to say about it, nothing to know about it. It's just there. You see, I am a scholar trained as a teacher in history, both ordinary history and intellectual history and, somehow or another, that background of historical knowledge and the full knowledge of another culture and of a native culture enables me to, I think, write more fully about the American culture. Which is mine by choice. You see, I'm really just in the same situation that Americans are in, only intensified. The American culture is still a development from the English culture, let's say European, though primarily from the English. Since I came from a place that was sort of a half-way point in the development from English to American, i.e., Canadian culture, it's a vantage point for understanding contemporary culture in America. That's why my books are, at the same time quite intimate in relation to American life, they're also somewhat distanced.

G: Space, this natural environment of Santa Barbara and southern California, seems quite important in your work. Why have you chosen this agrarian, natural setting for Archer to traverse?

M: It's the part that really interests me. Other people have done the city over and over again. You know, there's a certain advantage in getting out into the open a little more, where there's a little more dilution of people by nature and that sort of thing. I think this is the ideal mix, myself, for civilization. And I'm not alone in thinking that. I talked to Constantinos Doxiadis when he was here in Santa Barbara. He called attention to the fact that Santa Barbara was approximately the size and general shape of what he considered the ideal city, Periclean Athens. Same population. The fact that everything, downtown anyway, is within walking distance. The city's small enough so that everybody, so to speak, can get to know everybody else if he wants to. No high-rise pressing you down into the earth and cutting off the sky and the view. Doxiadis really said it was his conception, or corresponded to his conception of the ideal city.

G: There seems to be a slow-down, or calmness out here.

M: That's true, there is a slow-down, and an opening out. I mean you are exposed to space out here. You are not surrounded by people and buildings.

G: This area, Santa Barbara, is certainly almost an idyllic setting.

M: With a very high murder rate. We've got ten unsolved murders just along the beach in the last three years. Life in California does have a fairytale aspect. It seems unreal unless you get into the interior of it. Unless you really understand how people are living here, it looks like a dream. The fairytale aspect is that everything seems to be a delightful movie-like dream on the surface.

G: Nature and the landscape are a constant reference point in your Archer novels.

M: I just feel that man's connection with nature is indispensable to him. And a society or an individual literally goes insane if they lose touch entirely with natural rhythms and natural forces, both exterior and internal. And the two are in touch with each other. They speak back and forth to each other, external Nature and the inner nature of man. As Wordsworth said: "One impulse from a vernal wood can teach us more of man / of evil and of good / than all the sages can." Now that's an overstatement, but that's the sort of reference I'm going back to when I use Nature. And the destruction of Nature is a serious moral crime because it destroys man and his ability to live in the world.

G: That's why the offshore oil rigs and the recent oil spills must have affected you very deeply.

M: Well, (pause). It's been the most important external event in my life during the last five years. And I've written three articles and a book about it.

G: How do you write? What is the process behind a Macdonald novel?

M: I generally spend about six months preparing to write. I'll fill notebooks with ideas, plot developments, and so on. Generally, there will be several ideas for books going on simultaneously. Sooner or later I feel ready to start a book. I drop away the ideas that I'm not going to use, make a choice, and start writing. And I generally find that everything I've written in the notes gets absorbed into the book.

I really just write them the way I like them in the hope that somebody else will like them too. But I think that people like a rapid story clearly told, but also with some depth. The mind isn't satisfied, even the young mind, by an account of life that doesn't give the depths of life.

G: You mention that a "rapid story clearly told," is one of your goals as a detective novelist. But in your attempt to get at that goal you present some of the most complicated and finely wrought plots ever devised.

M: To me, the essence of the novel is its structure. It doesn't have to be as intricate as we're talking about. But you see, I get ideas that can only be worked out intricately. There is no way, for instance, that I could have written *The Chill* except in terms of that complex plot. It covers the whole lives of a number of people. There's just no other way to tell the story. And oddly enough, as I said, I get read by fifteen year-old kids and, I don't know how they do it, but they seem able to understand my books.

G: What do your novels turn on? Is it the story, the structure? Is it Archer? Chandler, for instance, placed a great deal of emphasis on his hero, Philip Marlowe. Do you feel that such focus is important in your novels?

M: Not nearly to the extent that Chandler's books do. That's one of the troubles with the Chandler books. He's too bound up with his hero, who is a self-projection, of course. And he doesn't move freely enough into other lives. He's constantly coming back to the subjective experience of Marlowe, who I don't find all that interesting. I find the other characters in Chandler's books more interesting, although Marlowe is a fine creation. I'm just speaking in terms of how I'd do it. And I really have tried to play down, to a certain extent, the personality aspects of the detective and to make him more a means of getting into the lives of other people. He represents the author, but not with the idea of blowing him up. He's essentially a narrator. A man who gets around in order to narrate, looking at it from just the technical point of view. And he's an eye. And an ear. He's a man too, but I'm not writing about him in that capacity so much. I leave out his private life. In fact, I become very impatient with detective stories that devote too much space to the private life of the author as represented by the detective. Many of the other characters are, at least, as interesting to me as Archer is. And many of them are just as representative of me as Archer is.

G: In an early novel of yours, *Trouble Follows Me,* the hero, Sam Drake, spends much of the closing chapter pointing out the importance of the gun. In your novel, *Underground Man,* there is extremely little emphasis on the gun or gunplay. In fact, I don't believe Archer ever carries one. Why this change in attitude towards the gun?

M: When I took up writing the books we're talking about, the form was essentially a novel of violence. That's what *Trouble Follows Me* is. It's a social novel with its dealings with the racial theme expressed in terms of violence. But as one develops, one tries other ways, perhaps more subtle ways, of dealing with the subject matter. I have, myself, an objection to guns. I hate the idea of there being so many guns floating around in our society constantly being used to kill people. You know, when you write about a person like Archer, I won't call him a hero, but he is intended to be a kind of middle representative of American man. And you want him to do the things that are representative in a good sense rather than a negative sense. In other words, I like him to be able to operate without violence, though he's sometimes subjected to it and he has to fight back. This is a concept that gradually grew over the years. It corresponds to real life, too. The detectives that I know don't carry guns.

G: Archer seems to be continually involved with broken marriages and, for the most part, finds himself in search of the missing pieces trying to put things back together again.

M: I'm profoundly concerned with broken marriages. I was the child of one. I'm sure that had a lot to do with it. Don't forget, though, that the Archer novels in general, and mystery novels in general, are about various kinds of brokenness. It's various kinds of social, psychological, and moral brokenness that leads to crime. In our society, which is virtually a society of broken marriages, (we have almost a fifty percent divorce rate) a man who's really trying to write honestly about the problems of the society will focus on some of these things. In other words, they're not just a personal interest, though they are that, they also reflect, or try to reflect, the truth of what's happening to society. We seem to be moving away from the traditional concept of marriage. And you write about what's there. You know, writers don't have much control over their material. It's there. And it's not only outside, but it's in them too.

G: Archer, too, is a product of a broken marriage.

M: I didn't realize how important it was going to be in the first book when I made him a divorced man, but it seems to have become a very central part of his life, his loneliness.

G: Archer seems to make little contact, other than official, with the opposite sex. Why the sexlessness of your detective fiction?

M: I'm deliberately, in my work, trying to get away from the idea, the central idea, that the private detective is a sex hero. I'm deliberately playing down that aspect because I'm interested in a different sort of image, model, and man. I'm trying to make him a man first. I'm also concerned with the fact that my books are read by everybody from age fifteen up. I started my life as a high school teacher, and I'm concerned with the kind of character I present. I'm not offering Archer as a model man, but I set limits to the things he does because he's a moral man. He's not a model of morality, but like several good private detectives I know, he's a better man than the people he has to work with. That's what makes him effective. He's in control of himself. He's not a moral ideal, not a paragon, but a guy that is fairly trustworthy. And he's not in it just for the money and he has a vision of the way things ought to be. Of course, these things are just signs that he's a human being. All human beings hate to lie. And all human beings have a vision of something good that they'd like to see played out in life. The only people who don't are the very sick and the criminal, who are essentially the same, that is the same group, the mentally sick people and the criminal.

G: In *The Moving Target,* the first Archer novel, Archer intimates that he is "a new kind of detective." What's new about him?

M: Well, I intended him to be both new and old. If there is any novelty in him in *The Moving Target,* I think it's in the fact that his explorations are essentially of people and their lives rather than of terrain and clues. He's a psychological detective. I can't claim that that's a wholly new development, but in the context of the American "hard-boiled" tradition, there is something a bit new about it. And later, of course, I was able to develop him in that direction.

G: What kind of guy is Archer?

M: Well, I've written eighteen books about him, and I've sort of covered the subject. But I consider him a man who's limited by his job and by his nature. He's not a great hero type either of the physical or the intellectual sense. He's a man who is in touch with the ordinary and content to be fairly ordinary. And at the same time he has moral interests and humane interests which are reflected not so much in what he does, but in how he does it. He takes his job seriously. I mean he's not just concerned with running down a criminal. He's concerned with the whole interrelationship of people that produces crime and is affected by crime. His primary interest is understanding other people's lives. And trying to make sense of them. Archer has two aspects. In one aspect he's an ordinary man, a private detective doing a not terribly well-paid job and working hard at it. And there's the other aspect of him where he's the representative of the novelist in the novel, and, in a sense, the mind of the novel. It's his observing mind in which things are put together and in which the whole novel exists, in a sense. So, he has, like all first-person narrator-characters, two aspects that have to be distinguished from one another. One is the man, the other is the voice of the novel, and readers don't seem to have any trouble making that distinction. They like a little literary sophistication. Even the fourteen or fifteen year-olds. It's true, though, there hasn't been very imaginative understanding of the nature of first-person narration in criticism. I've never seen it explained clearly. It's simple enough. What I've said was simple enough.

Archer really isn't the hero of these books, in the old-fashioned sense. He's more of a narrator and observer than hero, although he's on the scene the whole time. But what happens, happens essentially to a lot of other people, twenty or more people in every book. It's their story that he tells, not his own. You never get to know very much about Archer's life apart from his working life.

G: Archer refers to himself in a few places as a modern day Natty Bumppo. Does he function as a contemporary Bumppo?

M: Yes, of course. I think that the whole idea of the . . . let's call him the benevolent hunter, originated with Natty Bumppo. Natty didn't originate in Cooper's book, though. He originated in the men who existed behind the book. And Archer is, to a certain extent, a descendent both socially and literarily of those men. It's the western tradition. The west was in the east when Natty Bumppo existed. The west has gradually moved from the Atlantic seaboard to the Pacific seaboard.

G: Often in your books, the reader is treated to a glimpse of a revelation about himself and the society in which he lives. Archer, in fact, becomes as much a public eye as he is a private eye.

M: That's what a writer is supposed to be. I wouldn't describe myself as a seer, but I do have these moments of what I would call penetration in my life. I think all writers do. That's what makes them want to write. And, of course, what you see isn't always negative, but often highly positive.

G: Archer has better than average perception and penetrating abilities also.

M: Good detectives do. You have to remember, though, Archer is not just a detective, not just a fictional detective. He's also the narrator of a novel. So, he gets automatically endowed with all of the literary and imaginative qualities that the author has. Huckleberry Finn is a twelve or thirteen year-old boy. He's also a great poet. He's the vehicle of some of the greatest poetic prose ever written. Archer is more than himself. He's also the voice of the novel.

G: Julian Symons in his recent study of the crime novel, *Mortal Consequences: A History from the Detective Story to the Crime Novel,* has mentioned your repeated use of the Oedipal-Electra themes as evidence of your unwillingness to experiment with new themes and ideas. Do you think that this might be a valid criticism of your work?

M: Well, possibly it is, but it's a criticism that could be made of almost any serious writer. Every writer has his themes and follows them to the end. Of course, there's a compulsive return to certain themes, but that's not peculiar to me. There's the same compulsive return in the work of Patricia Highsmith, who is Julian Symons' heroine in his detective fiction. Symons' own work, though there are some returning themes, does try to go on to new territory every time.

The structure of my books has often been described as Freudian, meaning that what happens to you in early childhood is determinant. Though that's more than Freudian. People knew that long before Freud. But the peculiar tone and attitude in which these ideas are expressed, I guess, is Freudian. I'm certainly a disciple of Freud. Freud was a revelation to me, a major part of my education, and my wife's. But there have been other psychiatrists and analysts since that have been very influential on me and other writers. The existentialist school of psychoanalysis, for example.

G: Reading your novels, one is struck by the actionlessness of them. They are clearly from another mold than the typical ripsnorting mystery yarns.

M: That kind of fiction and the kind of fiction I write offer two kinds of satisfaction. One is essentially fantasy, and the other while it has its element of fantasy, is essentially realistic. That is, the satisfactions are the satisfactions you get from recognizing reality rather than from going off on some dream-adventure. I don't pretend that it's a lot of fun to be Archer.

G: Archer's attempts to understand people's lives rather than to trace step-by-step the development of a case seem to come out of a non-linear rather than linear sense of logic. He seems more interested in inter-relationships and patterns than linear deduction. Is he the appropriate hero for the McLuhan age of non-linearity? Is there a connection between Marshall McLuhan's ideas and your fiction?

M: Yes. I think there's some connection between McLuhan's ideas and my narrative practice. Of course, I've been a great fan of McLuhan for twenty years, ever since *The Mechanical Bride.* I know him. I've audited one of his courses. We exchange all our books. I'm complimented by the idea because McLuhan is one of our great modern "understanders," I think. I don't pretend to be. I don't pretend to be a major intellectual. And I'm not trying to write highly intellectual material. I, of course, have been trying to use the detective novel, this is not accidental, to use it and change it into a form that could be used to express new perceptions and new meanings including the new "wholenesses" that you have to pick up. You have to look at a scene and pick it up quickly, nowadays, because it's changing. And that's essentially what Archer is doing. That's why I have to keep writing new books. The scene keeps changing. It's changed enormously in the twenty-five years that I've been working on this, and so have I changed. Therefore, the books have changed.

I'm really trying to write about contemporary life. I've found the detective form useful for this. In fact, that's why I write in this form. The old linear novel just comes to pieces under the new conditions of life. I found I couldn't write about them any other way. I'm trying to set up typical patterns that can be used for understanding contemporary life. I'm not really offering the novel as a substitute for science, psychology, sociology, etc. Nevertheless, the novel is one of our most important tools for learning how to understand life and to apprehend it later. Isn't that true? It's almost traditionally over the last century that fiction has been the main tool of social understanding. If you wanted to stretch it a little, you could include drama and now, of course, the movies. We learn to see reality through the popular arts we create and patronize. That's what they're for. That's why we love them. Yearning for reality and the pleasure of it and the knowledge of it is the whole basis of art.

G: But the reality of the detective novel is often an exaggerated one. For instance, almost all detective novels focus on the crime of murder. Why murder and not some other crime?

M: It's the ultimate crime. It's the ultimate crime in a secular society, and the mystery novel is essentially the expression of a secular society. But it's really symbolic. Murder stands for various kinds of crime. And, in fact, in my books it reflects other kinds of crime. It's the objective correlative, you might say, of spiritual death. That's why I write about extreme situations such as murder. They are a metaphor for our daily lives. We live in extreme situations in the United States. We're close to the edge in many ways. Which is quite thrilling too. It's a nice way to live, if you can survive it.

G: Taking your Archer novels together, one might point out that your work is of epic magnitude.

M: No, I wouldn't say epic "magnitude," but epic in nature. You see, there are various sizes of epics. Some of the Icelandic and Norse sagas are not particularly big or particularly mythical. The *Saga of Grettir the Strong*, which is a very good one, and was very influential on me, is about a man who could have been an actual man and probably was. The essence of it, combined with his strength, was a kind of understated wit. One of the things you have in the back of your mind, hopefully, when you start a series is that it may turn out to be something that will take up and embody the characteristics of the society which you are writing about. That's what epic is for. That's what I have in mind. By epic, I don't mean something enormous or something terribly ambitious. I mean in the nature of it. A writer who can write a long novel or series of novels about a society and express it rather fully is doing a kind of epic work. Whether it's of great magnitude or not doesn't matter. Of course there are eighteen novels about Archer now. That's long.

G: Why use the detective novel to work out your vision of society?

M: Well, people should work on what interests and fascinates them. It seems to be the form that suits me. I don't find myself thinking in terms of straight novels. Perhaps it's because I have a very complex attitude towards society and towards life in general. And a somewhat "downbeat" attitude, at least superficially "downbeat." Though, I think, in general, the Archer books could be called hopeful. By definition, of course, the mystery novel is "downbeat." It has to do with crime, crime and punishment. I haven't run out of things to do in the detective form yet. I'll write what I feel like writing. I'll write what comes up to write.

G: What have your novels done for you personally?

M: I think they've deepened my understanding of life. They've made me, in recent years at least, a good living. They've made me into a writer instead of something else. I used to be a teacher. And while writing is a much lonelier life, it has satisfactions that you don't get out of teaching. For one thing, it's a rarer form of life. Let's put it this way, my novels made me into a novelist.

G: Do you get much response from your readers?

M: Yes. Generally they're friendly, very friendly. People just thank me for having written a book.

THE GENRE EXTENDED

Charles R. Carlisle

STRANGERS WITHIN, ENEMIES WITHOUT: ALIENATION IN POPULAR MAFIA FICTION

Crime and criminals have long been a mainstay in popular prose fiction, as can be seen in the sale of such popular novel series as Sam Spade, Shell Scott, and Mike Hammer. The Mafia, the organized crime syndicate imported in various ways from Sicily to the United States and elsewhere, has only in recent times become a serious addition to popular crime fiction.

Since the Kefauver investigations of the 1950's disclosed to the American public the existence of a flesh-and-blood crime syndicate of national proportions, and more especially since the publicity given to the expose of what he called *La Cosa Nostra* by Joe Valachi, a soldier in one of the powerful New York "families," the rise in popular interest in the Mafia has given birth to a considerable body of fiction about this Italo-Sicilian import to America.

In reading these works of fiction about the Mafia, one becomes increasingly aware of the way in which this body of popular literature fits into the overall structure of twentieth century literary production. Not only is it written now about events which largely have their history in this century[1]—at least where this country is concerned—but the majority of these novels develop one or more aspects of one of the most salient literary themes of our time: alienation.

Although alienation is not, of course, unique to this century, that this theme is an important literary concern in twentieth century *Welt-literatur* can be seen in the principal characters of novels published in almost any country, especially since the first World War—characters such as Joseph Heller's Yossarian, Capt. Pilli in Mario Tobino's *Il deserto della Libia,* Camus' Merseult, the priest in Unamuno's *San Manuel bueno, mártir,* and Joachim Mahlke in Günter Grass' *Katz und Maus,* to mention but a few.

These and other characters are portrayed in some state of alienation; from society as a whole, from some particular aspect of their national or ethnic ties, from friends, or from family. And it is within these levels of alienation that most of the *mafiosi* in post-1959 Mafia fiction are portrayed, Mario Puzo's *The Godfather* being one work which encompasses almost all of the variations of the theme of alienation found in the other popular novels about *L'onorata società,* "the Honored Society."

By their very rejection of the laws of contemporary society, *mafiosi* have alienated themselves from the formal structure to which the majority of the citizenry adhere. They dwell outside the law, largely apart from society. Their rejection of American society and its legal system is shown in *The Godfather* when Don Vito Corleone chides Amerigo Bonasera for having trusted in American legal justice before coming to the godfather for help:

> No. Don't speak. You found America a paradise. You had a good trade, you made a good living, you thought the world a harmless place where you could take your pleasure as you willed. You never armed yourself with true friends. After all, the police guarded you, there were courts of law, you and yours could come to no harm. You did not need Don Corleone. Very well. . . . Now you come to me and say, "Don Corleone give me justice."[2]

When the bereaved father protests that America has been good to him, that he wanted to be a good citizen, his daughter to be an American (Puzo, p. 32), Corleone replies, " 'Well spoken. Very fine. Then you have nothing to complain about. The judge has ruled. America has ruled. Bring your daughter flowers and a box of candy when you go visit her in the hospital . . . give me your word that you will put aside this madness. It is not American. Forgive. Forget. Life is full of misfortunes.' " (Puzo, p. 32)

Two levels of alienation from American society are shown in Don Corleone's words to the father of the rape victim: the rejection of the legal processes of American society and a scornful reminder of alienation steeped in Sicilian—and especially in Mafia—tradition. No true Sicilian, much less a *mafioso,* would forgive and forget. By previously avoiding Don Corleone, Amerigo Bonasera has chosen to be an American rather than a Sicilian, and in so doing he has made himself an object of the *mafioso*'s scorn. The alienation from American society of Don Vito Corleone and all those like him is not just formalistic; it has roots that lie deep in the traditions of the Sicilian people, be they *mafiosi* or not.

In *The Mafia Don,* Nick Zaccardi, the grandson of a dying *capo mafioso,* expresses similar thoughts while in training to replace his grandfather as the head of the Zaccardi's Mafia family. While traveling across the country to learn the extent of his responsibilities, he meets a young hippie girl who asks about the formal way he speaks, indicating that he seems to be a foreigner. "Nick smiled. 'Foreign to much that is American,

I suppose,' he said. 'But I was born here.' "[3]

The case of Nick Zaccardi has other parallels to *The Godfather* which show another aspect of alienation in Mafia fiction, in that Nick's rise in the Mafia family is very similar to that of Michael Corleone, the youngest son of Don Vito, who turns from rejection of the Mafia tradition to become a powerful, feared head of the family. Both young men are in love with American women when first introduced by the author, a fact which points out a level of alienation often found in Mafia novels: family dissent over breaks in tradition.

Michael is made aware of the family's feelings toward Kay Adams at his sister's wedding where both of them are virtually ignored by his father. Kay is an outsider, a non-Sicilian, and the family cannot consider her as a serious candidate for marriage, even though Michael himself is a renegade, ignoring his father's wishes that he not fight in World War II and joining the Marines. (Puzo, p. 17) Both are cast in the role of almost neutral observers to the goings-on at Connie Corleone's wedding, although Michael does not share Kay's unawareness of the family's situation.

Nick Zaccardi, soon after bringing his American fiancee to his father's baronial manse near the New Jersey marshes, meets a much more outward resistence to her presence by his family. Even as they approach the Zaccardi house, Nick anticipates their rejection by his family. "To them, she would appear as a porcelain American. Hardly enough tit to suckle a mouse, his father would say. His mother would look at the delicate shoulders, the boyish hips, the slender thighs, and shake her head in silent rejection." (Rae, p. 10) His brother, already a soldier in their grandfather's family, would make his reaction to Elly Saunders more bluntly: " 'Zaccardis should like women built like workhorses! Don't you know that Zaccardis only come to manhood back in Sicily after they had fucked a mare behind the stables?' " (Rae, p. 10) But the reactions to Elly's slender physique take second place to the most pressing objection which Nick's grandfather, the family *capo*, will have. "It was not the build of a woman that concerned Don Santo. He believed in the blood, and Elly was not of the blood." (Rae, p. 10)

This concept of blood differences is not only an aspect of the alienation of American *mafiosi* from non-Sicilian Americans, but is developed in some novels as an aspect of the separation of *mafiosi* from all others—even other Sicilians—to the point of almost Gothic Naturalism. *The Sicilian Heritage* by Jack Higgins is an example of this application of blood-alienation, in that its central character, Stacey Wyatt, is the grandson of "Vito Barbaccia . . . Lord of Life and Death,"[4] a *capo mafioso* still operating in Sicily.

Although the question of American *Vs.* Sicilian blood is developed in the novel (". . . it was made plain that the Wyatt blood in me was tainted. . . ." [Higgins, p. 7]), Wyatt discovers upon a return to Sicily that his blood, his Mafia blood, makes him a part of that "other Sicily" which is kept from the tourist brochures, and of which not all Sicilians are a part, by any stretch of the imagination. "To the visitor, the tourist, Sicily was Taormina, Catania, Syracusa—golden beaches, laughing peasants. But there was another, darker place in the hinterland. . . . A world where the key word was *omerta*. . . . Manliness, honour, solve your own problem, never seek official help, all of which . . . was the breeding ground of the Mafia." (Higgins, p. 54)

That the Mafia's children are alienated from even other Sicilians is pointed out to Wyatt when his lover-to-be reacts to the news of his being the grandson of one of the local *mafiosi*:

"Stacey's grandfather is something to do with his Mafia thing," Burke said. "Isn't that so, Stacey? He's going to see him tonight."

Hoffer frowned. "Your grandfather?"

"Vito Barbaccia," I said. . . .

Rosa Solazzo sucked in her breath and dropped her glass.

. . . Strange how the Barbaccia name affected people. And Rosa? Rosa had gone very pale and when I smiled at her she dropped her gaze, fear in those dark eyes.

Barbaccia—*mafioso*. I suppose that to her the two were interchangeable. When I tucked her arm in mine, she was trembling. (Higgins, pp. 62-63)

The *mafiosi,* then, are alienated by reason of birth and "profession" from non-Sicilians and from other Sicilians by their brotherhood in the union of *la Santa Mamma,* the Holy Mother, which is their bond against society and its institutions. An interesting aspect of this bond appears not only in *The Godfather*, which serves to typify Mafia literature in this period (if not an actual prototype in every case), but in others of these novels, as well. The bond which *mafiosi* have with the Mother Country is seemingly closer than a first glance at the Mafia's image of Big Business, Wall Street-after hours, and all of the other business-like, if not sinister, trappings of today's "Syndicate" would suggest. There is present in some of these novels the suggestion of an almost spiritual renewal which must be undergone and which can take place only on the soil of *Sicilia.* This is especially true in the case of the younger generation of potential *mafiosi,* of which Michael Corleone, the *don*-to-be in *The Godfather,* is a good example.

After killing an enemy of the family in a small Sicilian restaurant in New York (the ambience, if not the details, being reminiscent of many gangland killings to gain press coverage in recent years), Michael Corleone is smuggled out of the country to await the cooling off of his crime in Sicily. While this trip to the ancestral turf is primarily designed to avoid prosecution for murder, its effects on Michael are much deeper.

He has alienated himself from society by killing Sollozzo, his father's rival, and McCluskey, Sollozzo's ally on the New York City Police, and in this act Michael has "made his bones," has blooded himself in the name of the family. But this is not enough to turn Michael from all of his very American ways, traits which have previously alienated him from his father and the "extended family" of *don* Vito Corleone's Mafia associates and soldiers. This change takes place after his arrival in Sicily, although it is adumbrated much earlier in the scene at the hospital, after Vito Corleone has been shot.

Having gone to the hospital to see about his father's condition, Michael realizes that his father is virtually helpless. There are no bodyguards near, no soldiers, nor can police protection be counted on. He must do what he can for his father, his only ally being Enzo, the baker's helper, who owes the Godfather for not being deported after World War II as an ex-prisoner of war. The refugee from the Italian army is terrified, but Michael is strangely calm in the face of danger. A black limosine cruises past Michael and Enzo as they stand guard, unarmed, in front of the hospital. "The car seemed about to stop, then speeded forward. Somebody had recognized him [Michael]. Michael gave Enzo another cigarette and noticed that the baker's hands were shaking. To his surprise his own hands were steady." (Puzo, p. 125)

This calm in the face of danger takes Michael as far as "making his bones" against Sollozzo and McCluskey, but it is in Italy that his complete transformation is realized. His outward calm (a calmness noted in his father when Vito was of a similar age) and his coolness under fire indicate Michael's talent (again, an example of the "Mafia blood" motif) for the life of a *mafioso*. His return to the homeland of the *Onorata Società* makes the change complete.

At first, Michael feels very foreign to the people he encounters. He is, in effect, alienated from the old country people and their ways. Despite his dramatic introduction into "family" life in New York, that was still America. Sicily, however, is something else. He is "of the blood," but Michael Corleone, ex-Marine hero of the Pacific Theatre, has yet to become totally as one with his father's people and their way of life. It is a question of time:

> After five months of exile in Sicily, Michael Corleone came finally to understand his father's character and his destiny. He came to understand men like Luca Brasi, the ruthless *caporegime* Clemenza, his mother's resignation and acceptance of her role. For in Sicily he saw what they would have been if they had chosen *not* to struggle against their fate. He understood why the Don always said, "A man has only one destiny." He came to understand the contempt for authority and legal government, the hatred for any man who broke *omerta,* the law of silence. (Puzo, p. 324)

Time reveals these insights to Michael, but it is love that shows his having crossed the line from "Americanism," in the sense of his non-Sicilian thinking and reacting, to "Sicilianism," a trait that further develops the blood motif of the novel. When he encounters a lovely girl on one of his strolls through the Sicilian countryside, Michael goes to inquire about her at the nearest village and encounters none other than the girl's father. When the father reacts negatively to Michael's inquiries, breeding—and the months of "renewal" in Sicily—come quickly into play. Michael's envoy to the father returns with the man's reply:

Michael gave him a cold stare. Up to now he had been a quiet, gentle young man, a typical American, except that since he was in hiding in Sicily he must have done something manly. This was the first time the shepherds had seen the Corleone stare. Don Tommasino, knowing Michael's true identity and deed, had always been wary of him, treating him as a fellow "man of respect." But these unsophisticated sheep herders had come to their own opinion of Michael, and not a wise one. The cold look, Michael's rigid white face, his anger that came off him like cold smoke or ice, sobered their laughter and snuffed out their familiar friendliness. (Puzo, pp. 335-336)

Michael then summons the man to him, an order his two shepherd bodyguard-envoys quickly carry out. When the man is brought outside to Michael, the alienation of ordinary Sicilians from the *mafiosi* is underscored, as is the change in Michael which Sicily is making. Michael makes his proposal to the man in such a manner that the barrier between them is quite obvious to the poor innkeeper. He asks Michael if he is "a friend of the friends," to which Michael says no, thus disavowing a formal relationship with the Mafia.[5] Nonetheless, the innkeeper feels the difference between them, and agrees to let Michael call on his daughter for the purpose of courting her. This shows Michael's developing conversion.

The murder of his new bride seals it. Shortly after their honeymoon, Michael and his bride plan to take a ride in their car. Before Michael can stop her, his wife turns the ignition key and is instantly blown to bits by a bomb under the hood. His mentor in Sicily, Don Tommasino, tries to comfort Michael after the funeral, and it is then that Michael puts words to all that he has experienced in Sicily: " 'Tell my father to get me home,' Michael said. 'Tell my father I wish to be his son.' " (Puzo, p. 354)

This renewal of the blood (instincts?) by contact with Sicily is not unique to *The Godfather*, although Puzo develops the motif more successfully than most of the other writers who return one or more characters to the old country for such a revival of faith in *la Santa Mamma, la cosa nostra.*[6]

Despite the possibly salutary effects on the younger generation of a trip to Sicily for spiritual re-birth in family traditions and attitudes, one aspect of alienation is found in several of the popular fiction accounts of life among *gli amici*: the drifting apart of younger members from the ways of the older *mafiosi,* when the more modern, progressive, corporate business-oriented members refer to as "Moustache Petes." Even *La Cosa Nostra* has its generation gap.

This is developed to a degree in *The Godfather,* being shown as a rift in the Sicilian faction (Puzo, pp. 329-330), as well as in the American Mafia. Often it is no more than a desire on the part of the younger *mafiosi* to be less conspicuously un-American, as Tom Hagen's wishing his godfather would change from De Nobili brand *sigari toscani* to Havana-style American cigars (Puzo, p. 70), but it is usually a very wide hiatus of lifestyles and ultimate aims for the family business that divides the younger generation from the traditionalists.

In the *romanzi di mafia* written and published in the United States during the 1960's and '70's this aspect of the alienation theme has been used by several writers, to a great variety of degrees. Carlino's *The Brotherhood* develops this aspect of alienation as the primary thematic and argumentative structure of the entire novel, as does *War of the Dons,*[7] to a lesser degree. Ovid Demaris develops this aspect of the theme of alienation in *The Overlord*, treating it more as *leitmotif* than primary concern, but one excerpt from his book merits attention for the way it captures the "insider's view" of the Mafia Generation Gap:

Big Juice and Eddie Merelli went back a long way together, a half a century or more, back to the wild days of the rumbling 49-Mob, back to the time when the *patruni,* the big shots, were Moustache Petes from the old country, guys with a belly, feudal lords, *pezzi grossi,* and there was no horsing around, no joking in their presence, only *silenzio,* and you bowed and *bacio li mani,* kiss their hands, like they were the pope, and you had to go out and make your bones, you had to kill, before they gave you a godfather and took you into the family. Some of the dons didn't even speak *inglese,* and they said things like *buon viaggio,* have a pleasant journey, to the losers they put in boxes, always very polite and correct, *Il padrone, uomini rispettati,* and they really believed in *destino Sagiliano, destino Mafioso, destino d'onore.* Their homes were modest, gay in wop colors . . . with crocheted antimacassars over the fat furniture to protect against *quinzo* heads and hands, and the *signora* fetched great pitchers of cool red vino from the cellar and washed *Il padrone's quinzo* feet while he puffed on a little black *quinzo sigaro* and waxed eloquently on *i nostri giorni,* the old days, and grumbled on about *il giorno d'oggi* and all that was wrong with today. But the good old days were *finito* and nowadays a *matto del tutto,* a madman, like Big Juice, could be a *caporegime* and command great wealth and power simply because he was a bloodthirsty pervert, which to many old-timers was a sad commentary on the state of affairs in *l'onore Mafioso,* which in itself was a sad commentary on the recollective accurancy of senescence.[8]

The above is given as the attitude about the Moustache Petes *circa* 1970, and other books establish this attitude in earlier parts of the post-war era. The aging godfather in Leslie Waller's *The Family* laments the coming of this newer breed of *mafioso,* as he thinks:

There was a strain of softness, like a sustained violin note among the crash of brass. The young men in their twenties, and even in their thirties, these dunces were all soft between the ears. They had no *maschiezza,* no *virilita,* no balls.

Everything they had . . . had been handed to them on *una argenteria.* The silver platter had been loaded to overflowing with everything he, Don Vincenzo, and the men of his generation of the family had had to fight for. It fell into the baby-soft hands of these . . . *college* men without a struggle.[9]

This difference in attitude and lifestyle between the younger generation and the old country-oriented *mafiosi* extends even to the techniques of enforcement used by the two. The old school prefers to use violence and murder as a warning system to those who might wish to go against the Mafia, as much as to punish those already guilty of some offense against *l'onorata società.* A "classic" Mafia murder-with-a-message is shown in *The Overlord.* The case in point is an affront to the honor of the family of Tony Acuto by Ernesto, the fiance of Tony's older sister, who wishes to dissolve the engagement in order to marry more in keeping with his station.

The situation has all the makings of a Spanish *Comedia de pundonor,* a plot by Calderón or Lope de Vega. Tony's manner of cleansing the family honor with blood is, however, strictly Sicilian in execution. He has his sister arrange a last tryst with her suitor, who has allowed family pressures to blind him to the possible dangers of dropping a girl of the *famiglia* Acuto. The unfortunate Ernesto agrees to a last rendezvous in the hills with Gabriella, and, when the two are engaged in passionate love-making, Tony strikes, stabbing Ernesto when no resistance can be made. "Moments later . . . he carefully amputated the still warm testicles and watched as Gabriella forced them into her dead lover's mouth in a way that left the penis protruding from the slack lips." (Demaris, p. 109)

When a witness, a fourteen-year-old boy, testifies against Tony, causing him to serve two years in prison, this, too, is avenged in "classic," old world Mafia style. "On the day following his [Tony's] release from prison, the brutally mutilated body of the witness was discovered at the original murder site. This time there was a dead canary in the corpse's mouth." (Demaris, p. 109)[10]

The "New Mafia," however, is generally against such measures, preferring to give its "contracts," assignments for murder, to highly-trained assassins, called "mechanics," whose methods generally leave no suggestion of murder. Lewis John Carlino's *The Mechanic* deals with just one such hired assassin and gives the step-by-step procedures used by this type of syndicate enforcer. He is very good at what he does, and when approached to execute a Syndicate victim in a short period of time which might preclude his usual, methodical methods, Bishop (the mechanic) reacts in the negative: " 'Look, I'm not some Cleveland shooter. I don't cowboy.' "[11]

Bishop refuses "to cowboy," to use open gunplay without the finesse and subtlety which his training has given him. He is of the new breed, another example of the division within Mafia ranks brought on by inability or refusal to communicate or by the cultural gap created by the younger generation's lack of contact with the old world ways and mores left in Sicily, a gap made even greater by the technological and economic advances of the period following World War II.

Twentieth century literature, especially since the War, is characterized to a great extent by the theme of alienation in an absurd world. Mafia literature, popular novels written more as escape literature than as documentary of this sub-cultural aspect of American and European society, rather than providing an escape from the sense of alienation, is more symptomatic than not of this condition of our times. The *mafioso,* a man against society, is shown to be alienated not only from The Establishment, from generally accepted social behavior, but from his own kind, his fellow members of *l'onorata società* and even from his own blood relations, because of a variety of reasons. The action of these popular novels may provide the pedestrian reader some diversion from the quotidian cares of mortgage payments and the dullness of the routine of an impersonal, unvaried office job, but the sense of alienation is everywhere in Mafia fiction, either as the direct subject of plot and theme or, at least, as a repeated thematic motif underscoring the primary concerns of the author.

Richard Gid Powers

J. EDGAR HOOVER AND THE DETECTIVE HERO

There might be few political scientists who would be willing to go as far as Jacques Ellul in asserting that the mass media have assumed the traditional function of the leader in the mass society, but many have begun to suspect that mass politics and mass entertainments are governed by the same general laws. The result has been the development of a dramaturgical theory of politics in which Walter Bagehot's despised "dignified" part of government has assumed an ever more central place. "All the world's a stage," is more than a metaphor in contemporary political science and communications theory: it is an essential insight into the way power operates in the mass society, whether this is as you like it or not.

While political scientists have begun studying the importance of politics' dramatic aspect, other theorists have been working on a theoretical understanding of popular entertainment's impact on political attitudes. The Frankfurt school and the French semiologists have in their different ways outlined the part mass entertainment plays in constructing the symbolic reality within which mass politics operates.

This paper is an introduction to a study of one of popular politic's most successful practitioners, J. Edgar Hoover. It is not intended to pass for an adequate inquiry into the meaning of his role in American culture, but rather as an indication of the approaches that might be taken and the materials that might be examined in the course of a more elaborate study. It ought to be subtitled "An introduction to a case study in popular politics."

J. Edgar Hoover was a phenomenon without parallel in American cultural history. Hoover's career was played out in the full glare of publicity: it would be superfluous to serve up illustrations of the political power he acquired as head of the F.B.I. from 1924 until his death in 1972.

Reprinted from the JOURNAL OF POPULAR CULTURE, IX:2.

Few American politicians have ever held the popular imagination in as firm a grip as did Hoover, and none ever maintained his grasp so long. The sources of Hoover's control over rival political figures are just now being fully revealed, but those dossiers on hijinks in high places would have been blank charges had Hoover not been so secure in the public's esteem that he could denounce without fear of being splattered. It was Hoover's role as a public hero, a celebrity of the headlines, "Public Hero Number One" as one pulp called him in the thirties, that was the ultimate source of his power.

A public hero is no test-tube baby. He is the result of an almost sexual dialectic between a public whose needs, both practical and expressive, define the contours of the heroic role, and a public figure whose actions demonstrate his ability to fill that role. Therefore a figure like Hoover cannot be studied apart from the culture that nourished and rewarded him. Moreover, if we can learn why Hoover became a public hero and why there should have been available for him a heroic role as national symbol of law enforcement, we will at the same time be looking at the structure and political processes of the mass society and the role of such people as Hoover in defining and maintaining that system.

Hoover did not become famous until August 1933 when his name, picture, deeds and writing began suddenly to appear everywhere one looked in the mass media. He had, however, been head of what would ultimately be called the F.B.I. since 1924, and had been performing important functions within that agency ever since joining it in 1917. In comparison with his later fame, however, he had been performing his labors in an obscurity as deep as Grant's at Galena. In July 1933 he was unknown. A year later he was one of the most famous men in America. What had happened? What food of the gods did he consume?

The Federal Bureau of Investigation was founded in a blaze of publicity in July 1908. President Roosevelt was in a deadlock with Congress, as he had been throughout his elected term. His congressional relations consisted of mutual threats and recriminations, with both parties frequently expressing their disdain for each other before a public audience that thoroughly enjoyed the performance. In an effort to seize the initiative from Congress and to preserve his popular support as a dynamic leader in the face of his legislative ineffectiveness Roosevelt began an investigation of the corrupt involvement of important congressmen in an Idaho land fraud scheme. This was a scandal which happily involved several of Roosevelt's Republican enemies in the far West and also included his most hated rival, Senator Ben Tillman of South Carolina.

Because the Justice Department had no investigators of its own, Roosevelt and Attorney General Bonaparte had borrowed agents from the Secret Service of the Treasury Department. The obvious investigator, the General Land Office of the Interior Department, was thoroughly implicated in the scandal. The guilty congressmen, of course, were terrified at the prospect of this investigation, and the innocent were also very far from applauding, because with a President after congressional scalps raking over one's past assisted by an army of detectives, no one could be sure he would emerge unscathed. Their fear was especially acute because the President was turning over anything he uncovered to the press. Since Congress regarded Roosevelt's investigation of the Idaho land frauds as an attempt to discredit and intimidate it, the legislature defended itself by passing a law before adjournment for the summer of 1908 which ordered the Justice Department not to "borrow" detectives from other agencies.[1]

This was the opening Roosevelt needed. Branding Congress's action a *de facto* interference with a criminal investigation and flourishing his constitutional obligation to enforce the laws despite the efforts of crooked congressmen to impede him, he had Attorney General Bonaparte create the "Bureau of Investigation" within the Justice Department. Congress responded with wrath that called upon the Magna Carta, the Declaration and the Constitution to witness the heinousness of Roosevelt's assault on civil liberties. Unfortunately for the impact of their rhetoric, several of those who most stridently defended the right of Americans to go uninvestigated were soon behind bars because of this very investigation.[2]

The Bureau of Investigation was therefore the accidental outcome of a specific political controversy. It was founded to provide quick political profit for one particular president, profit which he could record in two ledgers. The first ledger was the private one: here Roosevelt collected facts about congressmen and other officials which they would rather not see the light of day. This aspect of the Bureau's work might be termed "elite discipline." The second ledger was public: here Roosevelt scored points with his supporters by posing as their champion in a crusade against the lawless both inside and outside of the government. This can be called "symbolic politics." In all of its subsequent operations the Bureau continued to work on these two levels, acting privately to preserve discipline among the elite leadership of the nation, and acting publicly to impress the masses with the government's importance as the nation's protector against the enemies of the people.

Why had it taken until 1908 for the branch of the federal government charged with enforcing the law to create its own investigative force? The answer is that not until Roosevelt's time was there a need for a national police: there was no "national crime" for a national police to police.

What is "national crime?" It is crime that for some reason has come to concern the entire nation rather than simply some locality, class or group within the nation. Throughout the nineteenth century there had been almost no such crime: New York, the West, industry or immigrants might have a crime problem, but the nation did not. Crime could not become national news because until the 1890s there was, except for national politics, no national news.

Crime had been a staple of American journalism since 1830 when Benjamin Day's New York *Sun* discovered what crime news could do for circulation. At that time, however, local readers were interested in *local* crime. When outrages like bombings or assassinations attracted more than local attention they were still seen as challenges to *local* order. They were the responsibility of local officials who might, however, become national heroes (Roosevelt himself as New York City Police Commissioner) or villains (Altgeld of Illinois) depending on how they handled their responsibilities. There was no shortage of crimes, but no national crime until two conditions were met: an interlocking network of news media that alerted the nation to local offenses, and an editorial policy that featured crime news and so depended on a constant supply of crimes (which the local market could not supply). By the mid-1890s both situations existed because of the press wars of Pulitzer and Hearst. A regular diet of crime news gathered from police blotters everywhere and shared by papers all over the country was creating the impression in the local reader that crime was everywhere and that, no matter how far away, it concerned *him.* Editors were then faced with the problem of making distant crime seem significant to the local reader; they found they could do this by treating crimes as facts not significant in themselves but significant as evidence proving the existence of a much more important situation, a crime problem. A crime problem thus came into existence once an audience had to be interested in crimes that concerned it only indirectly. In more recent years a "wonderful world of sports" became a reality when the local demand for sports news outran the local supply so that the audience had to be interested in new sources of sports entertainment imported from strange places and played by strange peoples. In both cases it was difficult to persuade the audience that it was directly involved in the particular crime or game under discussion. However it was possible to persuade the audience that as alert citizens or fans they ought to be concerned about "crime" or "sports." Therefore a rape in Arkansas could be presented as worth a Newark reader's attention because the outrage in the Ozarks was part of the "crime problem." Because of the new nationally integrated news media and their reliance on crime news the federal government by 1900 found itself with a national crime problem. Moreover it faced the question of why it was doing nothing about it.

Although there was no national crime problem before 1900, the federal government did face some similar challenges, challenges that were as abstract as the crime problem and that presented the government with a similar difficulty in formulating a response. In the nineteenth century there were three such cases, all three having to do with the emerging economic organization of American society. The first was the Jacksonian problem of the Bank; the second was the question of slavery; the third was the Gilded Age rise of the trusts. With the first and the last the government was able to deal successfully. The problem of slavery was one that evaded political solution.

In all three of these cases the American public was faced with a developing economic order that was creating real dislocations as well as a cultural sense of disorder and ineffectiveness. What Jackson was able to do with his veto of the Bank recharter in 1832 and Congress with its passage of the Sherman Anti-trust Act of 1890 was to fix the blame for the dislocations and cultural disorder on symbolic threats, the Bank and the trusts. The government was then able to perform acts or pass laws that convinced the public that the threats were under control. In both of these cases, of course, the symbolic reassurance provided by taming the banks and the trusts permitted the economic organization and development of the country to proceed without the interference of public opinion. The Great Compromise of 1820 had once been a symbolic solution for the question of slavery, but once Webster "nationalized" the problem of slavery in 1850 (in the opinion of the North) no further symbolic solutions could be found.[3]

If one believes that the Bank Veto and the Anti-trust Act had no effect on the economic structure of the country this kind of symbolic politics can seem negligible or contemptible. Nevertheless such acts of symbolic reassurance appear to be necessary if a government wishes to preserve its authority. A government maintains its hold on the public's loyalty by proving itself able to protect its citizens against threats. When a people feels threatened it does a government no good to plead that the threat is imaginary, that the Bank or the trusts are only symbols of a process that is causing distress, a process with which the government is unable to deal. To a symbolic threat there must be an appropriate symbolic response, and if one leader is too fastidious for this kind of witchcraft another will readily be found.

During the twentieth century national leaders found themselves constantly confronted with the sort of symbolic challenges that earlier had emerged only once in a generation. All kinds of problems that were essentially local in character and that could be dealt with effectively only on the local level were now collected, categorized and nationalized by the new national media of communications. National leaders found themselves having to learn how to deal with these new national problems even though the problems consisted of vast arrays of localized events which just a few years before had been universally considered to be exclusively local in character. Once a new "national" public was created by mass communications (replacing the old "federal" public) the national government found itself compelled to take a stand on every issue that came to concern the public, whether or not programs on the national level could have any effect on the problem.

Theodore Roosevelt was the first president to be faced with the new public of mass communications, and his by-now-clichéd description of the presidency as a "bully pulpit" was phrased in his own idiom, but it was no more than a fair description of the new role every president since him has had to play, making allowances for variations in personal style. Roosevelt had an opinion on everything, from coinage design and football to socialism and religion, and he needed no prodding to make his opinions known. Other presidents *have* needed prodding, but in all cases presidents have had to take stands on every issue of public concern, whether or not the president has any power to effect a solution. In fact the public seeks to fill the presidency with men whose reflexive tendency is to take stands. One student of this phenomenon has observed that "the public official who dramatizes his competence is eagerly accepted on his own terms. . . . Willingness to cope is evidently central. Any action substitutes personal responsibility for impersonal causal chains and chance. The assumption of responsibility becomes vital in a world that is impossible to understand or control."[4]

If high officials neglect ritual statements of concern in times of public alarm the result is widespread anxiety, or more precisely, anomie. It is one of the most important functions of the central authority (the president or his spokesman) to reaffirm popular conventions whenever they come under attack, particularly when the threat is symbolic. To neglect this duty is to risk the accusation of encouraging or approving the symbolic evil. Roosevelt's understanding of this principle can be seen in an incident that occurred in 1906 when newspaper readers were being diverted and scandalized by reports of free love and trial marriages being advocated by advanced thinkers and "new" women. Roosevelt's response was to ask Congress for a Constitutional amendment that would have extended federal authority to "the whole question of marriage and divorce" to safeguard "home ties" and oppose birth control.[5]

The Federal Bureau of Investigation was a byproduct of Roosevelt's need to have some way to pose as a symbol of law and order. It grew because the Bureau offered a convenient means for public officials who succeeded Roosevelt to strike similar poses and to express symbolic concern when new issues emerged to disturb the tranquility of the public imagination. The Bureau's function was to promote mass quiescence by fighting crime in whatever symbolic form the popular mind might imagine it.

This thesis gathers support from the events in 1910 that produced the first major enlargement of the Bureau's authority. For two years after the conclusion of the Idaho land fraud case in 1908 the Bureau was left with no duties except the investigation of crimes on Indian reservations. During these same years, however, a bizarre hysteria over white slavery began to develop which finally forced the government to make a symbolic response. No doubt there were prostitutes in the United States in 1910 and some senators probably knew where to find them. There certainly was also organized prostitution, and once again some congressman must have had first-hand knowledge of vice rings. But the newspapers had convinced the overheated public mind that the whores and their pimps were very nearly in control of the nation; the town prostitute was only the visible manifestation of a gigantic conspiracy, a secret network that worked its will over almost every aspect of American life. Stanley W. Finch, the head of the Bureau of Investigation at the time, told the congressmen that the Mann Act was needed because "unless a girl was actually confined in a room and guarded there was no girl, regardless of her station in life, who was altogether safe. There was need that every person be on his guard, because no one could tell when his daughter or his wife or his mother would be selected as a victim."[6] It did no good for authorities to point out that the white slavery conspiracy, at least in the magnitude suggested by Finch, was imaginary. To say this was to seem to make light of the real fears that were being expressed by means of the white slavery symbol, fears that traditional sexual morality and the sanctity of the home were under attack. The Mann Act of 1910 was the government's testimony that it shared the public's concern about morals, a concern that it expressed by symbolically opposing the symbolic expression of the public's fears. Years later Hoover himself would describe the intent of the Mann Act so as to lend support to this analysis. He said that it was an attack on "the problem of vice in modern civilization."[7]

Thus the Mann Act episode seems to follow the same pattern established in the previous examples of the Bank, the trusts, and the Idaho Land Fraud. An incoherent public anxiety finally comes to a focus in the form of some Menace that is the personification of the fear. The government then performs an action that indicates its potency in dealing with the personification of the fear, thus avoiding having to grapple with the source of the problem, because it is frankly not in the power of the government to do anything about it. When King Canute began giving orders to the waves his popularity probably soared. His subjects must have loved him because while his commands might not have any effect on the sea, they at least showed that the king cared and was *trying* to do something.

The Bureau was given the responsibility of demonstrating the earnestness of the government's enforcement of the Mann Act, which it did by selecting for arrest individuals who would generate the maximum publicity. The prize victim was Jack Johnson, the unpopular Negro boxing champion.[8] The Bureau never forgot the lesson it learned during its Mann Act days: he who defends popular morality will come to be defended *by* popular morality. In fact he *becomes* popular morality in the minds of those who cannot distinguish between a thing and its representation. Not one to let a good trick die, as late as 1947 Hoover was writing magazine articles with titles like "How Safe is Your Daughter?"[9]

Besides the Mann Act, the Bureau's most important jobs before its flush times in the thirties were the Slacker raids of April-September 1918 and the Red Scare raids of the winter of 1919-1920. To the threats posed by the Draft Dodger and the Red the Bureau responded with dragnets. In the first case it rounded up all men of draft age in several cities and held them until they could produce their draft registration; in the second it arrested all members of the predominantly foreign-born Communist Party with the intention of deporting them aboard "Soviet Arks." In both instances the publicity was feverish. There seem to be no national figures on arrests in the Slacker raids, but in New York City there were over 75,000 arrested, while the Bureau itself admitted that only one out of every two hundred was actually a slacker. In the Red Scare raids 10,000 were arrested but only 3,500 were prosecuted and only 700 deported.[10] The Bureau's handling of the Red Scare raids was J. Edgar Hoover's first important assignment. Hoover had become the Bureau's resident authority on radicalism and communism and had been the responsible author of the first official Bureau position paper on communism. He had been the head of the anti-radical General Intelligence Division of the Bureau since its inception in 1919. Hoover's first professional experience was defusing a symbolic threat through symbolic action. He learned early in his career the need for carefully managing the news media if symbolic action was to succeed in reassuring its audience.

There is little need to analyze the sorry details of the Slacker and Red Scare Raids. That has been done often and done well. The point is that the Bureau's work against the slackers and the Reds was of one piece with its war against vice in 1910, and that all of these actions prefigured the Bureau's work against the gangsters of the thirties. Each time the Bureau was the effective means whereby the law could be mobilized in a pageant of popular politics; through highly publicized dragnets the Bureau sought to demonstrate the government's opposition to unpopular behavior or opinions: "Vice," "Disloyalty," "Anarchy." Depending on whether attention is focused on the victim or the audience this kind of activity discourages nonconformity or encourages conformity and thus strengthens "organic" social solidarity.

When the law is used as an instrument of ideological repression it is in the nature of things that *those charged are always innocent.* What is being attacked by the law is an idea or a form of behavior, and individuals are accused not for their actions but because they have become symbols of proscribed ideas or behavior. But people have little control over whether or not they become symbols, nor can they fully determine what they come to *mean* to others. Their symbolic significance is controlled by the audience and its manipulators (politicians, journalists and policemen). Therefore the victims are not responsible for what has put them in jail or brought them to trial—that they have become symbols of dangerous cultural tendencies. If they have committed criminal acts, such acts function merely as illustrations of the evil they symbolically represent. From the earliest days, the victims of the Bureau have been prosecuted not for what they have done, but for what they have meant.

From 1908 until 1924, when Hoover assumed command, the Bureau was the highly visible expression of the government's opposition to sexual offenders, the unpatriotic, anarchists, communists and radicals (especially the I.W.W.). Why, then, did the Bureau lapse into a nine-year period of obscurity during the first phase of Hoover's directorship?

From the beginning the Bureau had its critics. Since almost invariably the *symbolically* guilty victims of the Bureau turned out to be *legally* innocent, the criticism had plenty of fuel to feed on. Indignation over the Bureau's misdeeds, however, would never have been enough to bring the Bureau down. The F.B.I. could (and did) defend itself by charging that defenders of its victims were really motivated by sympathy for the unpopular causes the victims represented. This argument often had a certain degree of validity and in any case was effective rhetorically.

What almost destroyed the Bureau was not its performance of ideological repression. Its other role was to silence the elite critics of government policy by amassing damaging information against them. It was in this role that the Bureau finally overreached itself. Harding's Secretary of the Interior and Attorney General used the Bureau to head off exposure of the scandals at Teapot Dome by trying to frame their most dangerous critic, Senator Burton Wheeler of Montana. When this came out at Wheeler's trial the history of the Bureau's activities against Congress was revealed. Totally disgraced, the Bureau lost its entire top leadership, and the new director was given the job of rehabilitating the Bureau by keeping it ostentatiously free of politics (both real and symbolic). The man who was given this housecleaning task was J. Edgar Hoover, and by all accounts he *did* concentrate until 1933 on keeping things clean. During these years he sought to identify the Bureau with science which was a powerfully anti-political symbol during the twenties, stressing new developments like fingerprinting and crime laboratories. But in 1933 a new set of conditions forced the government to bring the Bureau out of mothballs; a government desperate to reassert its authority and its effectiveness, and a new crime wave made up of front-page gangsterism.

The F.B.I.'s own historian, Don Whitehead, explains the sudden rise of the Bureau to prominence during the early thirties as a response to an abrupt change in public attitudes:

A kidnap-murder in New Jersey, a gang massacre in Missouri and a kidnaping in Oklahoma were the crimes of 1932-1933 which shocked the nation and, by their chain reaction, sent the F.B.I. into a strange kind of guerilla warfare against the armed forces of the underworld.

During the twenties most of the country had watched the growth of crime with a so-what attitude. Those fellows in the gangs, many people felt, were no worse than the thieves in dinner jackets who had been corrupting federal, state and local governments; about the only difference was that one group used guns and the other didn't. But this tolerance gave way to angry demands that something be done about the menace of the gangsters and racketeers. And the beginning of the change in attitude can be pin-pointed as to time and place.[11]

H. L. Mencken called the Lindbergh case the greatest newspaper story since the crucifixion, and in terms of sheer volume of newsprint he was probably right. When the Lindbergh baby was taken from the family's house in New Jersey on March 1, 1932 the event touched off such a wild craze of public interest that it seemed as though the business of the entire country had come to a stop while the nation participated in the manhunt through the pages of their newspapers. Three months later the Congress passed the Lindbergh Kidnap Law, which, as usual, responded to a crime wave by throwing the F.B.I. at it. On September 14, 1934, after publicity which had turned everyone involved into a celebrity, the case was broken, and two years later the kidnapper was executed. The principal hero of the case, Colonel Schwartzkopf of the New Jersey State Police, went on to star as the announcer for Phillips H. Lord's "Gangbusters" (*né* "G-Men") radio show.

The second incident that helped create the image of a new national crime problem was the "Kansas City Massacre" of June 17, 1933. This was a daring attempt to free a Missouri mobster from custody, a blood-bath in which three F.B.I. agents died. The "star" of this atrocity was "Pretty Boy" Floyd.

The third media event that precipitated the Bureau's reentry into the public arena was the kidnapping of an Okalhoma City oilman on July 23, 1933. The villain this time was "Machine Gun" Kelly, and according to the legend fostered by the Bureau it was Kelly who, during his arrest for this crime, gave the agents their "G-Men" nickname.

The public was fascinated by these crimes and, as a good Aristotelian audience, it demanded a cathartic response from the national government. The demand most frequently heard was that all local police be nationalized into a great national police force. The Roosevelt administration was at this time enjoying a great public relations success with its mobilization of American business in the N.R.A., and so such a solution must have seemed an appealing one to the New Dealers. Hoover, however, immediately saw that it would be dangerous to allow the government to shoulder the responsibility for dealing with crime. It would be difficult to prevent the public from fixing the government with this responsibility if there was actually a national police force. Writing at the time, Hoover observed that "The cry of the public is for Federal legislation and Federal prosecution of racketeers. It is perhaps not overlooked, but it is certainly underemphasized, that the problem is a state one."[12] Hoover was able to make his superiors see the validity of his position and so when it came time for Homer Cummings, Roosevelt's Attorney General, to make his recommendations to Congress on the federal response to crime he said

> it is distinctly not the duty of the Federal Government generally to preserve peace and order in the various communities of our nation . . . we need expansion of the federal penal statutes to include control over the unlawful activities of those who deliberately take advantage of the protection presently offered them by state lines in perpetrating their crimes.[13]

Congress was persuaded by Cummings' reasoning, and during the spring of 1934 it passed new crime laws that made it a federal offense to rob a federal bank, to cross state lines to avoid prosecution and to use interstate communications systems for extortion. These new laws also made *all* interstate kidnappings federal crimes and gave F.B.I. agents the right to make arrests and tote guns. These laws *seemed* to be drastic ones; writing in 1937 one observer thought that "in the brief span between 1932 and 1934 police work in this country underwent the most radical change in its history . . . these measures were revolutionary. They put the federal government, for the first time, into the business of punishing crimes of violence."[14] The truth about the New Deal response to the crime problem, however, was that it was both more and less than it seemed. In effect the federal government was putting itself in the position of being able to deal with the *crime problem* (that is, with the popular image of crime) while resisting being saddled with the responsibility for preventing *crimes.* This paradox is the key to Hoover's resistance to the national police force idea, a position from which he never deviated and which he reaffirmed consistently throughout his career. Hoover's unwillingness to have the F.B.I. perceived as a national police force with real crime prevention responsibilities later plunged him into difficulties first with the Kennedy brothers, who wanted federal "strike forces" against crime, and then with Nixon, who wanted his help with the "plumbers."

Hoover refused to allow the F.B.I. to be called a national police force and resisted the nationalization of local police under F.B.I. leadership because this would symbolize the federal government's acceptance of responsibility for the prevention of crime throughout the country. This would have been disastrous because within the limits imposed upon action by Hoover's free society ideology, nothing the federal government could do would have any real effect on the occurrence of crime throughout the nation. Hoover had only to review the disastrous history of the Prohibition Bureau to see what would happen to any federal agency given responsibility for controlling crime: the ineffectiveness of the government's anti-crime work would soon become apparent and the Bureau and its head would inevitably be blamed. Hoover understood quite well what real crime prevention meant, because in 1931 the Wickersham Commission had argued that a real effort to deal with crimes throughout the nation would entail a sociological and psychological rather than a moralistic approach. Hoover's own religious outlook made the sociological approach to crime abhorrent to him, but even if he had been persuaded of the approach's merits, he would have been justified in doubting whether American society would ever implement a program that called for some redistribution of wealth and an alteration of cultural attitudes and values. Hoover was undoubtedly correct in suspecting that *any* measures adopted by the federal government to lower the incidence of crime would be ineffective, and that such a demonstration of the federal government's ineffectiveness in such an important and sensational area as crime would have a thoroughly disillusioning effect on the public's confidence in the government. No—the federal government must resist at all costs the actual responsibility for preventing crimes; local governments must be made to seem responsible for their occurrence, while the federal government would undertake to deal with crime in the one form that it could not avoid: the symbolic image of the crime problem, a matter of public relations. To accomplish this Hoover adopted a three-part strategy.

First, he acquired complete control over the raw material of the public's perception of crime, crime statistics. The F.B.I.'s Uniform Crime Reports have been criticized on almost every possible methodological ground (although they have been recently given impressive and unexpected support as an accurate index to *variations* in the crime rate), but such criticisms are really beside the point. These figures allow the Bureau to be the *first* to interpret the meaning of the numbers in relative and absolute terms. The Bureau is the first to know what is happening to crime across the nation, and thus it is the first to say what the figures mean and who is to blame. Critics of the Bureau must then begin their side of the argument with a rebuttal, a rhetorically inferior position. This control over crime statistics the F.B.I. has maintained until the present.

The second aspect of Hoover's strategy was to keep the federal government's responsibility from extending to *crimes* (which he would force the local governments to cope with; their failure would be heralded by gibes from Hoover); he would limit the Bureau's jurisdiction to the crime *problem.* It was not difficult to see theoretically how this might be done, but to accomplish it took the knowledge of a master and the skill of an artist. Hoover's management of the crime problem depended on his insight into the fact that the public is not stirred by the large number of anonymous crimes that constantly occur. These attract only passing attention. The public is stirred by the individual, highly dramatic offense that seems meaningful because it seems to be a *symbol* of all crimes. By carefully overseeing the drafting of federal crime legislation Hoover restricted his responsibility to those few crimes that happen to be transformed by publicity into crime symbols. During the thirties these were kidnappings and bank robberies, during the forties and fifties spying and sabotage. Hoover well understood that, as George Orwell observed, "The average man is not directly interested in politics, and when he reads he wants the current struggles of the world to be transformed into a simple story about individuals."[15] Hoover made sure that he had to deal only with those crimes that were "simple stories about individuals," because these were the only crimes that mounted a direct challenge to the government's image of effectiveness. Hoover's method was to transform crime from a faceless and unmanageable chaos born out of thousands of obscure crimes into the sensational deeds of a few dramatic public enemies who could be dealt with according to a set of popular conventions featuring detection, chase, shoot-out and capture or death. Of course a rational manager of public opinion will not long rely on the vagaries of the popular press to provide him with his supply of symbolic criminals. Therefore Hoover hit upon the device of creating his own symbols by designating selected outlaws as "Public Enemies"; in the fifties this process was further rationalized by creating a never-ending supply of symbols by means of the "Ten Most Wanted Fugitives" list.

Once Hoover had perfected his management of symbolic crime, "real" crime could grow and fester, but the government would be off the hook. Crimes could be enumerated and evaluated by the F.B.I. and blamed on unpopular groups against whom the government could align itself with the public. Since crime was now symbolic, its causes must also be symbolic: ideas and practices offensive to conventional morality, all lumped together under the generic label of "disrespect for the law." Blame for the increase in crime could be charged against symbols of the scientific approach: criminologists, penologists, parole officers, lawyers and politicians; but perhaps one of Hoover's own lists should be cited: "Theorists, pseudocriminologists, hypersentimentalists, criminal coddlers, convict lovers, and fiddle-faced reformers." These were Hoover's enemies because their non-symbolic (or even naturalistic) attitude toward crime threatened the theatrical suspension of disbelief that let the public accept the front-page capture of a notorious gangster as an effective government response to the crime problem.

The third aspect of the Hoover strategy was the most important. Jack Alexander wrote in 1937 that the Kansas City Massacre convinced Hoover that "the mere quieting down of the kidnapping and bankrobbery scare was not enough but that an actual crusade was needed. . . . Someone had to become the symbol of the crusade, and the Director decided that, because of his position, it was plainly up to him."[16] Hoover was not a humble man, but more than vanity was involved when Hoover decided to turn himself into a national symbol of the law. This may in fact have been the only effective way of dealing with the symbol of national crime, because if Hoover could become a symbol of national law enforcement, then the effectiveness of the government's war on crime would come to depend not on what Hoover *did*, but upon what he *meant* in the public's imagination. According to Drew Pearson Hoover was able to accomplish this transformation of himself into a symbol through the efforts of a newspaperman named Harry Suydam, a publicist Homer Cummings hired for Hoover on Pearson's recommendation. Pearson recalled that Suydam "performed so spectacularly that within a year he had transformed Hoover, previously a barely known bureaucrat, into an omnipotent crime-buster whose name was familiar to every American."[17]

Louis B. Nichols, Hoover's third in command, recalls that Suydam worked for the Attorney-General and not for Hoover, and that Suydam's job was to build up the Justice Department at the Bureau's expense. Nichols argues that Rex Collier, a reporter for the Washington *Star*, wrote the first features about the Bureau, and therefore Nichols gives Collier credit for creating the public interest in the Bureau that later publicists exploited.

Before 1933 Hoover had written only one article that was circulated outside the Bureau, and that was a scientific essay on fingerprinting for the *Annals of the American Academy*. Beginning in August 1933 Hoover's by-line began to appear regularly in the mass circulation magazines (particularly *American Magazine*) and for the rest of the decade the rate of Hoover's writing approached one article a month. Usually credit was given to the "editorial assistance" of Courtney R. Cooper. His symbolic approach to crime thus became familiar to the readers of such magazines as *Parade, Reader's Digest, Scholastic* and the already-mentioned *American Magazine.*

During the 1930s the equivalents to the television talk shows for introducing new names to the public were the gossip columns, particularly those of Ed Sullivan and Walter Winchell. Hoover assiduously cultivated these writers, trading exclusive news for mention in their columns. This meant that his diet, hobbies and sports were all described in the daily papers. From these publicists Hoover learned how to pick up publicity by drinking at the Stork Club and vacationing at Palm Beach.

As a part of this process Hoover's appearance began to change. Hoover's photos before 1933 show a thin, pale, serious person with a camera-shy, inexpressive face and slicked down hair. He posed for these early shots working at his desk with pen in hand. After the build-up Hoover was characteristically photographed in action poses: with a machine gun, tennis racket, or fishing rod, or striding beside his heroic subordinate, Melvin Purvis. By 1944 the Bureau would be circulating an 8 x 10 publicity portrait by Karsh of Ottawa in which a relaxed, confident Hoover is dressed in a movie hero's three-piece suit. He knows how to dominate the camera and looks like a man sure of his celebrity status and in complete control of his image. The caption for the 1944 portrait has the kind of prose that a theatrical agent writes for his client:

> Tough and looks it, is MR. J. EDGAR HOOVER, Director of the Federal Bureau of Investigation of America, the most efficient anti-crime organization in the world. This stockily built chief has a sensational record for bringing public enemies of all kinds, including the notorious kidnapping gangs, to justice. The prevention of sabotage and espionage have since the war become major tasks of the F.B.I., and as a result of the exploits of his men, Mr. Hoover is the hero of all American schoolboys. . . . Besides many articles in newspapers and magazines, he has written a book, "Persons in Hiding." Mr. Hoover has a pleasant personality; is a bachelor; fond of sports; and collects Chinese antiques.

This publicity treatment during the mid-thirties quickly turned Hoover into, as producer Quinn Martin of "The Untouchables" and "The F.B.I." has said, "a star in his own right." Martin said that when he met Hoover in the fifties "I felt much as I did when I met Cary Grant—that this was a special person."[18] Publicity alone, however, could have done no more than make Hoover a very famous person and his Bureau a very notable force. Clearly something more than this happened to Hoover; he became more than a celebrity; he became "Public Hero Number One." During the thirties Hoover became more than just a famous person who fascinated the public because of what he did. He became vitally important to the American people because of what he *meant*, and his agency and its chief acquired a symbolic role in the culture.

What was Hoover's secret for turning public relations dross into mythic gold? The governmental woods in the thirties were full of ambitious men eagerly seeking the greatness of heroism. Why did Hoover succeed where so many others had failed?

It is no answer to say that these were hero-worshipping times, although they were. F.D.R.'s success in making himself into a tribal leader, a cultural symbol of solidarity more than a president, perhaps indicates that during the depression years the nation needed heroes who could counteract cultural disintegration. In fact during this decade it was not unusual for the symbolic roles of Roosevelt and Hoover to be linked together. Jules Feiffer remembers that as far as comic book readers were concerned, Roosevelt and Hoover were the eternal president and vice-president.[19]

Others before Hoover had sold themselves to the public as symbols of the "war on crime." Ole Hanson, Calvin Coolidge, and A. Mitchell Palmer were public officials who tried it, as did Allan Pinkerton among the free entrepreneurs. Where Hoover's method was different was that they had offered themselves to the public as heroes on the basis of their deeds, and so had to maintain their image by repeating their exploits until they finally ran out of new villains to vanquish; Hoover presented himself as the embodiment of a role and claimed to be a hero because of the role he filled and not because of the things he did. Once he had succeeded in identifying himself with this role he had merely to remind his public occasionally of it—the role would take care of the rest.

This may all sound mysterious. What was this prepotent role that did so much for Hoover and made him a political immortal in *saecula saeculorum*? What Hoover did was to adopt the guise of the detective hero, a pop culture figure who had a long and firmly established symbolic meaning in American iconography. Hoover managed to persuade the public that the F.B.I. agent was a real life version of the fictional detective hero that Americans idolized in their magazines, comic strips and radio shows. Therefore as the head of these amazing G-Men Hoover must be the greatest of them all, the archetypal detective.

More specifically, the detective hero upon whom Hoover modeled himself was the *action* detective of the story paper, dime novel and pulp magazine. Hoover adopted two approaches in working towards his goal of identifying his agents with the action detectives. First he highlighted the similarities between G-Man adventures and the exploits of Hawkshaw the Detective, Old Sleuth, Old Cap Collier, Nick Carter and Dick Tracy. Hoover's second means of mythologizing the F.B.I. (and by "Hoover" after 1933 is meant that corporate personality consisting of Hoover himself and the writers of the Crime Records Division) is even more interesting to the student of popular culture. Beginning in 1933 Hoover encouraged writers to use G-Men and Hoover himself as characters in the fictional detective stories appearing in pulp magazines, comics, movies and radio shows.

America's fascination with the fictional detective hero was almost a hundred years old when Hoover decided that such popularity was too valuable to waste on mere entertainment. Howard Haycraft's famous dictum that there could have been no detective stories until there were actually detectives is undoubtedly true. The first popular accounts of detectives began to appear shortly after the formation of the first professional detective detective agencies: around 1827 in England (the memoirs of the Bow Street Runners) and around 1829 in France (the memoirs of Vidocq). These early detective stories were eagerly read in this country where Edgar Allan Poe created the first detective short story in 1841, "The Murders in the Rue Morgue." This story appeared in "Uncle Sam," the first American story paper, a medium of entertainment that would prosper largely because of the steady diet of detective stories it could supply.

The attention of the standard histories of the detective story has been focused on what Poe called the story of ratiocination, or what has come to be known as the mystery. This is an artfully constructed tale in which a supremely intelligent hero guides the reader through a maze of clues in pursuit of a barely characterized murderer. In the mystery story the characterization of the detective is essential, as is the complexity of the plot and the subtlety with which it is unfolded. The nature of the crime and the characterization of the criminal are deliberately sketchy because too great an emphasis on these elements would detract from the excitement of the intellectual chase. This is the tradition that includes such masters as Poe, Doyle, Sayers, Ellery Queen, Rex Stout and Ross Macdonald, and it is the tradition that has attracted the attention of those intellectuals who write the histories of the detective story, which is only natural: this is the type of detective story that intellectuals read. But for every reader of Sherlock Holmes hundreds read Old Sleuth, Cap Collier or Nick Carter; for every reader of Dorothy Sayers there were dozens of *Shadow Magazine* or Doc Savage readers; for every Rex Stout addict there are thousands who follow the exploits of Mike Hammer.

The mystery story has been collected and chronicled and reprinted; no such loving care has been lavished on the other principal detective story tradition, the action story of the pulp magazines. These were seldom collected, and when a rare Nick Carter (now on microfilm) or Old Sleuth can be found the cheap basswood pulp crumbles upon reading. But in these fragile volumes of he-man stories the popular (as opposed to the high-brow) image of the detective was born. It was the pulp magazine detective who took hold of the public's imagination.

The appeal of the mystery story has been analyzed at length by critics like Edmund Wilson and scholars like William Aydelotte. Both agree that the mystery reader is presented with a substitute universe with fixed and reasonable laws in which all events are significant (because they are clues), one where knowledge is power since it is an act of knowing that solves the case. In other words, it is a world where thought *is* action, a paradise for the intellectual.

In the action detective story, on the other hand, knowledge is *not* power; power is power. As George Orwell has pointed out, the action detective story tends to be a celebration of the power principle. This is not to say that complex plots are never encountered in action stories, but when they are their function is different than in the mystery. The reader is not expected to enjoy unraveling the mystery along with the detective; rather he is expected to enjoy watching the *hero* overcome an ordeal, this time an intellectual one, just as he has enjoyed watching the hero overcome such physical ordeals as beatings, gunshots and Dido's embraces. The action story's plot need not be logical; it need not even be worked out completely at the end. The action detective does not untie the Gordian knot—he slices it through with a karate chop or a secret knife hidden inside a trick decoder ring.

Action detectives are faced with the mysterious and they overcome it not with science but with strength and trickery; when science is used it is only a superior sort of mumbo-jumbo. Gimmickry abounds in the adventure story: ventriloquism, disguise, specially equipped cars, oriental styles of dirty fighting.

The action hero is faced with a challenge, the capture of a criminal whose identity, method and motive may very well be known to the reader and perhaps even to the hero at the beginning of the story. Every element in the story is intended to demonstrate the difficulty of the inevitable capture, thereby proving the prowess of the detective. The action detective story is therefore a travesty on the epic form; it is a series of ordeals that exist only to be overcome by a hero with whom the reader identifies, a hero whose omnipotence the reader admires and comes to share. Since the action detective is a projection of the culture, his success is a demonstration of the culture's ability to repel all challenges. It is a ritual whose effect is to prove the strength of a culture and the weakness of those outside it. In other words it tends to increase that respect for the law that Hoover always maintained was the only real answer to the crime problem.

The mystery focuses on the *process* of solving the crime while the action detective story centers on the *capture* of the criminal. This makes the political symbolism of the action story more obvious than in the mystery. There are other differences as well. In the mystery ambiguities and eccentricities of character are not only tolerated: they are essential. Mystery heroes tend to be odd types, even defiant non-conformists. In the action story the hero is a purely projective culture hero; he must be an embodiment of all culturally admired values. In a class-structured or pluralistic culture he will be drawn only from the most admired class or ethnic types. Not only did Hoover have few non-whites in the F.B.I., but during the sixties he even began to make his long-standing requirement that applicants "look like agents" more specific: he began to demand that they conform to the "Zimmy image" (i.e., that they look like Efrem Zimbalist, Jr., star of *The F.B.I.* TV show).

Motive is one of the puzzles in the mystery, and in order to create suspense the motive, like the solution, must not be immediately obvious. In the action story evil character is the only permissible motive. The hero's motive for pursuing the criminal is the eternal hostility of good for evil. Nothing is allowed that might blur the clarity of this tension.

In short, the action detective story is an entirely different genre from the mystery. It emphasizes the criminal's capture and not his unmasking; it creates identification with the hero by making him a projection of cultural values; the plot is a series of ordeals by which a culture demonstrates its superiority over its enemies ("criminals"). These are the hallmarks of the *popular* detective hero, and a hundred years of loyalty demonstrates the depth of this formula's significance to the popular audience.

While there had been many action detective stories in American popular literature during the mid-nineteenth century, it was not until the first "Old Sleuth" story in George Munro's *Fireside Companion* in 1872 that a particular detective became famous. Story papers like *Fireside Companion* were the most important popular entertainment medium of the late nineteenth century. The field was dominated by two New York City publications, the *Ledger* of the fabulous Robert Bonner, and the *Weekly* of the long-lived firm of Street and Smith. It was in the *Weekly* that the career of the greatest of all action heroes was launched: Nick Carter in 1886. Nick Carter was created by John Coryell and then carried through over two hundred novels by Frederick Marmaduke Van Renselaer Dey (as late as 1943 there was a *Nick Carter, Master Detective* show, and today there are *new* paperback adventures of a *new* Nick Carter). The popularity of the story paper detective was astounding: by 1900 the British firm of the Aldine Company had over two hundred and fifty different detective heroes in its stable, including the "Demon Detective," "Fritz, the Bound-Boy Detective," "Old Stonewall, the Shadower," "Lynx Eyes, the Pacific Detective," and "Old Electricity, the Lightning Detective." The popularity and durability of the action detective hero was so great that he survived the medium that had made him famous. At the end of the century the story papers were replaced by the weekly pulp magazines devoted either to the adventures of a single detective (e.g., *The Nick Carter Weekly*) or to types of action stories (*Adventure, Detective*). During the second decade of the century the detective hero entered the comic strips (the first being *Hawkshaw the Detective* after Tom Taylor's play *The Ticket-of-Leave Man*). The great twentieth-century detective hero, *Dick Tracy*, arrived in 1929, the same year that *True Detective Mysteries*, the first radio detective show, went on the air. By 1930 the public's infatuation with the detective hero was almost manic. *Munsey's Detective Fiction Weekly* and Street and Smith's *Detective Story* and *Shadow Magazine* were only the leading detective pulps: there were dozens of others competing on the news-stands. On the back of cereal boxes Inspector Post implored kiddies to join the "Post Toasties Law and Order Patrol." This detective mania would continue throughout the thirties; there would be a *Sherlock Holmes* radio show as well as others starring Dick Tracy and Charlie Chan, while the decade would end with the *Superman* and *Captain Midnight* radio shows (both in 1940). Even today the popularity of the form on television is showing no sign of flagging.

What Hoover did was to infiltrate the action detective story. To do this he demonstrated the parallel between the actual cases of the F.B.I. and the plots of the action story. Then he persuaded writers, artists, film makers and other mass entertainment producers that they would do well to make F.B.I. agents the heroes of their fictional dramas.

To show the parallel between the work of the F.B.I. and that of the detective heroes, in 1933 Hoover began a series of articles and books that presented "true" cases of the F.B.I. These stories seem to be pointless publicity chasing unless Hoover's ultimate mythologizing strategy is kept in mind, and then a clear pattern emerges. In these magazine articles and books Hoover pointed out that the formulaic exploits of the detective hero were the everyday routine of the F.B.I. agent. In a 1937 speech, for example, he claimed that "life has been a great adventure for those of us who have been privileged to play a pioneering part in the field of progressive law enforcement."[20] In the action detective stories the hero is expected to know all crime fighting skills, and these constitute a rather conventionalized repertoire: fingerprinting, disguises, foreign languages, wire-tapping, stalking and tracking, unarmed combat and sharpshooting. It was Nick Carter's boast that he was the *master* detective, proficient in every means of combating crime. Therefore Hoover methodically went through all the detective routines and devoted one article to each of them, proving that the F.B.I. agent, or rather the Bureau itself as a collective hero, was also the master of all the traditional detective tricks. The moral of these "true cases from the files" is usually not explicitly stated, but it still cannot be missed. Hawkshaw, Sherlock Holmes, Old Sleuth, Nick Carter: all are rank amateurs compared to the agents of the F.B.I. Sometimes Hoover did draw the comparison: "there is no magic in efficient law enforcement, no Sherlock Holmes theorizing or fictional deduction . . . before science all things must fall, including the ramparts of criminality."[21] Hoover often argued that the cases he featured were significant because they posed theoretical challenges to one of the Bureau's scientific techniques. For example, one grisly piece described a gangster who had skin from his back grafted onto his fingers to defeat the Bureau's fingerprint system. Hoover seriously discussed this as a threat to the whole concept of scientific law enforcement, and so he carefully traced the methods the Bureau used to defend its system against this surgical refutation, and he drove home the point with stomach-turning photographs of the man's hands and back.

Hoover also had his publicists pre-package all the Bureau's major cases, so that when reporters came to write their stories about the F.B.I.'s exploits they would follow the approved adventure formula of clues, leads, colorful informants, crooks with nicknames, chases and gunfights. The Bureau's publicists also made sure that whenever the Bureau went after its man he was never perceived as merely a small-time crook. Like the Shadow, Nick Carter or Superman the F.B.I.'s criminals by definition had the status of "Public Enemies." They were major threats to society. When Hoover got finished with each F.B.I. case it was as good as a pulp magazine adventure, only better—it was real.

The Bureau Headquarters in Washington was turned into a shrine to the myth of the G-Man as detective hero. It was outfitted as an American Madame Toussaud's filled with death masks of criminals, tours of crime labs, trick-shooting, and fingerprinting for everybody. It was a Hall of Fame for detectives, and all the detectives so honored were G-Men.

Hoover worked hard during these years to make himself the personification of the Bureau. He publicized the number of his office phone as a direct link between any citizen with news of a kidnapping and the Director himself. He traveled about the country giving speeches invariably embellished with examples drawn from fresh cases still warm in the files. The publicity activities of the Bureau were feverish during the thirties, and were all calculated to create the impression that the Federal Bureau of Investigation was a veritable library of pulp magazine adventures. All of this was bait that could not fail to attract the attention of action story writers desperate for material, and before long writers everywhere were rising to the lure.

But Hoover was not one to wait for the fish to bite. He began very early to "plant" F.B.I. agents in fictional adventure stories by encouraging a friendly writer, Rex Collier, to go through the Bureau's files for material for the first of the fictional G-Men adventures, the comic strip "War on Crime." Next he went to work on Hollywood, and before long "Public Enemy" himself, James Cagney, was starring in *G-Men* as an apprentice being indoctrinated in Bureau ideology and trained in scientific crime-fighting. This was the beginning of a long list of G-Men movies that included *You Can't Get Away With It, The House on 92nd Street, Walk East on Beacon,* and *The F.B.I. Story.*

Rex Collier had been collaborating with the sensationally successful crime radio show writer, Phillips H. Lord. The result was *G-Men*, with its identifying announcement "Calling the Police! Calling the G-Men! Calling All Americans to War on the Underworld!" This show, popular as it was, represented one of Hoover's rare setbacks. Lord was too headstrong and too much of a hotshot to accept for long Hoover's heavy-handed attempts to maintain control over the show. By 1936 Lord had changed the name of the show to "Gangbusters," had stopped identifying the heroes as F.B.I. agents, and, to add insult to injury, had replaced the F.B.I. agent who announced the show with Colonel Schwartzkopf, Hoover's hated publicity rival from the Lindbergh case.

It irked Hoover that there was not a satisfactory F.B.I. show on radio. When the post-World War II *The F.B.I. in Peace and War* was not to his liking he finally produced his own, *This is Your F.B.I.* He appeared on the inaugural April 6, 1946 show himself. Eventually *Top Secrets of the F.B.I.* and *I Was A Communist for the F.B.I.* also featured agents as heroes.

Hoover's greatest success in infiltrating popular culture was in the pulp magazine field. The best of the pulp G-Man detectives was Norman Daniel's Dan Fowler, the F.B.I. hero of *G-Man Detectives Magazine.* Frederick C. Davis' entry was *Secret Operator #5 Magazine. The Feds* and *F.B.I. Detective* were also devoted to fictional G-Man exploits, and G-Man stories also appeared regularly in almost all of the other adventure pulps.

The editors of these pulps could count on getting personal letters of commendation from Hoover for running G-Man yarns that he liked, and William W. Turner has described how assiduously editors tailored their stories to conform to a formula that would win them such letters.[22] For especially meritorious work an editor might be favored with a guest editorial or a "scientific" article by the Director. The name "J. Edgar Hoover" on the cover of a pulp was money in the bank for a publisher, and so once the pulp editors understood the rules of the game they were eager to play.

Hoover's success in associating his agents with action detective heroes and in turn filling fictional detective stories with F.B.I. characters was prodigious, as evidence from every form of thirties popular entertainment demonstrates. In 1932 Post Toasties had premium offers enticing kids into Inspector Post's Law and Order Patrol. By 1937 it had become the Melvin Purvis G-Man Law and Order Patrol. By the early 1940s Hoover and F.D.R. were regularly appearing in the first panels of comics giving the superheroes their assignments, and then in the last panel thanking them for saving the nation (or civilization, which amounted to the same thing). Most impressive of all, during the 1930s G-Men joined baseball players in the greatest of all tributes to the popular (or at least boyhood) hero, the bubble gum card. The "G-Men and Heroes of the Law" card series had literally hundreds of brightly colored accounts of the F.B.I.'s successes in defeating famous gangsters. These examples could be matched by many others, but perhaps one more may as well be mentioned: in a last, sad effort to keep alive one of the greatest of all popular heroes, Jack Armstrong, the All American Boy, finally became an agent of the "S.B.I." the Scientific Bureau of Investigation. But there is no time for that.

By the winter of 1933 the mythic transformation of Hoover and the F.B.I. had begun, and within a few years it was very nearly complete: both had become legends. In the public mind the F.B.I. and its director had become confused with the fictional heroes of mass entertainment. If radio shows, comics and movies were part of the fantasy life of Americans, then Hoover and his men had occupied the station house in the American Dream. The effect on American culture of this mythologization was wide-ranging and it was profound.

The Bureau's approach to crime, both because of its history and because of the needs of the central government in a mass society, was that of symbolic management. It would seek to avoid responsibility for actual crimes but would deal with those symbolic offenses that had come to represent all crime in public opinion. The most important effect of Hoover's self-mythologization was to harden this approach into a national orthodoxy, thus effectively denying the nation the opportunity of dealing with crime realistically and scientifically.

The symbolic approach to crime has been discussed here as the central authority's defensive response to events that threaten to destroy its image of effectiveness. The symbolic approach has a *positive* content as well: it views crime as an attack on the collective sentiments and values that are the basic sources of solidarity in a culture. Hoover's ideology essentially consisted of ethnocentrism within the American tradition of Christianity and individualism, so it is not surprising to find that his actions derive from this ethnocentric theory of crime; it *is* surprising to find that at times he used rather sophisticated language to communicate this theory to the public. In a 1939 speech he defined democracy as "the dictatorship of the collective conscience of our people,"[23] and he pointed to the law as the defender of that dictatorship. Hoover meant that the *real* significance of crime was that it was a threat to social cohesion and so had to be punished in such a way as to reestablish the strength of the collective conscience which the crime had weakened.

If the mass media is the effective repository of the popular consensus, as De Fleur and others have argued, then Hoover's treatment of crime as a public relations problem grows logically out of his ethnocentric convictions. If social solidarity is the highest good (and for Hoover it was), and if public opinion is society's *sense* of social solidarity, then it is in the area of public opinion that crime's effects are most to be feared. If crime as an image in public opinion is left uncombated it will create the image of a weak or nonexistent social solidarity, and will ultimately affect behavior by weakening conformity. Hoover was hostile to scientific criminologists because they urged the public to reject approaches to crime which treated crime principally as a symbolic threat to social solidarity. As Durkheim once observed, to a defender of cultural integration like Hoover, "theories which refuse to punishment any expiatory character appear as so many spirits subversive of the social order . . . these doctrines could be practiced only in a society where the whole collective conscience would be very nearly gone."[24]

It is no easy task to impose a symbolic and ritualistic interpretation of crime on a modern and pluralistic society. There are too many people who refuse to treat the criminal as symbol: the American legal tradition tries to punish an individual only when he is personally responsible for his crime. Hoover, on the other hand, wanted to punish the criminal for his symbolic significance, scarcely a matter for which he is legally responsible.

The identification of the F.B.I. agent with the detective hero of the fictional adventure stories contributed importantly to Hoover's success in imposing the ritualistic view of crime on American public opinion. Law enforcement in the detective story is a ritual; the hero and the criminal are stereotypes who are not really responsible for what they do. Their actions are simply typifying gestures that indicate their significance as symbols of good and evil. By identifying his agent with the fictional detective hero, Hoover was able to use the public's acceptance of the fictional hero's symbolism and ritual behavior to justify his agent's symbolism and ritual behavior. He lent the agent to crime fiction and in return borrowed popular entertainment's ritual interpretation of the law as justification for his Bureau's symbolic response to crime.

The ritualization of reality through myth has been thoroughly studied by the French semiologists, and in particular by Roland Barthes. Barthes writes that:

> Myth does not deny things, on the contrary its function is to talk about them; simply, it purifies them, it makes them innocent, it gives them a clarity which is not that of explanation but that of a statement of fact. If I state the fact of French imperiality without explaining it, I am very near to finding that it is natural and goes without saying: I am reassured. In passing from history to myth, myth acts economically; it abolishes the complexity of human acts, it gives them the simplicity of essences, it does away with all dialectics, without any going back beyond what is immediately visible, it organizes a world which is without any contradictions because it is without depth, a world wide-open and wallowing in the evident, it establishes a blissful clarity: things appear to mean something by themselves.[25]

Martin Jay explains this same phenomenon another way when he states that in mass culture there is characteristically "the substitution of mythic repetition for historical development."[26] Since the leader who provides symbolic (read alternatively mythic) solutions is dispensing clarity and simplicity, the result can be mass quiescence and reassurance; intense gratitude and affection will be bestowed upon the symbolic leader who provides an orderly and meaningful world view, a world view that obviously violates Einstein's dictum that a theory should be as simple as possible, but no simpler. Murray Edelman argues that "emotional commitment to a symbol is associated with contentment and quiescence regarding problems that would otherwise arouse concern. . . . One of the demonstrable functions of symbolization is that it induces a feeling of well-being: the resolution of tension."[27]

It is possible that the cultural solidarity produced by Hoover's brand of symbolic reassurance was needed during the depression. Again quoting Edelman, "the leader's dramaturgical jousts with public problems make the world understandable and convey the promise of collective accomplishment to masses who are bewildered, uncertain and alone."[28] Certainly Hoover's contribution to the unexpected cultural solidarity that emerged in the United States during the depression ought not to be ignored by historians of the period.

Such solidarity, however, was purchased at a high price indeed. If crime has any sociological significance at all it is that some members of society either do not accept the values of society or that the structure of society makes it impossible for them to live by those values. In any case crime is an important index to the well-being of society, information about itself that a society can afford to ignore no more than a motorist can ignore his oil pressure gauge. For almost fifty years Hoover's real life police dramas excited the imagination of the American public. His rituals of crime and punishment reassured Americans that all was well in their society, that theirs was a moral universe, and perhaps every culture must have some means of providing this reassurance. But did Hoover contribute to the nation's understanding of itself, its problems and its needs? Or did he blind Americans to vital facts about their society and so help create a heritage of unresolved social tensions? It will be the answers to these questions that will finally fix J. Edgar Hoover's place in the history of American culture.

Mick Gidley

ELEMENTS OF THE DETECTIVE STORY IN WILLIAM FAULKNER'S FICTION

Faulkner must have had an affection for detective stories. At his death in 1962 more than twenty-five modern exercises in the *genre* were to be found on his library shelves. This is a significant number both in itself and because it exceeds that for, say, flying stories, a kind of fiction more commonly known to have held Faulkner's interest and in which he produced some of his own most important work. Amongst the prominent crime writers to have provided items for entry into *William Faulkner's Library – A Catalogue* are John Dickson Carr, Dashiell Hammett, Ellery Queen (Frederic Dannay and Manfred B. Lee), and Rex Stout; Joseph Blotner, the catalogue's compiler, justifiably draws attention to their presence–and to that of equally imposing figures like Carter Dickson (John Dickson Carr), Mary Roberts Rinehart, Dorothy L. Sayers and Georges Simenon.[1] With equal facility he could have singled out E. C. Bentley, Agatha Christie or A. E. W. Mason.

Yet when Jean Stein, in a *Paris Review* interview, asked Faulkner if he "ever read mystery stories" he veered away from the question's implications–as was often his way during literary discussions–and seemingly towards evasiveness, inconclusiveness; he replied, "I read Simenon because he reminds me something of Chekhov."[2] A year earlier, in 1955, he had employed the same gambit with Cynthia Grenier:

Question: I'd like to ask one more question on your reading if I may, do you read detective stories?
Faulkner: Well, I like a good one like *Brothers Karamazov.*
Question: Well, I was thinking of *Knight's Gambit.*
Faulkner: Oh, I think you can learn a lot from Simenon's stories. They're so much like Chekhov's.
Question: I guess maybe I'd better read Chekhov again.
(Faulkner and Interviewer eye each other a minute.)[3]

Reprinted from the JOURNAL OF POPULAR CULTURE, VII:1.

Such rejoinders, to use the parlance of detective fiction, may in fact be much smaller red herrings than they appear; they do reveal that Faulkner was well aware that there may be *elements* of detective fiction in much of the greatest literature. This is the viewpoint of Norman Shrapnel's essay, "The Literature of Violence and Pursuit," in which he demonstrates the closeness of vision between the best of crime fiction and some of the acknowledged great novels of the last hundred years.[4] With this idea in mind we could do worse than glance at one of Faulkner's own examples, *The Brothers Karamazov*: Dostoyevsky's novel is rightly revered for its infinitely more salient qualities, its psychological and ideological complexity and intensity; but it *can* be viewed–on an admittedly limited level–as a detective story or, more accurately, as a crime story concerning the murder of Feodor Pavlovich and the wrongful conviction of Dimitri. (Moreover, if I were less pressed for space I would offer James Sandoe's similar comments on Dostoyevsky's *Crime and Punishment*–or those of L. A. G. Strong showing several conclusive affinities of both structure and content between Faulkner's other example, Chekhov, and the best of today's crime short story writers.)[5]

Frequently on public occasions, in university classrooms and the like, Faulkner would be asked to name his favorite authors. Over the years his reply–the list of books and writers that he reeled off with such relish–hardly changed. Amongst novelists the names which appear most often are Balzac, Dickens and Conrad.[6] Now it is interesting to note, I think, that in her standard work *The Development of the Detective Novel,* A. E. Murch devotes a considerable amount of space to discussions of the generative influence on the modern detective story of two of these writers, Balzac and Dickens.[7] And Albert Guerard, in *Conrad the Novelist,* asks "how many modern experiments in structure–even those of Faulkner–owe something to the 'police take' and the later Dickens," hinting that some link with the *genre* could be forged for Conrad.[8] As Faulkner was able to point to the presence of a detective element in a book he read infrequently, *The Brothers Karamazov*–at first sight such an unlikely host–it is probable that he would not miss it in the works of writers he professed to love and know intimately. Indeed, I believe one of the characteristics which so endeared them to him is that feature we now associate perhaps primarily with detective fiction, the sense of surprise, shock, *dénouement.* Emily Whitehurst Stone, wife of Faulkner's friend Phil Stone, has described what Balzac meant to her husband and to Faulkner when they read him as young men:

> [they were] joyously outraged as Balzac consistently outwitted them with his superior insights into the human heart, into his characters who never did quite what [Phil and Bill] had expected. "I used to finish a book and throw it across the room," Phil says. "Because Balzac was right every time."[9]

And Stone has written elsewhere that Faulkner shared his opinion "that Balzac is the greatest writer who ever lived."[10] (Martin Turnell, in *The Novel in France*, records the following anecdote: " 'I wish,' [he] once said to a Frenchman, '. . . someone would explain to me what the French see in Balzac.' 'I read him,' came the reply, 'as I read Simenon.' ")[11]

Hence it should come as no surprise to learn that when Faulkner dictated a list of books to be acquired for the later use of his grandchildren he included not only his beloved Balzac, but also a thoroughgoing work of detective fiction (if of a unique kind), G. K. Chesterton's "Father Brown" stories.[12] And in his own library, as I suggested previously, there are many writers who, according to Mrs. Murch, contributed to the evolution of the *genre*—Bulwer-Lytton, Wilkie Collins, Poe, Eugene Sue[13]—or who represent some of the best in modern crime writing: Eric Ambler, John Buchan, Anthony Gilbert (Lucy Malleson), and Frances Noyes Hart. . . .

Faulkner could well look his interviewers in the eye.

Sanctuary (1931) is the novel which occasioned André Malraux's famous quip that in Faulkner we witness the intrusion of Greek tragedy into the detective story.[14] Actually, just as the term "Greek tragedy" seems slightly off target so, applied to *Sanctuary*, does "detective story." *Sanctuary* is not, strictly speaking, a detective tale. It is rather a crime story; the action and meaning of the novel center on the crimes committed by Popeye: the murder of Tommy "the feeb" and the unnatural rape of Temple Drake. And it is on this level, as a crime tale, that *Sanctuary* has inspired, or partially inspired, at least two other famous crime novels. At the lowest level of common interest, as George Orwell noticed long ago, Faulkner's work lies behind *No Orchids for Miss Blandish* (1939) by James Hadley Chase.[15] (We may note here that Faulkner, unlike Hemingway, has perhaps not been granted his full due as a formative influence on the development of the so-called "hard-boiled" school of writers.)

On a considerably higher plane, *Sanctuary*, I suspect, had some effect on Graham Greene's *Brighton Rock* (1938). I refer generally to the mood of the book and particularly to the creation of the boy gangster, Pinkie. Pinkie, if not impotent like Popeye, hates and fears what he calls "the game," sexual love. He is a petty but violent criminal with black-suited narrow shoulders and eyes as devoid of humanity as Popeye's. It is revelant to this conjecture—although providing no outright evidence to support it—that Greene's luke-warm review of *Absalom, Absalom!* (1936) does single out Popeye as a "memorable figure" from the range of Faulkner's pre-1936 characters.[16]

Julian Symons has written that the task of the serious modern crime novel is to "investigate . . . the springs of violence."[17] *Sanctuary*, of course, performs this task with, it might be said, deadly effect. What has less often been realized–except as ammunition for the charge of "decadence"–is that many others of Faulkner's major works have crime, frequently violent crime, at their core. Let me summarily list several of the more notable: Joe Christmas' murder of Joanna Burden in *Light in August* (1932)–and, in turn, his own "crucifixion" at the hands of Percy Grimm and the lynch mob; the shooting of Charles Bon at the gates of Sutpen's Hundred and, also in *Absalom, Absalom!*, the death of the chief protagonist himself, Thomas Sutpen, under the driving scythe of Wash Jones; in *The Wild Palms* (1939) Harry Wilbourne is incarcerated for the manslaughter of his mistress, Charlotte Rittenmeyer; Mink Snopes kills Houston in *The Hamlet* (1940)–and in *The Mansion* (1959) he returns from Parchman to avenge himself on Flem Snopes, the kinsman who had refused him aid at his earlier trial; lastly, in *Requiem for a Nun* (1951) the process of retribution and atonement is set in motion by the murder of Temple's child by Nancy Mannigoe. Moreover, moving onwards from the impending murder related through "That Evening Sun" or the lynching at the heart of "Dry September" (both from *These 13,* 1931), a similar mosaic of crime could be put together from the central events of many of Faulkner's most memorable short stories.

Sanctuary, as I have said, is not strictly a detective tale but a crime story. However, little attention has been paid to the figure in it who functions, to some extent, *as* a detective–and the same may be said of related figures in other novels. In *Sanctuary* it is Horace Benbow who acts as a detective; for example, when in his efforts to clear Goodwin he traces Temple to the Memphis brothel. And, of course, in the later *Requiem* Gavin Stevens puts Temple through a kind of third degree in order to detect for her, to reveal to her, the nature, the wilfully evil nature, of her past behavior. Even the jovial but shrewd V. K. Ratliffe behaves as a kind of detective when he muses over the barn burning in *The Hamlet*:

> I just never went far enough . . . I went as far as one Snopes will set fire to another Snopes' barn and both Snopeses know it, and that was all right. But I stopped there. I never went on to where that first Snopes will turn around and stomp the fire out so he can sue that second Snopes for the reward and both Snopeses know that too.[18]

In any consideration of Faulkner's relationship to detective fiction the story "Vendée" from *The Unvanquished* (1938) deserves special–if minor –notice. A. E. Murch records that the Leatherstocking tales of James Fenimore Cooper had a thrusting effect on the European detective story of the later Nineteenth century; Balzac and others adapted to the streets of Paris the procedure of tracking, tracking by disturbance of animal and plant life, traces of cloth on branches, etc.[19] When Bayard, Ringo, and Uncle Buck trail Grunby and his men through the wilderness, following a loose horse shoe, noting a disturbed snake, etc., their activities represent a small return in detective-type fiction to the forests from whence it came.

But the above detective elements, isolated briefly from Faulkner's fiction, are all matters of plot. Of primary concern in this essay are the ways in which the overt detective tales amongst Faulkner's work—such as the stories in *Knight's Gambit* (1949)—may illuminate the *structure* and *meaning* of some of his major novels. If we consider for a moment a generally recognized tendency of these major novels, analogies with detective fiction may be brought into focus. In his seminal essay of 1939, "The Novel as Form," Conrad Aiken noted that one of the principal characteristics of the style and structure of Faulkner's best work is the ability to deliberately *withhold meaning.*[20] Likewise, the skill of the detective author lies to a large extent exactly in the ability to conceal meaning—in the form of clues, motives, etc.—until he has prepared the reader to receive it. Many of the particulars to be investigated in the remainder of this essay amount finally to facets of this general characteristic common to both Faulkner and detective writing.

With two other scriptwriters, Faulkner worked on the screenplay of Raymond Chandler's nōvel *The Big Sleep* (1939).[21] The fact that the film—directed by Howard Hawks, starring Humphrey Bogart and Lauren Bacall—was successful with both the critics and the public on its release in 1946 shows, I think, that Faulkner understood the basic intentions of detective fiction, and the effects it should achieve. And, of course, as is more to the point, he demonstrated that he could create these effects in his own medium when he collected the tales—written at various times during the previous decade—published as *Knight's Gambit* (1949).

Knight's Gambit contains five stories and a novella of the same title. The first story is called "Smoke." An old proud and crotchety man, Anse Holland, is found dead, presumably killed by his horse. He leaves a peculiar will bequeathing his farm to one or other of his two sons—both of whom are estranged from him and from each other—if certain facts can be established by the local aged and respected judge. Then the judge is murdered, shot between the eyes in mysterious circumstances. Gavin Stevens, the detective hero of the stories in *Knight's Gambit,* unravels the motivation for the murder in a long court scene in which he substantiates a connection between the two deaths and then proceeds to allow suspicion to fall first on one of the sons and then on the other, alternately, until finally he is able to reveal the identity of the true murderer—who turns out to be a cousin we have seen virtually no reason to suspect but who, from a position of hindsight, is shown to have had excellent motives for committing the crimes.

In several respects "Smoke" can be viewed as a conventional detective story. Stevens, the detective figure, like many such heroes before and after him, is a lawyer and, as has often been noted, his characterization grew out of the other lawyer in *Sanctuary,* Horace Benbow. He is etched as somewhat eccentric, renowned for his garrulousness and to be revered both for his shrewdness as a human being and his erudition as a man of learning. He succeeds in solving the case by the application of a mixture of the two principal methods commonly employed by fictional detective heroes: logic, in the manner, say, of Sherlock Holmes, and intuition based on long observation of human traits—like, for instance, Father Brown. In court he presents his findings, replete with agonising digressions on various faults of human nature, with panache and as much attention to timing and histrionics as an Erle Stanley Gardner attorney. And he completes his revelation, extracts a virtual confession of guilt from the true murderer, by sheer trickery. Also, in common with numerous other works of this type, after the trial is over and the criminal's fate sealed, Stevens lets his listeners (and the reader) in on both the secret of his trick and the reasons for his suspicions. In the good conventional detective story no loose ends should remain untied. (Anse Holland's digging up of his wife's grave, although not explained, can be taken either as an illustration of Holland's warped state of mind or as the execution by Faulkner of a device also practiced and recommended by Raymond Chandler: the deliberate initiation of a false mystery.)[22]

Yet, as a detective story, "Smoke" does have some weaknesses. First there are two matters of verisimilitude. The trial is staged in the dead judge's chambers. Presumably this is to allow Stevens to make such casual yet devastating use of the judge's brass box—but how could all the members of a "grand jury" (plus onlookers) fit into such a small room? And just what kind of trial could it be? Also Faulkner devotes some skillful writing to showing that the judge's black servant had never failed to spot an intruder in more than seventeen years. Yet on the one occasion of the murder he somehow fails to open his eyes just because the hired "city" gangster walks extremely softly; having built up the impregnability of the chambers so forcefully, the reader expects a much more ingenious method of entry than mere quiet feet—something at least a fraction closer to Poe's fantastic offering in "The Murders in the Rue Morgue."

The clues which lead to the criminal's conviction raise a more theoretical question. Much of the pleasure aroused by classic detective fiction derives from the assumption that, though the reader is in possession of all the necessary clues, the detective will still most likely beat him to the solution. The reader enjoys testing his powers against those of the sleuth in what has come to be known as "fair play." But clearly this is only possible if the reader actually is in possession of all the necessary clues (I do not mean all the necessary *knowledge*; many detectives can only interpret the clues because they are aware of obscure facts, usually scientific or literary)—and this is decidedly not the situation in "Smoke." Only Stevens has all the clues; only he knows, for instance, that the cousin had shown any interest in legal means of acquiring Holland's farm, the objective behind the crimes. Thus Faulkner breaks the eighth of Monsignor Ronald Knox's nine rules (later expanded into "the Decalogue") for detective authors: "The detective must not light on any clue which he does not instantly produce for the inspection of the reader."[23]

"Smoke" has imperfections of another kind. In characterization it falls short of Faulkner's achievements in many of his non-detective stories of comparable length. Take the two brothers, Anse and Virginius Holland: one is excessively violent and the other extraordinarily mild. These are really the only aspects of their respective natures that Faulkner renders. In other words, in "Smoke" Faulkner seems positively to deprive his people of the complexity we expect them to exhibit. Now Poe, in "The Philosophy of Composition," declared that the plot must be planned in detail first and be throughout the primary area of concern, even to the exclusion of "style" and strong characterization.[24] This view has achieved wide acceptance amongst many modern authorities on detective fiction, including Somerset Maugham, S. S. Van Dine (Willard Huntington Wright), and Nigel Morland.[25] Bearing this teaching in mind, it is perhaps surprising that Faulkner—who professed to "follow" rather than dictate to his characters[26]—found anything congenial in the form at all; even if he was influenced toward it by Van Dine (see below), he would surely have known he was working against the grain of his abilities. But the number of detective stories he wrote shows that he did find something to his taste in the *genre.* Consequently, while in such a more or less "pure" detective story as "Smoke" he tends to write down to his readers, many of the detective elements which we have noticed in it, *when submerged or subsumed in other contexts,* would enable him to provide effects it is difficult to imagine him supplying by other means. We will have occasion to examine these effects as we move outwards from the other stories in *Knight's Gambit.*

"Monk" contains no evidence of any writing down. Its very first paragraph may be appreciated as a suitable credo for what follows:

> I will have to try to tell about Monk . . . a deliberate attempt to bridge the inconsistencies of his brief and sordid and unoriginal history, to make something out of it, not only with the nebulous tools of supposition and inference and invention, but to employ these nebulous tools upon the nebulous and inexpliquable material which he left behind him. Because it is only in literature that the paradoxical and even mutually negativing anecdotes in the history of the human heart can be juxtaposed and annealed by art into verisimilitude and credibility.[27]

—a credo for that matter less strained than some of Faulkner's similar comments at Stockholm and one which could be applied to all of his best work.

In Monk himself we are presented with a character who, though "a moron, perhaps even a cretin," is rich in eccentric inconsistencies, as highly developed a simpleton as we are ever likely to meet in fifteen or so pages. Faulkner interests us in this man and his fate. But, while two crimes occur and we naturally want to know how they came about (we never really believe that Monk, the accused, is guilty, or, more emphatically, responsible), the story is not strictly a detective one. Stevens is present, exercising his mental powers, but as a detective he discovers nothing; he stumbles across the truth by accident: a gross infringement of the form's "rules." Mainly Stevens serves as the agency whereby we learn more about Monk's fate and, as far as the *plot* is concerned, Monk's fate is what engages our attention. But Stevens also forms the medium through which the *meaning* of Monk's destiny registers. At the end of the story, after we learn that, yes, Monk is innocent, and that the man guilty of the second murder–due to the political corruption of the governor–will be reprieved, Stevens leaves the penitentiary sickened at man's injustice to man and the absurdity of man's predicament.

Such an effect is diametrically opposed to all the basic tenets of classic detective fiction which, inasmuch as it separates the sheep from the goats, usually restores the reader's faith in the ultimate efficacy of justice, in the stability of the social order.[28] Thus, as a detective writer, Faulkner is subversive. But then, to beg a question to which I will return at the end of this essay, this is surely precisely one of the qualities responsible for his high stature as a serious author. In *Sanctuary* we find it displayed in the extreme. There the figure in the position analogous to Stevens in "Monk" is, as I have stated, Horace Benbow. Benbow forms a sort of mirror through which the reader watches the horrific happenings at the Old Frenchman Place, Miss Reba's brothel, and the Jefferson courthouse. And the effect these events have upon Benbow's ideas is in turn reflected for the reader to absorb and, in all probability, share.

Admittedly, right from the opening of the novel Horace, unlike the average fictional sleuth, because of his disastrous marriage, is "straddling two worlds–the world of his illusions and [that] of his actual existence";[29] but his ideas (they become illusions definitely only later) are intact: God is a "gentleman," the rule of justice prevails, and society embodies civilized values. However, as he investigates he becomes sucked into the vortex of evil Popeye has stirred into action and learns that Ruby Goodwin, a whore, possesses more humanity than the Christian women of Jefferson, including his sister; that the District Attorney will twist the law for political advantage; that Temple can not only face him with "actual pride, a sort of naive and impersonal vanity"[30] in what she has done, but will actually lie in court; and that the spirit of the people of Jefferson can express itself in the lynching of an innocent man.

Though superficially it seems that the climax of Horace's disillusionment arrives when he concludes, Temple having babbled her tale, that

"Perhaps it is upon the instant that we realize, admit, that there is a logical pattern to evil, that we die" (p. 177) this judgment proves to be merely a stage along the way. It is too positive; there would still be something in the sanctuary. In reality the climax occurs when he senses that a logical pattern is precisely what the crucial events of a lifetime do *not* have: there seems no logical reason for Temple to so glibly condemn an innocent man to shield the impotent and twisted one who had raped her so unnaturally and killed her lover, Red. This is the action which defeats Horace, which translates him home to Kinston a "dead" man. I cannot envisage how else, how other than by the introduction of a quasi-detective (representing more or less the average man) to investigate the situation—that is, to get close to it—that Faulkner could register with such immediacy the evil at the heart of *Sanctuary*'s events. To paraphrase one of Knox's remarks about Chesterton's later Father Brown stories, if we read "Monk" or *Sanctuary* with interest it is not because they are good detective stories but because they are disturbingly good Faulkner.

"Hand Upon the Waters" is both fairly good Faulkner and an engaging detective story. In it Stevens proceeds from a hunch aroused by a piece of acute observation to arrange a trap for Lonnie Grinnup's murderers. The trap closes neatly—despite the fact that Stevens suffers a wound—and retribution is justly, if very harshly, apportioned. The method Faulkner arranges as a means of murder and body disposal—having the victim hung on a trot-line fishing hook below water—proves original, a worthy extension of the more macabre possibilities of crime fiction. Also, by allowing Stevens himself—the character we most identify with—to intervene physically in the story's action in the manner of a Hammett or Chandler hero (though emphatically more shyly, almost nonviolently!), Faulkner raises the level of suspense. Indeed, from the viewpoint of detective fiction there is only one weakness in the story: the reader receives no reason for Lonnie's killers to return to the scene of the crime (unless it be to look for whatever had made Stevens suspect them) and, equally, no cause for Stevens' certainty that they will be there. But these are minor blemishes.

"Hand" manifests some of the signs of Faulkner at his best. We are confronted, as in "Monk," with a range of sharply delineated characters: a "feeb" descended from one of Jefferson's original settlers; a deaf and dumb boy who becomes, ironically, the agent of justice; and a cold, expressionless, Flem Snopes-like criminal, a gambler who, for his own salvation, tries to restrain Boyd, the hot-headed killer with whom he is in league. Also, the ambience of the crime, the dilapidated shack out back in the wilds of the country, is evoked with a skill reminiscent of that employed in such earlier works as *As I Lay Dying* (1930) and *The Hamlet.*

Practically the same may be said of "Tomorrow," the tale of Jackson Fentry. Fentry descends from the hills to work in a lumber camp, falls in love with and "marries" a stranger, an already pregnant woman. When she dies in childbirth he returns to his father's farm with the child and devotes all his puny yet powerful energy, both emotional and physical, to raising him. Then the woman's kinfolks arrive to take the boy away from him; legally he is powerless to stop them and, in time, retreats into the impassive shell a routine harsh existence supplies. Many years later the child, now grown into a bullying braggart named Thorpe–"Bucksnort" to his neighbors–is killed and his slayer tried for murder. Fentry, as a member of the jury, will not bring in a verdict of innocent even though the case against Thorpe and for the defendant has been proved beyond all reasonable doubt. While from the outside Fentry seems a simple man, he operates with all the enormous complexity of one whose heart, to use the Stockholm words, is "in conflict with itself": justice against a dream of love.

The above summary however is *not* the narrative order of events, but the unscrambled chronological sequence in which they occur. Which is where the element of detection comes in. Stevens, counsel for the defense, cannot understand how the jury could fail to acquit his client. Finding out that Fentry was the obstacle to their doing so, he determines to discover why. He tracks down Fentry's father's farm but has to quit it at gunpoint. Then he seeks out the Fentry's nearest neighbors–before extracting more information from Fentry's employer during the time when he had met the pregnant woman. What these people divulge, when pieced together, reveals that "Bucksnort" had once been that boy on whom Fentry had expended so much love and hope.

The narrative order, the order in which we assimilate "Tomorrow," is perfectly appropriate to a detective story. On matters of principle Knox has this to say:

> It will be seen . . . that the detective story differs essentially from every other type of fiction. For the interest of the ordinary romance centers in the question "What will happen?" . . . But the interest of the detective story centers in the question "What has happened?" Ordinary fiction works forwards from the conditions of the plot to its consummation, *detective fiction works backwards from its consummation to its conditions.*[31]

In several respects this constitutes much too simplistic a distinction. But it is a useful one because it serves to highlight the affinity of approach between much detective fiction and a story like "Tomorrow" which, except for the mere *presence* of a detective figure, has no definite element of detective interest in it.

Such an affinity grows in importance when we consider Faulkner's achievement in *Absalom, Absalom!,* a novel that superficially, though full of crime, would seem to have equally little detective content. Knox's definition of the characteristic structure of the detective tale applies just as well to the situation presented in this novel as it does to "Tomorrow."

Everything has happened; Quentin Compson and Shreve McCannon want to know what has happened. In order to understand the central "consummation" of the plot–Henry's shooting of Charles at the plantation gates after they have survived the war's inferno together–Quentin and Shreve must work backwards, necessitating some unscrambling of chronology, to its conditions. On the simplest, most abbreviated level, the question lying at the heart of the novel that they must answer is one of motivation, Why did Henry kill Bon? Was it incest, or miscegenation, he feared?

Ursula Brumm has stated that Quentin acts as an historian in *Absalom.*[32] No analogy or metaphor, of course, is really comprehensive enough to explain Quentin's position in the novel; but, like that of historian, the image of Quentin as detective does, I think, guide us into this one sector of the book's luxuriant terrain. Because she feels Quentin possesses the necessary qualifications for the task, Rosa Coldfield applies for his assistance in the investigation of some mysterious events out at Sutpen's Hundred. He becomes interested in the situation and, like Stevens in "Tomorrow," he collects evidence–though on a grander scale than Stevens–from a variety of sources. Some of it is documentary in the form of letters, etc.; some derives from eye-witnesses–like General Compson and Rosa herself–who do not necessarily tell the whole truth; and a good deal of it, especially that from his own father, amounts to speculation or hearsay, local gossip. Also, he is able to interview Henry, one of the principal protagonists, and to receive from him a sort of death-bed confession. And thus, sifting through this massive file of information, he delves back into the past, right to where, as a boy, Thomas Sutpen, like Fentry, came down from the hills. In "Tomorrow" Stevens becomes the agency whereby the reader is able to view Fentry's later actions under the fullest possible light. In essentially the same way–though by immeasurably more complicated maneuvers (there being, in *Absalom,* more actions and actors)–Quentin performs this function in *Absalom.* But it goes without emphasis that Quentin performs at a more subtle and intricate level than Stevens, and to some of these greater complexities we will return.

"An Error in Chemistry" was first published in *Ellery Queen's Mystery Magazine* (1946) where it won second prize in the journal's first annual detective short story contest, missing the first prize by only one vote. The editors' citation states that they regarded it as a "strange story of almost pure detection . . . stylized, morbid, mystical, and sharply and brilliantly narrated."[33] We can hardly disagree with the second part of the citation. If in several respects the story is subject to the same criticisms as "Smoke," it does offer compensations for its relative shallowness: the magnificent rendering, for instance, of Flint's desire to give one last bravura performance with all the assurance he had once possessed as

Signor Canova, artist of illusion and make-up. But the first part of the citation deserves examination.

In this discussion I have tended to regard detective fiction, for convenience sake, as somewhat more of a fixed form than it actually is; increasingly, and enrichingly so, it moves beyond efforts to formulate rules for its construction. Nevertheless, "An Error," it seems to me, strays beyond the bounds of the most lenient definition because it contains hardly any *detection* at all; it resembles, rather, a mystery story. Stevens and the sheriff are able to capture Flint-Canova, who has assumed the identity of his murdered father-in-law, only because he makes an "error of chemistry" in his mixing of a whiskey toddy, an error even young Chick Mallison spots immediately. Consequently, if we are to agree with the whole of the editors' citation, i.e., to agree also that "An Error" deserves praise as a story of "almost pure detection," then we are constrained to broaden yet further our appreciation of "detection" to include what in the story passes or substitutes for detection.

In such an eventuality the factor which most forcefully impinges on our consciousness is the large amount of *conjecture* in the story. From the moment that Hub, the sheriff, appears to tell Stevens of Mrs. Flint's murder, Stevens, from his tilted armchair, with the barest minimum of information, begins to speculate in a manner reminiscent of his behavior on his first entrance into the Faulkner canon in *Light in August* (when he attempted, quite wrongly as it happens, to explain all of Joe's acts in terms of his "black" or "white" blood becoming dominant at various times). He conjures forth the emotions of the principal participants and then speculates on the causes of these—note—attributed emotions. And it is his conjecturing which draws the sheriff out, makes him match—or contradict—his suppositions with the facts of the case as he knows them. In other words, as a tool of detection, conjecture often precedes fact. During the first half of the story (pp. 110-121), Stevens' *speculating virtually takes the place of narration.*

This is precisely the situation in much of *Absalom*. From within the confines of their Harvard quarters Quentin and Shreve imagine the emotions of figures not familiar to them, often figures long dead. The following is an example picked practically at random:

> That was the day he [Sutpen] came to the office—[on] his one day of leave at home, came home with his tombstones. Judith was there and *I reckon* he looked at her and she looked at him and he said, "You know where he is" and Judith didn't lie to him, and (he knew Henry) he said, "But you have not heard from him yet" and Judith didn't lie about that either and she didn't cry either because both of them knew what would be in the letter when it came so he didn't have to ask, "When. . . .[34]

—a piece of pure divination on Quentin's part. Actually their roles are not so easy to circumscribe. Cleanth Brooks has produced an interesting table to show that Shreve, not Quentin, does the majority of the speculating.[35]

When this happens it is Shreve who can be likened to Stevens in "An Error"; he goads Quentin—who "knows" more of the facts than he does—to refute or match his suppositions with whatever evidence Quentin's memory allows to be dredged up for their joint inspection.

This process affects the reader. Confronted by conjectures—for example, that there was a lawyer in New Orleans counselling Sutpen's first wife or, more trivially (from "Knight's Gambit"), that the Stevens-Mallison chess game may be interrupted yet again—confronted by such conjectures the reader reacts more personally perhaps than he would if presented with facts. He turns them over in his mind, thinks, Is that so?, and thus approximates the position of the detective himself.

Furthermore, immersed in such a welter of possibilities and words, it ultimately becomes well-nigh impossible for the reader of *Absalom* to distinguish *between* facts and assertions. Quentin and/or Shreve, to advance the metaphor slightly, are like lawyers advocating points to a jury: a particular point may be disallowed, or cancelled by more concrete evidence, but each member of the jury has already heard it; it has registered and, to differing degrees for each member, becomes for the jury part of the case, part of the version of the case which each juryman believes and upon which he will base his final verdict. Conjecture becomes narrative. Each reader, in accepting or rejecting the various hypotheses raised for his deliberation, becomes actively involved in the composition of his own *Absalom, Absalom!*; he becomes, so to speak, his own detective, jury and, perhaps, judge.

The long crime-centered debates of *Absalom*—and, perhaps, the similar debate in Part Four of "The Bear" (*Go Down, Moses,* 1942) between Ike McCaslin and his cousin Cass—may be further clarified if we look at a convention of detective fiction more readily apparent in "Knight's Gambit." In the course of this novella Charles Mallison emerges as a sort of Watson to Stevens' Holmes. Although he narrates the opening stories in *Knight's Gambit* he remains far in the background, and "Tomorrow" and "An Error" see him granted only minimal exposure as a sounding board for Stevens; but in "Knight's Gambit"—rendered like *Absalom* in the third person—not only do his thoughts come to the fore but he plays a significant part in the actual detection: it is he who makes the connection between McCullum's killer horse and the Harriss estate, the wild horse being the means Max Harriss has chosen to eliminate Captain Gualdres.

Traditionally, the Watson-type finds himself in the dark, driven by curiosity to persistently ask questions in the hope of eventual comprehension. As the reader also finds himself in this state, he naturally identifies closely with both such a character and his questions. In *Absalom, Absalom!*, while we cannot assert that either Quentin or Shreve is fixed permanently in the role of a Holmes or a Watson, the reader's response nevertheless adheres to the pattern it would in the case of a detective novel: at any particular moment the reader identifies with whoever happens to be in the dark at that moment—and, furthermore, this constantly shifting identification serves to increase his already earnest participation generally in the ongoing process which makes the novel. . . .

"Knight's Gambit" itself is, I believe, the weakest piece in the volume. It seems decidedly—almost willfully—sentimental; this stricture applies no matter which way we interpret it, whether as the saga of Gavin Stevens (the "knight")[36] and his love for Mrs. Melisandre Harriss, as the unfolding of Chick Mallison's excitement and premonitions at the prospect of going off to war, or, even, as the portrait of an enigmatic Argentinian cavalryman, Gualdres. Consequently, I wish now to discuss only one feature of the novella, a feature that bears upon Faulkner and detective fiction and which ultimately, I think, points us towards interesting data on the origin of some of Faulkner's most notable characters.[37]

Stevens, Faulkner's Holmes in "Knight's Gambit,"[38] while actually occupied by very little real detective work, receives in this story his fullest delineation. Nevertheless, compared to the Gavin Stevens we meet in the later Snopes volumes, Faulkner's rendering of him here relies almost exclusively on the external facts of his career—his Phi Beta Kappa key, his Heidelburg degree, his country corn-cob pipe, and his "translation." In other Faulknerian contexts we would condemn this portrayal as shallow. But if we accept that in *Knight's Gambit* Faulkner is working more or less within the conventions of detective fiction then such a judgment needs to be tempered somewhat by whatever considerations this implies. I suggest that the Stevens encountered in *Knight's Gambit* is at one with the other conventions common to detective fiction thus far abstracted; he falls indeed into a recognizable line of literary-minded amateur detectives, into a line which includes the creations of, say, Dorothy L. Sayers, Michael Innes (J. I. M. Stewart), and S. S. Van Dine (Willard Huntington Wright). This alignment invites investigation.

Wright, the only American listed above, was an influential literary journalist during the interwar years. He theorized on painting, wrote an unreadable novel under his own name, collaborated with Mencken on *The Smart Set* and other projects, popularized the ideas of Nietzche and published a volume of aesthetics called *The Creative Will* (1916).[39] At about the time Stevens first entered the Faulkner canon in *Light in August* (1931), Phil Stone wrote to Louis Cochran about Wright's *The Creative Will*; "[It] constitutes," he said, "one of the most important influences in Bill's whole literary career."[40] Frances Blazer O'Brien has speculated on the effects Wright's aesthetics might have had on Faulkner[41] —and I think it is possible (granted more space than this essay permits) to press the parallels further than she does.

More pertinent to my purposes, O'Brien also goes on to suggest affinities between Faulkner's major novels and the detective fiction Wright produced under his pseudonym, "S. S. Van Dine." She isolates the following common features: the occurrence of murderous activities amongst close blood relatives; the material and moral degeneration within established families (she cites close parallels between the Compsons of *The Sound and the Fury*, 1929, and the Greenes of *The Greene Murder Case*, 1928); the frequent reiteration of such remarks as, "better for her [Temple] . . . and [the other protagonists] if [they were all] . . . removed, cauterized out of the old and tragic flank of the world" (*Sanctuary*, p. 176); and the gothic settings in which many of the crimes take place. Besides the above similarities between the two authors—several of which, I think, would repay further investigations—O'Brien also notes that in the published works of both we find maps. Van Dine was the very first of the many detective writers who have offered readers such data as a map of the scene of the crime(s) and a list of persons involved; it is notable that on the map included in *Absalom, Absalom!* we discover rather more emphasis on criminal activities—"Where Wash Jones killed Sutpen," "where Goodwin was lynched," etc.—than we do in the case of the later map drawn for *The Portable Faulkner* (1946), a fact which just might suggest the detective fiction of Van Dine as the original source of the innovation. . . .

It is surprising to realize that the most obvious and relevant comparison of all—that both Wright *and* Faulkner wrote detective stories—remains unremarked by O'Brien. Which is perhaps why she fails to point out what seems to me to be glaring similarities between Van Dine's detective hero, Philo Vance, and Gavin Stevens. Like Stevens, Vance is a highly educated dilettante—Ogden Nash wrote that for his erudition "Philo Vance deserves a kick in the pance"—and at the opening of *The Bishop Murder Case* (1929) we come upon him engaged on a "translation"—from Menander. Vance too will talk about anything at the drop of a hat, anything extraneous that is to the business of detection at hand, and he has what Van Dine calls "a tremendous flair for the significant undercurrents of the so-called *trivia* of life. . . ."[42]

As a detective Vance, of course, is ultimately extremely effective. In *Knight's Gambit*, Stevens is reasonably so. But Faulkner has said this of him:

> While he was . . . a country attorney, an amateur Sherlock Holmes, then he was at home, but he got out of that. He got into a real world in which people anguished and suffered, not simply did things . . . they shouldn't do. . . . That is, he knew a good deal less about people than he knew about the law . . . [or about what he had learned in his] passion for getting degrees, for trying this and that. . . .[43]

In other words, Stevens' Vance-like character is virtually bound to be ineffective in the "real world" of *The Town* (1957) and *The Mansion*—and this appears, for the most part, to be the case. Now it is interesting to observe that several other Faulkner characters (often thin and languid ones, sometimes bachelors or bachelor-types) exhibit a weakness for words (and classical learning) and are normally ineffective in the real worlds of the novels in which they appear—Rector Mahon in *Soldier's Pay* (1926), Gail Hightower in *Light in August,* the Reporter in *Pylon* (1935) and, wherever he surfaces, Mr. Compson. Therefore I think it quite conceivable that Van Dine's Philo Vance lies somewhere in their ancestry.

Whether or not Faulkner was—as V. K. Ratliff would say—"actively" influenced in particulars by a famous detective author of his formative and major years, I hope I have shown that *Knight's Gambit* only partially deserves its comparative neglect by Faulkner's critics and that its implicit ramifications certainly merit consideration for precisely the reason it has often been disregarded: its detective content. Indeed, Ellery Queen, rightly bemoaning the "snobbishness" of reviews like that of Howard Mumford Jones,[44] has seen fit to include it in *Queen's Quorum: A History of the Detective-Crime Short Story as Revealed by the 106 Most Important Books Published in this Field since 1845.* In the same work he also remarks that Faulkner's publisher's claim that it was his first detective piece is incorrect; "What," he asks, "was Faulkner's *Intruder in the Dust* if not a detective story?"[45]

Actually, Queen's view of *Intruder* is itself less than just. To be sure, in essence the novel's plot is a detective one. Like Silas Phelps in Twain's *Tom Sawyer, Detective*, Lucas Beauchamp suffers wrongful arrest for murder. He tells Chick Mallison how his innocence can be proved and the boy carries out his request to exhume the body of the murdered man—with the aid of Miss Habersham, a lady of ancient gentility, and Aleck Sander who, like Lucas, is black. In the opened grave—because the real murderer, following the trend set by Poe's Goodfellow in "Thou art the Man," has been covering his own tracks—they find the corpse of another man. This discovery leads in turn first to the belated detective activity of those supposedly responsible for justice in the community, Gavin Stevens and Sheriff Hampton, and eventually to the apprehension of the true criminal. Some aspects of the detective plot strain credulity, the most important one being that after the reader has experienced Chick's first encounters with Lucas it is hard for him to believe that such a man as Lucas—proud, contained, resourceful—would ever be gulled into the position which leads to his arrest. However, other aspects conventional to a detective story are handled with consummate skill: the sense of a severe time limit within which the detection must be completed, for instance, or the ritual explanation of what actually took place on the day of the crime. So, again reminiscent of Twain's story, the novel ends with a return almost to the state of affairs which obtained before it began: Lucas released to go his own lonely inscrutable way, Stevens out of old habit dispensing justice as he sees it (he tells Lucas to take flowers to Miss Habersham), Chick by his uncle's side in the law office, and the town enjoying its normal market day diversions. Business is as usual in Jefferson, Miss. Which sort of ending, as I have pointed out, is entirely appropriate for detective fiction.

Yet, in contrast to the almost comic *Tom Sawyer, Detective,* such a resolution for *Intruder* seems jarring, structurally unsound. I think we might seek some explanation for this through Faulkner's own account of the novel's inception and composition. He said,

> I thought an idea for [a detective story] would be a man in jail just about to be hung. [He] would have to be his own detective, he couldn't get anybody to help him. Then the next thought was, the man for that would be a Negro. Then the character of . . . Lucas Beauchamp came along. And the book came out of that. . . . But once I thought of Beauchamp, then he took charge of the story and [it] was a good deal different from . . . the detective story I had started with.[46]

Up to a point, the published novel bears out Faulkner's claims. As we have observed, its plot is basically a detective one. And for a time Lucas does seem to "take charge." Chick's eyes first rise to his composed "intractable" face from where he had slipped into the icy stream, and from then on Lucas determines the relationship; he refuses payment for his gestures of human kindness and treats the boy as he treats everyone else, with respect but without either arrogance or subservience, and honoring himself and others thus, he asserts his own individual humanity. But on his incarceration in Jefferson's jail he becomes impotent. In other words, as Leah Rothberg rightly points out, Faulkner endows Lucas with "all the characteristics of a hero—and then denies him the role."[47] This judgment hints at the complex of reversals which follow. Chick advances to the fore as Lucas recedes into the middle-ground and other concerns—all related—become grafted onto the novel: the position in the South of the Negro ("Sambo" as the novel unfortunately has it); what it means to be a white Southerner; the behavior and mental circumlocutions of lynch gangs, etc. Now all of these grafts are or become integral to other Faulkner structures—I am thinking particularly of *Light in August*—and we would not expect them to damage the organism, indeed sometimes they are its veritable flowers. Let us briefly follow the contours of one of them—the lynch mob—through *Intruder.*

From the moment that Lucas enters the jail no black people are to be seen on the streets; fear rules. Then the mob appears, quiet at first, "settling down," reminiscent of "holiday," their faces "myriad yet curiously identical in their lack of individual identity,"[48] menacing, signifying doom. Faulkner conjures forth the people so well in an increasingly terrifying vision that ultimately, to Chick's mind at least, their myriad faces do indeed become one composite Face, gross and evil, the Face of a mob certainly not to be deflected by one old lady knitting; to be simplistic, they could just lift her, knitting and chair, all intact, aside, and get at Lucas. Yet this does not happen. Presumably, in what constitutes another reversal, Faulkner cannot bring himself to follow the logic of the vision he has so powerfully presented. And this is not simply because the story would end if he did so. For what happens to the lynch mob reflects exactly the change in Chick's consciousness during the course of chapter nine. At the end of it, instead of being afraid, or engaged, or even ashamed of the gang of his own people prepared to kill an innocent man, he is ready to acquiesce in his uncle's opinion that it was only something to "regret." Chick listens to his uncle and the mob flee: the two occurrences side by side, internal and external changes, work to make the mob less menacing; Chick accommodates himself to the counter-vision that Stevens elaborates, a counter-vision which is concluded in italics (signifying both emphasis for the reader and the urgency of the words coursing through Chick's memory), a counter-vision which demands that only the South can, will, and should rectify the ills it has perpetrated on the black man (see pp. 215-217 especially).

Once this more benign view of affairs—more benign because the enemy is now not the evil lynch mobs of the South but the external forces who would interfere with the South—once this more benign view has become firmly established in Chick's and the reader's mind the only way to resolve the novel is what follows: Lucas is reduced to something of a buffoon "who *had got himself* into the position where they had *had* to believe he had murdered a white man" (p. 237, my emphasis), a buffoon who can actually await a receipt for his petty fees; the Jeffersonians once again become country people going about their humdrum business; and Stevens once more occupies the seat of justice. In sum, Faulkner reverts to the form of the detective story he had first envisaged—in order to circumscribe, contain, those forces which had tended towards wholesale conflagration, a conflagration too repugnant to endure.

I noted of "Hand Upon the Waters" that when Faulkner allows the character with whom the reader most identifies (Stevens) to physically intervene in the action, he raises the level of suspense because the reader fears for his safety during the period in which he courts danger. The same is true of Chick's intrusion in the dust—perhaps, due to his youthful vulnerability, more so. Now we know that Chick's detective ability, his willingness to endanger himself, arises intimately, directly, out of his confused personal and racial feelings *vis à vis* Lucas. And this factor receives additional emphasis from the fact that Stevens, who cares so much for justice in "An Error," abrogates such responsibility at the opening of *Intruder* when he accepts Lucas' guilt solely because Lucas is black.

These observations on *Intruder* have a direct relevance to—and signpost the superiority of—*Absalom* and *Go Down, Moses.* Quentin's investigations are intimately bound up with his conception of himself as a white

Southerner; indeed *Absalom* closes on his repeated and hysterical declaration that he does not hate the South. Similarly, when Ike searches back through the plantation ledgers to find the clue to what in his heritage was askew, the act is prompted by his sensitivity to the general wrongs committed by man in the South. They both embark on quests fraught, if not with physical danger, with extreme intellectual and moral tension, peril. Moreover, unlike Chick, each is damaged by the experience: Quentin ends up somewhat crazed and Ike impotent, impotent in several respects as "Delta Autumn" makes clear. And through all this the reader follows, submerged imaginatively in their anguish.

Thus when we consider Faulkner's own detective stories and his employment of several of the *genre*'s resources in his basically non-detective works, we are presented with a paradox. Some of the tales in *Knight's Gambit* and facets of *Intruder* demonstrate that he harbored the *potential* to carve himself a respectable niche as a detective author; moreover, we have seen that when subservient to the full force of his tragic vision—for example in *Absalom*—his quasi-detective story techniques are an immeasurably important factor in the creation of tragedy.[49] Yet these same methods, when employed for their own sake (as in "Smoke"), or when allowed to militate against anguish and tragedy (as in *Intruder*), result in what must be regarded, quite simply, as works of a lower imaginative order.

In other words, it is to Faulkner's credit that none of his works achieves actuality as a totally satisfactory pure detective story. In such works, as I pointed out earlier, practically everything should fall logically into place. Turning again to Ike's search through the ledgers, we witness a man who—albeit behaving analogously to the sleuth—investigates nothing less than the cause of the curse on his head, on the land, on the South. And he traces it back to enforced incest, which is to say, to where he began, to man's inhumanity, to an aspect of his abiding nature everywhere: his capacity for evil. Books born of such knowledge cannot be cleanly resolved. Faulkner shows at the end of *The Sound and the Fury* that reality only composes itself happily into a logical sequence in the mind of an idiot. We judge him great, I think, precisely because he habitually drove his fiction through this spurious order, this mask of order, to record —in ways sometimes difficult to understand and/or replete with contradictions, hysteria and, even, madness—a little of the ultimate mystery of man.

Douglas G. Tallack

WILLIAM FAULKNER AND THE TRADITION OF TOUGH-GUY FICTION

This study is not intent on proving the direct influence of particular tough-guy novels on William Faulkner but at providing a different perspective from which to examine one of his novels, *Sanctuary* (1931), and certain aspects of others. Tough-guy fiction was "in the air" at that time. As W. M. Frohock remarks, when discussing James M. Cain's *The Postman Always Rings Twice* (1934): "The historical importance of books like *The Postman* is that they were the ultimate exploitation of the climate of sensibility which also produced the best novels of Faulkner, Hemingway, Wolfe, Steinbeck, Farrell, and Dos Passos."[1] Consequently, by a loose comparative approach, in which tough-guy novels written after *Sanctuary* are still valid material, it is hoped to bring out those distinctive features of the genre which Faulkner used and adapted and, incidently, to show how he aided its reputation and development.

Tough-guy fiction is a product of a particular social context and a literary style and it reached its apogee in the thirties flourishing alongside, and indeed related to, the proletarian fiction engendered by the Depression.[2] Its most accomplished practitioners were Cain, Dashiell Hammett, Horace McCoy and, rather later, Raymond Chandler. However, there was a host of less skilful writers such as W. R. Burnett, Carroll John Daly, and Raoul Whitfield, many of whom rose to prominence in the pages of *Black Mask* and other pulp magazines of the twenties and thirties. It must be admitted, however, that tough or hard-boiled fiction was written to a commercially successful formula laid down, to a large extent, by Joseph T. Shaw, the editor of *Black Mask* during its most successful phase.

The pace of tough-guy novels makes detailed descriptions and evaluations of American society during the Depression rare, and jarring when they do occur. Nevertheless, the social background does provide a substructure for the action. The tough-guy writers relied on Prohibition and gangsterism, the Great Crash and the ensuing Depression for the materials of their stories. Thus, crime and violence are usual, though not vital ingredients. More significant is the overwhelming bias towards the lower social and economic levels as the sources for character and setting. According to Chandler, perhaps the most self-conscious of the tough-guy writers, "Hammett took murder out of the Venetian vase and dropped it into the alley . . . Hammett wrote at first (and almost to the end) for people with a sharp, aggressive attitude to life. They were not afraid of the seamy side of things; they lived there. Violence did not dismay them; it was right down their street."[3]

A brief consideration of Ernest Hemingway's short story, "The Killers" (1927), will serve as an approximate chronological introduction to the genre since it was such an immediate success that it undoubtedly influenced the body of tough fiction that followed. The style is monotonously simple with a carefully restricted vocabulary and short sentence constructions. The studied repetition of the gangsters' dialogue conveys their menace, while the syncopated rhythm suggests a dislocated and threatening society:

> "What are *you* looking at?" Max looked at George.
> "Nothing."
> "The hell you were. You were looking at me."
> "Maybe the boy meant it for a joke, Max," Al said.
> George laughed.
> "*You* don't have to laugh," Max said to him. "*You* don't have to laugh at all, see?"
> "All right," said George.
> "So he thinks it's all right." Max turned to Al. "He thinks it's all right. That's a good one."
> "Oh, he's a thinker," Al said. They went on eating.[4]

And so it continues, like a deadly vaudeville act. The effect of this style depends upon emphasis rather than width of reference. The immediate world forces itself upon the reader. Experience rules, creating the illusion of complete objectivity.

Hemingway's affiliations with the genre are considerable and beyond contention but Faulkner's relationship to it is limited and not immediately apparent. His characteristic style is complex while the tough-guy writer's is simple, and his novels are not bound by the limits of time, whereas the apprenticeship served by many of the tough-guy writers when writing for *Black Mask* had taught them to keep their narratives relentlessly in the present. Yet, *Sanctuary*, at least, can be discussed in the same terms as tough-guy novels, that is, as the union between a particular social context and a literary style. It also has the added qualification, unique in Faulkner's canon, of being a best-seller. Alice P. Hackett, in *70 Years of Best Sellers 1895-1965,* lists the total sales of *Sanctuary* as 2,080,985, compared with *The Wild Palms* (1939), his second highest seller with 1,534,371.[5]

The popularity of *Sanctuary* began in France, where it was an immediate success on translation in 1933. A French critic, Claude Elsen, refers to *Sanctuary* as the father of the "roman noire."[6] Certainly, the French saw the connections between Faulkner and the hard-boiled school. Leslie Fiedler, in *Love and Death in the American Novel,* comments, with some annoyance, on the proliferation of such terms as "hard-boiled," "neo-realist" and, as an umbrella term, "tough," which have been applied to the American novel and which denote it as somehow anti-literary.[7] Yet toughness is the very quality that the French critics of the thirties and forties so admired in the American novel. Between 1918 and 1950 there was, in Stanley D. Woodworth's phrase, "une invasion litteraire."[8] Saturated by novels of analysis, the French eagerly embraced the brutality of Cain's *Postman* and the nightmarish violence of Faulkner's *Sanctuary.* The influx of American novels which capitalized on the success of *Sanctuary* inevitably influenced French writers, including Albert Camus, whose novel *L'Etranger* (1942), owes something to Hemingway and even to Cain. Boris Vian adopted the pseudonym Vernon Sullivan, a writer supposedly banned in America because he had black blood, for *J'irai cracher sur vos tombes* (1946), a tough novel in the American style whose hero, Lee Anderson, is based on Joe Christmas. A reviewer in *Samedi Soir* writes:

> Vernon Sullivan dépasse de loin ses prédécesseurs par un réalism d'une crudité et d'une puissance d'évocation rarement atteint dans la littérature non spécialisée . . . Depuis Faulkner, dont le *Sanctuaire* parut en son temps le comble de l'audace et de la noirceur, les nouveaux venus tels que James Cain, Horace MaCoy [sic], Herbert Chase, Henry Miller, et, actuellement Vernon Sullivan, expriment d'une mannière de plus en plus brutale leur angoisse et leur révolte.[9]

In the U.S.A., however, *Sanctuary* was attacked on the one hand by "humanist" critics and on the other by Marxist critics, both of whom sought a positive statement of values in literature. Those reviewers saw far more similarities between Cain and Faulkner than this article will suggest. Critics seized on Faulkner's admission that *Sanctuary* was written for money. The details of its composition seem to be Faulkner's party-piece, which he dutifully recounts whenever questioned. In the Introduction to the Modern Library edition, Faulkner apparently dismisses *Sanctuary*:

> This book was written three years ago. To me it is a cheap idea, because it was deliberately conceived to make money.
>
> ....
>
> I took a little time out, and speculated what a person in Mississippi would believe to be current trends, chose what I thought was the right answer and invented the most horrific tale I could imagine and wrote it in about three weeks and sent it to Smith, who had done *The Sound and the Fury* and who wrote me immediately, "Good God, I can't publish this. We'd both be in jail."[10]

"Current trends" indicated a novel of violent crime with an element of detection. *Black Mask,* with Hammett as its star contributor, was enormously popular and influential in the late twenties. Faulkner, a friend of Hammett, was a great contemporary reader and also a devotee of detective stories, both of the classic English school and of the hard-boiled type currently gaining popularity in America.[11] Joseph Blotner's catalogue of Faulkner's library reveals the extent of his interest in this field. Hammett, McCoy, Ellery Queen, Georges Simenon and *Creeps by Night; Chills and Thrills,* edited by Hammett, vie on his shelves with the works of the earlier exponents of the detective story: Wilkie Collins, Edgar Allan Poe and Mary Roberts Rinehart.[12] According to Julian Symons in *Bloody Murder,* the success of the tough-guy novel shaded the detective story into the crime novel and the thriller.[13] Elements of all three are to be found in *Sanctuary.*

The success of *Sanctuary* might have led to it influencing other writers who were starting to produce stories of violent crime written in the tough style. In 1939 an Englishman, James Hadley Chase, borrowed the plot of *Sanctuary* for his best-selling "shocker" *No Orchids for Miss Blandish.*[14] On a higher level, Graham Greene's baby-faced killer, Pinkie, in his upgraded "Entertainment," *Brighton Rock* (1938), surely owes something to Popeye in appearance and degree of menace, if not in motivation.

The notoriety of *Sanctuary* did much for its sales but Faulkner has dispelled the notion that it is a mere "potboiler" by explaining that he virtually rewrote the novel, the first version of which had been completed in the early summer of 1929. He reminds a Japanese interviewer that the version published is the revised one:

> At that time I had done the best I could with it. The one that you didn't see was the base and cheap one, which I went to what sacrifice I could in more money than I could afford rather than to let it pass. The one you saw was the one that I did everything possible to make it as honest and as moving and to have as much significance as I could put into it.[15]

Michael Millgate has compared the published version and the galleys of the earlier *Sanctuary,* the *Ur-Sanctuary* as he calls it.[16] This reveals that the cheapness is not in the subject matter but in the writing and the structure. The notorious details of Temple's rape and the incidents that occur when she is installed in Miss Reba's whorehouse have been taken over from the original with very little alteration. In some respects the published version is more violent and horrific. Chapter XXIX, describing the burning of Lee Goodwin, is entirely new. The earlier version contains only a hint that he may be lynched but the actual event is never described.

It is apparent that the contents of *Sanctuary*, however sensational and exploitative they may appear, were of considerable importance to Faulkner. The novel depicts a frightening and stark view of modern life.

In the descriptions of sex it bears some comparison with T. S. Eliot's *The Waste Land* (1922). Both novel and poem seek values in an apparently valueless world. Eliot uses a series of comparisons with the past but Faulkner, contrary to his usual practice of invoking the older, less fragmented South, keeps the narrative remorselessly in the present. There are no family units in *Sanctuary* to give coherence. His deep and sympathetic involvement with the Compsons in *The Sound and the Fury* (1929) is supplanted by an almost cold and detached social interest in the sordid and violent aspects of contemporary society. Along with the recognized tough-guy novels, *Sanctuary* shows that a vision of violence, if it is closely related to its age, can be considered only too normal.

The depth given by a historical perspective is replaced by the dialectic of the detective story, which Faulkner uses as a vehicle in the search for values. The detective story describes a situation in which the criminal is placed in opposition to society. The former represents the aggressive source of evil and the latter, usually in the person of the Great Detective, its corrective. Detective fiction evokes crime and then purges it and is thus a completely safe form. It offers its readers a reassuring world in which the status quo is never really in danger. Social reality is also consistently ignored, particularly in British detective fiction, which clung to its country houses and Oxford Colleges despite the lengthening dole queues. According to Julian Symons, "The fairy-tale land of the Golden Age was one in which murder was committed over and over again without anybody getting hurt" (*Bloody Murder,* p. 104).

However, when society appears malevolent, threatening and uncontrollable as it did to an unprecedented degree in the age of "Bathtub gin and the crime wave,"[17] and the Depression, the dialectic must change. Raymond Chandler describes Dashiell Hammett's world as one "where a judge with a cellar full of bootleg liquor can send a man to jail for having a pint in his pocket . . . where no man can walk down a dark street in safety because law and order are things we talk about but refrain from practising" (p. 59). W. H. Auden recognizes that Chandler, himself, had moved away from "the guilty vicarage": "I think Mr. Chandler is interested in writing, not detective stories, but serious studies of a criminal milieu, the Great Wrong Place."[18] "The Great Wrong Place" appears in many guises throughout tough-guy fiction: as Hammett's Personville ("Poisonville") in *Red Harvest* (1929), Hemingway's Key West in *To Have and Have Not* (1937), and McCoy's Colton in *No Pockets in a Shroud* (1937). It is a world in which it is impossible to persuade witnesses to testify and in which respectable society is honeycombed with corruption and hypocrisy. It is the world of *Sanctuary* in which Horace Benbow struggles in vain to disperse the "smell of fear"[19] created so effectively by Popeye and to disentangle the intricate and soiled web that connects a Memphis brothel with the State capitol and the police force. At the centre of this web is the ubiquitous Clarence Snopes, who sells the same information three times.

The force of society pressing down upon the individual during the Depression was such that social deviance became common, especially among those without the resources to survive. Tough-guy fiction deals primarily with those born "across the tracks"[20] and therefore social deviance is common to most of its characters. When society is turbulent and violent the tough-guy is invariably cast as the hero or, at least, the central figure, whereas in a stable and more optimistic era he takes the villain's role.

The tough-guy has a few alternative roles in the fiction of the hard-boiled writers. He may be a tough detective, a gangster or an uncommitted loner. The purest form of the tough-guy is the last and he is to be found pre-eminently in the novels of Cain and McCoy, though the prototype is Hemingway's. After being "busted" by a brakeman, the young Nick Adams realizes that "You got to be tough" to survive on the road.[21] The quality of toughness, possessed completely by Harry Morgan in *To Have and Have Not,* is a reaction to a tough era rather than an adeptness with fists and guns. It is basically a means of protection rather than outright rebellion. Nevertheless, the exigencies of the situations described in tough-guy novels often make action the only answer. The heroes of tough-guy novels are the doers, not the thinkers. Hemingway sets up a contrast between Harry Morgan and Richard Gordon and it is made explicit by the contemptuous epithet flung at the latter by his wife: "You writer!"[22] Harry, on the other hand, has "cojones" and we learn that "since he was a boy he never had no pity for nobody. But he never had no pity for himself either" (p. 79).

In *Postman,* the hero, Frank Chambers, has only his tough veneer as protection against social and economic adversities. He is a dispossessed, disconnected wanderer, who is prepared to resort to crime to satisfy his very basic desires: food, money and women. Cain never analyses his hero's actions or the motives behind them. Frank's motives seem to be so simple that analysis would be incongruous. He is about to turn down the Greek's offer of a job at Twin Oaks Tavern but then he sees Cora. "Except for the shape, she really wasn't any raving beauty, but she had a sulky look to her, and her lips stuck out in a way that made me want to mash them in for her."[23] Sex is constantly linked to violence in Frank's mind and love is "like being in church" (p. 21).

In Horace McCoy's most famous novel, *They Shoot Horses, Don't They?* (1935), there is an interesting variation in that the tough-guy is a woman, Gloria Beatty. She is very much the product of her environment: a miserable childhood, reform school and finally down-and-out in Hollywood. She is an outcast, unemployed, and completely cynical. "This whole business is a merry-go-round," she tells Robert Syverton. "When we get out of here we're right back where we started."[24] McCoy continually emphasizes the contrast between Robert, a sensitive dreamer, and Gloria with her dreadful nihilism. Hemingway's protagonists may start out with a similar attitude to life but there is a belief, a code, to which they can aspire. This is never apparent in *They Shoot Horses.*

The heroes of Cain and McCoy are generally victims rather than aggressors and this pure version of the tough-guy is to be found in Faulkner in the characters of Lee Goodwin in *Sanctuary* and Joe Christmas in *Light in August* (1932). Lee Goodwin is a criminal but still a victim. He is less the exploiter of the opportunities of Prohibition than the exploited. As Benbow tells Miss Jenny, "They knew what he was doing, but they waited until he was down. Then they all jumped on him. The good customers, that had been buying whisky from him and drinking all that he would give them free and maybe trying to make love to his wife behind his back."[25] Ruby Lamar reminds Benbow that "people don't break the law just for a holiday" (p. 129).

Goodwin is unusual among tough-guys since he is "married." The tough-guy who is married is more vulnerable to the forces that oppose him. Harry Morgan would certainly be better off without the responsibilities of a family, though his attachment to Marie is never questioned. In *Sanctuary,* the anger of the townspeople is turned upon Ruby as well as upon Goodwin and so he can be attacked in more than one direction. In this respect, Popeye is invulnerable, as is Rico Bandello in W. R. Burnett's *Little Caesar* (1929). Rico is portrayed as a calculating person who "fought shy of any kind of ties."[26] Ruby and Marie represent one type of woman in tough-guy fiction; the other type is the Cain woman, the destroyer. Cora in *Postman,* Juana in *Serenade* (1937), and Mrs. Nirdlinger in the novella, *Double Indemnity* (1943), are all dangerous temptresses, who eventually help to destroy the hero. Hammett also sees women as the root of much trouble and in *The Maltese Falcon* (1930), Sam Spade finally has to put Miss Wonderly away. Robert Syverton comes to deeply regret meeting Gloria. "I try to do somebody a favour," he thinks, "and I wind up getting myself killed" (p. 15). The destroying woman in *Sanctuary* is Temple Drake. She is especially dangerous because she appears to be defenceless. Joe Christmas, who is the best example of a pure tough-guy in Faulkner, is also partly trapped by a woman, Joanna Burden. To form any sort of attachment or to lose the powers of self-control that the tough-guy usually possesses is tantamount to destruction.

Joe Christmas manages to survive thirty-three years by adopting the tough attitude which McEachern forces upon him. In common with all tough-guys, he has to absorb plenty of punishment but he must retain control over his feelings. For the tough-guy to show his feelings, even to himself, is to render himself vulnerable. Consequently, Joe is presented as an almost unfeeling character, who is stoical to an extreme, especially under the stern rule of McEachern. It is rare that we see inside the minds of tough-guy characters and Joe Christmas is no exception. Sometimes it is difficult to understand him. After killing Joanna Burden, his state of mind is indicated only by his strange sequence of actions in going into the woods, methodically destroying a supply of whisky and then reading a comic from the first page to the last. Similarly, Popeye's feelings when in gaol remain a mystery. All we have is the naked objectivity of his peculiar ritual involving the cigarette stubs. Of some relevance here is the connection between the American novel of the thirties and behaviourism, which is traced by Claude-Edmonde Magny in *L'Age du Roman Américain.*[27] Although this behaviourism is rarely employed systematically, there is in many tough-guy novels a bias towards a realism that reduces subjectivity to occasional sentimentality and limits knowledge to external observation. In brief, it involves the reduction of psychological reality to consequences. Joe Christmas is treated in this way, though he is never sentimental in the way that Frank Chambers is. The world of *Sanctuary* and the tough-guy novels is, in Camus' words, a "despairing world in which wretched automatons live in the most mechanically coherent way."[28] For instance, Temple's extreme mental disorder is described in purely physical terms: "She lay on the shuck mattress, turning and thrashing her body from side to side, rolling her head, holding the coat together across her breast but making no sound" (p. 66).

When Joe Christmas arrives at the sawmill in Jefferson he has all the characteristics of the rootless wanderer, "as though no town nor city was his, no street, no walls, no square of earth his home."[29] Later, Faulkner develops the metaphor of the lonely street to describe Joe's life:

From that night the thousand streets ran as one street, with imperceptible corners and changes of scene, broken by intervals of begged and stolen rides, on trains and trucks, and on country wagons with he at twenty and twentyfive and thirty sitting on the seat with his still, hard face and the clothes (even when soiled and worn) of a city man . . . The street ran into Oklahoma and Missouri and as far south as Mexico and then back north to Chicago and Detroit and then back south again and at last to Mississippi. It was fifteen years long . . . he was in turn labourer, miner, prospector, gambling tout; he enlisted in the army, served four months and deserted and was never caught. (pp. 168-169)

The metaphor of the lonely street is implicit or explicit in all tough-guy novels. The street may be semi-rural, as in Cain, or urban, as in Chandler. The latter connects his hero and the metaphor very closely in "The Simple Art of Murder": "But down these mean streets a man must go who is not himself mean, who is neither tarnished nor afraid" (p. 59).

By the time Byron Bunch meets him, Joe Christmas is completely hard and rejects friendship and kindness. He refuses Byron's offer of food as he had previously spurned all aid from Mrs. McEachern. Brown, the other newcomer to Jefferson, is just as much a wanderer but to be a tough-guy requires a particular attitude towards life. Brown does not bear the marks of such a cruel existence and so he is weaker and less self-contained. The difference between Brown and Christmas is apparent firstly in the way they shovel sawdust: the former is hurried, erratic and ineffective, while the latter works with a "brooding and savage steadiness" (p. 31). Secondly, Brown is a talker and is always liable to give away information about the still they are operating. Christmas is silent and in control of his tongue. After six months at the mill, "He still had nothing to say to anyone" (p. 28).

Tough-guy fiction has connections with the tradition of naturalism, not only in its style, but also in its acknowledgment of the doctrine of determinism. The growth of society and the economy was beyond the individual's ability to control it or even cope with it. In a very perceptive preface to the first French edition of *Sanctuary,* André Malraux touches on the same subject. "But there is the figure of Destiny," he writes. "An intense obsession crushes each of his characters, and in no case do the characters succeed in exorcising it. The obsession still hovers behind them, unchanging, summoning them instead of awaiting their summons." He concludes by calling *Sanctuary* "the intrusion of Greek tragedy into the detective story."[30] This applies equally to the characters of Cain and McCoy. In *Postman,* Frank and Cora are allowed some initial choices but it is soon apparent that they are trapped. They are out when the Postman, as the symbol of fate, calls the first time but he "always rings twice." As Cain remarks of *Postman*: "The whole thing corresponded to a definition of tragedy I found later in some of my father's writings: that it was the 'force of circumstances driving the protagonists to the commission of a dreadful act.' "[31] "It's a big airplane engine," Cora tells Frank, "that takes you through the sky, right up to the top of the mountain. But when you put it in a Ford, it just shakes it to pieces. That's what we are, Frank, a couple of Fords. God is up there laughing at us" (p. 93). Walter Huff, the hero of Cain's novella, *Double Indemnity,* is aware of something inside him which overcomes his reason: "I kept telling myself to get out of there and get quick, and never come back. . . . What I was doing was peeping over that edge, and all the time I was trying to pull away from it, there was something in me that kept edging a little closer, trying to get a better look" (p. 27). Edmond Wilson sees Cain as one of the "poets of the tabloid murder."[32] He notes that Cain is "particularly ingenious in tracing from their first beginnings the tangles that gradually tighten around the necks of the people involved in those bizarre and brutal crimes that figure in the American papers" (p. 21). His heroes are "always treading the edge of a precipice; and they are doomed, like the heroes of Hemingway, for they will eventually fall off the precipice" (p. 20).

In *They Shoot Horses,* McCoy reinforces the fatalism by revealing the outcome on the first page and then preceding each chapter with a fragment of the judge's pronouncement of sentence of death on the narrator. During the course of the novel the characters are creatures in a human circus obeying the commands of the ringmaster. They are owned by the promotors of the marathon dance contest who feed, clothe and manipulate them. Socks metes out punishment with a blackjack, or sometimes he shows mercy: " 'I forgive you—' Socks said, dropping the blackjack into his pocket" (p. 78).

Wyndham Lewis says of the characters in *Sanctuary* that they are "futilely energized and worked up to no purpose."[33] Destiny weighs heavily on every figure. Popeye is the prime agent of fate with his small automatic. At the Frenchman's Place Popeye's "black presence" lies on the house "like the shadow of something no larger than a match falling monstrous and portentous upon something else otherwise familiar and everyday and twenty times its size" (p. 96). Even in those parts of the novel when Popeye is not an actual presence, he cannot be forgotten. This is especially noticeable in those scenes when Benbow is talking to Goodwin in the Jefferson gaolhouse. Goodwin is trapped between society and the underworld and these two inexorable forces combine to kill him and thwart Ruby's attempt to perform a natural role as a mother and wife.

In *Light in August,* the victimized individual is shown to be subject to forces both within him and without him. As Wyndham Lewis states in *Men Without Art,* Joe Christmas "carries round a big doom with him" (p. 52). An unwanted orphan, suspected of being half negro, he soon becomes a victim of society. He is an outsider from the first but society, unwilling to let him be, forces him to rebel and then destroys him. Joe's struggle is to give his life some meaning. Fritz Lang's cinema provides a useful parallel, since he, too, mixes the voluntary and self-determining actions of the individual with the influence of destiny. Ultimately, the combination of environment and heredity do crush the individual. As Lang says, "the *fight* is important—not the result of it, but the revolution itself. Sometimes, maybe, with a strong will, you can change fate, but there is no guarantee that you can."[34]

The prime symbol of Joe's fate is the circle. "But I have never got outside that circle," he thinks. "I have never broken out of the ring of what I have already done and cannot ever undo" (p. 255). The main difference in this respect between *Postman*, for example, and *Light in August* is that the former employs a naive temporal determinism, in which Frank Chamber's actions gradually tighten the trap, whereas the determinism in *Light in August* is a mixture of history and psychology; in Malraux's term it is the "irreparable." Before killing Joanna Burden, Joe recognizes his fate: "he believed with calm paradox that he was the volitionless servant of the fatality in which he believed that he did not believe" (p. 210). The fatalism of the novel is developed by a curious technique, whereby characters such as Doc Hines and Percy Grimm are introduced apparently without reason, but later play important roles in Joe's fate. It is significant that Percy Grimm, the final agent in Joe's destruction, should be described five times as the tool of the Player: "He was moving again almost before he had stopped, with that lean, swift, blind obedience to whatever Player moved him on the Board" (p. 347). An interesting parallel use of the chess-board metaphor is to be found in one of T. H. Huxley's lay sermons. "The chess-board is the world," writes Huxley, "the pieces are the phenomena of the universe, the rules of the game are what we call the laws of Nature. The player on the other side is hidden from us. We know that his play is always fair, just, and patient. But also we know, to our cost, that he never overlooks a mistake, or makes the smallest allowance for ignorance."[35] The world of *Light in August,* as it affects Joe, at least, and that of *Sanctuary* corresponds to Huxley's chess-board metaphor quite closely.

The character of the pure tough-guy implies considerable social criticism which is often overlooked when these novels are evaluated. James T. Farrell, for example, criticizes Cain for exploiting "the material of life in America,"[36] which the French found so fascinating, but failing to make it socially significant. Alfred Kazin notes the similarities between proletarian and tough-guy fiction but is equally critical of Cain, describing him and others like him as "technicians of sensation," who popularized "the Broadway-Hollywood cult of violence."[37] It is difficult to deny that Cain does write in a sensational fashion but at the heart of his novels and those of Horace McCoy, there is a deep pessimism that can be compared with that expressed in *Sanctuary.* There is no recourse to an ideology such as Farrell and John Steinbeck possessed at that time. The dispossessed, disconnected wanderer appears as frequently in Nelson Algren, Farrell and Steinbeck as he does in the tough-guy writers but there is a code of shared values or a possible political solution in these writers that provide another dimension and consequently a source of hope. Whether in epigraphs taken from the Communist Manifesto, as in Algren's first novel, *Somebody in Boots* (1935), or in the conclusive speech of a Ma Joad, there is a source of hope that does not exist in the pure tough-guy novel. In *To Have and Have Not,* Hemingway attempts to graft a social message on to a very effective tough-guy novel and this almost ruins the whole novel. Harry Morgan is most convincing in the first half of the novel when he is solely tough and kills Mr. Sing, betrays twelve Chinese and contemplates killing his mate, Eddy. Wesley's rather overwrought criticism of Harry indicates the type of character the tough-guy needs to develop. " 'You don't care what happens to a man,' the nigger said. 'You ain't hardly human' " (p. 59). Having created such a character, Hemingway then begins to undercut all that Harry has stood for and this process culminates in Harry's dying message: "No matter how a man alone ain't got no bloody chance" (p. 178).

Such social comment is generally absent from the pure tough-guy novel, as is the tendency to elevate the common man to the rather artificial level of martyr. The tough-guy novel invariably ends with the unrelieved death of the tough-guy. Albert Van Nostrand, so severe on Cain, is surely over-generalizing when he states that "Popular fiction has always assured the reader about himself and his possibilities—that humanity is naturally good, that the individual counts for something, that he *can* improve."[38] The eventual death of Cain's criminal heroes may assuage the censor—"expedient reciprocity," Van Nostrand calls it—but at the end of *Postman* or even *Double Indemnity,* we hardly regard society as a moral victor over the tough-guy.

There is little hope for the main characters in these novels. In *Postman,* the rebirth by water scene precedes the final catastrophe and though Frank preaches his "on the road" philosophy, he only makes abortive attempts to free himself from Cora. In *Sanctuary,* after the death of Goodwin and the sentence of imprisonment on Benbow—"The light from his wife's room fell across the hall. 'Lock the back door,' she said." (p. 240)—Faulkner describes the absurd death of Popeye, which hardly reinforces Benbow's faith in "the law, justice, civilization" (p. 105), and he closes the novel with the awful emptiness and sterility of Temple sitting in the Luxembourg Gardens in "the season of rain and death" (p. 253).

The second version of the tough-guy is the gangster. His sociological birth is easy to explain: Prohibition, which made law-breaking inevitable and extremely profitable. He is the extreme version of the tough-guy. Unlike the pure tough-guy, the gangster is less society's victim because he organizes other anti-social forces and hits back. Camus' distinction between rebellion and resistance describes the difference between the gangster and the pure tough-guy. In a highly complex urban society, the free man is recognized as the hero, and in such a society the successful criminal is the obvious candidate. The earliest literary versions are to be found in Donald Henderson Clarke's *Louis Beretti* (1927), and of course, in *Little Caesar.* Again, Hemingway's "The Killers" contributed to the formation of the gangster's style. Whether Faulkner read all or none of these early gangster stories, he was certainly aware of the gangster and his conventions. The description of Red's lavish funeral in *Sanctuary* strikes just the right note of ridiculous incongruity. There is a perfect blending of solemnity and excess, spiced with underworld humour:

> "How about the Blue Danube?" the leader said.
>
> "No, no; don't play no blues, I tell you," the proprietor said. "There's a dead man in that bier."
>
> "That's not blues," the leader said.
>
> "What is it?" the second man said.
>
> "A waltz. Strauss."
>
> "A wop?" the second man said. "Like hell. Red was an American." (pp. 194-195)

Faulkner's gangster, Popeye, may have been based on newspaper reports of Popeye Pumphrey, a Memphis gangster. Alternatively, Carvel Collins claims in "A Note on *Sanctuary*" that the Temple-Popeye relationship and the characteristics of the gangster are drawn from the experiences of a girl whom Faulkner met in a nightclub in the mid-twenties.[39] Around the time that Faulkner was writing *Sanctuary* he was writing a short story called "The Big Shot," whose central character is a racketeer, Dal Martin, operating in a Southern city during Prohibition. A bootlegger called Popeye appears in the story, "a slight man with a dead face and dead black hair and eyes and a delicate hooked little nose and no chin, crouching snarling behind the neat blue automatic" (Millgate, p. 316).

The gangster has made himself at home in the tough world by imbibing its qualities in an exaggerated and theatrical form. They are reflected in his clipped speech, his comical appearance, and his incessant, nervous movements. Rico Bandello and Popeye share a number of characteristics. They are both small men of Italian origin who impose their will upon others. Faulkner makes an obvious distinction between Popeye and the other bootleggers, even Goodwin. When Van fights with Gowan, Tommy warns him: "You want Mr. Popeye to start guttin' us all with that ere artermatic?" (p. 59). Perhaps because of their dangerous existence, gangsters are rarely still. "Rico lived at a tension. His nervous system was geared up to such a pitch that he was never sleepy, never felt the desire to relax, was always keenly alive" (pp. 70-71). Popeye, too, is "jumpy" and quick to draw his automatic. All of these characteristics make up the style of the gangster. Faulkner's achievement in the creation of Popeye is to give the stylized gestures of the gangster a real horror. Popeye is a figure of parody but he is also a figure of dread. The gangster has an unnatural code, a life-denying code. He is above personal feeling. "You are cold," Mrs. Magdalena tells Rico. "Don't like wine. Don't like women. You are no good, Rico" (p. 36). Similarly, killing Tommy is no different to Popeye from killing Tommy's dog. In "The Killers," Nick's sense of shock is felt when one of the gangsters tells him why they are there. It is generally recognized that "The Killers" is about Nick's introduction to pure evil and it is much the same with *Sanctuary.* Popeye is one half of a dialectic that Faulkner sets up to indicate the loss of values in society. The other half is Benbow, an innocent like Nick. Popeye is Benbow's introduction to unadulterated evil and the fact that there is a "logical pattern to evil" (p. 176).

This introduces the third role for the tough-guy, the "hard-boiled dick," and the only one which does not appear in Faulkner, though his absence is significant. Faulkner's detectives, Horace Benbow and Gavin Stevens, are pre-eminently men of reason, related more to the traditional detective than the hard-boiled one. Dashiell Hammett's stories and novels sounded the death knell of the traditional detective story and ushered in the tough detective story or simply the crime story, as Julian Symons prefers to label it. The detective heroes of Hammett and Chandler prove that the successful detective must become part of the milieu in which he works and in order to survive there he has to be tough. The world that Hammett and Chandler write about is just as brutal as that of Cain and McCoy but the characters such as Marlowe and Spade are figures of order, however dubious their methods. It is a form of compromise. Philip Marlowe, as Chandler tells us in "The Simple Art of Murder," is a lonely man, an outsider, but he does have a place in society as its tough saviour, its latterday knight. In a less idealistic fashion this also applies to Hammett's ruthless private investigators, the Continental Op and Sam Spade. His two other famous heroes, Ned Beaumont in *The Glass Key* (1931), and Nick Charles in *The Thin Man* (1932), are different. The former, not having a definite role as the detective (though he functions as one) is nearer the pure tough-guy, while the latter, as a retired and well-off detective, most certainly has a place in society with his wife, and consequently he is not tough. Even Mickey Spillane's Mike Hammer, their degenerate successor, sees himself playing a definite role keeping America free of "hoodlums" and "reds." This relief is missing from Cain, McCoy and Faulkner.

Faulkner's detective in his grimmest work is Horace Benbow. He is the man who links the different milieux in his attempt to impose order on a lawless and corrupt society. However, he is unable to resist the evil that opposes him. Just as Nick Adams cannot thwart the killers, so Benbow is defeated by Popeye and by the corruption that emanates from the apparently respectable areas of Southern society. The contrast between Popeye, the tough gangster, and Benbow, the ineffectual detective, is apparent from the opening scene when the little man holds Benbow captive for two hours merely by staring at him. Later, Ruby listens to the lawyer's voice, "a quick, faintly outlandish voice, the voice of a man given to much talk and not much else" (p. 13). A tough world needs a tough detective but Benbow, a "talker," accomplishes virtually nothing. The evil overwhelms him from all sides. We feel that he is too articulate, too intellectual. After all the concrete similes that are applied to Popeye in the first chapter, Benbow uses a literary comparison: "He smells black, Benbow thought; he smells like that black stuff that ran out of Bovary's mouth and down upon her bridal veil when they raised her head" (p. 8).

The role of the detective in relation to the world in which he operates enables a general comment to be made about Faulkner's changed attitude to the world from the time of *Sanctuary* and *Light in August* to the time of *Requiem for a Nun* (1953), the sequel to *Sanctuary,* and *Intruder in the Dust* (1948). In these two later novels, as well as in the collection *Knight's Gambit* (1949), Benbow is replaced as the detective by Gavin Stevens. Faulkner is still writing the crime story and using it as a vehicle in the search for values, but these later works have no connection with the tough-guy tradition. A difference of twenty years and a new social context and we see Stevens as the organizer of the plot, a role Benbow was never able to master. The fatalism of *Sanctuary* and *Light in August* has disappeared. Evil is shown to be the responsibility of man and his salvation is in his own hands. Stevens garrulously explains away the menace of Popeye as a mental aberration: "He was a psychopath, though that didn't come out in the trial . . . I was there; I saw that too: a little black thing with an Italian name, like a neat and only slightly deformed cockroach: a hybrid, sexually incapable."[40] Gavin was also "there" during the closing stages of Joe Christmas' life but all his rationalism amounted to then was a naive, simplistic judgment that ignored the complexity of the case. Benbow could never be as confident or as specific as Stevens with Popeye, Clarence Snopes, Judge Drake, Eustace Graham and the Baptists lined up against him. In *Requiem* and *Intruder,* a detective story with an unsatisfactory denouement, Stevens seems to make explicit a "tamed" Faulkner philosophy. The theme of the Nobel prize speech, that man will endure, constantly intrudes itself into both novels. Faulkner has left the world of *Sanctuary* and the world of Joe Christmas, a world where toughness in its various forms was the only protection against society's injustices and hardships, and has entered a world where reason seems to prevail and Gavin Stevens can, all too easily, pronounce his panacea: "What we are trying to deal with now is injustice. Only truth can cope with that. Or love" (p. 77).

It is difficult to decide where content finishes and style takes over in tough-guy fiction. In Hammett's work the style and technique are almost the subject. It is a style that is objective to an extreme, eschewing psychological interpretation and feelings, and concentrating instead upon externals. Hammett, Chandler, Cain and McCoy all used the first person narrator at various times because they felt that it reduced "interference." Cain explains his reasons in the Preface to *Double Indemnity*:

> For if I in the third person faltered and stumbled, my characters in the first person knew perfectly well what they had to say. . . . I make no conscious effort to be tough, or hard-boiled, or grim. . . . I merely try to write as the character would write, and I never forget that the average man, from the fields, the streets, the bars, the offices, and even the gutters of his country, has acquired a vividness of speech that goes beyond anything I could invent (pp. 9-10).

On the occasions when a third-person narration is used the tough-guy writer attends closely to details, however insignificant. The opening page of *The Maltese Falcon* contains three detailed descriptions of the appearances of characters. It is this approach which accounts for the lack of emotion in these novels. In *Red Harvest,* the Continental Op awakes from a dream-filled sleep to find himself apparently the murderer of Dinah Brand. Instead of an outburst of shocked fear or anger, there is a minute description of the scene. He notes that "The pick's six-inch needle-sharp blade was buried in Dinah Brand's left breast." The factual account continues: "She was lying on her back, dead. Her long muscular legs were stretched out towards the kitchen door. There was a run down the front of her right stocking. . . . The kitchen clock said seven-forty one."[41]

This style is not generally associated with Faulkner, yet in *Sanctuary* much of the effect derives from the use of sharp physical images. This is very evident in the Memphis episodes and in the opening scene, which has an almost intolerable immediacy about it. *Sanctuary* begins as many tough-guy novels begin, with a contingent but sharply described situation and the atmosphere is allowed to grow out of it: "From beyond the screen of bushes which surrounded the spring, Popeye watched the man drinking" (p. 5). Throughout the scene that follows Faulkner consistently describes Popeye in close detail, employing concrete images: "a man of under size, his hands in his coat pockets, a cigarette slanted from his chin. His suit was black with a tight, high-waisted coat. . . . His face had a queer, bloodless colour, as though seen by electric light; against the sunny silence, in his slanted straw hat and his slightly akimbo arms, he had that vicious depthless quality of stamped tin." With eyes like "two knobs of soft black rubber," Popeye is an artificial man and the style reflects this (pp. 5-6). Fiedler describes him in *Love and Death* as "the spawn of urban alleys, Prohibition, and the hysteria of the Great Depression" (p. 322). When he spits in the stream he seems to pollute it and it is apparent that he is ill-at-ease in this isolated area of Yoknapatawpha County. When an owl suddenly swoops Popeye claws for his gun and later, Tommy tells Benbow that when his dog startled Popeye, the little gangster shot it.

In *The Rebel,* Camus explains that the technique of the tough-guy novel "consists of describing men by their outside appearances, in their most casual actions, of reproducing, without comment, everything they say down to their repetitions and finally by acting as if men were entirely defined by their daily automatisms" (p. 230). Hammett perfected this technique and Faulkner uses it in *Sanctuary.* He objectifies Popeye by assigning to him certain mannerisms and a distinctive appearance. He has a peculiar skill in lighting cigarettes and then allows the smoke to curl across his face. He also has a disturbing habit of making sudden silent appearances, often in doorways. These and other external characteristics give him an automaton quality, which is reinforced by his curt, repetitious statements. The conversations involving Popeye are terse, clipped interchanges, which show how accurately Faulkner can write tough dialogue:

> "Didn't I tell you to get on down that road?" Popeye said.
> "Me an' him jest stepped down hyer a minute," Tommy said.
> "Did I tell you to get on down that road, or didn't I?"
> "Yeuh," Tommy said. "You told me." (p. 40)

To talk at any length in the gangster's world could be dangerous. Popeye's spare diction relates to his fast, nervous existence. He is virtually inarticulate but in a very different way from Faulkner's idiots and simple characters. Popeye is pure action and style.

The elevation of action over analysis is particularly evident in the chapters describing Temple's confinement at the Old Frenchman's Place. Faulkner's technique is akin to that of the Hollywood thrillers, which were inspired by the tough-guy novels. Temple is subjected to a series of multiple shocks that are almost cinematic in execution. She dashes from one room to another and then out of the house into the outbuildings. Her frantic motion is suddenly arrested by a moment of paralysis, like a grotesque game of musical chairs. She turns to find Popeye standing silently in a doorway, cigarette smoke drifting across his doll-like face; or she comes "eye to eye" (p. 76) with a rat, which then leaps at her. Other incidents which produce a similar "terrific" effect are Red's corpse rolling, as if in slow-motion, out of the coffin, or Miss Reba's dogs crouching in "terrific silence" beneath Temple's bed. This is followed by an account of Temple "cringing" and "thrashing furiously" but helplessly as Popeye approaches (pp. 124, 127).

These rather unusual aspects of Faulkner's art probably led Robert Penn Warren to cite *Sanctuary* as the best example of one of three distinct techniques that he discovered in Faulkner. According to Warren, *Sanctuary* is characterized by "a tightly organized plot, a crisp, laconic style, an objective presentation of character—an impersonal method."[42] Joseph T. Shaw would have approved of such a novel. Yet, Faulkner's greatest achievement in *Sanctuary* is the blending of this tough style with a more poetic, symbolic style. The latter is never intrusive to the point where it disturbs the surface tension but it is the method Faulkner uses to expand the meaning of his novel. The personal menace of Popeye, for example, is expanded into a universal evil. It is obvious that Popeye's revenge on Red is inevitable when Temple sees him waiting in his long touring car. "When they passed it Temple saw, leaning to a cupped match, Popeye's delicate hooked profile beneath the slanted hat as he lit the cigarette." And then the objective description is briefly abandoned: "The match flipped outwards like a dying star in miniature, sucked with the profile into darkness by the rush of their passing" (p. 192).

The same combination of realism and poetic images is apparent in the account of Temple's arrival at Miss Reba's brothel. Faulkner captures the sentimentality and sordidness of the surroundings by objective description, such as he uses throughout the Memphis episodes:

> She [Miss Reba] had just returned from church, in a black silk gown and a hat savagely flowered; the lower half of the tankard was still frosted with inner chill. She moved heavily from big thigh to thigh, the two dogs moiling underfoot, talking steadily back across her shoulder in a harsh, expiring, maternal voice.
>
> "Popeye knew better than to bring you anywhere else but to my house. I been after him for, how many years I been after you to get a girl, honey? What I say, a young fellow can't no more live without a girl than . . ." (p. 115)

Faulkner then suggests that outside this world, the world of the whole novel, is a different existence, symbolized by the weak sunlight which filters through:

The narrow stairwell turned back on itself in a succession of niggard reaches. The light, falling through a thickly-curtained door at the rear of each stage, had a weary quality. A spent quality; defunctive, exhausted—a protracted weariness like a vitiated backwater beyond sunlight and the vivid noises of sunlight and day." (p. 115)

Albert Camus criticizes the tough American novel for its presentation of a one-dimensional universe and it must be conceded that in its attempts to present stark reality certain levels of existence are ignored. Faulkner, however, proves himself adept at reproducing those elements of the tough-guy style which enable him to capture the sordid reality of a Memphis brothel, or the "smell of fear" that pervades the Old Frenchman's Place, but he combines this sensing through experience with the need to see beyond the immediate context.

In one of the Nagano interviews, Faulkner criticizes Hemingway for being unadventurous: "I rated Hemingway last [among their contemporaries] because Hemingway through good fortune or through good preceptor, had developed a style where he was quite at home, where he did not make mistakes, and that he did not risk as we've risked" (p. 61). Faulkner was not content to function as near to the tough-guy tradition as Hemingway because the style was inappropriate to his usual subject. However, the tough-guy elements in *Sanctuary* and *Light in August* suggest that Faulkner recognized that the tough-guy novel, for all its faults, succeeded in capturing the reality of Depression and crime-dominated America, and in conveying the effect of that tough environment upon that ubiquitous character, the American individual. In both these novels Faulkner shows that he, too, can write in a tough fashion for a particular purpose, though his panorama is not narrowed by his use of tough-guy conventions.

Steven R. Carter

ISHMAEL REED'S NEO-HOODOO DETECTION

I

In a 1973 interview, Ishmael Reed argued that his book *Mumbo Jumbo* should have won an Edgar since "it was the best mystery novel of the year,"[1] and maybe he's right. There is little doubt about the high quality of his novel. It won a deservedly warm critical reception, including a laudatory front page assessment in the *New York Times Book Review* and a nomination for the National Book Award. Virtually all the critics used such terms as "original," "amusing" and "broad in scope."

The problem is whether or not this humorous experimental work can be classified as a mystery. *Mumbo Jumbo* features two detectives, a climactic confrontation between detectives and villains, and a "solution" to both a murder and a missing text case. However, it also includes a reconstruction of the Jazz Age, a commentary on the Harlem Renaissance, a capsule summary of Western and African cultural history, and a political, religious, and social satire on White and Black America.

If we accept the intelligent and useful definitions which Julian Symons offers in *Mortal Consequences,* then *Mumbo Jumbo* lies well outside the basic mystery categories of the detective story and the crime novel. Reed's novel is little influenced by either "a pleasure in employing a conjurer's sleight of hand" or "an appetite for violence."[2] In addition, Symons would probably ex-clue-d *Mumbo Jumbo* from the mystery field on the same grounds on which he eliminated Dostoievski's *Crime and Punishment* and *The Brothers Karamazov* since it too moves "in mystical regions where spiritual truths are being considered."[3]

However, Symons' categories may not encompass the full range of mystery fiction. If, as he theorizes, one of the two mystery forms has evolved from the other, might not a third mystery form evolve from the previous two? Moreover, if, as Symons believes, the crime novel has moved away from the rigid patterning of the detective story toward a more flexible and "serious" approach, might not the new form developed from these two become open-ended and experimental? In the light of the latter conjecture, a novel like *Mumbo Jumbo* could be considered a further extension of the mystery genre into the realm of "serious" literature.

Ishmael Reed is aware of the past—and often still present—scholarly condescension toward mysteries. In the introduction of *19 Necromancers from Now*, his anthology of innovative minority writing, Reed comments:

> I was to learn that White authors, as well as Afro-American authors, are neglected by the American university. Before I arrived at Berkeley, there was no room in the curriculum for detective novels or Western fiction, even though some of the best contributions to American literature occur in these genres.[4]

He is attracted to detective fiction for the same reason he is drawn to slang; he views it as a form of popular expression scorned by the standard bearers of a repressive culture.

More importantly, Reed regards the mystery novel as a vehicle for getting at other mysteries, such as "the mysteries of the American civilization."[5] which he wishes to de-mystify, and the mysteries of Voodoo (the Haitian form of the African Ju-Ju), which he seeks to redefine and reactivate. He calls his own viewpoint Neo-Hoodooism, acknowledging that it is a personalized Afro-American variation of Voodooism, and links all versions of Voodoo to ancient Egyptian religious myth. Significantly, he refers to "Neo-Hoodoos" like himself as "detectives of the metaphysical about to make a pinch."[6] The offender sought for arrest is the god Jehovah, and, by extension, the whole of White Western civilization. In Reed's eyes, the central conflict of our time is between two churches: the Western church, Shadow-ed by a glum Christ, and the African church, inspired —but not presided over—by a dancing Osiris.

Obviously, Reed is after bigger game than individual evil-doers. The capture and punishment of the murderer Hinckle Von Vampton has little importance in itself; Reed does not cater to that kind of puzzle buff. Even though he has developed an inverted mystery plot around Von Vampton, Reed's focus is on the Western civilization's spiritual illnesses embodied in H.V.V. He is less concerned with the killing of Abdul Hamid than with H.V.V.'s attempt to manipulate and dilute Black culture by determining who will speak for the "Negro." He is also disturbed by H.V.V.'s uptight espousal of Pragmatism—Hinckle can only relate to Whites and Blacks who prefer power, honor, wealth, and respectability to the spiritual release of boogieing—and by H.V.V.'s penchant for leading crusades against ways of life he can't dig. Ultimately, Reed traces Von Vampton's offensiveness less to his destructiveness than to his ego-tripping; Hinckle is the corrupt defender of the holier-than-thou putdown.

But Hinckle is a small fry. Reed wants to get the Big Bosses: Uncle Sam, Kaiser Bill, John-David-Nelson Rockefeller, the whole Judeo-Christian mob. His method is a startling reworking of traditional detective techniques:

When I said that [*Mumbo Jumbo*] was going to be a "straight" book, I meant I would follow the classical detective story or mystery form, follow it more closely than I had the western or gothic form of my two previous novels. . . . The form is described in a headline of the *New York Times*, Monday, June 25, 1973: "Search for Suspects of Slain Policeman Provides Classic Example of Detective Work." A detective defined it as an investigation that included several lucky breaks and ingenious piecing together of seemingly unrelated bits of information.[7]

On the literal plot level, the two Neo-Hoodoo detectives, Black Herman and Papa LaBas, piece together such details as a newspaper photo of H.V.V. wearing his Knight's Templar pendant, the Knight's Templar seal on top of the box in which the murdered Abdul Hamid received the Jes Grew Text, the Haitian's warning that an evil white man would soon create a pseudo-spokesman for the Jes Grew Movement, and the information that H.V.V. is about to introduce "the only Negro poet with any sense."[8] The lucky break occurs when T. Malice mentions the Cotton Club while Papa is pondering the meaning of Abdul's cryptic message about American-Egyptian cotton.[9] Once Papa LaBas finds the box at the Cotton Club, he deduces that H.V.V. was the Knight Templar librarian who found the Jes Grew Text in the Temple of Solomon, carried it with him for a thousand years, lost it to Abdul Hamid, and killed Abdul in a futile attempt to retrieve it. Naturally, this type of plot is not meant for the fussy logician or the sobersides:

You can have a lot of fun with this book. For example, in the 1940s the detective or mystery movies always had a form or formula where the detective would assemble all the characters involved in the crime, give a summary of how it happened, and then point to the guilty person. Well, that's what I did in *Mumbo Jumbo*, only I exaggerated. You're supposed to laugh when the detective goes all the way back to [ancient] Egypt and works up to himself in reconstructing the crime. When he finishes the summary, everybody's asleep.[10]

On a deeper level, though, the entire novel is a metaphysical and social puzzle which the reader has to fit together. One minute Reed describes the activities of the art-nappers, the next he quotes from a book on dancing by Irene Castle, and the third he analyzes the war in Haiti; but he is not creating a crazy-quilt pattern. He merely seems to be sewing a patchwork from such diverse elements as several distinct stories involving different sets of characters; quotations from books on witchcraft, rock and roll, the depression, etc.; and a mixture of "real" figures like Jacques de Molay and Black Herman and imaginary figures like Hierophant 1 and Papa LaBas. In reality, Reed centers all his "clues" around the conflict between the Jes Grew Movement and the Wallflower Order. The detectives' reconstruction of Hinckle's crime, though comically long and partially a put-on, supplies the final pieces to this larger puzzle.

Papa LaBas's reconstruction suggests that from the time of Osiris to the present the Jes Grew Movements have had their main effect on Blacks, though Browns, Reds, Yellows, and even Whites have often joined in with their own steps when the spirit shook them. According to LaBas, the essence of Jes Grew is a willingness to let the spirit grab you and take you where it wants, to open yourself to the creative forces of the universe and expose yourself to other levels of reality. As LaBas's creator stated in another context:

> . . . Arthur Koestler said that strict determinism is dead in physics. He went on to say that there are other levels of reality than those we see with the eyes of the common man or the scientist. I think that the traditional hoodoo physics were always amenable to that possibility. Later what happens is that the conjure man becomes a buffoon and loses his powers. This was a very sorry episode for blacks in this country when the decline of the conjure man occurred, when blacks went North and were exposed to all the ideas of Europe. They seemed to lose this kind of wonder and became materialists.[11]

Reed's Jes Grew conjures the spirits—and that lost sense of wonder—through shake it, don't break it dancing. He argues that such dancing is grounded in ancient rituals which were sparked by a magical conception of life. He is particularly drawn to the fertility rituals which combined a powerful and joyful sexual impulse with a profound respect for the forces of nature. He feels that these ritual dances allowed men to express their awareness of the power held by the gods and by nature and their desire to align themselves with this power. He worries that modern variations on these dances may be mistaken for mere entertainment if men forget the origin of the dances. The knowledge of the history of this kind of dancing—and of other features of contemporary Black culture—is the Text which Jes Grew needs in order to reach its full development.

A word of caution, however, about Reed's belief in the loas (spirits). One of the epigraphs at the beginning of *Mumbo Jumbo* is Zora Neale Hurston's statement on the origin of a new loa: "Some *unknown phenomenon* occurs which cannot be explained, and a new local demigod is named." The unknown phenomenon may be either outside or inside man. In a book which is listed in Reed's bibliography at the end of *Mumbo Jumbo*, Maya Deren argues that the loa are "principles" such as "life, death, love or affinity, war or conflict, etc."[12] She also asserts:

> . . . one might reconstruct the origin of Voudoun as follows: that the Haitian—or, more properly, his African ancestor—observed the universe, both nature and man as part of nature, and, in its operation, discerned certain major and recurrent principles; that he distinguished between the principle of the thing and the thing itself and remarked that the material objects or phenomena are transitory or destructible and singular, whereas the principles themselves are persistent and pervasive, or immortal; that he consequently estimated these latter as of an order superior to matter; and,

finally, that it is this superior order—these principles to which he himself is subject—which he conceives of as divinity.[13]

The best example in *Mumbo Jumbo* of a loa viewed as principle or natural phenomenon occurs in an incident involving one of Papa LaBas's assistants. Earline, who wears a scarf picturing a heart stabbed by a dagger after her boyfriend starts neglecting her, forgets to feed the loa of passion (Erzulie). The loa retaliates by filling her with a sudden desire for a happily married trolley car operator. After her brief but exuberant flings with both the trolley operator and Black Herman, Earline is restored to a sense of harmony with her world. Reed's own guiding spirit is clearly the loa of humor, and he tells us that ancient African sculptors too brought "side-splitting, bellyaching, satirical ways . . . to their art."[14]

Reed's main reason for favoring the Afro-American forms of hoodoo, jazz, and shake it dancing is the amount of freedom they permit for individual expression within the context of a meaningful group experience. He notes that "Neo-Hoodoo is not a church for ego-tripping—it takes its 'organization' from Haitian VooDoo of which Milo Rigaud wrote: 'Unlike other established religions, there is no hierarchy of bishops, archbishops, cardinals, or a pope in VooDoo. Each oum'phor is a law unto itself, following the traditions of VooDoo but modifying and changing the ceremonials and rituals in various ways.' "[15] Similarly, jazz combines a basic melody begun by the entire group with subsequent inventive variations by individual members of the group. Finally, shake it dancing lets people share the same dance floor, respond to the same music, and perform some motions in common, while developing their own style and making a personal contact with the spirit.

In contrast, the Wallflowers (otherwise known as Western Civilizers) enclose and inhibit. Order is their keystone, a weight on the soil and on societies. The Wallflower Order aims at control over mind, body, self, emotions, nature—and other men. Instead of following "the ancient Vodun aesthetic . . . which bountifully permits 1000s of spirits, as many as the imagination can hold,"[16] the Wallflowers seek "to interpret the world by using a single loa"[17]—theoretically Christ, but in reality the loa of reason. (The two Neo-Hoodoo detectives also employ reason, but they couple it with their intuitions, called Knockings).

The Wallflowers embrace reason as a tool for insuring their power. For example, their reason enables them to categorize things pragmatically and to stigmatize and weaken potential troublemakers. Unlike the artnappers who feel that art should be integrated into the daily life and religious practices of a culture, the Wallflowers believe that art should be placed in intellectual cells to hinder people from being moved by it. The Wallflowers also use their reason to create instruments of destruction to keep people in line. However, the Haitian Benoit Battraville warns that Western civilization has created a new technological loa which feeds on the crimes that have been committed through misuses of its powers. Appropriately, Battraville intends to punish Hinckle Von Vampton and "Safecracker" Gould, the two military men and saboteurs working for the Wallflower Order, by letting their own beloved technological loa destroy them.

Like Reed's main plot, the contrast between the Jes Grew Movement and the Wallflower Order is probably also a conscious exaggeration, but this matter—and the question of the accuracy of his historical account—can be debated elsewhere.[18] The point here is that the mystery novel is well adapted to a world view which makes a sharp distinction between opposing ways of life and which pictures one as overtly healthy and the other as surreptitiously destructive; fictional detectives often ferret out hidden villains. At no point does Reed have to chop up or limit his ideas to fit them into a procrustean literary mold. Instead, he has chosen the genre best suited to his vision and has adapted it to meet his special needs. In doing so, he has immersed the reader in a puzzle which is far more than an intellectual game. As a result, his novel is not a distortion of the mystery form, but rather a valuable extension of it.

Reed has produced a unique blend of forms; his book is at once an inverted detective story, a mystery parody, a satire, a historical survey, a metaphysical statement, a cinematic fiction (with quick cuts and fast dissolves), and a serious novel which employs the mystery form in striking new ways. However, the two ingredients which hold the blend together are his world view and his personalized version of the mystery novel. He has therefore joined a growing number of contemporary writers who have sought to reshape the mystery form to accommodate their own hignly individual purposes. Some of their independent, nontraditional mysteries are Thomas Pynchon's *V,* Chester Himes's *Blind Man with a Pistol,* Mark Smith's *The Death of the Detective,* Joseph McElroy's *Lookout Cartridge,* Richard Brautigan's *Willard and His Bowling Trophies: A Perverse Mystery,* Colin Wilson's *Necessary Doubt,* Muriel Spark's *Robinson,* Kobo Abe's *The Ruined Map,* Manuel Peyrou's *Thunder of the Roses,* Alain Robbe-Grillet's *The Erasers,* Michel Butor's *Passing Time,* Carlo Emilio Gadda's *That Awful Mess on Via Merulana,* Hans Hellmut Kirst's *The Officer Factory* and *The Night of the Generals,* and Per Wahloo's *The Thirty-First Floor* and *The Steel Spring.* One could also cite several short stories and novellas by Jorge Luis Borges, Julio Cortazar, Mircea Eliade, and John Fowles. In view of such works, the MWA (and Julian Symons) ought to consider a new category—The Experimental Mystery. Then, if they go this far, they could take the further justificable step of making Ishmael Reed the first Experimental Mystery Grand Master.

II

Reed's latest novel, *The Last Days of Louisiana Red,* comes close to being a straight crime novel a la Ross Macdonald and Chester Himes. Close, but not quite. Consider this partial list of characters: Antigone, Minnie the Moocher, T. Feeler, and Amos and Andy. Consider also that the detective, again Papa LaBas, seeks advice from a psychic baboon named Hamadryas and a messenger who stands on the right hand side of Osiris (the right hand signifies the Rada rites in Voodoo). Consider further that Papa LaBas, like Orpheus, rescues a girl from the land of the lecherous dead. Clearly Reed has lost neither his comic touch nor his interest in technical experimentation.

His central plot, however, is a straightforward whodunit. Reed conceals the identity of Ed Yellings' killers until close to the end, though he gives the reader a fair chance to guess who they are. Like Ross Macdonald and James Jones (in *A Touch of Danger*), he makes effective use of foreshadowing. For example, when Papa LaBas lectures Ed's younger daughter, Minnie Yellings (Reed's pun is intentional), about the numerous collaborations between White men and Black women, he also prepares the reader for the revelation that the phony White radical Max Kasavubu and the phony Black mammy-figure Lisa have been sleeping and conspiring together for ten years. (Max's involvement with a woman has already been established by his remark to himself, "Then I can really retire. My baby and me."[19] Also, Minnie early raises the question of what Nanny Lisa does on her every other Thursday off,[20] and the reader eventually learns that Lisa met Max on those days.)

Another good example of foreshadowing is LaBas's reference to Marie Laveau's "domestic spy network"[21] since this reference hints at Nanny Lisa's domestic spying against Ed Yellings. Nanny Lisa was spotted while going through Ed's drawers, though she claimed she was only looking for change to pay the paper boy. Thus, when the messenger of Osiris informs LaBas that a spy from the Louisiana Red Corporation got close to Minnie and gained access to Ed's papers, she indirectly but unmistakably points a finger at Nanny Lisa. LaBas intuitively fits all this together when he looks through the yellow pages for a domestic and suddenly realizes how close the domestic Nanny Lisa has been to Minnie.

The biggest clue to Lisa's part in the crime comes when the messenger tells LaBas that the key to Ed's death is Doc John. Her immediate meaning is that Ed carried on and extended Doc John's Voodoo practices and that he therefore became a dangerous rival to the Louisiana Red Corporation. However, since she implies that the murderer is someone opposed to Doc John, she again points to Nanny Lisa who poisoned Minnie's mind against Doc John—and all men—by telling her stories about how Marie Laveau continually triumphed over him.

Like Dashiell Hammett in *The Maltese Falcon*, Reed keeps the reader from becoming too absorbed in this relatively simple puzzle by drawing his attention to other things. Using the same kind of razzle-dazzle that

Bill S. Ballinger practiced in *The Tooth and the Nail* and *The Longest Second,* Reed juggles three separate plots which ultimately merge. Sometimes his center ring contains Papa LaBas investigating Ed's death and carrying on Ed's work; sometimes it provides a forum for Chorus to retell the story of how Antigone upstaged him; and sometimes it permits Andy and George "Kingfish" Stevens to demonstrate their mooching techniques. On the literal level, the three plots converge when Ed's daughter Minnie helps Andy and Kingfish in a skyjacking and then launches a tirade against the passenger Chorus who identifies her as Antigone. On the figurative level, the plots merge when the reader realizes that Minnie is an updated version of Antigone and that her protest activities are spiritually akin to the Kingfish's parasitical begging since she shouts down the "real" voice of the people whom she claims to represent.[22] The solution of Ed's murder provides another significant basis for the merging on the figurative level.

The motive for Ed's killing is important. Ed opposed mooching in every form, and began to teach a group of men and women how to think and act independently. With the aid of Doc John's example and techniques, Ed was on the brink of discovering a means of overcoming the most debilitating form of dependence on others. The so-called revolutionary leaders who wanted an oppressed people to become hooked on them could not tolerate this kind of competition. Exit Ed.

In Reed's eyes, the Whites in power welcome the attempts at leadership by violent and divisive figures like Minnie and Street Yellings (who resembles Eldridge Cleaver). Reed argues that "Louisiana Red was the way [oppressed workers in general and revolutionaries in particular] related to one another, maimed and murdered one another . . . while above their heads . . . billionaires flew in custom-made jet planes."[23] He also condemns mooching as a specialized form of the spiritual disease which he calls Louisiana Red and asserts that:

> The Kasavubus, Sallys, Feelers and Rookies are among all "oppressed people" who often . . . have their own boot on their own neck. They exist to give the LaBases, Wolfs and Sisters of these groups the business, so as to prevent them from taking care of Business, Occupation, Work. They are the moochers who cooperate with their "oppression," for they have the mentality of the prey who thinks his destruction at the fangs of the killer is the natural order of things and colludes with his own death. The Workers exist to tell the "prey" that they were meant to bring down killers three times their size, using the old morality as their guide: Voodoo, Confucianism, the ancient Egyptian inner duties. . . . Doc John, "the black Cagliostro," rises again over the American scene. The Workers conjure and command the spirit of Doc John to walk the land.[24]

Reed believes that oppressed peoples have a better chance of eliminating their oppression if they build their cultures and struggles on the independent strengths of individual members rather than on the collective weaknesses of all. His metaphor for this approach is gumbo, a dish which can be made in "*many varieties*" by cooks "with equal ability."[25] He wants each person to strive to develop his own creative powers to the fullest rather than to lean on others or to settle for sterile imitation.

Reed uses a new recipe for gumbo in *The Last Days of Louisiana Red*, though it bears much in common with the recipe he worked from in *Mumbo Jumbo*. He still stresses the need to welcome the existence of men's multiplicity of talents and to see that men with a variety of interests and abilities may work separately for a mutual cause. He also emphasizes the importance of seeking durable values in prewestern and nonwestern sources like ancient Egyptian religion and Voodoo. However, he has thrown in a dash of Confucianism, and this has given the mixture a slightly different flavor. Instead of continuing to focus on spontaneous, boisterous outbursts of joy, Reed pictures the quieter pleasures of sitting in a night spot like Solomon Grundy's where Art Fletcher "plays a soft piano"[26] and of playing chess at the Toulouse restaurant where people of all races and all classes gather. Moreover, he indicates that people should show consideration for each other and that such consideration should preclude "talking loudly" to the "annoyance of their fellow customers" in a public establishment.[27] The chief virtues he heralds this time are industriousness, creativity, self-reliance, courteousness, concern for genuine victims of oppression, respect for "mystery,"[28] and the readiness to "party" after your work is done.

One major ingredient of Reed's gumbo has remained the same: his interest in the mystery novel. As before, Reed's motivation in using his own version of the mystery form is to point up how to detect and control a spiritual disease (in this case, Louisiana Red and its subsidiary disease, Moocherism). In pursuing his larger aim, however, Reed provides many of the traditional rewards of mystery fiction.

Julian Symons' definitions of the detective story and the crime novel fit most of the works he discusses in his insightful and stimulating survey of mystery fiction. The interested reader would gain a lot by studying his definitions at length in the opening section of the chapter on "Crime Novel and Police Novel" in *Mortal Consequences*. However, there may be a third category which Symons has overlooked. This category, experimental mystery fiction, can be defined as follows: 1) it combines elements of detective and crime fiction with the devices of mainstream and/or experimental fiction; 2) it reshapes the elements of detective and crime fiction to fit a personal vision; 3) it usually examines the mysteries of the spirit and/or the skeletons in the closets of societies (it generally aims at exposing the spiritual weaknesses of entire societies rather than ferreting out the hidden villainy of a single individual; it is closer to metaphysics and sociology than to intellectual gamesmanship and psychology); 4) it may or may not resolve any puzzle or problem it poses; and 5) the detective and crime novel elements must play a major role in the work as a whole. The last term of this definition might exclude such borderline cases as John A. Williams' *The Man Who Cried I Am,* William Melvin Kelley's *Dunsfords Travels Everywheres,* John Gardner's *The Sunlight Dialogues,* and J. P. Donleavy's *A Singular Man.* Like any other literary definition, though, this one is far from airtight and ought to be used very flexibly.

If my definition has any validity, then Ishmael Reed should be considered one of the foremost practitioners of experimental mystery fiction. If it is not valid, then Reed can at least be viewed as an important modern writer whose work has been profoundly influenced by both the detective story and the crime novel.

NOTES

Jan R. Van Meter

[1] Eugene Ionesco, *Victims of Duty,* quoted in Kenneth Burke, "Dramatic Form—And," *TDR*, 10 (Summer, 1966), p. 57.

[2] Burke, *Counterstatement* (Berkeley: University of California Press, 1968), p. 34.

[3] Philip Slater, *The Glory of Hera* (Boston: Beacon Press, 1968).

[4] William O. Aydelotte, "The Detective Story as a Historical Source," *Yale Review,* 36 (Fall, 1949), p. 76.

[5] Ross Macdonald, *The Underground Man* (New York: Bantam Books, 1971), p. 26.

[6] Raymond Chandler, *The Simple Art of Murder* (New York: Ballantine Books, 1972), p. 20.

[7] Aydelotte, p. 84.

[8] Geraldine Pederson-Krag, "Detective Stories and the Primal Scene," *The Psychoanalytic Quarterly,* 18 (1949), pp. 207-214; and Charles Rycroft, "A Detective Story: Psychoanalytic Observations," *The Psychoanalytic Quarterly,* 26 (1957), pp. 229-245.

[9] Pederson-Krag, p. 213.

[10] Rycroft, p. 231.

[11] Edmund R. Leach, "Magical Hair," in *Myth and Cosmos: Readings in Mythology and Symbolism,* ed. John Middleton (Garden City: The Natural History Press, 1967), pp. 77-107.

[12] Ross Macdonald, Quoted in John Leonard, "Ross Macdonald, his Lew Archer, and other secret selves," *The New York Times Book Review,* 1 July 1969, p. 19.

[13] Macdonald in Leonard, p. 19.

Elliot L. Gilbert

[1] Clair Sterling, "Get it While You Can," *San Francisco Chronicle Sunday Punch,* 16 January 1972, p. 5.

[2] "Butor's Use of Literary Texts in *Degrees,*" *PMLA* (March 1973), 314.

George Grella

[1] A. E. Murch, *The Development of the Detective Novel* (London, 1958), p. 11.

[2] "The Simple Art of Murder," *The Art of the Mystery Story,* ed. Howard Haycraft (New York, 1947), p. 230.

[3] *Ibid.,* p. 230.

[4] "Why Do People Read Detective Stories?" *The New Yorker* (October 14, 1944), p. 76.

[5]John Williams, "The 'Western': Definition of a Myth," *The Popular Arts,* ed. Irving and Harriet A. Deer (New York, 1967), p. 202.

[6]This is the consensus of an overwhelming majority of historians, critics, writers, and readers. For pre-Poe detective themes and types (known to initiates as the incunabula) see Miss Murch's book, Note 1.

[7]For detailed accounts of this development, see Murch, *op. cit.,* Haycraft, *Murder for Pleasure* (New York: D. Appleton-Century, 1941) and *The Art of the Mystery Story,* and Julian Symons, *The Detective Story in Britain* (London: Longmans, Green, 1962).

[8]"A Cosmic View of the Private Eye," *Saturday Review* (August 22, 1953), p. 7.

Geraldine Pederson-Krag

[1]H. Haycraft, *Murder for Pleasure* (New York: D. Appleton-Century Co., Inc., 1941).

[2]Leopold Bellak, *Psychology of Detective Stories and Related Problems.* Psa. Rev., XXXII, 1945.

[3]Edmund Bergler, *Mystery Fans and the Problem of Potential Murders,* Amer. Journal of Orthopsychiatry, XV, 1945.

[4]Hans Zulliger, *Der Abenteurer-Schundroman.* Ztschr. f. psa. Pädagogik, VII, 1933.

[5]Edith Buxbaum, *The Rôle of Detective Stories in a Child Analysis.* The Psychoanalytic Quarterly, X, 1941.

[6]Otto Fenichel, *The Psychoanalytic Theory of the Neurosis* (New York: W. W. Norton & Co., Inc., 1945).

[7]Freud, *A Neurosis of Demoniacal Possession in the Seventeenth Century.* Coll. Papers, IV.

[8]Margaret Mahler s., *Pseudo Imbecility, the Magic Cap of Invisibility.* The Psychoanalytic Quarterly, XI, 1942.

[9]Marie Bonaparte, Notes on the Analytical Discovery of the Primal Scene. In *Psychoanalytic Study of the Child, Vol. I.* (New York: International Universities Press, 1945).

[10]Freud, *A Phobia in a Five-Year-Old Boy.* Coll. Papers, III.

[11]Freud, *From the History of an Infantile Neurosis.* Coll. Papers, III.

[12]Marie Bonaparte, *Edgar Allan Poe* (Paris: Éditions Denoël et Steele, 1933).

[13]Cf. Hanns Sachs, *Edgar Allan Poe.* The Psychoanalytic Quarterly, IV, 1935, p. 294, and Marie Bonaparte, *The Murders in the Rue Morgue.* The Psychoanalytic Quarterly, IV, 1935, p. 259.

[14]Mary Chadwick, *Notes Upon the Acquisition of Knowledge.* Psa. Rev., XIII, 1926.

Patrick Parrinder

[1]Four vols., ed. Sonia Orwell and Ian Angus, London 1968. Hereafter referred to as *CEJL.*

[2]George Orwell, "Grandeur et Décadence du Roman Policier Anglais," in *Fontaine,* nos. 37-40 (Algiers, 1944), pp. 69/213-75/219. Hereafter referred to as GD. Quotations from this article, which are in my own translation, are included by kind

permission of Mrs. Sonia Orwell. Mrs. Orwell has, however, informed me that in the absence of the original text she is not prepared to authorize the publication of a full English version of the essay.

[3]GD, p. 69/213.

[4]Orwell mentions the following volumes: *The Adventures of Sherlock Holmes* (1891) and *The Memoirs of Sherlock Holmes* (1894) by Sir Arthur Conan Doyle; *Max Carrados* (1914) and *The Eyes of Max Carrados* (1923) by Ernest Bramah; and *The Singing Bone* (1912) by R. Austin Freeman.

[5]GD, p. 71/215.

[6]*CEJL*, iv, pp. 19-22.

[7]*CEJL*, iv, p. 19.

[8]GD, p. 75/219.

Edward Margolies

[1]"Raffles and Miss Blandish" in *A Collection of Essays* (Garden City, New York: Anchor Books, 1957), p. 147

[2]On occasion, however, the three gentlemen have had to trail their enemies themselves, thereby incurring physical risks. Indeed in at least one instance, "The Adventure of the Illustrious Client," Holmes had illegally entered an apartment in order to steal evidence. But by and large persons of Holmes's ilk much prefer to remain in the background.

[3]Dashiell Hammett: *The Maltese Falcon* (New York: Knopf, 1930).

[4]Mickey Spillane: *I the Jury* (New York: E. P. Dutton, 1950).

[5]Norbert Davis, "Don't Give Your Right Name" in *The Hardboiled Dicks,* ed., Ron Goulart (Los Angeles: Sherbourne Press, 1965), pp. 29, 30.

[6]John K. Butler, "The Saint in Silver" in *The Hardboiled Dicks,* ed., Ron Goulart (Los Angeles: Sherbourne Press, 1965), p. 74.

[7]For a fuller discussion, see Edward Margolies, "The Thrillers of Chester Himes," *Studies in Black Literature,* I (Summer 1970), 1-11.

[8]*A Rage in Harlem* (London: Panther Books, 1969), p. 51.

D. F. Rauber

[1]The earliest significant example I have found of the Sherlock Holmes type of deduction is in Chapter II of Voltaire's *Zadig,* and Voltaire was, of course, greatly influenced by the English empiricists. In connection with rationalism, it is worth noting that the type of detective story under study remains emotionally sterile, even when—as in Holmes and Wolfe—the center of attraction moves away from the pure intellectual puzzle type established by Poe and continued by writers such as Agatha Christie, A. A. Milne, and Freeman Wills Crofts. For example, sex and love are virtually absent from the stories. Both Holmes and Wolfe are blatant misogynists, and even Archie Goodwin, who is theoretically a lover and an expert on women, forms no real emotional attachments. Only Watson marries, but Watson was never a real member of the club.

[2]Quotations from A. Conan Doyle are from *The Complete Sherlock Holmes,* preface by Christopher Morley (New York, 1938). All Wolfe quotations are from *A Right To Die* (New York, 1964).

[3]Edmund Wilson, "Why Do People Read Detective Stories?" in *Classics and*

Commercials (New York, 1950), pp. 232-3. Wilson errs in his designation of Cramer; as Wolfe fans know the proper formula is "Inspector Cramer of Homicide South."

[4] Louis de Broglie, *Physics and Microphysics,* trans. Martin Davidson (New York, 1955), p. 110.

[5] Robert L. Fish, in his *The Incredible Schlock Homes,* parodies these chains of reasoning with great effect. He constructs the same elaborate structures, which turn out always to be right, but only accidentally and for completely the wrong reasons.

[6] Bertrand Russell, *Wisdom of the West* (New York, 1959), p. 378.

[7] Edward Condon, "Physics," in *What is Science?*, ed. James R. Newman (New York, 1961), p. 109. Condon goes on to say that the particular difficulties which prompted Hilbert's joke have since been solved, "but little progress has been made in interpreting the fundamental problems of atomic theory. . . . On balance, Hilbert's judgment is at least as true today as it was when he made it."

[8] Only at the end, in the stories written under the shadow of the First World War, does Holmes' confidence falter. In "His Last Bow: An Epilogue of Sherlock Holmes," the great detective says: "Good old Watson! You are the one fixed point in a changing age. There's an east wind coming all the same, such a wind as never blew on England yet. It will be cold and bitter, and a good many of us may wither before its blast. But it's God's own wind none the less, and a cleaner, better, stronger land will lie in the sunshine when the storm has cleared." (p. 1155) Nowhere else, to my knowledge, does Holmes criticize his society.

[9] Wolfe's isolation emerges even more clearly if we compare him with what is probably his literal source in the Holmes stories, Mycroft Holmes. Mycroft, it will be remembered, is the lethargic and withdrawn brother of Sherlock. On the surface he appears to be exactly like Wolfe, but we learn that rather than being a recluse as Wolfe is—the man who deliberately cuts himself off from society—Mycroft is the still unmoving point at the dead center of the Empire. As Holmes explains to Watson: "All other men are specialists, but his specialism is omniscience. We will suppose that a minister needs information as to a point which involves the Navy, India, Canada and the bimetallic question; he could get his separate advices from various departments upon each, but only Mycroft can focus them all, and say offhand how each factor would affect the other. . . . In that great brain of his everything is pigeon-holed and can be handed out in an instant. Again and again his word has decided national policy." ("The Adventure of the Bruce-Partington Plans," p. 1076) In other words, Mycroft is actually a precursor, not of Nero Wolfe, but of the modern central computer.

Ronald Ambrosetti

[1] Eric Ambler, *A Coffin For Dimitrois* (New York: Bantam Paperbacks, 1972), p. 10. All subsequent references are to this edition.

[2] Eric Ambler, *Journey Into Fear* (New York: Bantam, 1972), p. 52. All subsequent references are to this edition.

[3] Eric Ambler, *The Intercom Conspiracy* (New York: Bantam, 1970), pp. 22-23.

Allen B. Crider

[1] Philip Durham, "The *Black Mask* School," *Tough Guy Writers of the Thirties,* ed. David Madden (Carbondale, Illinois, 1968), p. 55.

[2]Carroll John Daly, *The Snarl of the Beast* (New York, 1927), pp. 11-12. All future references to Daly's work are to this edition and are included in the text.

[3]Some critics of the mystery novel have blamed the excesses once referred to as "Spillanism" on later hard boiled writers, particularly Dashiell Hammett. As this quotation shows, however, from Daly to Spillane is a step with no intermediates.

[4]Williams only talks about it, however. Hammett's Continental Op *did* shoot a woman, in the knee, in "The Gutting of Couffignal" (1925).

Kay Weibel

[1]Leslie A. Fiedler, *Love and Death in the American Novel* (Revised Edition, New York, 1966), p. 83.

[2]Alice Payne Hackett, *70 Years of Best Sellers: 1895-1965* (New York, 1967), p. 64.

[3]Hackett, pp. 12-13.

[4]For comparisons between the hard-boiled heroes, see Archie H. Jones, "Cops, Robbers, Heroes and Anti-Heroines: The American Need to Create," in *Journal of Popular Culture* (Fall 1967); John G. Cawelti, "The Spillane Phenomenon," in *Journal of Popular Culture* (Summer 1969); and Etta C. Abrahams, "Where Have All the Values Gone?: The Private Eye's Vision of America in the Novels of Raymond Chandler and Ross Macdonald," (an excerpt from Abrahams' Ph.D. dissertation, Michigan State University, 1973), presented to the Popular Culture Association Conference, May 1974.

[5]Bestsellers in 1951 with wartime settings included: *From Here to Eternity,* by James Jones; *The Caine Mutiny,* by Herman Wouk; *The Cruel Sea,* by Nicholas Monsarrat; and *Melville Goodwin, U.S.A.,* by John P. Marquand. Listed in Hackett, p. 187.

[6]See Chronology of Spillane novels at the end of this paper for publisher and publication dates of the novels referenced.

[7]Emma S. Woytinsky, *Profile of the U. S. Economy: A Survey of Growth and Change* (New York, 1967), p. 32.

[8]*Ibid.*

[9]Hackett, p. 202.

[10]*Ibid.*, p. 184.

[11]Bureau of the Census in cooperation with Social Science Research Council, *Historical Statistics of the United States, Colonial Times to 1957* (Washington, D. C., 1960), p. 218. In cities of 25,000 or more population, based on 1950 census data, the number of major offences (defined as murder, negligent and non-negligent homocide, robbery, aggravated assault, burglary and auto theft) increased between the years 1937 and 1957 from 276,426 to 457,370.

[12]The three books referenced were among the top ten bestsellers between 1950 and 1952.

[13]John Kenneth Galbraith, "The Economics of the American Housewife," in *Atlantic Monthly* (August 1973), pp. 78-83. See also, Galbraith, "How the Economy Hangs on Her Apron Strings," in *Ms.* (May 1974), p. 74 ff.

[14]This, of course, is the subject of Betty Friedan's *The Feminine Mystique* (Dell, New York, 1963). I consider it significant that no serious attempt has been made by educators or publishers to refute Friedan's charges.

[15]Television was saturated with images of the young mother during the 1950's. "The Adventures of Ozzie and Harriet," "Make Room for Daddy," "Bringing up Buddy," "The Donna Reed Show," "Stu Erwin Show," "The Real McCoys," "Father

Knows Best," "Lassie," "Leave It To Beaver," and "Life With Father," to name only a few of the most popular series, all featured attractive mothers of young children or teenagers who played important roles each week solving their family's problems. Programs are listed each year beginning in 1952 in Charles S. Aaronson, Ed., *International Television Almanac* (Quigley Publications, New York). It is interesting to note by way of comparison that during the current (1973-74) television season, only three weekly series feature families with children or teenagers in starring roles: "The Waltons," "The Brady Bunch," and "The Partridge Family."

[16]U. S. Department of Labor, Wage and Labor Standards Administration, pamphlet titled "Trends in Educational Attainment of Women," Washington, D. C., 1969; U. S. Department of Labor, *1969 Handbook on Women Workers* (Woman's Bureau Bulletin 294), Washington, D. C., 1969. See also William L. O'Neill, *Everyone Was Brave* (Chicago, 1969), pp. 304-305, and Evelyne Sullerot, *Woman, Society and Change* (New York, 1971), pp. 55, 198.

[17]U. S. Department of Labor, *1969 Handbook on Women Workers,* pp. 9-17.

[18]Friedan, pp. 185-189.

[19]*Ibid.* See also A. E. Seigel and M. B. Hass, "The Working Mother: A Review or Fesearch," in *Child Development,* 34:538 (1963).

[20]Theodore Peterson, *Magazines in the Twentieth Century* (Urbana, 1964), pp. 204-205.

[21]*Ibid.*, pp. 141-142.

[22]In *70 Years of Best Sellers,* Hackett gives total copies sold for each bestseller. Fiction sales outdistanced nonfiction until 1950, when the current trend toward higher sales of nonfiction books began.

[23]Hackett, pp. 184-211. Between 1950 and 1959, there were twenty-five top ten bestsellers in the domestic area.

[24]This analysis is based on my reading in the novels of Mary Stewart, Victoria Holt and Phyllis Whitney, the most popular authors of the modern woman's gothic romance formula.

[25]Marjorie Rosen, "Popcorn Venus: Or, How the Movies Have Made Women Smaller Than Life," in *Ms.* (April 1974), p. 47.

[26]The University of Chicago Law Review, "Dirty Words and Dirty Politics," in Frederick M. Wirt and Willis D. Hawley, Eds., *New Dimensions of Freedom in America* (San Francisco, 1969), pp. 71-80.

[27]Peterson, pp. 316-317.

[28]Cawelti, "The Spillane Phenomenon," p. 12.

R. Jeff Banks

Although almost all the Spillane books cited have appeared in hard-covers, the more readily available paperback editions are used as sources.

[1]Michael Brett, "Chapters 10 and 11," *Kill Him Quickly, It's Raining* (New York: Pocket Books, Inc., 1966), pp. 115, 145.

[2]See any espionage novel by Graham Greene, Len Deighton, John le Carre, Jimmy Sangster or Donald Hamilton for the serious. The agents in these books operate generally in foreign lands whose version of the Establishment is entirely inimical. They represent Establishments on "our side" which are hardly distinguishable in their relationships to the agents from those to which they are actively opposed. The works of Ted Mark, Clyde Allison, Lawrence Block, the first few in the Rod Damon series by Troy Conway, the two books ghostwritten for Dagmar by Lou Cameron, and Carter Brown's *Seidlitz and the Super Spy* are among the best of the

humorous and satiric. These books satirize the genre and socio-politico-economic forces predominant in Western life. Certainly many other examples, both serious and comic, will come to mind, if the reader is well read in this field.

[3]Mike Hammer does this in Chapter 8 of *Vengeance Is Mine,* to an arresting officer from the District Attorney's office who has just rudely prevented him from smoking.

[4]Mike Hammer does this in the opening chapter of *The Twisted Thing.*

[5]John G. Cawelti, "The Spillane Phenomenon," *Journal of Popular Culture,* III (Spring 1969), 8.

[6]These ingredients abound in *Vengeance Is Mine, The Big Kill, One Lonely Night,* and *The Snake.*

[7]Mickey (Frank Morrison) Spillane, "Chapter 3," *I, the Jury* (New York: NAL, 1948), pp. 24, 28-29.

[8]Spillane, "Chapter 3," *Kiss Me, Deadly* (New York: NAL, 1952), pp. 26-28.

[9]Spillane, "Chapter 5," *Kiss Me, Deadly,* pp. 39-40.

[10]Spillane, "Chapter 9," *Kiss Me, Deadly,* p. 109.

[11]Spillane, "Chapter 11," *Kiss Me, Deadly,* p. 127.

[12]Spillane, "Chapter 10," *One Lonely Night* (New York: NAL, 1951), pp. 165-167.

[13]Spillane, "Chapters 4 and 7," *Survival Zero* (New York: NAL, 1971), pp. 43-44, 96.

[14]Spillane, "Chapter 6," *Survival Zero,* p. 70.

[15]Spillane, "Chapter 7," *One Lonely Night,* p. 116.

[16]For adverse critical comment, see the Cawelti article cited above, Kingsley Amis, "Chapter 2," and "Appendix C: Sadism," *The James Bond Dossier* (New York: NAL, 1966), pp. 25, 121-122; George Grella, "Murder and the Mean Streets," *Contempora,* I (March 1970), 14-15; practically any newspaper or magazine review of any Spillane book which was written by a practicing detective story writer, but especially those by Anthony Boucher (William A. P. White) prior to his friendly treatment of *The Delta Factor.* The reader will find that it is Hammer's sadism, the surest proof of his claimed "toughness" which is most often and most emphatically objected to.

[17]See *The Big Kill,* Chapter 5; *Kiss Me, Deadly,* Chapters 7 and 9; *My Gun is Quick*, Chapters 3, 11, and 13; *The Snake,* Chapters 3 and 7; *Survival Zero,* Chapters 6, 8, 9, and 10.

[18]Norman Mailer, *Miami and the Siege of Chicago* (New York: NAL, 1968), pp. 174-175. Spillane's own words, in the reverie of one of his minor heroes, provide an interesting restatement of this idea. "There is something peculiar about those on the stiffer sides of the fence, the law and the punks. In some ways they seem to look alike sometimes. They work in the same areas in the same profession with the same people, and it gets to them so they adopt common mannerisms and expressions and deep in the back of their eyes is buried a mutual hatred." Those are the ruminations of Joe Scanlon, police lieutenant and hero-narrator of *Killer Mine.* They appear in "Chapter 6," page 50.

[19]Spillane, "Chapter 4," *The Day of the Guns* (New York: NAL, 1965), p. 28.

[20]Spillane, "Chapter 4," *The By-Pass Control* (New York: NAL, 1967), p. 47.

[21]Spillane, "Chapter 5," *The Death Dealers* (New York: NAL, 1966), p. 50.

[22]The number of articles listed in *The Reader's Guide to Periodical Literature* under the two headings most significant to this statement, "U. S. Police" and "Police Dogs," rose dramatically, from always fewer than ten to: 16 in the 1959-61 volume, 14 in 1961-63, and 18 in 1963-65. While no attempt was made to read all of them, this writer's general impressions were: (1) the content shifted markedly from descriptive concern with procedures and personality profiles to attempts to evaluate the

police as beneficial or detrimental to society; (2) the critical tone in the earliest period of increased interest was primarily unfriendly; (3) the later articles were more likely to be friendly, but if they were unfriendly they had a tendency to link the police with the John Birch Society (most often) or with other Radical Right groups which had become defenders of the police—such identification was of course an attempt to discredit the favorable magazine articles.

Especially recommended as exemplifying the anti-police side are:

Fred J. Cook, "Corrupt Society," *Nation,* June 1, 1963.

Paul Hoffman, "Police Birchites and the Blue Backlash," *Nation,* Dec. 7, 1964.

"Birch Policemen," *Commonweal,* December 18, 1964.

Recommended for the pro-police side are:

R. & E. Brecher, "Don't Take the Police for Granted," *Parents Magazine,* March, 1964.

"Thin Blue Line," *National Review,* August 11, 1964.

F. Sondren, "Take the Handcuffs Off Our Police," *Reader's Digest,* Sept., 1964.

The only objective account of the controversy this writer was able to find was "Storm Around U. S. Policemen," published anonymously in *Senior Scholastic,* January 14, 1964.

[23] Spillane, *Me, Hood!* (New York: NAL, 1969), pp. 10-11.

[24] Spillane, *Me, Hood!* p. 70.

[25] Spillane, "Chapter 5," "Return of the Hood," *Me, Hood!*, pp. 115-116. The "patriot" label is rejected by Tiger Mann in *Day of the Guns* (p. 20), but he seems to hint at acceptance of it in *Bloody Sunrise* (p. 148), and he muses briefly about how the Founding Fathers and other illustrious historical patriots would regard Martin Grady's organization in *The Death Dealers* (p. 24). In *The By-Pass Control,* he applies it to a man willingly co-operating with him (p. 51).

[26] Spillane, "Chapter 8," *The Deep* (New York: NAL, 1962), pp. 90-91.

[27] Spillane, "Chapter 1," *Killer Mine* (New York: NAL, 1968), p. 16.

[28] Spillane, "Chapter 2," *Killer Mine,* p. 27.

[29] Spillane, "Chapter 1," "Man Alone," *Killer Mine,* pp. 85-86, 95.

[30] Spillane, "Chapters 6 and 7," "Man Alone," *Killer Mine,* pp. 119, 138, 147, and 155.

[31] Spillane, "Kick It or Kill!," *The Tough Guys* (New York: NAL, 1969), pp. 9, 14, and 45.

[32] Spillane, "Chapter 1," *The Delta Factor* (New York: NAL, 1967), p. 12.

[33] Spillane, "Chapter 12," *The Delta Factor,* pp. 175-176. The author's flamboyant endings of *One Lonely Night* and especially *The Big Kill,* are commented upon in the Cawelti article cited earlier. However, they probably will get well deserved treatment in an article as interest in popular fiction continues to grow. They must certainly be one of the keys to Spillane's "phenomenal" and continuing popularity.

[34] Spillane, "Chapter 1," *The Flier* (London: Corgi, 1964), pp. 11-13.

[35] Spillane, "Chapter 3," *The Flier*, p. 27.

R. Gordon Kelly

[1] Dashiell Hammett, *The Maltese Falcon* and *The Thin Man* (New York: Vintage Books, 1964), pp. 55-57.

[2] *Ibid.*, p. 57.

[3] John D. MacDonald, *The Executioners* (New York: Simon and Schuster, 1957). The novel later served as a basis for the movie *Cape Fear,* which starred Gregory Peck as Samuel Bowden and Robert Mitchum as Cady.

In an appropriately fortuitous fashion, MacDonald himself suggests that an emphasis on the themes of precariousness and vulnerability is not misplaced. The initial draft of this essay was complete when the *John D. MacDonald Bibliophile No. 17* carried his reply to a reader concerned that violence in fiction such as MacDonald's might be causally linked to increasing violence in American society. MacDonald concluded his reply with a passage from his novel *The End of the Night*, ". . . an interior monologue by a father whose daughter has been slain by a quartet . . ." of young, casual killers. A "realist," the father wonders, nevertheless, whether the tragedy is in some remote way his fault. But it is not, he decides, for

> . . . Life is random. Luck is the factor. The good and the evil are struck down, and there is no cause to look for reasons. There is a divine plan, but it is not so minute and selective that it deals with individuals on the basis of their merit. Were that so, all men would be good, out of fear if nothing else. Those unholy four could have gathered up a tart in front of a bar. They happened to take Helen. It was chance. No blame can be assessed. . . . (*John D. MacDonald Bibliophile No. 17,* March 1972, p. 10.)

[4] *The Executioners,* p. 190.

[5] *Ibid.,* p. 11.

[6] *Ibid.,* p. 65.

[7] *Ibid.,* pp. 12, 14, 64, 106-107.

[8] *Ibid.,* p. 43.

[9] *Ibid.,* p. 185. A similar feeling of exultation in the death of an enemy is evident in the conclusion to the recent Sam Peckinpah film *Straw Dogs.*

[10] *Ibid.,* p. 190.

[11] Indeed, the novel may be read partly as an effort to undermine a deeply rooted assumption: namely, that an individual's experiences are necessarily related to his moral nature—that a person somehow deserves what he experiences or that a person's experiences are somehow linked causally to his previous behavior. Bowden learns, of course, that he has not caused, in any important sense, the attacks on his family. Certainly the attacks are not related to any moral weakness or failure; they are in no way deserved by him or by his family. He need feel no anguish that he is somehow responsible for what happens, including Cady's death—nor is he to feel guilt for shooting Cady.

[12] In another essay, I have suggested that an attenuated and selective naturalism may be traced in the work of several recent science fiction writers. MacDonald seems to be another popular writer in whose work this tendency can be seen. "Ideology in Some Modern Science Fiction Novels," *Journal of Popular Culture,* II (Fall 1968), 211-227.

[13] *The Executioners,* pp. 52-53, 120, for example.

[14] *The Social Construction of Reality* (Garden City, New York: Doubleday and Company, 1967), pp. 96-102, 148-149. See also Peter Berger's first chapter in *The Sacred Canopy* (Garden City, New York: Doubleday and Company, 1969).

[15] A remarkable instance of "reversion" may be found in Loren Eiseley's recent *The Unexpected Universe* (New York: Harcourt, Brace and World, 1969). Eiseley recalls a young woman whom he had met while doing field work in Nebraska. The prominent physical characteristics ascribed to her are virtually identical to those assigned to Cady by MacDonald. Their meaning, however, is totally different. For the anthropologist, the girl is a haunting symbol of a gentle race long since displaced by the more aggressive *homo sapiens.* In her eyes he sees, not sullen viciousness, but the enormous span of time separating her, although she cannot know it, from her true home and kind. Pp. 219-227.

Charles R. Carlisle

[1]That the Sicilian Mafia is centuries old is, of course, common knowledge. For histories of this element in Sicilian culture, *Cf.*, among others: Salvatore Francesco Romano, *Storia della Mafia,* (Verona: Arnoldo Mondadori Editore, 1963); Norman Lewis, *The Honoured Society,* (London: Collins, 1964); and Frederick Sondern, *Brotherhood of Evil: The Mafia,* (New York: Farrar, Straus, and Cudahy, 1959).

[2]Mario Puzo, *The Godfather,* (Greenwich, Conn.: Fawcett Publications, Inc.), p. 31.

[3]George William Rae, *The Mafia Don,* (New York: Pyramid Books, 1972), p. 121.

[4]Jack Higgins, *The Sicilian Heritage,* (New York: Lancer Books, 1972), p. 7.

[5]For an explanation and history of this euphemism for the Mafia, *amico degli amici* ("friend of the friends"), *Cf.* Luigi Barzini, *The Italians,* (New York: Grosset and Dunlap, 1969), pp. 266-267.

[6]Among these are: Lewis John Carlino, *The Brotherhood,* (New York: New American Library, 1969); and Jack Higgins, *op. cit.*

[7]Peter Rabe, *War of the Dons,* (Greenwich, Conn.: Fawcett Publications, 1972).

[8]Ovid Demaris, *The Overlord,* (New York: New American Library, 1972), pp. 42-43.

[9]Leslie Waller, *The Family,* (New York: New American Library, 1969), p. 113.

[10]This method of dealing with informers, those who violate *omertà*, is graphically portrayed in the Paramount film version of Carlino's *The Brotherhood,* an example of the old world style being employed in America by local (New York) *mafiosi.*

[11]Lewis John Carlino, *The Mechanic,* (New York: New American Library, 1972), p. 115.

Richard Gid Powers

[1]This account follows Willard B. Gatewood, *Theodore Roosevelt and the Art of Controversy* (Baton Rouge, 1970), Ch. VIII.

[2]For these speeches see Max Lowenthal, *The Federal Bureau of Investigation* (New York: William Sloan, 1950), Ch. I.

[3]For a full discussion of this theory see Murray Edelman, *The Symbolic Uses of Politics* (Urbana, Illinois, 1964).

[4]Edelman, p. 70; p. 78.

[5]Henry R. Pringle, *Theodore Roosevelt* (New York, 1956), p. 333.

[6]Quoted in Lowenthal, p. 15.

[7]J. Edgar Hoover, quoted in Lowenthal, p. 19.

[8]See Howard Sackler's play *The Great White Hope* for a fictional account of this.

[9]*American Magazine* 144 (July, 1947).

[10]Lowenthal, Ch. 4; Chs. 14-23; Robert K. Murray, *Red Scare* (Minneapolis, 1955).

[11]Don Whitehead, *The F.B.I. Story* (New York: 1956), p. 92.

[12]Quoted in Whitehead, p. 97.

[13]Quoted in Whitehead, p. 102.

[14]Jack Alexander, "Profile, The Director," *The New Yorker* 13 (September 25, 1937), p. 22.

[15]George Orwell, "Raffles and Miss Blandish" in *A Collection of Essays* (New York, 1954), p. 153.

[16]Alexander, p. 24.

[17]Quoted in William W. Turner, *Hoover's F.B.I.* (New York: Dell, 1970), p. 105.

[18]Quoted by Turner, p. 118.

[19]Jules Feiffer, *The Great Comic Book Heroes* (New York: 1965), p. 48.

[20]J. Edgar Hoover, "The Adventure of Scientific Crime Control," in *Vital Speeches* (July 1, 1937), p. 562.

[21]"Scientific Crime Control," p. 561.

[22]Turner, p. 121. Characteristically, pulp editors picked Hoover's writings out of the public domain (*Congressional Record* or press releases). Thus, according to Louis B. Nichols, the pulps' use of Hoover material was "tolerated" but not "encouraged."

[23]J. Edgar Hoover, "Fifty Years of Crime," in *Vital Speeches* (January 1, 1939), p. 509.

[24]Emile Durkheim, *The Division of Labor in Society* (New York, 1933), p. 108.

[25]Roland Barthes, *Mythologies* (New York, 1972), p. 143.

[26]Martin Jay, *The Dialectical Imagination* (Boston, 1973), p. 187.

[27]Edelman, p. 38.

[28]Edelman, p. 91.

Mick Gidley

[1]"Introduction," *William Faulkner's Library – A Catalogue* (Charlottesville: University of Virginia Press, 1964), p. 9. In the catalogue itself books are listed alphabetically by author under each national literature represented. At one of the University of Virginia class conferences Faulkner claimed that detective stories were all over his house because his *children* enjoyed them (*Faulkner in the University,* eds. Frederick L. Gwynn and Joseph L. Blotner, New York: Vintage, 1965, p. 141). However, publication dates and other factors in the books concerned simply do not tally to any notable degree with such a view of their acquisition; moreover, Robert Coughlan has reported that between bursts of creative activity Faulkner liked to relax with "a mystery story" (*The Private World of William Faulkner,* New York: Harpers, 1954, p. 101).

[2]Interview reprinted in *Lion in the Garden: Interviews with William Faulkner 1926-1962,* eds. James B. Meriwether and Michael Millgate (New York: Random House, 1968), p. 251; also in *William Faulkner: Three Decades of Criticism,* eds. Frederick J. Hoffman and Olga W. Vickery (New York: Harbinger, 1963), p. 78.

[3]*Lion in the Garden,* p. 217.

[4]Supplement to *TLS,* June 23, 1961, 1-2.

[5]For Sandoe see "Dagger of the Mind," *The Art of the Mystery Story,* ed. Howard Haycraft (New York: Farrar, Straus, 1946), p. 256. For Strong see "The Crime Short Story," *Crime in Good Company,* ed. Michael Gilbert (London: Constable, 1959), pp. 157-159.

[6]See *Lion in the Garden,* pp. 49, 72, 111, 217 and 251, and *Faulkner in the University,* pp. 50, 150, 231-232.

[7]London: Peter Owen, 1958, pp. 51-59 and 92-102 respectively.

[8]Cambridge, Mass: Harvard University Press, 1958, pp. 88-89.

[9]"How a Writer Finds his Material," *Harper's Magazine,* November, 1965, 158.

[10]Letter from Phil Stone to Louis Cochran, printed in "Early Notices of Faulkner by Phil Stone and Louis Cochran," by James B. Meriwether, *Mississippi Quarterly,*

XVII (1964), 141.

[11] London: Hamish Hamilton, 1950, p. 211.

[12] *Catalogue,* plate facing p. 6.

[13] See Murch, early chapters. The following also contain interesting material on the precursors of Conan Doyle: Howard Haycraft, *Murder for Pleasure: The Life and Times of the Detective Story* (London: Peter Davies, 1942), pp. 1-45; Dorothy L. Sayers, "Introduction," *Great Short Stories of Detection, Mystery and Horror* (London: Gollancz, 1928), pp. 3-31; Julian Symons, *The Detective Story in Britain,* No. 145 in Writers and their Work Series (London: Longmans, 1962), pp. 10-13; H. Douglas Thompson, *Masters of Mystery* (London: Collins, 1931), chpater 1; E. M. Wrong, "Introduction," *Crime and Detection* (London: World Classics, 1921), pp. iv-xx. I list these exhaustively because I am indebted to them also for notions on the *form* of detective fiction.

[14] "A Preface for Faulkner's *Sanctuary,*" *La Nouvelle Revue Francaise,* November 1, 1933; reprinted in *Faulkner: A Collection of Essays,* Robert Penn Warren, ed. (Englewood Cliffs: Prentice-Hall, 1966), p. 274.

[15] George Orwell, "Raffles and Miss Blandish" (1944), *A Collection of Essays* (Garden City: Doubleday, 1954), p. 145.

[16] "The Furies in Mississippi," *London Mercury,* March, 1937; reprinted in Warren, ed. *Faulkner,* p. 277. It has been pointed out to me that Mme. Claude-Edmonde Magny has remarked on Faulkner's possible affect on Greene in *L'Age du roman american* (Paris: Editions du Seuil, 1948), p. 151 n.

[17] "The Face in the Mirror" in Gilbert, ed., *Crime in Good Company,* p. 132.

[18] New York: Random House, 1940, p. 101.

[19] *The Development of the Detective Novel,* pp. 42-52.

[20] *The Atlantic Monthly,* November, 1939; reprinted in *Three Decades,* pp. 135-142.

[21] James B. Meriwether, *The Literary Career of William Faulkner* (Princeton: Princeton University Library, 1961), p. 157.

[22] *Raymond Chandler Speaking,* eds. Dorothy Gardiner and Katherine Sorley Walker (London: Four Square, 1966), p. 61.

[23] Ronald Knox, "Detective Stories" (1929), *Literary Distractions* (London: Sheed and Ward, 1958), p. 191. Symons provides a succinct account of the "rules" and the revolt against them in *The Detective Story in Britain,* pp. 22-28.

[24] *Selected Writings,* ed. David Galloway (London: Penguin, 1967), p. 480.

[25] Maugham, "The Decline and Fall of the Detective Story," *The Vagrant Mood* (London: Heinemann, 1952), pp. 108-109; Van Dine, "The Great Detective Stories" (1927), in Haycraft's The Art of the Mystery Story, pp. 38-42; in Morland's *How to Write Detective Novels* (London: Allen and Unwin, 1936), p. 57.

[26] See, for example, *Faulkner in the University,* p. 141.

[27] *Knight's Gambit* (New York: Random House, 1949), p. 39. Subsequent page references are to this edition.

[28] Cf. *Raymond Chandler Speaking,* p. 58. Chandler writes that punishment for the criminal "has nothing to do with morality. It is part of the logic of the form. Without it the story is like an unresolved chord in music." Also, to be fair, it must be stressed that since the second World War many detective works, in attempting greater realism, do not portray justice as accomplished.

[29] Edmonde L. Volpe, *A Reader's Guide to William Faulkner* (London: Thames and Hudson, 1964), p. 142.

[30] *Sanctuary* (London: Chatto and Windus, 1952), p. 172. Other page references are to this edition.

[31] *Literary Distractions,* p. 185. My emphasis.

[32] In an unpublished paper presented at the University of Sussex, December 11, 1968.

[33] Quoted in *The Literary Career*, pp. 33-34.

[34] New York: Modern Library, 1951, pp. 270-271. My emphasis.

[35] *William Faulkner: The Yoknapatawpha Country* (New Haven and London: Yale University Press, 1963), pp. 432-436.

[36] Cf. Chandler's Marlowe in *The Big Sleep* (London: Penguin, 1948), p. 153; "I looked down at the chessboard. The move with the knight was wrong. I put it back where I had moved it from. Knights had no meaning in this game. It wasn't a game for nights."

[37] Other features of the novella–and of the collection in general–are admirably discussed in Albert Gerard, "Justice in Yoknapatawpha Country: Some Symbolic Motifs in Faulkner's Later Writings," *Faulkner Studies*, II (Winter, 1954), pp. 49-57 and Michael Millgate, *The Achievement of William Faulkner* (London: Constable, 1966), pp. 265-270.

[38] Faulkner himself called the Stevens of *Knight's Gambit* an "amateur Sherlock Holmes" (*Faulkner in the University*, p. 140).

[39] For biographical details on Wright, see Haycraft, *Murder for Pleasure*, pp. 163-168; S. S. Van Dine, "Introduction," and W. S. Braithwaite, "S. S. Van Dine–Willard Huntington Wright" in S. S. Van Dine, *Philo Vance Murder Cases* (New York: Scribners, 1936), pp. 1-28 and 29-45 respectively.

[40] In Meriwether, "Early Notices," p. 141.

[41] "Faulkner and Wright, Alias S. S. Van Dine," *Mississippi Quarterly*, XIV pp. 101-107. She discusses briefly Wright's views on the essential loneliness of the writer, on diction, on time, and on Balzac's method of creation.

[42] Quoted in Murch, p. 225. For a composite "biography" of Vance see Y. B. Garden (presumably Wright), "Impressionistic Biography" in *Philo Vance Murder Cases*, pp. 46-73.

[43] *Faulkner in the University*, pp. 140-141.

[44] Jones, "Loyalty and the Tiresias of Yoknapatawpha," *Saturday Review of Literature*, XXXII (November 5, 1949), p. 17.

[45] London: Golancz, 1953, pp. 107-109.

[46] *Faulkner in the University*, p. 142.

[47] "William Faulkner and American Humor," unpublished dissertation (Hebrew University of Jerusalem, 1968), p. 270. Miss Rothbert's comparison between *Intruder* and *Huckleberry Finn* is both penetrating and fascinating (pp. 266-283).

[48] New York: Random House, 1948, p. 137. Subsequent page references are to this edition.

[49] For a similar reading to my own on this and certain other points, see Warren French, "William Faulkner and the Art of the Detective Story" in French ed., *The Thirties: Fiction, Poetry, Drama* (Deland, Florida: Everett Edwards, 1967), pp. 55-62.

Douglas G. Tallack

[1] W. M. Frohock, *The Novel of Violence in America* (Dallas: Southern Methodist University Press, 1958), pp. 21-22.

[2] See David Madden, ed. *Tough-guy Writers of the Thirties* (Carbondale and Edwardsville: Southern Illinois University Press, 1968) and *James M. Cain* (New York: Twayne Publications, Inc., 1970).

[3]Raymond Chandler, "The Simple Art of Murder," *The Atlantic Monthly*, 174 (December 1944), 58.

[4]Ernest Hemingway, "The Killers," *Men Without Women* (London: Jonathan Cape, 1961), p. 84.

[5]Alice P. Hackett, *70 Years of Best-Sellers 1895-1965* (New York: R. R. Bowker Company, 1967).

[6]Claude Elsen, "Faulkner et le roman noire," *Réforme*, 16 February 1952, p. 7.

[7]Leslie A. Fiedler, *Love and Death in the American Novel* (London: Paladin, 1970), p. 23. Subsequent page references are to this edition.

[8]Stanley D. Woodworth, *William Faulkner en France: (1931-1952)* (Paris: M. J. Minard, 1959), p. 11.

[9]*Samedi Soir,* 7 December 1946, p. 8.

[10]*Essays, Speeches and Public Letters by William Faulkner,* ed. James B. Meriwether (London: Chatto and Windus, 1967), pp. 176-177.

[11]I am obliged to Mick Gidley for sight of his article, "Elements of the Detective Story in William Faulkner's Fiction," prior to its publication in the *Journal of Popular Culture*, 7, 1 (Summer 1973), 97-123.

[12]Joseph Blotner, *William Faulkner's Library: A Catalogue* (Charlottesville: University Press of Virginia, 1964).

[13]Julian Bymons, *Bloody Murder: From the Detective Story to the Crime Novel: A History* (London: Faber and Faber, 1972), chapter 10. Subsequent page references are to this edition.

[14]George Orwell, "Raffles and Miss Blandish," *Decline of the English Murder and Other Essays* (London: Penguin Books Ltd., 1972), pp. 63-79.

[15]*Faulkner at Nagano,* ed. Robert A. Jelliffe (Tokyo: Kenkyusha Ltd., 1962), p. 65. Subsequent page references are to this edition.

[16]Michael Millgate, *The Achievement of William Faulkner* (London: Constable, 1966), pp. 113-123. Subsequent page references are to this edition. See also, Linton Massey, "Notes on the Unrevised Galleys of Faulkner's *Sanctuary*," *Studies in Bibliography*, 8 (1956), 195-208.

[17]Frederick Lewis Allen, *Since Yesterday: The Nineteen-Thirties in America* (New York: Harper and Brothers, 1940), p. vii.

[18]W. H. Auden, "The Guilty Vicarage: Notes on the Detective Story," *Harper's*, 196, No. 1172 (1948), 408.

[19]Raymond Chandler, "Introduction," *The Smell of Fear* (London: Hamish Hamilton, 1965), p. 9.

[20]Horace McCoy, *No Pockets in a Shroud* (London: Penguin Books Ltd., 1962), p. 47.

[21]Ernest Hemingway, "The Battler," *In Our Time* (New York: Charles Scribner's Sons, 1958), p. 68.

[22]Ernest Hemingway, *To Have and Have Not* (London: Penguin Books Ltd., 1971), p. 146. Subsequent page references are to this edition.

[23]James M. Cain, *The Postman Always Rings Twice* (London: Panther, 1964), p. 8. Subsequent page references are to this edition.

[24]Horace McCoy, *They Shoot Horses, Don't They?* (London: Penguin Books Ltd., 1970), p. 72. Subsequent page references are to this edition.

[25]William Faulkner, *Sanctuary* (London: Penguin Books Ltd., 1970), p. 102. Subsequent page references are to this edition.

[26]W. R. Burnett, *Little Caesar* (London: Nicholas Vane, 1967), p. 72. Subsequent page references are to this edition.

[27]Claude-Edmonde Magny, *L'Age du Roman Américain* (Paris: Éditions du Seuil, 1948), chapter 2.

[28]Albert Camus, *The Rebel,* trans. Anthony Bower (London: Penguin Books Ltd., 1971), p. 231. Subsequent page references are to this edition.

[29]William Faulkner, *Light in August* (London: Penguin Books Ltd., 1970), p. 25. Subsequent page references are to this edition.

[30]André Malraux, "A Preface for Faulkner's *Sanctuary,*" *Yale French Studies,* No. 10, pp. 92 and 94.

[31]James M. Cain, "Preface," *Double Indemnity* (London: Corgi Books, 1965), p. 13. Originally published as *Three of a Kind* (London: Robert Hale, 1945). Subsequent page references are to the Corgi edition.

[32]Edmund Wilson, "The Boys in the Back Room," *Classics and Commercials: A Literary Chronicle of the Forties* (New York: Farrar, Straus and Company, 1958), p. 21. Subsequent page references are to this edition.

[33]Wyndham Lewis, *Men Without Art* (New York: Russell and Russell Inc., 1964), p. 49. Subsequent page references are to this edition.

[34]Peter Bogdanovich, *Fritz Lang in America* (London: Studio Vista Ltd., 1967), p. 38.

[35]T. H. Huxley, "A Liberal Education," *Lay Sermons, Addresses and Reviews* (London: MacMillan, 1899), p. 28.

[36]James T. Farrell, "Cain's Movietown Realism," *Literature and Morality* (New York, 1947), pp. 79-89.

[37]Alfred Kazin, *On Native Grounds: An Interpretation of Modern American Prose Literature* (New York: Harcourt, Brace and Co., 1942), pp. 388-391.

[38]Albert Van Nostrand, *The Denatured Novel* (New York: The Bobbs-Merrill Company Inc., 1960), p. 81.

[39]Carvel Collins, "A Note on *Sanctuary,*" *Faulkner: A Collection of Critical Essays,* ed. Robert Penn Warren (New Jersey: Prentice-Hall Inc., 1966), pp. 290-291.

[40]William Faulkner, *Requiem for a Nun* (London: Penguin Books Ltd., 1970), p. 120. Subsequent page references are to this edition.

[41]Dashiell Hammett, *Red Harvest* (London: Penguin Books Ltd., 1963), p. 145.

[42]Robert Penn Warren, "William Faulkner," *William Faulkner: Three Decades of Criticism,* ed. Frederick J. Hoffman and Olga W. Vickery (East Lansing: Michigan State University Press), 1960, p. 122.

Steven R. Carter

[1]John O'Brien, "Ishmael Reed," *The New Fiction: Interviews with Innovative American Writers,* ed. Joe David Bellamy (Urbana, Illinois: University of Illinois Press, 1974), p. 132.

[2]Julian Symons, *Mortal Consequences: A History–From the Detective Story to the Crime Novel* (New York: Schocken Books, 1973), p. 55.

[3]Symons, pp. 54-55.

[4]*19 Necromancers from Now,* ed. Ishmael Reed (Garden City, New York: Doubleday & Co., 1970), pp. xiii-xiv.

[5]O'Brien, *New Fiction,* p. 133.

[6]Ishmael Reed, "Neo-HooDoo Manifesto," *Conjure* (Amherst, Massachusetts: University of Massachusetts Press, 1972), p. 24.

[7]O'Brien, *New Fiction,* p. 132.

[8]Ishmael Reed, *Mumbo Jumbo* (Garden City, New York: Doubleday & Co., 1972), p. 191.

[9]Cryptic messages have been a standard device in mysteries since Poe's "The Gold Bug." Also, the references to the Cotton Club and the Dancing Bales recall

another mystery, Chester Himes's *Cotton Comes to Harlem.*

[10]O'Brien, *New Fiction,* p. 132.

[11]O'Brien, "Ishmael Reed," *Interviews with Black Writers,* ed. John O'Brien (New York: Liveright, 1973), pp. 176-177.

[12]Maya Deren, *The Divine Horsemen: The Voodoo Gods of Haiti* (New York: Dell Publishing Co., 1972), p. 89.

[13]Deren, p. 88.

[14]Reed, *Mumbo Jumbo,* p. 96.

[15]Reed, *Conjure,* p. 21.

[16]Reed, *Mumbo Jumbo,* p. 35.

[17]Reed, *Mumbo Jumbo,* p. 24.

[18]In O'Brien, *Interviews with Black Writers,* p. 179, Reed said that his novel *Yellow Back Radio Broke-Down* "is really artistic warfare against the Historical Establishment. . . . So this is what we want: to sabotage history. [The apologists for Western culture] won't know whether we're serious or whether we are writing fiction. They made their own fiction, just like we make our own. But they can't tell whether our fictions are the real thing or whether they're merely fictional."

[19]Ishmael Reed, *The Last Days of Louisiana Red* (New York: Random House, 1974), p. 84.

[20]Reed, *Louisiana Red,* p. 61.

[21]Reed, *Louisiana Red,* p. 139.

[22]The irony is multiple here since Reed stresses throughout that Chorus, the supposed voice of the people, has always been a fictional character. Reed believes that no group of people can be represented by a single voice.

[23]Reed, *Louisiana Red,* p. 7.

[24]Reed, *Louisiana Red,* p. 172.

[25]Reed, *Louisiana Red,* p. 3.

[26]Reed, *Louisiana Red,* p. 59.

[27]Reed, *Louisiana Red,* p. 45.

[28]Reed, *Louisiana Red,* p. 126.